CW00734825

A LONG TIME
IN MAKING

A LONG TIME IN MAKING

The History of Smiths

By

JAMES NYE

OXFORD

UNIVERSITY PRESS

OXFORD

UNIVERSITY PRESS

Great Clarendon Street, Oxford, OX2 6DP,
United Kingdom

Oxford University Press is a department of the University of Oxford.
It furthers the University's objective of excellence in research, scholarship,
and education by publishing worldwide. Oxford is a registered trade mark of
Oxford University Press in the UK and in certain other countries

© Smiths Group PLC 2014

The moral rights of the author have been asserted

First Edition published in 2014

Impression: 1

All rights reserved. No part of this publication may be reproduced, stored in
a retrieval system, or transmitted, in any form or by any means, without the
prior permission in writing of Oxford University Press, or as expressly permitted
by law, by licence or under terms agreed with the appropriate reprographics
rights organization. Enquiries concerning reproduction outside the scope of the
above should be sent to the Rights Department, Oxford University Press, at the
address above

You must not circulate this work in any other form
and you must impose this same condition on any acquirer

Published in the United States of America by Oxford University Press
198 Madison Avenue, New York, NY 10016, United States of America

British Library Cataloguing in Publication Data
Data available

Library of Congress Control Number: 2014933293

ISBN 978–0–19–871725–6

Printed in Italy by
L.E.G.O. S.p.A.

Links to third party websites are provided by Oxford in good faith and
for information only. Oxford disclaims any responsibility for the materials
contained in any third party website referenced in this work.

DEDICATION

The products that made Smiths a highly-regarded manufacturer and a household
name in the twentieth century were created by tens of thousands of workers
across dozens of factories. In a corporate history such as this, the individual
names and faces of all those workers are largely hidden from plain view,
but as some mark of their vital role this volume is nevertheless
dedicated to their collective endeavours.

Foreword

Continuous reinvention

The history of the Smiths Group exemplifies the evolution of British manufacturing industry in the past hundred and more years. So much has changed in the world of today's relative peace and prosperity that one might be forgiven for concluding the past has little to tell us about the present. Not so. Globalization and the acceleration of changes in communication create new challenges for Smiths, but the history of its ability to adapt to enormous changes in industrial development shows Smiths is a group well versed in coping with change. Smiths has played an important role in this evolution of British industry and now stands as an exemplar of the ability of our great companies to find new ways to develop in the world beyond our own shores; today the Group is dominated by its overseas activities.

Before James Nye began work on this history, the board of Smiths Group gave him unrestricted access to its archives; it has not, however, sought to influence what he has written, or the opinions he has expressed in any way. He has written a fascinating history that will make Smiths come alive to a new audience whilst at the same time intriguing those who did not fully understand the company's origins.

From jewellery, to clocks and watches, to the motor industry, to aerospace and beyond, the history of Smiths shows a group restless in its pursuit of tomorrow. From origins in retailing to today's conglomerate of major businesses encompassing medical devices, detection equipment, pipeline seals, flexible hosing and connectors, the company has travelled a long road, never afraid to reinvent its shape and direction. Throughout this journey the company has always had a focus on high-quality engineering—making products that exemplify the skills of its workforce and satisfy the demands of its customers. Those customers have come from a very diverse range of industries and themselves catalogue the changing fortunes of the Western economies. In this story we can see the rise and fall of a variety of industries which have caused the company to have to be nimble and imaginative in meeting new demands. There is a strong theme of very successful innovation underlying all that Smiths has achieved.

The company has also not been afraid to use the capital markets to assist in its continuous evolution, with a number of major transactions shaping and reshaping the business. At times this has been an acquisitive strategy, though by contrast, when judging others are better owners of Smiths' assets, the company has not been timid about disposals. It has been blessed with fine leaders who have had an unsentimental vision about the way forward, always keeping the core skills of high-quality engineering and innovation at the forefront of the company's evolution. 'Adapt or die', the saying goes—Smiths has shown how to adapt most successfully. The process continues to this day and no doubt our successors will be looking at a very different Smiths over the next twenty-five years. Its future shape will also reflect, I am sure, the same opportunism and eye for the future that was exhibited all those years ago by the founding Mr Smith.

James Nye brings the story up to the appointment of Philip Bowman. Almost immediately the new chief executive faced the turmoil of the financial crash of 2008. Speculative external expectations that he would embark on a structural realignment went unfulfilled as he focused on the traditional core skills of improving performance by paying attention to the operational details of good manufacturing and selling processes. In doing so he delegated authority to the business presidents and returned them to their home markets, with only the detection business remaining to be led from the UK. The Group has also invested more heavily in the emerging economies of the Far East and in research and development. At the same time, the board has had to wrestle with legacy issues associated with the asbestos liabilities of John Crane Inc. (from the TI transaction) and the effects of abnormally low interest rates on the pension liabilities of the Group. Nonetheless the return from Smiths shares has outperformed the market by over 60 per cent in the past eight years, a testament to the skills of the management in improving the operating profitability of the Group.

It was in this period too that Smiths closed its Finchley Road offices, downsizing to occupy a small floor in a modern building on Victoria Street. It also appointed its first ever women to the board—Anne Quinn, a New Zealander with a background in LNG with BP, and Tanya Fratto, a US citizen with a career in General Electric. They joined Sir Kevin Tebbit, formerly Permanent Secretary of the Ministry of Defence; Bruno Angelici, formerly with Astra Zeneca; and David Challen, who has had a long and distinguished career in investment banking. A new finance director, Peter Turner, completed the board on John Langston's retirement, and new presidents were appointed to the divisions.

Now as the Group reaches the centenary of its stock market debut, financial and economic conditions appear to be beginning to improve in the developed markets, so that opportunities once again to shape the Group towards areas of profitable growth are likely to present themselves, and I am confident that Smiths will extend its long history of continuous evolution.

I hope all those who read this history will share my pride in this successful evolution of one of Britain's finest companies and the achievements of those who have worked for that success.

Donald Brydon
Chairman (2004–13)

PREFACE

Smiths Group (formerly Smiths Industries) is one of few major engineering companies in the FTSE 100 index. Founded in 1851 as a small family business, it now employs some 23,000 people worldwide, and is valued at more than £5bn.

This book charts the history of the company—providing evidence along the way to explain how and why it has survived for more than 160 years. From beginnings in the jewellery trade, a bold move in the early twentieth century took it into motor accessory manufacture, followed by aero instruments, which in turn led to an involvement in clockmaking (and later watchmaking). In the late 1950s, a link across technologies introduced a medical devices business, and later developments brought specialist activities supplying ducting and high-integrity connectors. Such evolutionary change did not, however, all derive from thoughtful planning—serendipity played a role as well, for example in the recent creation of a threat detection business and the acquisition of what has become the most profitable element of the modern company—John Crane—a specialist in seals for the oil and gas industries.

Smiths' long-term survival and adaptability offer a compelling counter-narrative to the broad 'declinism' that characterizes descriptions of British post-war industry, found in much business history of the 1980s. Indeed, its choice of different business sectors highlights the point that, while some industries were failing in the latter part of the twentieth century, others were flourishing.

Business historians, following the lead of Alfred Chandler, have brought the focus a long way back from individual companies in order to explore wider themes and issues, and this 'new business history' has brought fresh energy and insight to the field. But as David Jeremy cautions, the close review of individual enterprises supports the wider analysis of commerce, so that 'the single-company history remains as essential to "new" as much as to "old business historians"'.[1] This is surely true in the case of Smiths, with a story sufficiently rich and long it offers multiple such comparisons. Its narrative history offers useful data and information to aid wider research into questions such as the legitimacy of conglomeracy as a business model, the creation and maintenance of corporate culture, issues of succession, the effects of mergers and the questionable value placed upon targeted synergies, even the role of serendipity, and much more.

As to a framework, this book is arranged in a series of chronological narrative chapters, and a final reflective conclusion. The chapters generally cover periods of one to two decades, defined by particular major developments, or challenges faced by the company—for example, the economic crisis following the boom in 1920 and the

---

[1] David Jeremy, 'New Business History?', *Historical Journal*, 37/3 (Sept. 1994): 717–728.

company's near collapse followed by slow recovery, or the 1970s crisis in the motor industry and the company's response in exiting the sector. A comprehensive history of light engineering in the UK is not attempted, but sufficient material is included to set Smiths' particular efforts in a broader context. The reader may be assisted by the various appendices, which offer (i) a simplified family tree (useful when untangling which Samuel Smith is which); (ii) a simple graphic presentation of the life cycles of various business lines; (iii) the principal financial data for the company since 1914; (iv) a list of companies acquired and sold, plus key formations; (v) a list of the key officers over time (helpful in keeping track of successive management generations); and (vi) a list of interviewees.

The story is necessarily largely a managerial one—while there are occasional bird's-eye view insights into the world of the shop-floor, they are rare, and the scope of the book therefore cannot encompass much of the daily lives of the thousands of workers who populated dozens of Smiths factories over many decades. But a general observation based on many letters and e-mails received during the research for the book—and on conversations among groups of animated Smiths pensioners—is that an immense pride exists within the wider Smiths community, a pride in both the inventive and manufacturing genius of the firm, but also in the atmosphere fostered between colleagues in those factories.

What unfolds in these pages is a story that begins with several generations of the Smith family amassing a fortune in retail, and becomes, by the mid-twentieth-century, that of a large manufacturer, in which control had slowly been ceded to new shareholders and managers. It describes a transition from an entrepreneurial, individually driven enterprise to a modern company led by a largely non-executive board making a series of discrete capital allocation and divestment decisions, with some echoes of the private equity model. There have been different drivers of change—for example the need to adapt the business model to the increasing scale required to retain or grow market share—and the business model adopted in any one period would often have been unrecognizable to the management of another.

Smiths was stamped indelibly by two world wars, which offered both challenges and opportunities, as the business adapted to large-scale munitions and instrument production—each post-war period bringing its own severe consequences and a further need for reinvention. From the 1940s to the 1960s, Smiths dominated the marketplace in motor accessories, clocks, and watches, but by the 1970s, international competition based on higher productivity and better technologies hit its core markets, forcing yet more renewal and adaptation.

Over the past forty years Smiths has continued to reinvent itself, developing wide-ranging industrial, medical, and aerospace businesses, emerging in the twenty-first century as a strong and diverse player in international markets, carrying out a controversial merger in 2000 and as recently as 2007 succeeding in shocking markets again by thinking the unthinkable and divesting itself of aerospace, the business most observers considered to be dominant. The centenary of the company's flotation on the London stock market, marked by the publication of this book, is an ideal time to reflect on the firm's history, and the people whose decisions helped to shape it.

ACKNOWLEDGEMENTS

It has been immensely satisfying and hugely enjoyable to uncover the rich history of Smiths, and tremendous fun to meet the fascinating cast of characters who granted me interviews. I am therefore extremely grateful to Philip Bowman and Donald Brydon for their sponsorship and support of this history, and to Neil Burdett, a Smiths stalwart of more than thirty years and my main contact, who was a wonderful help throughout the process, making introductions and fielding requests for information. Many thanks also go to Professor Richard Roberts for first introducing me to Smiths, and for his support on the project and review of the manuscript.

A good number of the actors featured in the later chapters gave me hours of their time in interviews—their names are all listed in the schedule of interviews at Appendix VI and they have my sincere thanks for answering a lot of impertinent questions with such good humour, and for being so candid in their responses—in particular, Keith Butler-Wheelhouse, Alan Hornsby, Sir Roger Hurn, and John Thompson went out of their way to answer countless follow-up questions. Most of all, David Flowerday provided considerable input, and the last three chapters owe a great debt to his careful guidance and correction, in addition to which the handling and charting of data relies substantially on his patient assistance.

I was in touch with many other ex-Smiths personnel, who provided information or checked my facts. Barry Jones, formerly of Portex, offered historical insights, and my thanks also go out to Cliff Alder, Bruce Alexander, Ron Cripps, Geoff Evans, Peter Graham, John Langston, Trevor Leader, Einar Lindh, David Miller, the late Dick Snewin, Dennis Williams, and Chris Wilson. Marcus Beresford was vital to the fascinating story of 'Lucy'. Over the phone and in detailed correspondence he painted an invaluable picture of events from the 'coal-face' of the motor industry, under the new Thatcher government. From Lucas, I am grateful for comments from Sir Anthony Gill, Jeffrey Wilkinson, and Keith Wills, while former civil servants Sir Gordon Manzie and Michael Cochlin were generous with their time.

Beyond Smiths' own records, other archives proved important. I am very grateful for the kind cooperation of David Townend in locating historic Smiths images. Caroline Shaw of the Schroder Archive was enormously helpful in finding Smiths-related material and granting me access. Thanks as always go to the helpful staff at Kew. Stephen Potter and Lucy Tann helped at Southwark Archives with early background detail, as did Krzysztof Adamiec, Rebecca Florence, and Rachel Freeman at the Church of England Record Office. Thanks also to Guy Hannaford of the Hydrographic Office for dealing with obscure enquiries on early Smiths instruments. In early car lighting, I was helped by Peter Card, the acknowledged authority. In the museum world, various curators kindly responded to enquiries: Alison Morrison-Low of the National Museums of Scotland; Rory McEvoy of the Greenwich Royal Observatory; Patrick Collins of the National Motor Museum; Neil Handley at the British Optical Association Museum; and Luke Clark at Watford Museum.

Among librarians, I would like to thank Alan Midleton at the BHI, Cathy Wilson and Jason Canham at the RIBA Library, Trevor Dunmore at the RAC, the staff of the Guildhall Library, and Lucas Elkin of Cambridge University Library. In Watford, Chris Hillier and Chris Cooksey of the Watford and District Industrial History Society, and Stella Merryweather of the West Watford Local History, were all helpful in uncovering the story of Robert Benson North's businesses.

The early life of Alan Gordon-Smith was illuminated with the help of Stephen Goldsmith, historian of Christ's College; Nick Maag, a horological researcher in Switzerland who researched the Biel apprenticeship for me; and Alan Piper of the Brixton Society. Further detail of S. Smith & Son, the jewellers, was found with the help of staff at the National Association of Goldsmiths. The extraordinary life of Cyril Aldin Smith was uncovered with the help of Graham Smith (his great nephew) and Aurel Sercu, a battlefield historian. Tony Edwards, munitions expert, also kindly gave freely of his knowledge. Simon Merrick provided amusing and vivid memories of his eccentric uncle, 'Pluto' Leader.

At the newspapers, extracts from *The Times* are courtesy of NewsSyndication.com, kindly mediated by Simon Pearson, while George Newkey-Burdon generously dug in the *Daily Telegraph*'s clippings archive for my benefit. The book reveals a number of important networks of contacts, and these were no less important in researching it. I am particularly grateful to my friends Jonny Macdonald and Michael Meade, who effected many important introductions in the City. In horological circles, I was privileged to have access to the considerable knowledge of Jonathan Betts, Alun Davies, Arthur Mitchell, David Penney, and David Read, while Keith Scobie-Youngs was generous in lending original photographs and glass slides.

Uncovering material on Speedometer House was eased by the help of my friends Julian Hind of Farebrother and Nigel Desmond of Bride Hall; as well as Richard Bowden at Howard de Walden and Alison Kenney of the City of Westminster Archive. Enquiries into legal disputes were aided by John Lyons and Polly Sprenger of 18 Red Lion Court. Jane Ridley, Edward VII's biographer, kindly corresponded on the King's cars and driving habits, while the tale of the Queen of Siam's pearls benefited from Bruce Margrett's and Alyson Hartley's input. The material on Lawrie Nickolay owes much to Graham Stevenson, convener of the Communist History Group, and his introduction to Stella Nickolay, who very kindly let me study Lawrie's papers in detail, illuminated further by her childhood memories.

Duncan Needham offered valuable guidance on the broader UK economic background to parts of the story. In unravelling Smiths' troubles in the 1920s, I was enlightened by two wise credit experts—Clive Christensen and Guy Pigache. David

Turner of Citywire facilitated other City introductions. The discussion of corporate life was enriched by the usual deep insights of Campbell Fleming, James Hoare, and James Naylor. The latter, together with David Rooney, spent countless hours reviewing each chapter and discussing ideas for invaluable improvements and clarifications. I am deeply grateful to both of them for the huge amount of time they both devoted to helping me.

In discussing the financial performance of the firm over the last few decades, I met with a number of helpful City analysts, but would single out Sandy Morris, who has surely covered the company for longer and in greater depth than anyone else. He not only granted an interview but also spent a long time on the phone discussing matters further. Extra pairs of research hands were available in the person of Anders Mikkelsen of King's, and my assistants Suzy Kirby and, more recently, Sarah Urquhart-Briggs, who cheerfully helped input data, tracked down sources of information, visited archives on my behalf and generally provided practical support. Coming back to Smiths itself, I am grateful to all those people who over two years unlocked safes and stores, helped me dig out material, brought coffees, and looked after me handsomely. I am extremely grateful for the significant editorial freedom I have been permitted, but it should be noted the views and opinions expressed, the characterizations of people, and the interpretations of events, are wholly my own.

Projects of this sort become overwhelming, meaning time normally devoted to family and friends suffers. I am therefore deeply grateful to Luci, Hero, and Otti for putting up with some severe disruption to the normal patterns of family life over the last two years, especially in missed holidays, but I very much look forward to making up for it.

Contents

List of Figures

LIST OF TABLES

List of Plates

ABBREVIATIONS

AEU	Amalgamated Engineering Union
AUEW	Amalgamated Union of Engineering Workers
BCM	*The British Clock Manufacturer*
BCMA	British Clockmakers Association
BFCC	British Foreign and Colonial Corporation
BHI	British Horological Institute
BLEU	Blind Landing Experimental Unit
BLMC	British Leyland Motor Corporation
BMC	British Motor Corporation
BMH	British Motor Holdings
BTG	British Technology Group
BWCMA	British Watch and Clock Manufacturers Association
CAV	C. A. Vandervell
CBI	Confederation of British Industry
CCS	Common Core System
CH1/2 etc.	Cheltenham factory 1, 2, . . .
CILG	Component Industry Liaison Group
CSEU	Confederation of Shipbuilding and Engineering Unions
DATAC	Development Areas Treasury Advisory Committee
DBB	*Dictionary of Business Biography*
DHSS	Department of Health and Social Security
DoI	Department of Industry
DSO	Distinguished Service Order
ECWM	English Clock and Watchmakers
EEF	Engineering Employers Federation
EFA	Eurofighter
ELMS	Electrical Load Management System
FQIS	Fuel Quantity Indicating System

GMWU	General and Municipal Workers Union
HUD	Heads-up display
HUMS	Health and Usage Monitoring System
LCC	London County Council
MA1/2 etc.	Motor Accessories factory 1, 2, ...
MAP	Ministry of Aircraft Production
MoS	Ministry of Supply
MRCA	Multi-Role Combat Aircraft
NPL	National Physical Laboratory
NRDC	National Research and Development Council
OAPEC	Organization of Arab Petroleum Exporting Countries
OEM	Original equipment manufacturer
ONC	Ordinary National Certificate
P/E	Price/earnings
SEC	Smiths English Clocks
SIFAN	Smiths Industries air movement businesses
SIMS	Smiths Industries Medical Systems
SMA	Smiths Motor Accessories
SMAA	Smiths Group archive
SMMT	Society of Motor Manufacturers and Traders
TSA	Transportation Security Administration
TUC	Trades Union Congress
WCM	*Watch and Clockmaker*

CHAPTER 1

....

1851–1899
Elephant and Castle to the Strand

....

By his great tact and ability, combined with a most genial manner, he soon made a good solid foundation for the making of a solid business.

(*South London Chronicle*[1])

INCREASING wealth across society supported strong growth in the jewellery business from the mid-nineteenth century. In the 1860s, J. S. Wright highlighted the trade's flourishing nature, attributed to the 'vastly increased wealth of England and her colonies', as well as the discovery of gold in Australia and California, and the 'desire for personal adornment', all of which combined 'to give an unparalleled prosperity to this branch of industry'.[2] Industrialization of manufacture in English jewellery was centred in Birmingham, and Wright claimed that, directly and indirectly, it provided more employment than any other trade in the city. Elkingtons, an important local manufacturer and supplier, increased its workforce from 400 in 1851 to 2,000 by 1887, its trade boosted by success at the 1851 Great Exhibition and successive fairs.[3] The advanced production methods of Birmingham firms such as Elkingtons broadly transformed luxuries into affordable items, largely intended for an increasingly wealthy middle class.

The mass-produced items from Birmingham and elsewhere were mediated to the public by large numbers of independent and family-owned retail high-street jewellers, and though much of the history of Smiths is associated with the later motor age, the story starts among the bustle of nineteenth-century markets and horse-drawn traffic with the establishment of one such retail jewellery shop.

It was in the year of the Great Exhibition itself, 1851, that Samuel Smith opened a new jeweller's shop at 12 Newington Causeway, in London's Elephant and Castle district, selling a range of 'general merchandise' as well as clocks and watches—perhaps even some items made by a young Joseph Lucas, apprentice at Elkingtons.[4] A century later, the local area was to be largely obliterated by a combination of air-raids and subsequent post-war redevelopment, but in the mid-nineteenth century Newington Causeway was a prosperous thoroughfare.[5] Mayhew conjures a vivid picture, describing a walk he took along the

> wide business street, and one of the main ones on the Surrey side of the river, where, especially in the evenings, a good deal of shopping is carried on . . . The south side of Newington Causeway . . . is crowded with shops, the street being lit up nearly as clear as day. [There were] milliners' shops, with their windows gaily furnished with ladies' bonnets of every hue and style, and ribbons of every tint; and drapers' shops with cotton gown pieces, muslins, collars, and gloves of every form and colour.[6]

In addition there were gin-palaces, boot and shoe shops ('fancy shoes as well as plain'), upholsterers, and chemists 'with their gay-coloured jars flaming like globes of red, blue, green and yellow fire'. Mayhew was looking for the seamier side of life, but found 'many respectable people take their evening's walk along this cheerful and bustling thoroughfare, which is a favourite place for promenading'. It was a bustling and thriving street in which Samuel, as the *South London Chronicle* put it fifty years later, 'made a good solid foundation for the making of a solid business'.

But Samuel had not been born near the Elephant—his roots lay over the river, and the opening scenes of the back story involve another Samuel Smith, a Spitalfields potato merchant and his wife Charlotte, née Burden. Married at St Marylebone's church in 1810, they had the first of ten children in 1815. Two died in infancy, but it was the third son, born in 1826, who was to take his father's name—and thus the true founder of the Smiths' empire arrived on the stage. The Spitalfields merchant died when his son Samuel was just 17, and the young man eschewed the family potato business, crossing the Thames to become a silversmith instead.[7] The richly interconnected world of merchants and dealers in the south London markets provided ample opportunities for young people to meet and in 1849, at the age of 22, Samuel married 19-year-old Amelia, the daughter of Joseph James Assender, a fellmonger, in Bermondsey.[8] With both sets of parents in the market trade, it is hard to see significant financial help coming from them, but Samuel had succeeded in advancing into the more prosperous middle classes—the young couple were the first to move into a newly built house at 2 Richmond Street, in Southwark, the first in a line of seventeen terraced houses, which survive to this day.[9] The house offered two rooms each on two main floors, a basement and attic—space enough for a single servant. The newlyweds' neighbours included a mix of professions, from coal merchants, through drapers and accountants, to the secretary of a mining company. It was a comfortable middle-class street, close to affluent London Road, which ran down to Newington Causeway.

Settled in comfortable home surroundings, it was not long before the Smiths' first child was born—another Samuel—on 11 September 1850. Registering the birth, the father now described himself as 'pawnbroker', but it was the only time he ever did so. If the Richmond Street house was comfortable, it may soon have felt a bit cramped. More children followed quickly—indeed the couple had twelve children between 1850 and 1869. It is not clear when the family moved, but by 1861 they had relocated to a larger house, at 65 Brixton Hill, now with five children.

Moving to a road coloured yellow on Booth's Poverty Map—upper-middle class, wealthy—here they were largely surrounded by a similar group of well-to-do professionals, drawn from medicine, commerce, and the City. It was common in these larger and wealthier houses to have more than one domestic servant, and Samuel and Amelia now had three, including a page.

There was wealth enough to send one of the younger sons, Joseph James, to Thanet Collegiate School, but Samuel junior instead joined the family business at the Newington Causeway shop in the late 1860s. Father and son are both described as jewellers in the 1871 census, where young Samuel, now 21, appears with eight sisters, ranging in age from 19 down to just 2 years old. Established in business and at home, his father became an active vestryman and participant in civic life from the mid-1860s in the local parish, 'Newington Vestry', helping to oversee the relief of poverty and the administration of workhouses and eventually joining the main governing board.[10]

It was probably in 1867 that Samuel senior (or perhaps now father and son together) expanded the business from the single shop at 149 Newington Causeway, acquiring the lease on No. 153, two doors away. The business was now divided, with No. 153 set up as a separate opticians, dealing not only in glasses but all the optical instruments, lanterns, and so forth. In an unregulated environment, the Smiths could act as dispensing opticians, the volume sale of reading glasses offering a profitable side-line.

From 1855, stamp duty had been removed on newspaper advertising and this led to a significant increase in its use by retailers in most fields. Broadly, advertising moved from the promotion of individual events and specific sales to the emergence of long-running campaigns, which had the effect of developing 'brands'—such that the public became familiar with the name of a retailer through its regular appearance—Samuel Smith was no exception and by the 1860s his advertisements appeared regularly in local newspapers, chiefly the *South London Chronicle*.

There is a scholarly debate over some of the motives of advertisers, for example over the degree to which advertising was aimed at the aspiring working classes, and to what degree, in the wake of the spectacle of the Great Exhibition and the increasing volume production of consumer goods, including jewellery, there was a desire to stress both the availability and affordability of supposed luxury items.[11] For those who could not afford to buy items outright, the rental market also offered a potentially lucrative avenue for the retailer. Advertising emphasized the vastness of the selection available, and affordability. The massing together of dozens of objects, both in advertisements and in window displays, had the effect of suggesting both luxury and attainability. Samuel's block advertisements in the *South London Chronicle* filled a column, claiming 'prices considerably less than usually charged for articles of the same merit and value', and he was not ashamed to list his prices: 'solid gold Albert chains from 17s 6d to £20' and 'The Celebrated Railway Timekeepers, £1 17s 6d each'. A standard fashion in mourning was to wear a carved brooch in ivory, and the Smiths offered these, as well as 'tortoiseshell and gold jewellery'. The advertisements were tailored to the seasons—for example, at Christmas and New Year 1868, the business headed its advertisements with a 'well selected stock of optical goods, comprising magic lanterns, dissolving views, stereoscopes, microscopes, opera glasses', as well as barometers, thermometers, and botanical microscopes—the magic lanterns and dissolving views could even be hired out.[12] Much else could be hired. If you needed to rent 'plate', i.e. silverware, the Smiths had it—indeed the portfolio on offer extended to providing entertainment for 'evening parties, consisting of first-class Dissolving Views of Palestide, Astronomical, Comical, Conjuring Tricks, and Ventriloquism'.[13] Fashionable, lively dinner party and salon life in south-east London—or aspirations towards it—were enhanced by goods on offer from S. Smith of Newington Causeway.

Despite the rhetoric employed in advertisements and the bold shop-front signing, the family business of Samuel Smith fell within Defoe's definition of tradesmen from London and the south—'shopkeepers, who do not actually work upon, make, or manufacture, the goods they sell'. They formed part of the most common strand of retail jeweller, present on the high street, yet with little in-house workshop capacity. It was important to maintain what Clifford described as the 'myth of the maker', prevalent also in the goldsmiths' trade.[14] Items were badged by the manufacturers with their retailers' names, and presentation boxes naturally featured the retail name.

The two shops (Nos. 149 and 153) straddled that of a piano dealer, but consolidation beckoned in around 1869–70 when the Smiths acquired No. 151, probably subletting No. 149 to Frederick Jones, charmingly described as a 'fancy draper'.[15] With fully adjoining premises, a trend gradually up-market was in evidence and in the early 1870s the trade of 'diamond merchant' began moving up the masthead of Smiths' advertisements, followed by the trades of jeweller, watchmaker, and silversmith. Advertisements now featured 'every description of English and French Clocks'. Diamonds had been discovered in South Africa in 1866, and the consequent exploitation of these had boosted the London trade, with various jewellers—notably Streeter of Bond Street—building their fortunes on the back of it.[16]

Go west, young man

> *A very Fine Stock of Diamonds, mounted and unmounted. An extension assortment of 18ct. Gold Jewellery, Watches, and Chains. A great variety of Dining and Drawing Room Clocks. An extensive assortment of Silver and Plated Goods. A large stock of Jet and Fancy Jewellery.*
>
> (Advertisement, 1872[17])

In the 1860s, the finest London jewellers had begun installing arcaded shop-fronts and dazzling displays, making themselves stand out from other trades—these were the opulent plate-glass temples of Tessier's, Asprey's, Benson's, and Hunt & Roskell.[18] The Smiths moved up-market, opening in the West End by 1872, now trading as S. Smith & Son, diamond merchants, at 85 Strand, taking over a ground-floor shop from fellow silversmith, Henry Henderson. 85 Strand sat at the east corner of the Strand and Cecil Street, which ran south towards Embankment Gardens (below Savoy Place). While

'S. Smith & Son' suggests this was a joint enterprise of father and son, Samuel junior was most likely the driver. His address changed to 26 Cecil Street, bringing him into the heart of the fashionable West End, and making him an immediate neighbour of the historic and distinguished chronometer firm of Frodsham's at 84 Strand, on the opposite corner of Cecil Street. The founding Frodsham had died, but his sons, Charles and Harrison Mill Frodsham, had inherited the business and would have been well known to Samuel—in fact in later years a number of common ties emerged between them. So from the mid-1870s onwards, the shops of Frodsham's and Samuel Smith guarded the Strand entrance to Cecil Street.

There was nothing parochial about the young Samuel Smith's approach to advertising. For example, he took out a box advertisement of several inches in the *Anglo-American Times* over several months from August 1872 to June 1873, addressed 'To Americans in London', offering 'a very Fine Stock of Diamonds, mounted and unmounted', together with clocks, plate, jet, fancy goods—'ALL GOODS AFTER THE AMERICAN STYLE'. Appealing to the shy or uncertain buyer, perhaps, he adds 'Every Article Marked in Plain Figures and at the Lowest Cash Price.'

The Smith–Aldin alliance

One of the great moguls of the Victorian building world.

(*Survey of London*[19])

Samuel settled into family life at the same time, marrying Annie Aldin in 1873. Her father's occupation appeared on the marriage certificate simply as 'builder', but this was deceptive. Charles Aldin was no ordinary jobbing builder—in fact he was a 'mogul' of the building world and 'a very successful speculative builder with many years' experience of house-building'.[20] By the early 1860s, he already employed over 400 men and fifty-five boys, while the family lived in a large house on King's Road in Clapham Park, with four servants and a separate lodge and stables for the coachman and housemaid. Annie had grown up in comfortable circumstances, and indeed was married from 7 Roland Gardens, at the heart of the development her father was engaged in at his death in 1871, and which her brothers carried through in the balance of the 1870s and 1880s. Although Aldin senior endured his share of the troubles common to speculative builders, he nevertheless amassed a fortune to leave to his children.

Just a few months after Samuel and Annie's marriage, a second alliance between the Smiths and Aldins was forged when William Aldin, second son to Charles, married Samuel's eldest sister, Amelia Jane. It is interesting to consider the benefits these marriages brought Samuel and his business. Charles Aldin's estate in 1871 amounted to close to £160,000 (2010: £11.5m), including substantial leaseholds in Kensington, largely divided between his two sons (Samuel's new brothers-in-law). The will also established a trust for Annie's benefit, endowed with £10,000 (2010: £690,000), but her brothers would have ceded control of the funds on her marriage, boosting Samuel and Annie's finances just at the time he was expanding in the West End.

At the end of 1873, with two children married off during the year, Samuel (elder) was in the Isle of Wight, possibly convalescing since his health began to fail that year. To round the year off, December saw the birth of Samuel and Annie's first son: Herbert Samuel Aldin Smith. He was the first of several to preserve the Aldin name, reflecting the importance of the link between the families.

The elder Samuel's health suffered over the next year or so, and one account suggests that, owing to resulting anxiety, Samuel junior took over the business from 1873.[21] Samuel senior went downhill quickly from around November 1874 and died, aged just 48, in February 1875, at Wilton House on Brixton Rise, with his son-in-law, William Aldin, present.[22] Samuel junior was now left in sole charge of the family business, with a presence both at the Elephant and in the West End.

Newington Causeway

The most attractive promenade in the south of London.

(Annual Report of Newington Vestry[23])

The whole area around the Elephant and Castle was being developed and improved, one feature being Spurgeon's enormous Metropolitan Tabernacle, built in the 1860s. The Smiths had consolidated several premises on Newington Causeway, and the shop lay in a row of buildings belonging to the Ecclesiastical Commissioners, but a report in 1873 revealed 'the premises are old and nearly worn out'.[24] The solution was to grant existing tenants new long leases if they would build anew—to which Samuel and his neighbours agreed in 1873. Work started in 1874 and 'the improvement was completed by the end of February 1875 . . . it has now become the most attractive promenade in the south of London'.[25] This coincided with the late stages of the elder Samuel's final illness, and the eighty-year lease for the much improved new premises was completed with his executors—Samuel junior and his brother-in-law William Aldin.[26]

The redevelopment gave S. Smith & Son a classic double-fronted, heavily glazed jeweller's shop-front with plenty of display space for its wares. A later account tells us 'the show-rooms are fitted up and appointed in superior style, the mahogany fittings, massive plate glass show cases, and large mirrors giving a fine effect to the interior'.[27] On completion of the works, the lessees of 131–161 Newington Causeway (including Samuel and his fellow executors) received permission from Newington Vestry to erect fifteen column lamps along the pavement in front of their shops, designed to support large fabric blinds extending from the shop fronts over the front pavement.[28] In all this, Samuel may not have been the only driving force in the business. His mother, Amelia, was a survivor, living all the way through to 1924, and a description of the Smiths' business at the Elephant from the 1890s mentions the 'late Mr Samuel Smith, since whose decease about twenty years ago it has been conducted by his widow, Mrs Smith, who is now the sole proprietress'.[29]

With his mother running the Newington Causeway shop, Samuel could concentrate on building the West End business. In 1882, Samuel added a second shop on the Strand, at No. 9, close to Trafalgar Square at the western end. This was to become the most famous of the firm's West End premises. The census returns and occasional newspaper crime reports provide the names of some of the staff that populated the shops—among them was a young man destined to play a vital role in a dramatic episode some twenty years later, Frank Weaver Margrett, who probably joined in around 1886, as a junior assistant.[30] There were many other staff from these early days whose names unfortunately go unrecorded. The census records provide only some bare bones, and occasional police reports on burglaries and thefts generally add only a limited amount of additional context—although, as we shall see, the forensic detail that sometimes accompanies a crime can provide rich material.

On the family front, by the summer of 1877 Samuel and Annie had moved home again, to Oakbrook on King's Road in Clapham, the street where Annie had grown up. A second son arrived, Cyril Aldin Smith, another bearer of the Aldin name, and destined for distinguished service in the Great War. This was also the year that the Hon. C. S. Rolls, William Morris (later Viscount Nuffield), and Louis Coatalen (prolific automobile designer) were all born—key figures in the future motor industry and contemporaries of the next Smith generation.

With another daughter in between and sticking with a pattern of a child each two years, 1881 brought the birth of the most significant son in this story, and another motor man, Allan Gordon Smith, followed finally by Reginald Aldin Smith, the last of Samuel's children.

Diamonds

> *IF YOU WANT DIAMONDS*
> *Buy by weight*
> *Of the pioneers of this system of business the*
> *ASSOCIATION of DIAMOND MERCHANTS*
>
> (Advertisement, 1896[31])

The importance of the diamond business in Samuel's growing empire has been forgotten, probably because it gradually faded away and there was no lasting industrial legacy. But in the 1880s and 1890s, fine stones occupied a large part of his time, as they did with contemporaries such as Edwin Streeter, one of the best known specialists in fine gems operating in late Victorian London.[32] If the move from the Elephant to the Strand was a move up-market, so too was the move to acquire premises at 6 Grand Hotel Buildings, on the Strand, very close to Trafalgar Square and both central and prestigious, formerly the showrooms and workshops of noted 'art goldsmith' John

Brogden, whose designs had won both medals and plaudits at international exhibitions in Paris in 1867 and 1878. After his death, Christie's sold the whole contents and Samuel stepped in, acquiring the lease and perhaps some of the stock-in-trade and goodwill.[33]

Samuel's business from this site, 6 Grand Hotel Buildings (see Plate 4), went under the name of the Association of Diamond Merchants, unincorporated, from 1885 onwards. But this was not the only diamond merchants' business Samuel established. Winding the clock forward to 1894, Oliver Seeley worked as an assistant in one of the Strand shops, and must have been doing well, since in December 1895 Samuel brought him into a partnership agreement, along with eldest son, Herbert (aged just 22), thus forming the Diamond Merchant's Alliance.[34] Samuel then took out a lease on 68 Piccadilly, installing Seeley as manager, with Herbert as his assistant (see Plate 7).[35] They 'were to receive a weekly salary and a commission upon the profits of the shop should they exceed a certain sum'.[36] In the context of rents, salaries, and profits, the question naturally arises as to the state of Samuel's finances, but little is known. Continued expansion suggests profitability or at least cash-generating ability over the long term, and the single trace of any external financing located to date is a mortgage raised on the Newington Causeway lease in 1886.[37]

From the mid-1890s there were now two notionally separate diamond merchants in the Smith empire, on Trafalgar Square and on Piccadilly. As regular newspaper reports testify, one of the features of an involvement in the diamond and jewellery trade was the number of robberies, involving all the Smith businesses, over many years. Only months into the operation of the Association of Diamond Merchants, Samuel was the victim of an attempted theft. A customer tried to distract an assistant and steal a packet of diamonds, but a hidden system kept customers under surveillance.[38] Perhaps Samuel should have been flattered to be targeted by John Colton, the thief, as Scotland Yard revealed it had 'an intimation from Pinkerton's Detective Agency in New York that he was one of the most expert diamond thieves living'.[39]

Over at the Diamond Merchants' Alliance, Herbert and Seeley found themselves under the spotlight, accused of negligence by Samuel's insurers over a burglary at 68 Piccadilly in October 1897, involving £7,500 in jewels, including a single pair of earrings valued at £3,000 (2011: £265,000), apparently left out of the safe overnight.[40] The haul also included 300 diamond and pearl pins, 15 pearl necklaces, 30 pear and diamond pendants, 6 diamond necklets, 40 diamond rings, 40 diamond bracelets, and yet more diamond watches, combs, and studs.[41] This was a robbery large enough to be reported as far away as New York, and one newspaper suggested that the safe had been tried, without success, and that it contained 'property worth £150,000' (2010: £13.3m).[42]

There was another business in the empire. The Newington Causeway shop had been both jewellers and opticians, carrying on a trade in all sorts of optical devices, as well as spectacles, sold off the shelf and without regulation. Up in the West End, on the south side of the Strand, between Samuel's shop near Trafalgar Square and the premises on the corner of Cecil Street, William Gregory had a shop at No. 51 Strand from around 1881, trading as an optician and scientific instrument maker, and later also as a photographer's. Again, like Samuel, it is extremely likely that his business was really that of retailer, adding his nameplate to binoculars, opera glasses, telescopes, micro-scopes, and other items, many examples of which survive to this day. Gregory hit a rocky patch in 1889 and filed for bankruptcy, allowing Samuel to step in and acquire what the receiver advertised as 'the whole of the valuable Stock of an optician and mathematical instrument maker, together with the office furniture, fittings, cases, an iron safe, book debts etc'.[43] Samuel kept Gregory on as manager, offering a wide range of optical related goods and services, a stone's throw from his jewellery and watch businesses on the busy Strand. During the 1890s, Gregory was to become well-known as a studio photographer, and for taking several thousand pictures of many regiments in the army.[44] It was a classic association, echoed in Regent Street in the close proximity of the prolific London Stereoscopic & Photographic Company and the Goldsmiths & Silversmiths.[45] In common with these firms, the stock-in-trade of Samuel's businesses was the paraphernalia of aspiring middle-class Victorian home life. If Samuel could supply watches, jewellery, purses, and other adornments for the person, his employee William Gregory could provide the portrait photographs to adorn the mantelpiece and dressing table.

So we can see that Samuel divided his businesses. Except for Gregory's, all the shops would have sold watches and jewellery, but the Grand Hotel Buildings and Piccadilly branches were slightly more anonymous, without Samuel's name above the door, and probably selling higher value items. The oldest son, Herbert, was placed squarely in the diamond business at an early age and Cyril, the next son, was also to become involved in the next incarnation of the Diamond Merchant's Alliance, as we shall see in the following chapter. With the eldest son involved, based in the more expensive premises, it is natural to conclude that, at least in Samuel's mind, the diamond business was the flagship within his retail empire.

The watch trade and the development of the Smiths brand

> *Allow me to congratulate your noble craft on such attainments and thank*
> *God for having given such wisdom and skill to men as he has bestowed on*
> *you and some of your skilled brother artists.*
>
> (J. Townsend-Trench, J.P. to S. Smith & Sons,
> 21 December 1896[46])

Diamonds are by their nature anonymous. Watches, by contrast, proudly bear a signature on their dials. They are also relatively long-lived items of personal jewellery, and the long-term twentieth-century cultural legacy of Smiths is much bound up in watches, of different sorts from different ages.

It is worth recalling here that the wristwatch started coming into common use in the Edwardian era, with many advertisements featuring it—often for women rather than men. But by far the most common form of 'portable time' was still the gentleman's pocket watch, frequently worn on a chain that fixed at the other end to a waistcoat or coat lapel. Ladies also carried similar watches, of a smaller size. For example the

Illustrated London News of 1895, referring to Smith & Sons, reported that 'the present fashion of wearing the watch on the corsage has caused the production of some very beautiful patterns and designs'.[47]

The situation for the watch industry in the United Kingdom in the last quarter of the nineteenth century offers parallels with the situation faced by the management of Smiths a century later, both in the watch and motor industries, where developments and changes in foreign-led mass production would have a large impact in the home market. The marketplace confronting Samuel Smith was, like many, comprised of a mass market, for which the cheapest goods were a natural fit; a smaller middle market, looking for something more individual, of better quality and finish, and therefore a higher price; and finally an elite and exclusive band, requiring the very finest.

Leaving aside his broader jewellery business, when the younger Samuel Smith started in business (*c.*1870), there was no mass production of watches in the UK. This emerged much later, although by the 1870s in the United States visionary engineers were imitating the mass production methods of the Springfield Armory, honed in the recent revolutionary war. Series production watches emerged in that decade in the United States, and Switzerland in particular woke up fast to this development and began pushing its own watchmaking trade in the same direction. But the United Kingdom trade body, the BHI, and its short-sighted membership dug in their heels and refused to modernize. The UK industry operated on the 'craft system', in which separate components of a watch (or clock) were made by different specialists operating in an interlocked fashion. Directories for the late nineteenth century show lists of entries for dial-makers, case-makers, spring-makers, hand-makers, and indeed different makers for each of many component elements. Expert opinion suggests that, even in 1900, a mid-range English-made watch could be the final product of upwards of more than forty specialists.[48] There was therefore no single 'maker'—instead the name on the dial, which we are tempted to think of as the maker, should really be thought of as the controlling mind in the production of the watch.

Having set the scene, we can dispel a long-standing myth. The older and younger Samuel Smith did not make watches, but they did add their names to the dials. Few survive with the Newington Causeway address, but thousands still bear the address No. 9 Strand, or Trafalgar Buildings. Of these, large numbers are actually Swiss imports, but badged for Smiths. Many of these are high-quality objects, made by firms such as Heuer or Jeanerret.

Smiths were not unaware of the importance for many customers to wear an 'English Made' product, and although we will encounter an interesting tension in the definition of what is English made or not, it is clear Smiths could also turn to a handful of large-scale producers of English watches. These notably included Rotherham's and Williamson's, both of Coventry, each with outlets in Clerkenwell, allowing for easy access to the West End shops of their customers, such as Smiths. J. H. Seager, originally of Williamson's, wrote many years later, 'as a lad it was part of my job to take messages or parcels from my firm in Clerkenwell to Mr Samuel Smith in the Strand'.[49]

All these suppliers, whether English or Swiss, could provide finished watches, showing 'S. Smith & Sons, 9 Strand' on the dial and indeed the firm's name engraved into the decorative and shiny back-plates of the watches. This was standard business practice, and Smiths' former neighbours, Frodsham's, along with other famous names such as Dent, and Benson (probably Smiths' main competitor), were all engaged in exactly the same practice—essentially that of retailer, not manufacturer.

Which is not to say there was not some in-house expertise. It was possible for Samuel to order watches in any state of completion, and there may have been small final elements of the watch-timing process completed by an employee, on the premises, partly in order to justify the strong claims that the firm made, on the surface of things, to make their own watches.

This last point occurs most forcibly when we consider the very top of Smiths' market—the precision timepieces, or pieces with significant complications (tourbillons, chronographs, and split-seconds timers). These luxury pieces were an important part of the 'brand' and were used to establish a strong reputation for quality and exclusivity.

The Kew trials

> That is the hope and object of all competitions. Sheep and cattle for the million are not represented at Islington. Hacks and cab-horses do not race at Newmarket. Only select scholars stand for the Ireland scholarship or the Porson Prize.
>
> (*The Times*[50])

In 1884, the decision to start testing timepieces at the King's Observatory Kew provided Samuel with a marketing edge for the watches he sold from 9 Strand. With marine navigation dependent upon accurate timekeeping, it was important for prospective purchasers (e.g. the Admiralty) to know that timepieces had been rigorously tested. The first rating test commenced in May 1884, occupying forty-five days, during which time watches were tested for eight periods of five days each, in different temperatures and positions, scoring points out of 100. The result from the tests was expressed both in class, viz. Class A, and also by the numerical score, often together with a narrative, e.g. 'Especially Good'.

This returns us to the issue of Samuel establishing his 'brand'. In April 1884, the Superintendent of the Kew Observatory, Mr Whipple, wrote to *The Times*, announcing that 'in order to answer a demand hitherto unsupplied in this country . . . the Kew Committee of the Royal Society have affiliated . . . a department which will rate Watches for either makers or the public on very moderate terms'.[51] The relatively short letter looks innocuous enough, and simply informative. That there was more behind the scenes is suggested by a significantly longer editorial piece a few days later— almost what might these days be termed an advertorial, and something that S. Smith & Sons were to repeat verbatim in their later catalogues, although there is no direct evidence of their hand, however much we may suspect Samuel's input. The editorial contained a significant puff for the English watch industry, with colourful rhetoric about the doom to which indifferent products were condemned in the trials, and the exalted status to which successful watches would be elevated. Hence the cry that 'Hacks and cab horses do not race at Newmarket'. Competition would improve the quality of all watches on the market, since 'the striving after excellence among the few is found to reproduce itself in a corresponding aspiration among the many'.

S. Smith & Sons submitted watches for trial in the latter part of 1884 and were rewarded amply with a letter to *The Times* in December 1884, again from Mr Whipple the Kew Superintendent, in which he asks the editor

> to chronicle as a noteworthy event in horological science, that we have just been able to award our highest possible certificate, a Class A, especially good, to a Watch submitted to us by a London firm, the cost of which is by no means so great as that frequently paid by gentlemen for a reputed good Watch.[52]

Following the previous pattern, of Whipple writing to *The Times*, followed a couple of days later by more positive editorial, it was revealed in *The Times* of 10 January that the 'makers' of the watch were S. Smith & Sons, 9 Strand.[53] This was excellent advertising, especially since the report continued by saying it was suggested the tests 'were thought so severe as to be practically impossible of attainment by any save specially constructed Watches, which could be produced only at fabulous cost'.

Having established a reputation with this initial coup, Smiths would continue to feature their continued success in Kew tests thereafter. In the late 1890s, another supportive editorial piece appeared in *The Times*, alerting readers they could view at Messrs Smith and Son, in the Strand, 'a remarkable watch' which had just scored 'extraordinarily high marks'. The message was clear—'seeing that English manufacturers have lost so much of the cheap watch trade, it is satisfactory that they can hold their own, and more than hold their own, in those of the highest class'.[54] All excellent advertising that enhanced Smiths' reputation.

Yet they did not make the watches. The finest quality watches and chronometers were made for S. Smith & Son (and Frodsham's, Dent, and other famous retailers) by firms, largely based in Clerkenwell, such as Golay, Baume, Bonniksen, and others, including significantly Nicole Nielsen & Co. of Soho Square.[55] From 1888, this distinguished chronometer firm was majority-owned by Harrison Mill Frodsham (neighbour in business to Smiths in the Strand) and Robert Benson North, who was to be highly important to Smiths in the first decade of the twentieth century. North was a very talented practical watchmaker and craftsman, but also a designer and inventor with a business sense, who would develop volume production capacity that Smiths would utilize. He took over control and management of Nicole Nielsen from 1899.

Smiths' success at the Kew trials rested on being able to source high-quality watches from Nicole Nielsen and other similar manufacturers, leaving Smiths the final task of bringing the watch 'to time' through a series of exacting adjustments carried out in the Strand by its in-house experts in 'springing and timing', as the trade might describe it.[56]

The importance placed by Smiths on their success at Kew is evidenced by the fifteen pages they devote to the whole subject in their *Guide to the Purchase of a Watch*, which appeared first in 1895 and in several subsequent editions. Occasionally, such publicity paid off handsomely. A good example was 'a split-seconds minute recorder watch' which Smiths sold 'to a well-known society man of Boston USA' for £450 in 1899, reported in depth in the *Daily Mail*.[57] The puffing newspaper report tells us the watch apparently took five years to make and a year to regulate sufficiently to score highly at Kew. But this was a product of a Soho Square precision manufactory, not Samuel Smith's Strand basement.

In the same way, Smiths popularized their 'Non-Magnetizable Watches'. Again, many pages of Smiths' catalogue were devoted to the subject, offering the dire warning that 'a journey on an electric railway may render a Watch useless for time-keeping purposes'.[58] Having painted such a risky picture, Smiths of course nevertheless had the solution. They could demagnetize the prized (though 'demoralized') possessions of their clients. And of course they could also sell an entire range of non-magnetizable watches—most watches offered at the Strand could be offered in a non-magnetic version at extra cost.

This product once more depended upon the efforts of an outside designer and manufacturer—in this case, one of Coventry's most distinguished makers, Alfred Fridlander, who supplied Smiths with a large number of watches, including examples shown at the 1892 Crystal Palace Electrical Exhibition, for which a gold medal and diploma were awarded.[59]

Interestingly, the highlighting of their success in Kew trials can be seen positioning S. Smith & Sons at the prestige end of the market. The publication of their *Guide to the Purchase of a Watch* elicited a strong response from the public. When they advertised it in the *Daily Courier* in 1896, they received postal applications for the catalogue by 12 o'clock the same day.[60] Yet interestingly another separate initiative attracted a different market—perhaps more the aspirational buyer—which was the introduction of instalment payments for watches. By the end of the 1890s, we see the offer of watches for sale against monthly or quarterly instalment payments, for UK residents only, and also the offer of a 5 per cent reduction for cash and immediate purchase.[61] Other firms in other markets were trying the same mass marketing, and among the London jewellers, Smiths were in company with Goldsmiths', Bensons, and Sir John Bennett—the Smiths advertisements in the *Illustrated London News* highlight 'The Times Encyclopaedia Britannica system of payment by monthly instalments', under a banner 'Immense Increase in Business'.[62]

Demolition, demolition, demolition

> *Great Sale of Jewellery—No Reasonable Offer Refused.*
> (*South London Chronicle*, 1897[63])

The 1870s had seen the demolition of the Newington Causeway premises and their rebuilding. Sometime in 1894, Samuel's West End neighbours, Frodsham's, received official notice of the intention to demolish their premises at No. 84 Strand, along with nearby buildings, all part of the 'Cecil Hotel Development Scheme', promoted by the infamous financier Jabez Balfour.[64] Building commenced, right next door to Smiths, which must have caused significant upheaval until completion of the first phase, but then the luxury hotel opened on 6 May 1896 and probably provided valuable new business.[65]

Back at the Elephant, where Samuel's mother had been running the business, it was reported in the press in 1897 that the trust under which the Newington Causeway property had been held after the elder Samuel's death was to expire and that the premises would pass to the Capital and Counties Bank, with a consequent need to liquidate the stock. The Smiths held a large sale, covering the front of the building with a large sign, announcing 'Great Sale of Jewellery—No Reasonable Offer Refused', and the store finally closed on 31 December 1897, bringing to an end the association with Newington Causeway (see Plate 3).[66] Amelia, Samuel's mother, was now 67 and if she had not already let go the reins of the business, surely she did now. She retired to 73 Ritherdon Road, in Tooting, with four of her daughters, where she was to see out the rest of her life.

Towards the end of 1898, Samuel Smith would have been in negotiation with the owners and developers of the Cecil Hotel next door. Having swallowed up the west side of Cecil Street, now there was a move to expand the footprint of the hotel towards Waterloo Bridge, and this would now absorb the east side of Cecil Street, and with it S. Smith & Sons on the corner. It was time to make another move, but this time it would be more far-reaching, as we shall see in the next chapter.

Family life in the 1890s

> *Mr F. C. Willis also examined the debtor at length as to various business transactions and his expenditure for the benefit of ladies who had lived under his protection.*
>
> (*The Times*[67])

If Samuel had dynastic visions both for the family and the business, the marriages of his children will have exercised his mind. In 1890, as he turned 40, the decade that was to unfold ahead offered much promise. He seems to have being living in comfort at home, with six healthy children, three of them now teenagers. His business empire gives every impression of being successful and expanding, in what was a prosperous decade of growth in trade and commerce. The middle years (1895 in particular) were a boom time, with the stock market showing a huge rise, largely on the back of the explosion of the South African gold market and the speculative mining companies to which it provided the spark. Against this backdrop, the Smith children grew up in prosperous circumstances and they probably had opportunities and freedoms that Samuel had not enjoyed.

The three eldest children all married before the turn of the century. First was Ethel Annie, aged 21 when she married Herbert Pigott Froy, who came from a wealthy family of builders' merchants based at Brunswick Works in Hammersmith. Residents of Hammersmith will know the name Froy from the drain covers that still populate their streets. In due course Herbert went on to run the family firm, incorporating it in 1909 and then floating part on the stock market in 1935.[68] With Ethel's marriage we see another link between the Smith family and the broader building trade.

Samuel's eldest, Herbert, was next, marrying Lilian Maud Cave in 1897. Lilian was one of eight daughters and four sons to Edward Jarvis Cave, 'a man of more than usual drive and energy' and, perhaps unsurprisingly given an apparent pattern emerging, 'a very large speculator in building in the City and elsewhere'.[69] Isobel Watson's meticulously researched account describes how Cave blazed across the heavens with his sons building the 'large mid-city mansion block' in Hampstead in the 1890s, amassing a considerable fortune at the same time. But he was to come spectacularly unstuck in 1900 when an illiquid market made it impossible to continue to finance his speculative building activity and unpaid suppliers of materials took action. Bankruptcy proceedings, reported in detail in *The Times*, took care of any wealth that might once have been amassed, but also unearthed the secret double-life Cave had been living, with 'expenditure for the benefit of ladies who lived under his protection' and another family in Camden—clearly a man with more energy than most. All four Cave sons were involved in the building business, and three of them were also to fail. Marrying into the Cave family (and another important Smith would do so) certainly provided spectacle, with scandals and bankruptcies followed by Lilian's sister Madge becoming Olympic figure-skating champion in 1908.

Finally, Cyril Aldin Smith married Mabel Sayer in 1897. This was perhaps at first glance a more unconventional marriage—none of the parents acted as witnesses and perhaps did not even attend. Cyril was still 20 and Mabel only 19, so unusually young to be married in their respective families' social circles—Mabel's father was a successful and prosperous brandy shipper.[70] Within a short time, Cyril's choices in life would no doubt have both sets of parents raising their eyes to the heavens. The family business therefore soon faced a traditional problem of succession planning.

The end of the Victorian era

> *This is a story of a future built on the foundations of the past; of the aim of a great enterprise based on the tradition and reputation of those who have gone before us—the Smiths of England.*
>
> (Foreword, *The Smiths of England*[71])

Three generations of Samuel Smiths saw great advancement in their fortunes over the course of a century from the 1790s to the 1890s—from potato merchant to diamond merchant—from Spitalfields to Piccadilly. In this chapter we have seen some of the material wealth being accumulated as residential and commercial addresses gradually move up-market. This was against a backdrop of a changing London landscape, where building enterprise was undertaken speculatively on a grand scale by characters such as the Aldins and the Caves, using materials from suppliers such as the Froys. It is a typical Victorian London story of mercantile commerce, in which we glimpse characteristic extended family and business networks. With the bedrock of new streets and new houses being laid down, so retailers such as the Smiths populated the stores on the high streets. While there might be a large manufacturing future ahead of them, the Smiths were at this stage simply adept at mediating between the wealthy ladies and gentlemen of the Strand on the one hand, and on the other the unseen skilled craftsmen, bench hands, and small-scale mass manufacturers who actually fabricated their products. For those who judged the retail trade correctly, there were ample rewards. For example, when Samuel Smith's neighbour William Tarn died in 1875, his department store at 165–173 Newington Causeway had allowed him to build a personal fortune of nearly half a million pounds (2010: £37m). But with wealth, responsibilities and concerns arrive in tandem, and we explore some of these in the next chapter, as one century gave way to another.

Notes

1. 23 Oct. 1897, 8.
2. J. S. Wright, 'The Jewellery and Gilt Toy Trades', in Samuel Timmins, *The Resources, Products and Industrial History of Birmingham and the Midland Hardware District* (London: Robert Hardwicke, 1866), 452–62.
3. Shelagh Wilson, 'Art and Industry: Birmingham Jewellery or "Brummagem"?', in Kenneth Quickenden and Neal Quickenden (eds), *Silver and Jewellery* (Birmingham: UCE, 1995), 43.
4. No. 12 renumbered as no. 149.
5. The site was 'totally destroyed by enemy action in 1941', Ecclesiastical Commissioners archive, ECE/7/1/95012.
6. Henry Mayhew, *London Labour and the London Poor* (London: Griffin, Bohn, 1862), iv. 333–4.
7. No apprenticeship records have been located.
8. A dealer in hides; *London Gazette* (8 Oct. 1833), 4.
9. Built 1849–52 by Garland and Christopher, in classic yellow stocks. English Heritage ID 470827.
10. Southwark Archives, *Minutes of St Mary Newington Vestry Governors and Guardians* (1865–6), 261–2, 299; *South London Chronicle* (22 Apr. 1865), 6; (29 Apr. 1865), 2; (24 June 1865), 3; (7 Apr. 1866), 2, (18 Apr. 1868), 5.
11. See e.g. Roy Church, 'Advertising Consumer Goods in Nineteenth Century Britain: Reinterpretations', *Economic History Review*, 53 (Nov. 2000), 621–45.
12. Dissolving view: a projector with two or more lenses, allowing slides to be dissolved from one to another (e.g. night into day); *South London Chronicle* (4 Jan. 1868), 7.
13. *South London Chronicle* (4 Jan. 1868), 7.

14. Helen Clifford, 'The Myth of the Maker: Manufacturing Networks in the London Goldsmiths' Trade', in Quickenden and Quickenden, *Silver and Jewellery*, 5–11.
15. Post Office directory (1872).
16. Patrick Streeter, *Streeter of Bond Street* (Harlow: Matching Press, 1993), 59–66.
17. Advertisement for S. Smith & Son, 85 Strand, *Anglo American Times* (31 Aug. 1872), 25.
18. Kathryn Morrison, *English Shops and Shopping: An Architectural History* (London: Yale University Press, 2003), 63.
19. *Survey of London*, xli. *Brompton* (1983), 149; xlii. *Kensington Square to Earls Court* (1986), 395.
20. See 'Roland Gardens', *Survey of London*, xli. *Brompton*, 149–55.
21. Wilfrid M. Cann, 'Smiths Industries Limited: A Chronological Record', unpublished manuscript (1962, revised 1967/8), 2 vols, i. 15.
22. *South London Press* (13 Feb. 1875), 7.
23. Southwark Archives, *Annual Report of Newington Vestry* (1874–5), 29.
24. Cluttons to George Pringle, Whitehall Place (15 Jan. 1873), ECE/7/1/95012.
25. Southwark Archives, *Annual Report of Newington Vestry* (1874–5), 29.
26. Letter, White Barrett to the Commissioners (21 June 1875), ECE/7/1/95012.
27. Wilfrid Cann, 'Robert Lenoir 1898–1979', unpublished manuscript (1980), 97.
28. *South London Chronicle* (9 Jan. 1875), 5.
29. Cann, 'Lenoir 1898–1979', 97.
30. Census (1891); *The Straits Times* (24 May 1912), 7.
31. *The Times* (10 Nov. 1896), 10.
32. Streeter, *Streeter,* passim.
33. The sale is reported widely, but see e.g. *The Times* (22 Apr. 1885), 16.
34. *The Times* (17 July 1894), 3.
35. *The Times* (29 June 1896), 4.
36. *The Times* (11 Aug. 1898), 3.
37. Ecclesiastical Commissioners, ECE/7/1/95012.
38. *The Times* (8 June 1886), 4.
39. *The Times* (15 July 1886), 4.
40. *The Times* (11 Aug. 1898), 3.
41. *The Church Weekly* (5 Nov. 1897), 889.
42. *Westminster Budget* (5 Nov. 1897), 3.
43. *The Times* (2 Nov. 1889), 16.
44. *Pall Mall Gazette* (5 May 1893), 7.
45. Charlotte Gere and John Culme, *Garrard* (London: Quartet, 1993), 52.
46. Testimonial, Smith & Sons, *Guide to the Purchase of a Watch* (London: Smith & Sons, c.1900), 24.
47. *Illustrated London News* (14 Dec. 1895), 742.
48. David Penney, personal communication.
49. Cann, 'Chronological Record', i. 66.
50. 28 Apr. 1884, 9.
51. *The Times* (25 Apr. 1884), 10.
52. *The Times* (26 Dec. 1884), 8.
53. *The Times* (10 Jan. 1885), 11.
54. *The Times* (5 Nov. 1898), 6.

55. See e.g. the range of actual manufacturers of Frodsham's pieces, Vaudrey Mercer, *The Frodshams: The Story of a Family of Chronometer Makers* (Ticehurst: AHS, 1981), appendix X.

56. Smiths employed Charles Heap and George Mortimer Cole in this role—two distinguished craftsmen.

57. *Daily Mail* (6 Apr. 1899), 7.

58. Smith & Sons, *Guide to the Purchase of a Watch, with illustrations* (London: Smith & Sons, c.1900), 29.

59. Advertisement, *Daily Mail* (12 Dec. 1896), 8.

60. *Daily Mail* (14 May 1896), 1.

61. See e.g. the advertisement for the 'Strand' watch, *Daily Mail* (23 Apr. 1899), 8.

62. See e.g. *Illustrated London News* (2 Sept. 1899), 338.

63. 23 Oct. 1897, 8.

64. See Mercer, *Frodshams*, 168. For the Cecil Hotel, see *The Times* (31 Oct. 1895), 14.

65. *The Times* (19 May 1896), 16.

66. *South London Chronicle* (23 Oct. 1897), 8.

67. 9 Nov. 1900, 13.

68. *The Times* (4 July 1935), 20.

69. Isobel Watson, 'A Very Large Speculator in Building: The Double Life of EJ Cave', *Camden History Review*, 24 (2000), 26–31, in turn quoting C. Dalton, 'Mountjoy's Inn, Fenchurch Street', *Topographical Record*, 27 (1995).

70. Census (1901).

71. S. Smith & Son, *Motor Accessories Catalogue* (London, 1910).

CHAPTER 2

···

1899–1913
A New Business Emerges

···

During all this long time we have suffered with galling impatience that knowledge of the infinite superiority of machinery, which it has always had, and always will have, over all kinds of animal power, specially in the matter of traffic.

(Harry Lawson[1])

WITH these triumphalist words, the serial company promoter Harry Lawson raised a toast at the Metropole Hotel in November 1896, at the end of the 'Emancipation Run'—the first London to Brighton run, commemorating the new law permitting motor-cars on the highways. Lawson, collaborating with Ernest Hooley (archetypal promoter and serial bankrupt), had been the epicentre of the Coventry cycling boom of the mid-1890s, and as that market began to go off the boil, he set his sights firmly on creating and sustaining a new boom, in the fledgling motor market—a market in which Hooley floated Dunlop in 1896 for £5 million (2010: £450m).[2]

While Lawson quickly crashed and burned, the transition from cycling boom to motor-car boom was unstoppable, many motor firms notably having their roots in the cycling industry, often in Coventry—Humber, Hillman, Rover, Riley, Swift, and many more.[3] Likewise, many motor pioneers and promoters started out as cycling champions—S. F. Edge and William Morris to name just two—Morris later proving critically important to Smiths.

Following the Emancipation Run, the number of cars in the UK rose from a handful to 23,000 a decade later (see Figure 2.1). By 1910–11, Morris was convinced 'there was going to be a big demand for a popularly priced car', having witnessed already for years the capacity of the market to absorb the products of a chaotic new industry, characterized not by vertically integrated manufacture, but assembly of components sourced from 20,000 small engineering firms located in Sheffield, Birmingham, and Coventry, already employing some three-quarters of a million people.[4] Joseph Lucas & Co., its main business line in cycle parts—called Cyclealities—moved early, developing Motoralities from 1901 onwards.

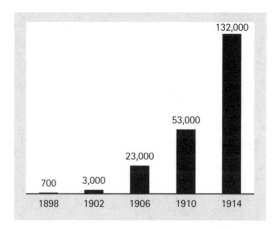

FIGURE 2.1 Number of cars in the UK (1898–1914).
Source: National Motor Museum

In London, Samuel Smith was concerned about succession planning and his inheritance. The firm was dabbling in motor watches, but he probably imagined Gordon would continue in diamond-merchanting and jewellery. Gordon had other ideas and was much taken with the fast emerging motor industry. From 1903–4, he began to focus on motor accessory factoring, laying the foundations for a wholly new business which would come to supplant his father's retail empire within a short space of time.

Into the twentieth century: the pace increases

> 'The outlook so far as the price of diamonds is concerned,' observed
> the manager of S. Smith & Son, Limited, 9 Strand, to a 'Daily Mail'
> representative yesterday 'is exceedingly doubtful.'
>
> (Daily Mail, 10 October 1899, 3)

The 'manager' talking to the *Daily Mail* was probably Samuel, commenting a week after the beginning of the Boer War and speculating about the prospects for the diamond market if the Kimberley diamond mines were to shut. Prices might well escalate, but he also revealed to the reporter that he had been made an attractive offer by a large syndicate for his whole stock the previous April. The evidence suggests the nouveau riche Samuel had a lot on his mind that year—probably reflecting on the journey from a small jewellery business in south-east London to a series of West End showrooms and much accumulated wealth, with its attendant burdens.

The difficulties of estate planning for the richest tier in society have attracted study, but work remains to be done on the rising class of bankers and merchants who made their modest fortunes in the late Victorian and Edwardian periods.[5] In the case of

Samuel, we can speculate on his thinking. He never knew his grandfather and his father died before 50. In considering Samuel's actions in 1899, it is worth considering the issue of mortality. Samuel was close to the Aldins, his brothers-in-law, who were near his own age, so it will have come as a shock when William died, aged just 43, in 1892. Two years later, Charles died at 50. William Froy, father-in-law to Samuel's eldest daughter, who had built up a substantial business, died in 1897. Samuel's children were now young adults, and he would turn 50 in 1900—it would have been natural to consider succession planning and inheritance issues. Although he was not to die for a number of decades, the evidence, including the small size of his eventual estate, suggests he acted early to pass his wealth on to the next generation.

Samuel's father had forged his own path, setting up in a new business, without any sibling involvement. Samuel had continued that business—the 'son' in 'S. Smith & Son'—but his only brother, Joseph James Smith, was not included. The latter set up his own jewellery business, in Putney and then Peckham. But Samuel involved all his sons, with the elder two brought into the diamond-merchanting side of the business in their early twenties. The younger two would also eventually become involved, so Samuel's intentions appear clear—that his sons should be closely gathered around him in business, not moving off into separate spheres of their own.

Another influence on Samuel's thinking would have been the risks to which unincorporated businesses or partnerships were exposed. In the case of the Aldin family business, Samuel and Annie had been direct beneficiaries of Charles Aldin's will back in the 1870s. But over 90 per cent of the estate, some £150,000 (2010: £10.9m) passed to William and Charles, who carried on the family building business. The continued development of Roland Gardens occupied the next twenty years, during which time this and other projects gradually absorbed all the capital in the Aldin building partnership. The young Aldins did not accumulate capital as their father had done, they burned through it. Samuel will have seen the whole process unfold. He was an executor to William's will in 1892, where the estate amounted to just £2,500. He will have known Charles's estate amounted to considerably less in 1894. Not long after, the sole remaining partner in the building firm was bankrupted, so a business that had significant capital in the 1870s dwindled to nothing in twenty years. Bankruptcy was a very public affair and where significant sums were involved it was common for a report of the examination to appear in *The Times*. Thus Samuel, who probably knew the details intimately in any case, could not have avoided reading that the last partner standing 'ascribed the insolvency of the business to the heavy drawings of his late partners [Samuel's brothers-in-law]' and that 'the business had been profitable throughout, but the drawings had exceeded the profits made'.[6]

Samuel's son Herbert had married into the Cave family in January 1897. Cave senior walked the tightrope of speculative building, always heavily demanding on cash-flow, and Samuel had an insight, since his eldest daughter had married into the Froy family of builders' merchants, a business that operated by extending deferred payment terms to builders. Between his children and their spouses, intelligence on E. J. Cave's financial situation would have been forthcoming well ahead of the bankruptcy that was to break in 1900.[7]

Turning to the older sons, though Herbert and Cyril were involved in diamond merchanting in the late 1890s, this did not last for long, and Cyril in particular soon made a bold break. Samuel may have already detected by late 1898 that dynastic plans for the Smiths' jewellery business might unfold unevenly.

Finally, we have seen Samuel would have been negotiating the surrender of the lease of 85 Strand to the developers of the Cecil Hotel towards the end of 1898. Here we can see a tangible physical event which may have acted as a spur to his thinking. Once more there would be a clearance sale, once more a new shop to set up. It might be a relatively small rearrangement within the business, but having made a number of such moves in recent years, Samuel may have wanted to make longer term arrangements going forward.

It seems reasonable to hypothesize that a cocktail of concerns over mortality, the risks of personal bankruptcy, possible concerns over the career hopes of his eldest two sons, and the need to move premises yet again might all combine to suggest a radical new course of action for Samuel in early 1899. But before outlining this, it is important to introduce another of the key actors in the Smiths narrative.

The return of the chosen one

> *His presence being required in the family business, Allan Gordon Smith*
> *returned from Switzerland.*
>
> (Cann, 'Chronological Record'[8])

Like his elder brothers, Gordon (as Allan Gordon was known early on) attended Christ's College, Finchley. Here he was an outstanding sportsman, playing for the school in the first XV in rugby, the first XI in both football and cricket, taking first place in many athletics events over his school career, including running (100, 110, and 220 yards), high jump, and putting the weight—he even won diving and swimming competitions.[9] Leaving Christ's in 1897, he likely joined his father in the Strand before travelling to Switzerland in April 1898 to start what should have been a three-year watchmaking course at the Westschweizerisches Technikum in Biel (Bienne).[10] His sporting reputation is further bolstered by the claim that, while there, he and another Englishman formed the local Association Football Club.[11]

An enduring mystery is the story of Gordon's return from Biel. He would have completed his first year towards the end of March 1899, but he was called back to London, perhaps accounting for Walton's description of his time abroad as 'an intensive apprenticeship in Switzerland'. He had hardly begun, so later public relations occasionally stretched the truth with claims he completed a thorough apprenticeship.[12] Despite his short stay, Gordon appears nevertheless to have forged relationships that proved critically important in later years. Given events unfolding in London, the suspicion is that Gordon's recall coincided with a corporate reorganization, as the firm moved into new premises at 104 Strand in early 1899—added to which his father Samuel was probably less interested in his son acquiring true watchmaking and bench skills than having someone to help manage the business. If it was already obvious that Herbert and Cyril were not cut out to be managers in the jewellery trade, perhaps the reverse was true of Gordon, and his father needed him close at hand.

Limited liability

The twelfth annual smoking concert, promoted by the Association of Diamond Merchants, including the well-known firms of Samuel Smith and Son, W. Gregory & Co, and the Diamond Merchants' Alliance, was held on Saturday night at the Hotel Cecil, under the presidency of Mr Samuel Smith.

(*The Echo*[13])

Samuel incorporated four companies at the end of March 1899:

* Association of Diamond Merchants, Jewellers and SilverSmiths Limited
* S. Smith & Son Limited
* Diamond Merchants' Alliance Limited
* W. Gregory & Co. Limited

All four companies shared a number of features. The initial shareholders in all four cases were: Samuel and Annie Smith, Herbert and Lilian Smith, Cyril Smith, Herbert and Ethel Froy (Samuel's daughter). In each case, Samuel transferred the relevant shop lease, plus stock and other assets, into a company, in exchange for fully paid ordinary and preferred shares. He took all the preferreds personally, plus all the ordinaries save for one each allotted to the other family members. No new equity was raised, and no cash consideration passed, so in effect Samuel merely drew the cloak of limited liability around a series of businesses. The end result is shown in Table 2.1.

The nominal consideration can be taken with a pinch of salt and does not necessarily represent fair value. That said, Samuel was at liberty to pick any numbers he liked, so the proportional relationship between share capitals is suggestive. On this measure, the Association of Diamond Merchants was apparently valued at nearly three times as much as S. Smith & Son, the watch, clock, and jewellery business—worth remembering as the businesses evolved over the next twenty years.

Samuel stamped his authority on the new companies, taking the role of 'governing director', which reserved practically all executive authority to himself, and from the share structure and the wording of the articles it is clear these four companies were in essence simply different aspects of 'Samuel Smith Limited'.

Table 2.1 Limited liability companies formed (1899)

Company	Lease Assigned	Nominal Consideration	Shares Allotted to Samuel
Association of Diamond Merchants, Jewellers and SilverSmiths Ltd	68 Piccadilly	£120,000	11,994 £5 ordinaries 12,000 £5 prefs
S. Smith & Sons Ltd	9 Strand 104 Strand	£45,000	4,394 £5 ordinaries 4,400 £5 prefs
Diamond Merchants' Alliance Ltd	No. 6, Grand Hotel Buildings	£19,970	1,993 £5 ordinaries 2,000 £5 prefs
W. Gregory & Co. Ltd	51 Strand	£6,000	5,994 £5 ordinaries 6,000 £5 prefs

Source: TNA: BT31/16169/61324 and 16170/61325/6/7.

Exposition Universelle, Paris 1900, and Glasgow 1901

> *The ladies who constantly surround the magnificent display of precious stones and pearls are continually breaking the tenth commandment.*[14]

Gordon's first major role was running the stands for the family businesses at the 1900 Exposition Universelle in Paris, where S. Smith & Son won bronze in the watch and clock class, while the Association of Diamond Merchants also took bronze, in a class dominated by maharajahs and other dignitaries from India.[15] A year later, Gordon was in charge again, with a single but much larger stand at the Glasgow International Exhibition for the Association of Diamond Merchants, showing clocks and watches, silver and jewellery, and winning a prize medal and diploma.[16] Returning in triumph, Gordon became manager at 68 Piccadilly—his (probably unreliable) brother Herbert meanwhile having disappeared from the scene. A significant recruit that year was Charles William Nichols who joined as Gordon's assistant and secretary, destined to become one of the most critical members of Gordon's team. Another key player, Primus Otto Dorer, joined in 1903. The son of a clockmaker from Baden, Germany, and a gifted technician and inventor, he was to be vital to Gordon in the development of countless Smiths products over several decades (Plate 5).[17]

The end of an era: the dawn of another

> *Victoria's mourning . . . set standards of etiquette that could only be satisfied by the purchase of specific clothes, jewellery and personal accessories.*[18]

A famous Smiths folk memory relates to the death of Queen Victoria. In the wake of Albert's death, Victoria had created a fashion both for black clothing and black funereal jewellery, ideally made from Whitby jet. As the end of the nineteenth century neared, so observers increasingly predicted the demise of the ageing monarch. Samuel apparently gradually amassed a large stock of jet jewellery, so that when Victoria finally died in 1901, the ladies of the West End flocked to his shop, earning him a significant one-time profit—a good anecdote, but no evidence has yet emerged.

If fashions in mourning jewellery had ossified because the Queen had lasted so very long—'no one knew any longer what should be worn'—there was another facet to S. Smith & Son's business in the new century that was distinctly forward-looking.[19] The Strand firm began altering its focus away from personal accessories and more towards adornments for motor-cars. With the coronation of the new King, the firm started offering an 'automotive' version of the long-standing 'Strand' model of watch for £4 4s (2010: £355), with an 8-day movement and an unusual and memorable pear-shaped case.[20] While motor-car clocks were an obvious item for a firm that regularly secured high marks for watches at the Kew trials, Samuel and Gordon were about to achieve their finest marketing coup with the introduction of the speedometer, but to set the context, we need to turn the clock back a few years.

Emergence of the car

> If the Bill became law during the present Session, he believed it would undoubtedly develop a very great, and, having regard to their experience in connection with bicycles, quite possibly an enormous trade, and give a vast amount of employment to the people of this country. ['Hear, hear!'] He thought it was even possible that these motor cars might become a rival to light railways—[laughter]—and that they were not at all unlikely to tend to decrease railway fares.
>
> (Hansard[21])

The firm had ridden the cycling boom with a range of speed indicators and timers, working hard to have their chronographs and timers used at any sort of race meet. In 1903, S. Smith & Son proudly proclaimed it had provided the official timing of the Gordon Bennett Race, bringing out a special commemorative clock.[22] Dashboard clocks for motor-cars were an obvious and easy addition to the range and by late 1903 Smiths even offered an 'automobile timepiece' with a 'tiny electric battery which will afford a thousand flashes to illuminate the dial in the darkness'.[23] But it was also natural to consider what other instruments could be sold for motor-cars, especially since a critical issue, over which there was much argument, was that of speed. There was another factor. With a background in the West End jewellery trade, some of the target clientele would already be familiar. Each Christmas the firm managed to get a good range of their goods covered in the 'Ladies' Pages' of the *Illustrated London News*, and it was there in December 1902 that the 'Motor Speed Chronograph' made an appearance, 'which enables the driver to time his speed exactly by the mile posts'.[24] This might well have made a handsome present from the lady of the house to her automobilist husband, but frankly did not offer cutting edge technology—something much better was needed.

The Edwardian Smiths succeeded in leaving to posterity the idea that they invented the first speedometer. The truth lies more in the firm being the first to sell large quantities of speedometers—and accurate ones at that—and the key to their success is clear. Where the credit should lie for the practical development of early speed indicators offers a research project in its own right, but various inventors and mechanics advertised their newly patented devices in magazines such as *Autocar* in the early years of the century. Smiths had already started advertising their motor watches in the growing motor press and it cannot have escaped their attention that, early in 1904, advertisements in *Autocar*, close to Smiths' own on the page, were appearing for an increasing variety of speed indicators—for example, from Jones, Staunton's, and Vulcan—often with 'knocking copy' directed at the competition.[25] Smiths advertised their old 'motor speed chronograph', calling it a 'speed indicator', but it was not in the same league.[26] All this was to change dramatically within months, as Smiths were busy behind the scenes.

Crystal Palace 1904

> Attention may be directed to the improved speed indicator of Messrs. Smith and Sons, the watch-makers to the Admiralty. There is every reason to believe that this most ingenious device will give a reading, not approximately, but absolutely correct . . . if the belief be correct, the invention is almost as welcome on moral as on scientific grounds.
>
> (*The Times*[27])

The venue was the Society of Motor Manufactures and Traders' motor show at Crystal Palace in February 1904. Smiths' publicity machine was in operation, as this supportive report in *The Times* shows—no other speed indicators warranted a mention—though there was plenty of competition, some of it covered in the more specialist press.[28] *The Car* was positive, describing the 'considerable attention' attracted by this 'most promising' new device, while *Autocar's* 'Guide to the Show' praised this 'improved type', recording that 'on stopping the car the hand at once returns to zero'.[29]

These motor shows were scaled-down versions of the Paris and Glasgow international exhibitions at which Smiths enjoyed success. The motor world was dominated by larger-than-life racing drivers such as Selwyn Edge, who had his own large stand at the show, showing Napier cars, while Dennis Brothers apparently took nearly £30,000 worth of orders (2010: £2.5m). In the heady petrol- and leather-scented atmosphere, the driven and intensely sporty and social Gordon will have thrived, with his assistant, the equally clubbable Charles Nichols, whose first show this was, but who would soon be living and breathing motor accessories.[30]

Following the death of Edward VII, a book of reminiscences by his driver, Charles Stamper, appeared—ghost-written by Dornford Yates.[31] The account of accompanying the King on every car journey from July 1905 is a highly entertaining picaresque tale, filled with amusing vignettes. Allowing for some licence, Stamper reveals Edward as genuinely interested in the finer details of the stable of motor-cars he assembled from June 1900 onwards. Stamper notes 'I had to arrange for the purchase of the cars and all accessories', and it may be that the previous mechanic did the same.[32]

The legend that survives in Smiths folklore has Edward VII asking Gordon Smith for a device to tell him how fast he was going in his car. The King was interested in maximum speeds, regularly travelling the seventy-mile run to Newmarket 'at a good pace', congratulating his engineer on a 'Fine run, Stamper. Fine run'.[33] A year before Stamper took up service, in 1904, it is clear the King had a speedometer installed (see Plates 8, 9). The ledger of speedometers delivered by Smiths in 1904–5 is preserved in its archive and opens with a magnificent first entry, in Gordon Smith's handwriting (see Plate 10):

No.1 H.M. The King, Buckingham Palace 18–28hp Mercedes Aug [1904]

The Prince of Wales followed suit the following February. In May 1905 it was the turn of the Princess of Wales' car, with the Queen's car completing the picture in October. This flurry of patronage allowed Smiths to apply for, and receive, a royal warrant in early 1907. Looking back, on the surface of it, there was no occasion when the King might have chatted to Gordon Smith, aged 23, and requested a speedometer—far more likely it was Stamper's predecessor, and that when the King's order for a new Daimler was placed at the time of the motor show, in mid-February 1904, a speedometer for the existing Mercedes was also ordered.[34]

Folklore also has it that Gordon had a hand in designing that first speedometer, assisted by Primus Otto Dorer. The true story is much more complex and reflects the all-important relationship between manufacturer and retailer. In Chapter 1 we met Robert Benson North of Nicole Nielsen, makers of many of the finest and complicated watches Smiths retailed. Despite this, following market practice, Nielsen's remained behind the scenes—it was the Smith name on the dial. The Smiths' clock catalogue boldly claimed the firm had factories in Coventry and at Soho Square, but in reality these belonged to Samuel's suppliers. The speed indicator fitted to the royal Mercedes is easily identifiable and was without doubt made by Nicole Nielsen, tying in with Mercer's account, which claims that 'in 1904 the firm Nicole Nielsen & Co. Ltd began to manufacture speedometers at 14 Soho Square'.[35] Unlike Smiths in the Strand, where some light finishing and adjusting could be done, 14 Soho Square had three floors set out for the complete manufacture of precision mechanical objects, using lathes, mills, presses, drills—indeed a full machine shop on one floor and a polishing shop on another.[36]

North had realized how important a speedometer was for the new motorist and having developed an initial model, he apparently mentioned his invention to Smiths, who then contracted to take his entire output.[37] A later in-house account makes it clear it was Gordon who was enthusiastic for the new product line, not his father. Samuel, despite disapproval, was also still firmly in charge and insisted it was his name that appeared as co-patentee alongside North's on a patent for 'Improvements to Speed Indicators'.[38] This was filed the day after the Crystal Palace show opened and it seems likely that in late 1903 the two houses would have been tying up a supply deal.

Faced with a willing buyer of all his output, and perhaps without any natural sales outlet, it was expedient for North to accept an exclusive arrangement with Samuel. But as with all the watches and clocks that Smiths carefully badged and engraved to show its name, so it had to ensure the public associated its name, and its name only, with the product. With North's name kept out of the limelight, the story of Smiths' royal speedometers could be cemented. Finishers and adjusters at Smiths could work on watches in-house, and in a similar vein the firm did not simply introduce their speedometer customers to the manufacturer—they arranged the fitting as well.

A number of interesting snippets about the early speedometer business survive in the ledger, including the names of various subcontractors and suppliers. While the bulk of the ledger details sales, the last few pages reveal scribbled pencil accounts for the fitting operation, including details of the fitters, one of whom was Charles Mears. Clerkenwell-born, he was 16 in 1901, working as an 'engine room lad', and living next door to a watch finisher in Islington, perhaps the source of an introduction to Smiths. By late 1904 he was spending time fitting speedometers, and seven years later, in the 1911 census, he ended up being one of a handful of people in the country whose trade was entered as 'speedometer fitter'.[39]

Back in 1904, the pencilled accounts reveal he was paid £1 12s per day for this work (2010: £135). A manifest of available tools includes a brest drill brace, wrench, pliers, calipers, even two cold chisels (so he meant business), and much else besides. There must have been a workshop, although whether it was in, or close to, 9 Strand is unclear. Certainly Mears travelled about for his work, not just in London, but all over the country, as his fares to Liverpool, Inverness, and Melton Mowbray show.

Taking a typical day—18 November 1904—Mears had an appointment at 10 a.m. to attend the De Dion Bouton company at 10 Great Marlborough St, to install a speedometer for their customer, Captain Sheppard, who wanted it 'fixed at the side of a motor watch to be supplied'. For each ledger entry we are given the customer (sometimes the coachbuilder, maker, or dealer), make of car, and some critical dimensions since each speedometer had to be calibrated to the car in question. In addition to his wages, Mears claimed for 6s 3d in expenses that day (2010: £36).

By 1905 the pace of installations had stepped up. Mears was spending three to five days per month on installations, but volume was increasing and the gloriously named St John Cameron Denne Collard was added as another fitter. On the income side, Smiths developed a range of speedometers over time, but pricing was generally of the order of £10 for a single unit (2010: £840). Judging by the pencilled accounts, Smiths charged 10 shillings for Mears or Collard to do the fitting (2010: £42).

Automobilists and aristocrats

And yet though the number of cars has made for a certain democracy, the lineage and history of the pleasure vehicle is essentially aristocratic.

(*Fine Arts Journal*[40])

S. F. Edge's memoirs remind us cars were delivered minus lamps, horn, windscreen, hood, spare wheel, speedometer, and other now essential fittings—leaving an obvious market opportunity Samuel and Gordon could target.[41] Their jewellery businesses in Piccadilly and the Strand sold prestige items to Edwardian high society and the 1904–5 speedometer sales ledger shows they continued to do so with their new product. Starting with the entry for the King, it includes other members of the Royal Family, and many other notables, including Lady Harmsworth, John Pierpoint Morgan jnr (who took three)—even W. S. Gilbert (who took two). However, it was unlikely that many sales would be direct to such clients. Most speedometers went to main dealers and coachbuilders, the single largest client being Gamages department store in Holborn. A breakdown of the main buyers for the period appears in Table 2.2.

From August 1904 to November 1905, Smiths fitted approximately 1,300 speed indicators, the pace of installation increasing notably. In December 1904, their advertisements finally dropped images of the old-style chronograph and instead showed a picture of the Nicole Nielsen indicator, adding the legend 'As supplied to H.M. the King'.[42] This cannot have failed to boost orders and production capacity at Soho Square would have been under pressure, so North established new factory premises in Hagden Lane in Watford, probably relocating all speed indicator production there to

Table 2.2 Top ten speedometer clients (1904–1905)

	Speedometers purchased
Gamages	90
Wallis & Watson	69
J. A. Lawton & Co. (coachbuilders)	40
FIAT	25
Hooper & Co. (coachbuilders)	23
Daimler Motor Co.	16
Rolls & Co.	12
London Motor Garage	12
Jarrott & Letts	12
Argyll Motors	12
Cannstadt Mercedes	8

Source: Original speedometer orders records (1904).

meet demand. This would in turn soon fail to keep up with Smiths' sales, but before we consider the further development of the motor side of their business, we can catch up on family life and how it was unfolding in the background.

Family life 1899–1913

> Last July Mr Smith and a lady stayed at the Star Hotel together. The lady was not Mrs Smith.
>
> (*Auckland Star*[43])

Around 1901, Samuel's increasing wealth allowed him to move to a substantial six-storey mansion, at 39 Holland Park, where the household grew to encompass seven staff, including a butler. Neighbours included City bankers, lawyers, merchants, civil servants, stock exchange members and brokers—and many living on their own means. Servants outnumbered family members in Holland Park.

In early 1904, Samuel moved on from the grand mansion to a more modern apartment in the recently built block at 38 Hyde Park Gate—downsizing significantly. But though the flat was retained in the family, he and Annie moved on again relatively soon, c.1909, this time to The Croft on Totteridge Green, a house built by T. E. Colcutt, a successful Victorian architect, for himself, c.1895, described as 'very picturesque Late Victorian with three ranges and a court, roughcast, with Tudor windows somewhat *à la* Voysey'.[44] Again this was a prestigious area, but though Samuel was accumulating wealth, he was also transferring it to his family, whether by gift, or salaries and dividends, judging by the lifestyles and addresses of his children.

Among those children, we can anticipate Samuel would have been happy with Gordon's progress after his return from Switzerland, with the firm's new business and the valuable exhibition medals which adorned the firm's catalogues, advertisements, and shop-fronts. Back in the 1870s, two Smith siblings had married two Aldin siblings, forging a link with the building trade. In 1897, Herbert had married Lilian Cave—now Gordon pulled off the double by marrying her sister Hilda Beatrice Cave in 1904, a marriage that was to last till Gordon's death in 1951. A first child, Ralph, future chairman of the firm, was born the following year.

His older sons, by contrast, probably had Samuel tearing out his hair. Cyril had married young, in 1897, but by 1901 the census conjures the affluent spectacle of comfortable new family life. Living at The Holt in Morden, Mabel and Cyril had five servants, including a gardener and two nurses, presumably to look after Doris, their 2-year-old daughter. Cyril started in the family business, but in 1903 took his wife and daughter off to New Zealand, to Waingaro in Waikato, where Mabel stayed in a hotel while he worked on a farm several miles away.[45] When Mabel sued for divorce in December 1906, she told the court Cyril had been distant from her since the arrival of Doris, and that 'he frequently remained away all night'. Everything came to a head with her discovery of photographs of another woman and a crumpled note to a newspaper, asking for the insertion of a small advertisement—the method Cyril used to communicate with his lover. With the necessary evidence supplied by Bella, housemaid of Waikato's Star Hotel, the marriage was annulled, leaving Doris with Mabel and some financial support. Cyril returned to the UK soon after, but not before representing the home firm at the 1907 International Exhibition in Christchurch, New Zealand, securing gold medals in both the jewellery section and the watches and clocks section.[46]

Herbert and his wife Lilian Maud also enjoyed a comfortable lifestyle, with a couple of properties—a house on West Hill in Putney and Flat 38, Avenue Mansions, in Hampstead, part of a development by Lilian's father, the prolific E. J. Cave. They were living there in 1901, with a baby and three servants including a nurse. But this was also a marriage that would not survive and there is some evidence for Herbert abandoning Lilian to go and live in Canada, perhaps around 1909–10. He was back by 1913, but did not rejoin his family.[47] Samuel had set him up as a partner in the Diamond Merchant's Alliance, but it was presumably clear by the time of the 1904 motor show that he had ideas in other directions. In November 1904, *The Car* published Herbert's letter detailing his journey in a newly acquired 'Rexette' from the Coventry factory back to London.[48] From the significant puff he gives it, and the offer of trial runs, we can guess this was the beginning of a commercial arrangement. A surviving pictorial letterhead from 1905 shows a splendidly moustachioed Herbert, detailing his London agency for Rexettes ('King of Little Cars') and of course for 'Messrs S. Smith & Son's Renowned Speed Indicators'.[49] His 'consulting offices' were at the familiar 9 Strand address, so while he had left his father's jewellery business, he was camped out there for business reasons. It was in February 1905 that his second child was born—Reginald ('Rex'), who was to serve as a divisional director with Smiths in later life.

For Samuel, we can speculate that by 1904–5 his original plans for his children's careers were not panning out. Cyril had left for New Zealand and Herbert was moving into the motor world—a world that Gordon too was fast adopting. This was a world which brought into existence a degree of conflict in society, and in many ways the Smiths business would neatly position itself at the centre of that conflict and exploit it.

The Automobile Association rides out

> For a long time discontent has been smouldering in some of the committees of the Automobile Club.
>
> (*The Car*[50])

For many, motor-cars were loud, dirty, and dangerous. As Passmore reports, the result was that 'Captain Mowbray Sant of the Surrey police set in place a trapping mania that soon was raising hundreds of pound in speeding fines.'[51] Someone who took action was Charles Jarrott, pioneer motorist, racing driver, and one half of Jarrott & Letts, motor-car importer and significant early client of Smiths for speedometers (see Table 2.2).

Jarrott commented that 'between the general public and the police we were having a most unpleasant time and a very expensive time'.[52] Discontent smouldered at the Automobile Club because its members were divided in their reaction to Jarrott's establishment of patrols designed to help motorists evade police speed traps—and in the summer of 1905 Jarrott led a militant splinter group to form the Automobile Association.[53] Membership increased rapidly and included Herbert Smith, who was elected to the Executive Committee, alongside, among many others, Selwyn Edge.[54] Soon Herbert was writing to the secretary, Clifford King, proposing his father as a committee member, a position Samuel was to take up for a year.[55]

In the conflict between the motorists, including militant activists such as Jarrott and Edge on the one hand, and the wider anti-motor-car public on the other, S. Smith & Son were uniquely positioned to play a key role, with a strong vested interest. On the back of royal endorsement and favourable coverage, and the fact their speed indicator was accurate, they provided the ideal weapon in a battle fought out from behind hedges on the main roads (where policeman hid with stopwatches) and in the courts, where the defendant offered the evidence of an accurate instrument.

It was remarkably effective. It was possible to argue the police method of measuring speed involved significant 'personal error' and flawed technique, but the knockout blow was the speed indicator—'The silent witness again saves an unjust conviction' as the firm's catalogue trumpets.[56] Court cases were reported throughout 1907, 1908, and 1909 in which motorists (often a chauffeur) were acquitted, having been summoned for speeding. Smiths introduced a couple of refinements in 1906, improving the quality of the 'evidence'.[57] The first was an additional hand, registering the highest speed attained, and this was further refined, c.1910, with a key-operated lock that prevented the chauffeur's access to the reset button. A second was the offer of a supplementary ('duplex') speedometer, fitted in the rear compartment, allowing the passengers to bear witness. By 1910, Smiths could fill two whole pages of their catalogue with an exhaustive list of court cases their clients had won, thanks to the 'Perfect' speed indicator—the brand name adopted from the very beginning (see Plate 11).[58]

Watford: a model factory

> *A press visit was made on Friday week to Messrs. S. Smith and Son's speedometer factory at Watford, which we have no hesitation in saying is one of the most up-to-date and best organised, as, indeed, it must be one of the most completely equipped works of its kind extant.*
>
> (*The Car*[59])

The 1904–5 ledger shows that sales latterly exceeded a hundred per month and 1906 saw the business expanding out of all recognition. For Smith (and North) it would have been hugely valuable to have secured sales to the royal family and wheels were in motion to secure a royal warrant. But North was also working to improve the speedometer, applying in late 1905 for a patent covering improvements.[60] It was most likely this design that was entered in the speedometer trials conducted by the Automobile Club in early 1906, but under the name of Kirby, North's factory manager.[61] The entry was described as 'experimental' but romped home with a special gold medal and topped the merit table. It was an excellent technical endorsement, and *The Times* was understandably confused when it reported that 'some of the best makers of speedometers kept aloof in this case', meaning Smiths. However, *The Times* concluded, Smiths

> hold an unofficial certificate worth many gold medals, in the shape of a letter from a motorist containing these words:- At my recent case at the South-Western Police-court . . . with the aid of your speed indicator there was not the slightest difficulty in satisfying the magistrate that, by their crude methods of timing, the police had greatly over-estimated the pace of my car, and the summons was dismissed.[62]

Despite the success of Kirby's speed indicator being widely reported, it was not long before Smiths added to their advertisements the claim that *its* model had won a special gold medal in the 1906 trials. As 1907 dawned, Smiths could add the distinction of its first royal warrant to all advertising, and with endorsements coming in left, right, and centre, sales were tremendous.[63] Indeed, the advertisements claimed 'The Sale of the Perfect Speed Indicator exceeds that of all other makes put together', and in November 1906 it received orders for 1,671 speed indicators *for that month alone*.[64]

Existing capacity could not support this level of demand and North therefore significantly expanded operations with a new second section at the Hagden Lane manufactory. With a site and plant value claimed to be £20,000 (2010: £1.7m), he now employed around one hundred staff, mostly men drawn from his native Yorkshire.[65] The factory was ready enough for a press visit, and Samuel orchestrated excellent coverage. On 31 May 1907, after a lunch for about sixty over which he presided at the Trocadero at Piccadilly Circus, cars took the guests out to Watford. The party included Earl Russell, Colonel Bosworth, Stenson Cooke of the AA, and representatives of the many motoring journals. Here they were treated to an extensive tour of 'one of the most completely equipped works of its kind extant', where 'the firm's output exceeds more than 100 instruments a week'.[66] A charming photograph of more than a dozen cars, each with a uniformed driver, drawn up outside and waiting for the return journey, appeared in *Motor* later that month.[67] Conspicuous in the shot are the large letters on the side of the brick building—Smiths Patent Speed Indicator Factory—but comparison of the picture with an original held by the North family shows the wording has been touched in on the negative. Once more we see Samuel ensuring the buying public associated his name with the product. The factory visit was written up in glowing terms in more than a dozen journals, including the *Tatler*.

A good team spirit was fostered between the West End and Watford and Gordon Smith was the prime mover behind sporting events and works outings arranged to bolster camaraderie. In June 1906, there was a joint Smiths/Nicole Nielsen staff sports day, held at The Ship Hotel in Pinner, featuring a cricket match and tug-of-war (both 'Staff *v.* Factory'), wrestling, and many mentions of 'refreshments' — so much so that the programme includes 'Next morning – headache'.[68] This developed into an annual tradition and a programme survives for the 'Second Annual Sports' between Smiths and 'affiliated business houses' in the summer of 1907, just after the press tour.[69] The event was under the presidency of Samuel Smith, and the stewards included his children and all the senior staff from 9 Strand and the other shops, while Robert Benson North presented a silver cup in the obstacle race. The same year there was also a football match between 9 Strand and the Watford factory, won by the former, with Gordon scoring two goals—a team photo survives (see Plate 6).[70]

By October 1906, advertisements claimed sales of over 5,000 speedometers in eighteen months.[71] Gordon's football team-mate and right-hand-man, Charles Nichols, became the firm's first travelling salesman that year, selling clocks, speedometers, and accessories, touring the country in a three-cylinder 8/11 hp Panhard Levassor car. Remembering this car, Sydney Walton later claimed that Harold R. Buckland, who started his distinguished Smiths career in 1906 as 'assistant chief packer and cleaner up', 'hired a growler and took fifty speedometers and bartered them for S. Smith & Sons' first motor car'—a car that Nichols swiftly commandeered as 'he knew the sales advantage of good and effective display'.[72] All this was against further increases in production and sales, which reached 100 per week in 1908.[73] Making a push into the international market, Gordon travelled to New York to represent the firm at the Madison Square Gardens motor show in January 1907, where the speedometer was shown for the first time in the United States market, leading on the line that 'Smiths speedometers have been supplied to half the Crowned Heads of Europe'.[74] Perhaps to make a holiday he took Hilda, but also Robert Benson Kirby from Watford and Charles Mears the fitter.[75]

An Aladdin's cave, full of wonders

Mr Sam, a genial white-haired Victorian, sent me downstairs to Mr Gordon, his son, in what, to me, was a veritable Aladdin's cave, full of wonders—coach lamps, clocks, gauges, long boa-constrictor horns—some with several bulbs and notes for coach-horn effect, and much more besides.

(J. H. Seager, *c.*1908[76])

The speedometer dominates the account of this period of Smiths' history because it was the accessory with which they achieved major sales and widespread brand recognition, but it also allowed them to develop a broader business across the whole field of motor accessories, and thence to launch a major business.

In-house manufacturing would eventually dominate, but from 1904, when the motor accessories department started, there was nearly a decade of business just as a motor factor—finding the components that automobilists wanted and selling them from 9

Strand or by means of a large and fully illustrated catalogue, like the watches, clocks, purses, and jewellery. A strong start had been made—the next challenges were lighting sets and carburettors.

In the case of the carburettor, the most important individual in the story is Vernon Anthony Trier, one half of the firm Trier & Martin, formed in 1906.[77] Vernon, born Werner Anton, was a prolific designer and inventor, securing nearly eighty patents over forty years. Trier Brothers had offered automotive lubricants at early motor shows, but in 1906 Vernon joined forces with his close neighbour, Helmuth Paul Martin. The pair were the principal investors in the new firm, alongside other family members and local connections, drawn from the 'wealthy enclave' that was 'Little Germany' in Camberwell.[78] They established the Trinity Works at 101 New Church Street, Camberwell, developing improved ignition devices, a carburettor, a magneto, and acting as suppliers (probably not makers) of lamps. Trier & Martin's carburettor quickly formed part of the Smith stable of accessories, performing well in the 1913 RAC test.[79] Trier would join Smiths towards the end of the Great War, but another carburettor designer, Herbert William Spiller joined earlier, in 1910, and worked on in-house development and refinement.[80] While independent still at this stage, there were increasing ties between Smiths and Trier & Martin, and a variety of accessories made in Camberwell appeared in Smiths' catalogue. A notable difference in treatment of the carburettor versus North's speedometers was that Smiths made clear they were offering the 'T & M patent' device, rather than hiding the identity of the designer, suggesting exclusive rights were involved.

The situation in lighting was more complex.[81] By the time Smiths were developing their motor business, various manufacturers had already established their own brand in the marketplace and Smiths could therefore only act as an agent and retailer, in competition with the likes of Dunhill and Gamages. Their range, largely of the acetylene-gas type, included B.R.C. 'Alpha' lamps from France, British-made versions from the well-known 'Bleriot' range, and 'Rushmore' lamps from the United States. Some lamps were badge-engineered exclusively for Smiths, for example, by J. R. Oldfield and Powell & Hanmer of Birmingham. In anticipation of the way the motor accessories industry was to develop, it is worth mentioning that a continued emphasis on acetylene-gas lamps, versus electric, was not solely because bulb filament technologies were not advanced—there was also the considerable income to be made from continuing the regular supply of carbide of calcium, not something the experienced retailer would ignore.

Electric side and tail-lamps came from C. A. Vandervell's factory in Acton (which later became part of Lucas). Also electric, and technically advanced, were lamps supplied by Sylverlyte (1909) Limited, for a relatively short period, c.1909–12.[82] These had the innovative feature of a patented deep bulls-eye lens into which an electric lamp could be inserted, offering both fog penetration and a lack of glare—a key desideratum in contemporary lamp technology.[83] While Smiths may not have had exclusive rights to these, they nevertheless featured them prominently and press coverage was positive—perhaps suggestive of journals hungry for advertising revenue.[84]

More important to Smiths was the 'Goldenlyte' acetylene-gas lamp—which sounds superficially similar to but has no connection with the Sylverlyte model—important on the basis that Smiths invested in its production. Here the technology depended on a technique devised in the 1890s by the prolific inventor Sherard Cowper-Coles, allowing the deposition of thin films of metal ('sherardizing'). This was used by his Reflector Syndicate Limited to produce thinly gold-plated lamp reflectors—hence 'Goldenlyte'— which were produced for Smiths, perhaps exclusively from c.1908, at 5 Hythe Road in Willesden.[85] Two versions were entered in the RAC vehicle illumination trials of July 1909 and performed well.[86] On the back of this, and with echoes of previous press coverage we saw for the Watford factory, Samuel knew what to arrange, using his home at The Croft as a base:

> Quite an interesting, instructive and enjoyable little function took place last week, when about a couple of dozen gentlemen, including a number of pressmen, fore-gathered at dinner at Totteridge, near London and subsequently attended a dem-onstration of the new Goldenlyte head-lamps . . . dinner over, the company were driven in Goldenlyted cars to the scene of the tests, where, writes our representative, a car stood staring into the darkness with one white and one yellow eye.[87]

Testing the new yellow lamps against the traditional white version, the press were suitably convinced of the lack of glare and the reach of the beam and Smiths were able to assemble enough positive copy, culled from various motor journals, to fill an eight-page advertising brochure for Goldenlyte lamps, with key supportive phrases picked out in bold. All well and good, but in 1911 there was a new development. Just after the press event, Samuel and Gordon Smith registered the trademark 'Goldenlyte' and then cooperated with the Reflector Syndicate and Arthur Field Burman to form a new company, Goldenlyte Limited, on 22 December.[88] Burman was a 'metal spinner and reflector maker' operating from the Avon Works, Windmill Street, Birmingham.[89] He and Gordon were the two key directors of the new firm, based at Avon Works, which raised new funds, but also issued one-fifth of its ordinary shares, fully paid, to S. Smith & Son. An agreement was entered into between Smiths and the new firm under which it was licensed to use the trademark, and Smiths committed to schedules of minimum purchases of lamps, acting as sole agents worldwide, save for the United States.[90] Alongside the supply of other well-known makes of lights, Smiths now had a captive design of their own, and one that had good brand recognition and positive press, though it had chosen to pursue the traditional acetylene technology, while the rest of the market—for example, at Joseph Lucas—was coming to the view that electric lighting offered the best path forward.

In addition, other firms were of course not blind to the opportunities presented by the rapidly expanding motor industry and its attendant accessory business. William-son's of Coventry, a major watch manufacturer and supplier to Smiths, will have followed North's production of speedometers with interest. Smiths might be well ahead in the market, but other brands were also being sold and Williamson's took the plunge and started its own production. This did not sit well with Smiths.

J. H. Seager of Williamson's takes up the tale—having described the Aladdin's cave that was below street level at 9 Strand:

> When I started work with my old firm, in 1908, they had stacks of speedometers and parts in their basement and I was informed they were to be destroyed as infringing a Smiths patent.[91]

The event was remembered in the late 1940s by Charles Tucker, son of one of the Williamson directors:

> What leg they had to stand on, I never knew, but my father, little dreaming of the future of the motor car industry and, what was more important to him then, jealous of the large number of watches we were then making for Mr. Samuel Smith... decided we could not afford to upset Mr. Samuel Smith, and decided to stop making speedometers and keep to our clocks.[92]

Perhaps a fatal decision—since as we shall see Williamson's were absorbed by Smiths in 1930.

The Queen of Siam's pearls

> *Scotland Yard, Singapore and Siamese police had to admit themselves baffled by this theft, which probably stands unequalled in its daring and audacity. So cleverly was the theft carried out that the pearls might well have vanished for all the trace they left.*
>
> (*Straits Times*[93])

One of the events that overshadowed the years 1909–12 for Samuel Smith and his family and staff was the extraordinary case of the 'Queen of Siam's Pearls', or the 'Siam Jewel Case' as it was alternatively known—not least for the financial strain it may have placed upon the business. Echoing stories from the pages of Conan Doyle, newspapers around the world reported the matter in sensational terms, and were still writing about it in the 1930s, more than twenty years later.

We met Frank Weaver Margrett in Chapter 1, joining S. Smith & Son back in 1886, around the time the Association of Diamond Merchants was formed. He worked his way up through the business and was a manager by *c.*1908, when the firm sent him out to the Far East as their representative in several locations—principally Bangkok and Singapore.[94]

The new venture did not have an auspicious start. In June 1908, despite a historic relationship with Garrard's (the Crown jewellers), the Chamberlain of the Siamese Royal Household started negotiations with the Association of Diamond Merchants, on behalf of the Queen of Siam, for a pearl rope necklace, to contain 242 pearls, with a value of £8,200 (2010: £667,000). There was one 'magnificent large pearl of a beautiful pink hue which was specially purchased as a centre stone'.[95]

I myself (Mr Smith says, in telling his story) undertook the building of the rope, and a beginning was made with one central pearl of fine colour and lustre, weighing 19 ¼ grains and worth £250.[96]

The order was placed in January 1909.[97] It took until May to find the necessary calibre of pearls and to assemble the rope, which was packed in a leather box, encased in a zinc-lined outer wooden case, soldered closed, and then fastened further with hoop-iron, 'sealed with impressive red wax seals'.[98] Shipped from Southampton on the Nordeutscher Lloyd steamer *Lutzow*, with Margrett and Reginald Smith (Samuel's youngest son) also on board, the box arrived at Bangkok on 18 May 1909, but on examination was found to be empty, having been carefully and unobtrusively cut open.

The necklace was insured through Lloyds and a claim immediately filed, and thus began a three-year hunt across the world to trace the culprit, and the missing pearls. The Lloyds underwriters refused to pay out, arguing there was no evidence where the pearls might have been missed. The Association employed private detectives, but to no effect. To maintain its reputation, Smiths assembled a second rope within months and made good the Queen's loss. Samuel Smith later reported that three years later

We had almost given up hope of hearing anything more about the pearls when we got a message from the Straits to say that a man named De Boseck was selling pearls, and had sold thirty-three to a dealer in Singapore. This was interesting because De Boseck was the head wharfinger at Bangkok when the pearls arrived.[99]

The second lucky break was that De Boseck 'had taken to the Turf' in Singapore and was raising money through the sale of pearls or borrowing against them as collateral. With long international telegrams, costing as much as £10 each (2010: £800), backwards and forwards, it was clear the single central pearl had been identified. A game of cat and mouse ensued, with warrants issued for De Boseck's arrest. He evaded capture in Indonesia and Ceylon, but was eventually traced to a house in the Commercial Road in London. After extradition to Singapore he eventually stood trial in March 1912, being convicted of theft and sentenced to two years' hard labour. The detailed reports of the trial appeared in many international newspapers, revealing sensational matters while the witnesses were on oath, including the smuggling of additional jewels by members of the royal household, but close to home was the revelation that a commercial rival of Smiths, Robert Mosley, working for Alexander Clark & Co., the Oxford Street jeweller, had alleged in writing to the Siamese royal house that the theft was all a put-up job by Smiths—a libel that led to the issuance of successful proceedings.[100] Smiths had also issued proceedings against Lloyds for failure to pay under their policy, but on securing De Boseck's conviction, the claim was finally settled with an increased payment of £10,000 to cover Smiths' expenses (2010: £770,000).[101]

It was this settlement that finally prompted a celebration dinner in honour of Frank Margrett, now a director of the firm, on 6 November 1912. By way of thanks for 'successfully unravelling the mystery of the disappearance of the pearl necklace', Samuel, Gordon, Cyril, and Reginald Smith presented Margrett with a loving cup of early English design, engraved with an appreciative commemoration and facsimiles of their signatures. The *New York Times* account concludes 'that Dumas never conceived anything more full of romance than that which surrounds the mystery of the Queen of Siam's Pearls'.[102]

Speedometer House

> *From cellar to roof it is a hive of industry—so light, so clean, so active.*
> *Aloft under the tiles, men and boys sit at benches where delicate little drills*
> *and grinders help them to construct the more minute parts of the popular*
> *Smiths speedometer.*
>
> (*The Auto Motor Journal*[103])

At the beginning, Samuel probably saw the motor accessories business in retail terms, utilizing the familiar technique of outsourcing production and aiming for volume sales, ensuring the public saw only the Smiths name. The business grew quickly—from April 1911, separate accounts had been kept for the motor accessories division, with turnover for that year exceeding £80,000, giving net profits of nearly £8,000 (2010: £635,000).[104] With Goldenlyte Limited, Smiths had their first taste of manufacturing in 1911, but no doubt 1912 was the year the decision was taken to make a bold move away from outsourcing and to bring production in-house—to create a complete and vertically integrated business, manufacturing, selling, and even fitting the accessories.

The decision to manufacture left Robert Benson North, now a committed speedometer maker, without his main client. He met the challenge head-on through developing a new brand, 'Watford', leading with a newly designed speedometer, patented by his colleague Albert Rutherford at Charles Frodsham's.[105] North launched a bold advertising campaign—describing the 'British Made Watford Speedometers' as 'the very latest conception of the well-known firm which has been manufacturing Speedometers in large quantities for the Trade since 1904'.[106] For the prestige market, North and Rutherford had options through their ownership of Charles Frodsham, and we see Frodsham-badged speedometers and clocks emerging at this period, sold from their Dering Street premises.

The Howard de Walden estate owned much of the block on the north-west side of Great Portland Street, from Devonshire Street to Weymouth Street. Between 1911 and 1913 the successful West End developer Charles Peczenik built several large buildings here, using Robert Angell as architect for 171–177 (Devon House) and neighbouring 179–185, replacing the buildings of Mitchell Lewis, British Lion Motor Co., and the Pytchley Autocar Co.—all possibly Smiths clients.[107] Somehow Smiths and Peczenik found each other, and with negotiations complete in August 1912, Smiths secured a forty-two-year lease on 179–185 from 25 March 1913, 'on exceptionally favourable terms', naming the building Speedometer House (see Plate 13).[108] 'Motor Row' was becoming the motorist's Mecca and it was natural for Smiths to move its new business there. The scale of its ambitions matched the scale of the development—it was later described as 'specially constructed' for Smiths use, but this will have referred to the fit-out. The building survives to this day, with 'a fine stone front' and 'is an excellent example of the architect's work in obtaining the maximum amount of space and light'.[109] It provided eight floors of 8,000 ft^2 each, with space on the fourth and fifth floors for 'electrically driven plant', the 'larger machine tools, some of them costing nearly £300 each' (2010: £23,000), for the manufacture and testing of speedometers.[110] A floor was also taken in neighbouring Devon House for speedometer production and a later account describes P. O. Dorer and Thomas Waterfield spending several years assembling the speedometer factory.[111] Teams of women could work in the ample light provided by upper floor windows to engrave speedometer dials, while the first floor was for despatch, and the second and third offered warehouse space. On the ground floor, the influence of the retail jeweller was keenly in evidence—contemporary images show bevelled mirrors, Turkish carpets, and glazed mahogany showcases filled with gleaming motor lamps, combining to create an opulent temple for the well-heeled motorist. A model Daimler chassis completed the effect, allowing lighting sets to be mounted for evaluation.[112] Below ground, but apparently well-lit and ventilated, there was space for twenty or more cars to be worked on and fitted with new instruments, while partitioned off work-shops were home to carburettor manufacture. A building on this scale could accom-modate a substantial workforce, and within months Smiths' staff would grow from the handful in the Strand to more than 300.

At the front of the building, the second floor had large projecting window balconies for which Angell needed special permission.[113] These were adorned with four large crests showing some of the firm's seven royal warrants, while the clerestory glazing of the ground floor showroom windows featured the names of the main product lines. True to form the firm made sure the motor journals were well briefed and from late July to early August 1913 a series of illustrated articles appeared, showing the impressive scale and arrangement of the new headquarters. We can see the first traces of Samuel Smith's influence waning in a concluding note in *The Motor* that 'any bona fide motorist who is interested can usually rely upon the courtesy of Mr A. Gordon Smith, the organizing head of this great business, to issue a permit for him to inspect the work in the course of procedure'.[114]

How Smiths financed the move to Great Portland Street and the substantial capital cost is unclear, but a rationalization of the existing portfolio of premises, coupled with some bank financing are the likely main sources of capital used. Dennis Barrett's later obituary for Gordon Smith talks of the 'great shock' brought by the Great War, 'because of the big commitments he had undertaken' which might refer to bank financing.[115]

Symbolically, the long-standing premises at 9 Strand were given up later in the year, to be demolished and rebuilt by J. Lyons & Co. as a tearoom. The sale of a wide range of jewellery, watches, clocks, and all the showcases, fixtures, and fittings stretched over four days in December, leaving the firm with two West End jewellers' premises at Trafalgar Square and 68 Piccadilly.[116]

Thus the transition occurred—from the retail diamond merchant's business of the 'genial white-haired Victorian' Samuel Smith, with an Aladdin's cave in a Strand basement, to Allan Gordon Smith's flagship on Edwardian Motor Row, vertically integrated, manufacturing, retailing, and fitting motor accessories for a demanding market. But such growth was capital intensive, and though largely a family concern till now, the time had come to raise funds from other sources, opening up another phase in the development of the business. As 1914 neared, plans everywhere were being mapped out.

NOTES

1. *The Times* (16 Nov. 1896), 7.
2. Ernest Terah Hooley, *Hooley's Confessions* (London: Simpkin, Marshall & Co., 1925), passim.
3. Peter Thorold, *The Motoring Age: The Automobile and Britain 1896–1939* (London: Profile, 2003), 67.
4. *DBB*, 'Morris, William Leonard', iv. 334; L. J. K. Setright, *Drive on! A Social History of the Motor Car* (London: Granta, 2004), 25–6.
5. Elite wealth has been studied by, among others, W. D. Rubinstein. The middle classes have received more recent attention from scholars such as Green and Rutterford, with an additional focus on issues of gender, but the analysis relates more to testamentary disposition than earlier estate planning. See e.g. David R. Green et al., 'Lives in the Balance? Gender, Age and Assets in Late-Nineteenth-Century England and Wales', *Continuity and Change* (July 2009), 307–35.
6. *The Times* (26 July 1894), 14.
7. *The Times* (9 Nov. 1900), 7 and (4 July 1901), 7.
8. Cann, 'Chronological Record', i. 36.
9. Stephen Goldsmith, *The History of Christ's College: The Victorians* (forthcoming).
10. Programm (Biel: Schüler, 1898) [prospectus]. Term started on 12 Apr. 1898, according to the *Journal Suisse d'Horlogerie*.
11. *PIVOT* (Aug. 1947), 3.
12. Sydney Walton, 'A Brief History', unpublished manuscript (1945), 9. Gordon's 'thorough apprenticeship', in *Souvenir of your association with S. Smith & Sons (M.A.) Ltd* (London: Smiths, 1934).
13. 13 Mar. 1899, 2.
14. *Glasgow International Exhibition 1901: The Official Guide* (Glasgow: Charles P. Watson, 1901), 39.
15. *Report of His Majesty's Commissioners for the Paris International Exhibition 1900*, P.P. 1901, Cmd. 629, 630, ii. 301.
16. *PIVOT* (Aug. 1947), 3; *Glasgow Official Guide*, 39.
17. *Smith's Home Journal* (Dec. 1937), 7.
18. Charlotte Gere, *Jewellery in the Age of Queen Victoria* (London: British Museum, 2010), 125.
19. Gere, *Jewellery*, 78.
20. *Illustrated London News* (9 June 1902), p. x.
21. Henry Chaplin, *HC Deb* (30 June 1896), vol. 42, c. 438.
22. *The Car* (4 May 1904), endpapers.

23. *Illustrated London News* (5 Dec. 1903), 862.

24. *Illustrated London News* (6 December 1902), 862.

25. *Autocar* (16 Jan. 1904), 5A; (23 Jan. 1904), 2A and (23 April 1904), 33.

26. Smiths' *Autocar* advertisements, starting Jan. 1904.

27. 15 Feb. 1904, 4.

28. e.g. *The Engineer* (19 Feb. 1904), 186, detailing the Elliott Brothers' indicator.

29. *The Car* (2 Mar. 1904), 44; *Autocar* (13 Feb. 1904), 216.

30. Cann, 'Chronological Record', ii. 50.

31. C. W. Stamper, *What I Know: Reminiscences of Five Years' Personal Attendance upon His Late Majesty King Edward the Seventh* (London: Mills & Boon, 1913).

32. Stamper, *What I Know*, 9.

33. Stamper, *What I Know*, 8.

34. *Motoring Illustrated* (27 Feb. 1904), 353.

35. Vaudrey Mercer, *The Frodshams: The Story of a Family of Chronometer Makers* (Ticehurst: AHS, 1981), 202.

36. Mercer, *Frodshams*, 201.

37. Mercer, *Frodshams*, 202.

38. Walton, 'A Brief History', 9; *PIVOT* (Aug. 1947), 3; patent GB3,684 (13 Feb. 1904).

39. 'Charlie' Mears later worked for Daimler—*PIVOT* (Oct. 1948), 29.

40. 35/7 (July 1917), 483.

41. S. F. Edge, *My Motoring Reminiscences* (London: Foulis, 1934), 270.

42. *Autocar* (3 Dec. 1904), p. xviii; (17 Dec. 1904), p. xvii.

43. 4 Dec. 1906, 5.

44. Nikolaus Pevsner and Bridget Cherry, *Hertfordshire*, 2nd edn (Harmondsworth: Penguin, 1977), 366. Now listed Grade II, English Heritage described it as 'an excellent essay in the "Old English" style'.

45. *Auckland Star* (4 Dec. 1906), 5.

46. *Auckland Star* (27 Mar. 1907), 7.

47. Information courtesy of Graham Smith, Herbert's grandson.

48. *The Car* (9 Nov. 1904), 381.

49. SMAA.

50. 9 Mar. 1904, 70.

51. Michael Passmore, *The AA: History, Badges and Memorabilia* (Princes Risborough: Shire, 2003), 4.

52. Quoted in Hugh Barty-King, *AA: A History of the First 75 Years of the Automobile Association 1905–1980* (London: Automobile Association, 1980), 60.

53. Peter Thorold, *The Motoring Age: The Automobile and Britain 1896–1939* (London: Profile, 2003), 42.

54. Barty-King, *AA*, 65.

55. Cann, 'Chronological Record', i. 54; Herbert Smith to C. King (15 Aug. 2012), SMAA.

56. S. Smith & Son Ltd, *Motor Accessories Catalogue* (London: Smiths, 1910), 10.

57. See e.g. *The Car* (6 June 1906), p. ii.

58. S. Smith & Son, *1910 Catalogue*, 10–11.

59. 12 June 1907, 175.

60. Patent GB19, 713 (1905).

61. *Autocar* (10 Mar. 1906), 296; results (2 June 1906), 708.

62. *The Times* (5 June 1906), 12.

63. The 'by appointment' tag appears first in *Autocar* (5 Jan. 1907), p. xxviii.

64. *Autocar* (26 Jan. 1907), p. xxviii; (5 Jan. 1907), p. xxviii.

65. *The Motor Trader* (5 June 1907), 630. See also *The Car* (12 June 1907), 175; *Automotor* (8 June 1907), 807.

66. *The Car* (12 June 1907), 175.

67. *Motor* (18 June 1907), 622.

68. 'Programme' (16 June 1906).

69. 'Programme' (29 June 1907).

70. Cann, 'Chronological Record', i. 61.

71. *The Car* (3 Oct. 1906), 289.

72. Walton, 'A Brief History', 8–9; the story also appears in *Smiths Home Journal* (June 1938), 4.

73. Cann, 'Chronological Record', i. 64.

74. *Motor Age* advertisement, date unknown.

75. Manifest, *SS New York* (29 Dec. 1906 to 5 Jan. 1907).

76. Cann, 'Chronological Record', i. 66. The basement (Aladdin's Cave) served as Smith's 'Warehouse and Despatch Dept.' and consisted of 'a number of cupboards'. See *Smith's Home Journal* (Feb. 1938), 3.

77. TNA: BT31/17788/89152.

78. Christine Lattek, *Revolutionary Refugees: German Socialism in Britain, 1840–1860* (London: Routledge, 2006), 19.

79. *Autocar* (13 Sept. 1913), 482, 484.

80. Spiller assigned patent GB191,463 of 1910 to Smiths, for 'improvements to carburetters', and many succeeding patents.

81. Comments here rely heavily on input from Peter Card, a leading authority in early motor-car lighting.

82. TNA: BT 31/12365/97716 and BT 31/12864/104237. The vehicle of company promoter James Stuart Burns, the firm was being wound up in 1912; *London Gazette* (26 July 1912), 5576. If the glass lenses were manufactured overseas, perhaps in Bavaria, supply issues likely emerged at this stage.

83. Patents GB5,191 (1904) and GB10,696 (1908).

84. They are reviewed in *Autocar* (4 Sept. 1909), 370.

85. TNA: BT 31/6249/44269. These were also the premises of Cowper-Coles Engineering Co.

86. *Autocar* (21 Aug. 1909), 290–1; *The Car* (25 Aug. 1909), 68.

87. *Motor World* (24 Feb. 1910), quoted in S. Smith & Son reprint.

88. Trademark no. 318080, registered 17 Mar. 1910, in Class 13. TNA: BT 31/20387/119430.

89. *London Gazette* (13 Dec. 1901), 8871.

90. TNA: BT 31/20387/119430. Minimum quantities were 1,000 projector-type Goldenlyte lamps and 3,000 gold mirrors, each year.

91. Cann, 'Chronological Record', i. 66.

92. *Horological Journal* (Jan. 1948), 23.

93. 17 May 1936, 4.

94. S. Smith & Son (Siam) Ltd, prospectus (Nov. 1917), TNA: BT 31/23831/148530.

95. Charlotte Gere and John Culme, *Garrard* (London: Quartet, 1993), 50; *Straits Times* (17 May 1936), 4.

96. *Lloyds Weekly News* (1 Dec. 1912), 6.

97. *Singapore Free Press and Mercantile Advertiser* (16 May 1912), 317.

98. *Wanganui Chronicle* (30 Apr. 1912), 3.

99. *Lloyds Weekly News* (1 Dec. 1912), 6.

100. *Straits Times* (24 May 1912), 7.
101. *Singapore Free Press and Mercantile Advertiser* (18 Nov. 1912), 6.
102. *New York Times* (9 Nov. 1912), C5.
103. 2 Aug. 1913, 964–5.
104. *Prospectus* for S. Smith & Son (Motor Accessories) Ltd (1913).
105. Patent GB14,617 (1909).
106. *Autocar* (4 Jan. 1913), p. xxiii. The North family recalls legal action against Smiths for breach of contract, but no further evidence has been traced.
107. *St Marylebone Borough Council Rates* (April–Sept. 1913), Ward 7, p. 58. Westminster Archives.
108. *Survey of London*, xlii. 99–116; *Prospectus, S. Smith & Sons (Motor Accessories) Limited—£50,000 ordinary shares* (London: 1914). The lease also included a floor of Devon House next door. See also *Prospectus* (1914).
109. *Motor* (29 July 1913), 1215.
110. *Auto Motor Journal* (2 Aug. 1913), 964; *The Times* (30 July 1913), 22.
111. *Smith's Home Journal* (Aug. 1938), 3. Waterfield was one of four members of the family at Smiths.
112. Peter W. Card, *Early Vehicle Lighting*, 2nd edn (Princes Risborough: Shire, 2004), 37.
113. *St Marylebone Borough Council Minutes* (3 Oct. 1912), 467, and (28 Nov. 1912), 35.
114. *The Motor* (21 July 1913), 1198.
115. *Smiths Times*, 1/10 (1951), 1.
116. *The Times* (12 Dec. 1913), 14.

CHAPTER 3

....

1914–1928
Flotation, War, Boom and Bust, Recovery

....

The well-established nature of the business is evidenced by the fact that the names of upwards of fifteen thousand (15,000) customers appear on the books of the Motor Department of the Vendor Company.

(*Prospectus*, 24 July 1914)

WHEN the Great War broke out in 1914, numerous small engineering firms soon commenced armaments work, although the organization of 'controlled establishments' only became formalized in the spring of 1915 with the emergence of the Munitions of War Act. A good example, and a trading partner of Smiths, was the brass founder, Newman Hender of Woodchester, which had only recently invested in new plant and machinery, ideally suited to munitions production, so it rapidly abandoned its traditional products. Smiths, Newman Hender, and many other firms quickly geared their entire production to the war effort, but post-war faced a vast hurdle to remobilize their enlarged workforces and heavily specialized operations towards peacetime work. Despite a natural feeling of entitlement to the fruits of peace, large numbers of firms failed as the immediate post-war boom rapidly came to an end, following the imposition of restrictive monetary policy, with both prices and wages, which had seen strong inflation over five years, declining from 1920—a time of 'unaccustomed bleakness'.[1] Newman Hender was an early casualty.[2]

Having moved from retail to manufacture by 1913, Smiths' West End operation was irrelevant for munitions, supplanted by a new factory complex at Cricklewood from 1915, funded by new external equity. Post-war, Smiths continued to expand rapidly through acquisition and raised further equity and debt in the process—equity that was almost entirely lost over the coming years, while the debt remained a millstone until 1927. The firm's survival owed much to careful management of business relationships—most of all with its banks, who were supportive if controlling—and also owing much to the guidance of the firm's accountant, Hubert Marsh.

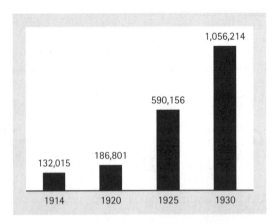

FIGURE 3.1 Numbers of cars in the UK (1914–1930).
Source: National Motor Museum

Gordon's early decision to focus on supplying the motor vehicle industry proved profitable—given the concentration by most makers on vehicle assembly rather than integrated manufacture, leaving room for the specialist component maker. Vehicle manufacture showed marked growth, increasing by a factor of five in the 1920s alone (see Figure 3.1), and despite occasional reverses was the only one of the so-called 'new' industries to sustain net investment through the depression at the end of the 1920s.[3] The firm succeeded in maintaining its dominant market share and once the costly mistakes of 1920–1 had finally been absorbed, profits grew commensurately, so that by the end of the 1920s Smiths was well-positioned to expand and diversify once more.

The stock market flotation and then significant wartime expansion were accompanied by a move from family to public ownership, and then the gradual emergence of professional management, but the Smiths retained tight control. With Samuel now marginalized, it was Gordon's vision that propelled the company forward. By the end of the 1920s, with a secure base established, he started to diversify again, not in components supply, but into the arena of vertically integrated manufacture of end products—the recreation of a British clockmaking industry offered a tantalizing goal.

Stock market flotation: July 1914

> *An interesting industrial venture makes its appearance this morning in the shape of S. Smith & Sons (Motor Accessories) Ltd . . . Largely increased profits are expected as a result of the extension of the business, and it is satisfactory that the management will be in the same hands as before.*
>
> (*Financial Times*[4])

In November 1913, a few months after Smiths established their new Great Portland Street factory and showrooms, the motor show took place at Olympia. That Smiths had captured significant market share is obvious—of 200 cars there, 169 sported a Smiths speedometer, still the instrument that defined the firm's presence in the market.[5]

To date, Samuel had financed the business. But with rapidly expanding sales, the time had come to bring in more equity, especially as the product range was still incomplete, lacking, for example, an electric self-starter. But perhaps he also wanted to create some distance between his original jeweller's business and the motor accessory cuckoo, fast outgrowing the nest. He had divided his businesses between corporate entities in 1899, and it was time to repeat the process. Alternatively, it may have been Gordon who pressed hard to carve out his new business line.

Whichever, the result was the formation of S. Smith & Sons (Motor Accessories) Limited on 15 July 1914, and the transaction commemorated by this book: the flotation of the firm with an initial public offering of shares on the London stock market, on 21 July.[6] The £100,000 capital of the firm was divided, with half the shares offered to the public— an offer that was oversubscribed—and the other half issued fully paid to the old S. Smith & Sons, in exchange for its transfer of the whole motor accessory business.[7] The old and new firms shared the same management—with Samuel as chairman and Gordon as managing director on £1,000 per annum. Other key players were Charles Nichols (sales), Reginald Aldin Smith (carburettors), and George Arnold (exports). Francis Cotterell ('Cotty'), long-time company secretary in the other family firms, obliged once more.

Floating on the stock market was typically profitable for the promoter—in this case S. Smith & Sons took the role and charged a 5 per cent underwriting commission, an additional 1¼ per cent 'over-riding commission', and a further £5,700 to cover preliminary expenses—so a total of £8,825 or 17.6 per cent of new cash raised. True, the parent had some expenses of its own (£1,640 in sub-underwriting fees), but *The Economist* commented tartly that 'the preliminary expenses absorb rather a large proportion of its capital'.[8] The *Financial Times*' view was on balance positive, concluding that, though 'the speculative element cannot be ignored, the shares seem a hopeful lock-up investment of their class'.[9] The irony of 'lock-up' would soon emerge with the five-month closure of the Stock Exchange from 31 July.

At the end of July 1914, Samuel owned pretty much half of the new firm, and a diverse group of investors owned the rest. While other family members had executive positions, they had very little equity in the business, so at this stage little had changed from previous years—the business effectively belonged to Samuel Smith. The business plan, by contrast, was Gordon Smith's, and straightforward—build on existing success with the speedometer and carburettor, develop new products in-house, and expand market share.

The Great War begins

Now came four tremendous years in which the Smiths of England turned from the plough-share to the sword.

(Sydney Walton[10])

In mid-1914, no one knew, post-Sarajevo, how serious the situation in Europe might become. The flotation occurred on a day when the Austro-Serbian crisis was still developing, making the oversubscription remarkable, given that July saw stock markets falling, diplomacy failing, and international tension escalating.[11] Just over a week after the float, to stem outflows of gold, Bank Rate was increased rapidly, hitting 10 per cent on Saturday 1 August. Monday was a bank holiday and the new Smiths board met on the Tuesday—yet this was another non-business day since the bank holiday was hastily extended for an unprecedented three further days. The new firm decided to move funds around in the wake of the Bank Rate change, but across town from these domestic deliberations the government was busy that Tuesday issuing an ultimatum demanding Germany's respect for Belgium's neutrality—an ultimatum that was rejected, leading to war being declared as of 11 p.m.

The board met again on Friday, coming up with its first responses to circumstances. These were short-term and focused on retaining cash—for example, stock purchases were suspended, and invoices over £50 would be held over, taking advantage of the national moratorium, but the dramatic move was to put the factory workforce on half-pay. By 20 October, the directors had evolved a more measured plan. Having cut wages in half, a scheme of rebates was introduced under which withheld wages would be released if production targets were met—which they were, by year-end, and the scheme was cancelled in March 1915.[12] Cash flow was nevertheless under pressure and a £15,000 bank overdraft was arranged—Samuel and Gordon providing a £10,000 personal guarantee.[13]

A strategic and typically optimistic move was the formation of branches or agencies in 'the most important British Colonies and Foreign Countries', first, in New Zealand, South Africa, and Java, 'with a view to capturing the trade which until then was largely in the hands of the Germans'.[14] Russia, Australia, and the Dutch East Indies soon followed, with George Arnold despatched to make local arrangements.[15] In London, it was decided to shelve plans to manufacture magnetos and that 'the Company was not justified in incurring further expenditure in connection with the electrical starter', thus abandoning one of the principal goals of the flotation.

After little more than a year, Great Portland Street was creaking at the joints. There were worries over stock levels, particularly Trier & Martin lighting sets, and daily stock inspection was introduced.[16] More significant was the loss of space to an entirely new activity. In December 1914 the firm secured a contract from the War Department to produce 50,000 friction tubes, used in firing breech-loaded artillery guns.[17] Cann's account recalls 'a small plant was installed in the basement... for making fuses for the Admiralty', suggesting the drive-in space designed for the fitting of accessories to customers' cars was sacrificed.[18] From early 1915, the firm also produced 'fuze indicators' (a form of slide rule) for use with 4.5 inch howitzers, and aerial incendiary darts ('flechettes'), used by British seaplanes against German airships. Geoffrey Conduit, then a young mechanic, later recalled a thrilling night-time delivery of darts, driven to Dover by Gordon Smith in his open-top tourer.[19]

By March 1915 'it was absolutely necessary that to allow for the great expansion of the business further premises should be acquired' and the interim measure proposed was to take more space in Devon House next door and to knock through between buildings.[20] The 'great expansion' meant 'Government orders for munitions and large quantities of lighting sets, signalling lamps, aeroplane accessories, etc.' received at the end of 1914, and a later account in *PIVOT*, the in-house magazine, suggests 'the Admiralty asked that another factory should be built for the manufacture of fuses'.[21] In April 1915, a month before the 'shell crisis' exploded, Gordon took decisive action, buying land in Cricklewood and instructing Robert Angell (architect of Speedometer House) to draw up plans for a factory.[22] Covering slightly more than an acre (0.4 ha), it was constructed remarkably quickly, and occupied by August.

The admiral at the Front

> We learn that Mr. C. A. Smith, a director of S. Smith & Sons (Motor Accessories) Ltd, who safely went through the bombardment of Antwerp, has received a commission in His Majesty's Forces.
>
> (*The Commercial Motor*, 1914[23])

A large initial wave of volunteering in the UK saw more than 750,000 men enlist by the end of September 1914, and the Smiths workforce played its part—'There are now 40 of Messrs. Smith & Sons staff at the Front or in training, and one of these, Mr Manby, who was wounded during the battle of Mons, is reported to be making favourable progress in hospital towards recovery'—but Cyril Aldin Smith was the only family member. We met him last in Chapter 2, leaving the family business for farming in New Zealand, but he returned with a new (second) wife, spending time as a director of a West End art gallery, and was back in the family business by mid-1913.[24]

Despite circumstances, the protection of intellectual property continued at the Western Front during the war—witness Captain Peter Nissen's patent for his portable building, filed as he served in the Royal Engineers in 1916.[25] Cyril was at the heart of some similarly fascinating interaction with Great Portland Street in 1915–16. A month into the war saw him enlisting, on 26 September, as a second lieutenant (RM) in the Royal Naval Division.[26] Predictably, he joined up as a 'motor owner driver' with a 20hp Straker Squire, equipped no doubt with Smiths motor accessories, and accompanied, at least latterly, by a black spaniel dog.[27] London omnibuses and assorted motor-cars, including Rolls Royces, were shipped across the Channel and found their way to Antwerp, being used in the early October evacuation, and a regimental history records Cyril 'in charge of a convoy of 'buses with the Royal Naval Division, whence he escaped to France'.[28] Apparently 'he seized the opportunity of an officer requiring to be taken up to join his unit, to make his way with his car to the front', and now commissioned as a temporary lieutenant in the Royal Naval Volunteer Reserve, he was lent to the 6th Infantry Division, where he made a name for himself. Major-General Marden described Cyril as 'consumed with a good healthy hatred of the enemy', keen to make a practical contribution, so much so that 'he devoted the greater part of the time he was with the Division to experimenting with bullet-proof shields on wheels to be propelled by manpower, a sort of embryonic tank'. These experimental infantry shields were probably made in Great Portland Street, and draft wording survives, confirming the commercial terms under which Cyril and his design collaborators at the Front would cede to Smiths the manufacturing and sales rights for an 'infantry shield' in return for a 10 per cent royalty on the cost price—a patent was secured later that year.[29]

Cyril was a risk-taker and further evidence emerges in that, on 21 July 1915, using the infantry shield (and somewhat overenthusiastically encouraging his comrades from a position forward of the shield) he was hit in the neck by a bomb splinter, resulting in his being invalided home by hospital ship.[30] Perhaps by reason of his leadership he had acquired the nickname 'Admiral' and Marden suggests this gave rise to the name 'Admiral's Road' for the track where Cyril was hit.

On his return to France, Cyril became engaged in the use of Bangalore torpedoes—lengths of tubing enclosing explosive charges—used for clearing battle-field obstructions. He trained 'an authorized party which had long existed under the name of the 6th Division Shield Party' and was engaged in a series of 'raids and minor enterprises' against the enemy lines.[31] There are detailed reports of overnight actions from March 1916 designed to enter the German lines and capture a prisoner, dependent on Cyril and his men's torpedoes. That these may have also been under experimental development, like the earlier shield, with the help of Smiths' workshops, is suggested by a resolution that 'the forms of application for Patents for Improvements in or relating to Devices for clearing Wire entanglements . . . be signed'.[32] Cyril's actions in March earned him the DSO and he travelled to London in early June to receive his medal from the King, returning immediately.[33] On the night of 9/10 June he was part of a raiding party that ran into trouble near Ypres and was reported missing. A letter from his commanding officer to Samuel a few months later records:

> I can assume that he earned his distinction several times over. Always jolly, he was welcomed by everybody. The dangerous work which he was daily carrying out with explosives was just suited to his temperament. I used to tell him that I should have to chain him down.[34]

Correspondence records Samuel's enquiry after Cyril in September and a response from Captain Brady of the 6th Division making it clear there was no hope.[35] Further correspondence between Gordon, the Admiralty, and the War Office reveals Gordon as executor, tidying up Cyril's affairs, in December. The Straker Squire car had long been worn out, though the spaniel had survived and was in the care of a transport officer. Other personal effects were naturally lost, including a touching reminder of the jewellery business—apparently Cyril had returned to France from his investiture ceremony with a small gold replica of his DSO, no doubt arranged for by his father and brothers—but destined nonetheless to be lost, like its owner, in Flanders fields.

Financing: 1915–1916

The Treasury has been consulted under the notification of the 18th January 1915, and raises no objection to the issue of the within-mentioned shares.

(*Prospectus*, August 1915)

Rewinding slightly, the firm had spent approximately £60,000 on the Cricklewood works and additional plant installed at Speedometer House, leading inevitably to a need for further financing. In August 1915, the capital of the firm was doubled with a further share issue, entirely taken by the proto-investment bank, the British, Foreign and Colonial Corporation (BFCC).[36] This was the vehicle of Frederick Szarvasy, a successful Hungarian banker who later made his name with the recapitalization of firms such as Marconi. In the July 1914 flotation, Clifford Turner had acted for Smiths, and he in turn was close to Szarvasy, probably leading to the introduction.[37] Szarvasy as financier and Turner as the corporate lawyer par excellence were both to prove critically important over the succeeding decade.[38] A month later, BFCC resold the shares in the market at a premium, reported on positively by the *Financial Times*:

> A new prospectus, especially one covering an issue of Ordinary shares, is somewhat of a rarity these days, but that of S. Smith & Sons (Motor Accessories) Ltd., which makes its appearance this morning is justified, both on patriotic and business grounds.[39]

This was the first in a series of capital increases (summarized later in Table 3.3), all of which diluted the family's interest, concentrated almost entirely with Samuel, who seems to have subscribed for no further equity after the flotation.[40] It might have been patriotic for investors to take up the latest issue, but Gordon was feeling the pressure:

> Owing to the large increase in the business of the Company, to the erection of the new factory, and to Government orders he had been working practically night and day and had been unable to take a day's holiday for two years.[41]

The minutes detail his *cri de cœur* that he was overstretched, particularly with regard to 'superintendence of the Counting House and of the Company's finance of which he thought he should be relieved'. After 'a long discussion' Gordon agreed to extend his service agreement through to 1922, with an 80 per cent increase in salary. Samuel (now 65) stepped into the fray by agreeing to take over as 'financial manager' for five years.

Having replenished the coffers, further expenditure was immediately under way, with all sorts of challenges emerging—for example, Gordon had to deal with 'the insufficiency of the female lavatory accommodation at the Cricklewood Factory and also the difficulty of assembly' in September 1915, leading to significant alterations and extensions to the new works. Shortage of space was a constant theme.[42]

The work was at least profitable, even allowing for excess profits tax, but with turnover doubling to near £400,000 in 1916, and orders in hand exceeding £500,000, yet more working capital was needed, and in October 1916 BFCC underwrote further equity, taking issued capital to £300,000, now three times the original total—further diluting the family's stake.

Continued growth and acquisitions: 1916–1918

> The directors are pleased to state they have experienced no labour diffi-
> culties and that the female labour employed has given satisfaction.
>
> (1916 annual accounts)

Rapid expansion of the Cricklewood factory in 1916 led to a doubling in staffing, to 2,000, mostly women (see Plate 14). It was not Smiths' first experience of women employees, however—under the classic gendered approach, believing women were solely possessed of the nimble and dextrous fingers for certain work, the production of speedometer dials had always been undertaken by women at Great Portland Street. The Cricklewood works manager later commented:

> One no longer need question the emancipation of women. A glimpse at the Carburetter Test Room with its intelligent girls busily engaged in taking strict readings ... all goes to prove that whatever grave injustice may have been done to the sex throughout the ages, now they are fully recognized.[43]

While the work was intensive, Gordon maintained Smiths' extra-curricular traditions. Access to an athletics ground was secured and a club formed—sport was actively encouraged, with annual traditions being made of a competition over which Gordon would preside, with his wife Bea awarding cups and prizes; there was also a works outing to bolster morale and a dinner for senior staff at a West End hotel.[44]

On the production front, a new speedometer was under development, but the carburettor was the main focus of attention in mid-1916. A new design could handle a mixture of 80:20 paraffin:petrol, offering a 60 per cent saving in consumption, so discussion in Great Portland Street centred on significantly increasing output.[45] What the firm could not develop in-house, it had to acquire. Smiths had sold Trier & Martin's equipment for several years, and partly to bring the business in-house, but also to secure the dedicated service of Vernon Trier (who had dropped the Germanic name Werner), Smiths acquired the firm in April 1917, leading to the development over the next two years of a combined starting and lighting set—a major product line.

Looking beyond cars, the next acquisition Gordon identified was the business of Frederic (Eric) Hollocoombe Clift, a gifted inventor with a substantial number of patents to his name, most notably for airspeed indicators.[46] These were manufactured by 300 staff at a small works in Bronnley's Corner Warehouse on Warple Way in Acton (home to many motor businesses) which Smiths acquired, together with patents and goodwill in September 1917—arguably the inaugural moment of Smiths' involvement in aerospace.[47]

At the Cricklewood central works, munitions and instrument production was relentless—and volumes would exceed all expectations. The friction tubes contract from March 1915 had nominally been for a notional maximum of 260,000 per annum, yet in late 1918 Samuel Smith reported the firm had made 'no less than approximately eight millions'.[48] Walton claims that 'large orders were secured from the Governments of France, Russia and Italy [for] a multitude of accessories, including millions of fathoms of wire rope'.[49] Other products included kite balloon winch-indicators, and Smiths 'Tankometers', fitted to all British tanks.[50] Exports through the 'colonial' network had been an early strategic goal, and large numbers of items (magnetos, tyres, instruments, etc.) were shipped overseas, though from 1919 these rapidly proved unsaleable as war-related demand ceased, so Smiths' name was removed and items cleared in any way possible. Little further detail of Smiths' wartime operation has emerged—it simply turned out vast quantities of mass-produced materiel alongside thousands of similar small engineering firms. When the minutes later reported on machinery replacement, there are occasional references to plant being worn out through twenty-four-hour operation over several years.

Other problems emerged towards the end of the war. A flaw in commission arrangements meant some agents were paid on a percentage of sales, with no reference to profits. Herbert G. Teagle, agent in New Zealand since 1915, was covering all the costs and actually losing money, leading to the October 1918 decision to form a new subsidiary, Smith & Teagle Ltd, allocating Teagle one third of the equity.

Remarkably, among all this war-related activity, Samuel still had grand ambitions for the jewellery business. In September 1917, he formed S. Smith & Son (Siam) Limited. With a view to selling fine jewellery in the Far East—even in the middle of the Great War—the £20,000 initial share issue was to finance 'large and important showrooms at Bangkok', to advance the fine stone business in 'Siam, Straits Settlements, Malay Peninsular, Dutch East Indies', and to develop an agency for the motor accessories business.[51] Our hero from the affair of the Queen of Siam's pearls, Frank Margrett, joined Gordon and Samuel ('recognised as one of the best judges of precious stones') on the board, travelling to Bangkok. But the business was never to prosper, with a receiver appointed in 1923 and winding-up commencing in 1926—though it was not for want of networking, given the composition of its shareholder list, which by mid-1918 included Siam's Grand Chamberlain, the ministers for both justice and war, customs officials, and a panoply of princes and princesses.

A short-lived boom as the Great War ends

The company had filled its part in the helping on to victory, and there was no
reason why they should not gain their fair share of the fruits of that victory.

(*The Economist*[52])

Thus Samuel Smith addressed the general meeting just over a month after the armistice. At an EGM in February 1919, to ratify a further share issue (see Table 3.3), Samuel
was bullish—'We have made our plans for the future. We want this new money, and we
must make sure of getting it.'[53] Increased funding supported an international
network—still at the heart of the firm's strategy—indeed Samuel told the shareholders
'it might interest you to know that the turnover at our branches during the past 12
months has equalled the total turnover of our entire business, home and export, during
1913–14'. But despite the bravura there is a telling admission of the change that peace
had wrought. He told shareholders:

> There is, however, one marked difference in dealing with many thousands of
> customers compared with having as your chief customer the Government. It is
> easier to finance a large turnover in the latter case than in the former.

The broad mood of optimism and the worldwide drive to replenish stocks led many
firms to expand rapidly. Interest rates were low, purchasing power was increasing, and
manufacturers like Gordon saw attractive opportunities to meet pent-up demand.
Gordon soon announced a new acquisition—M-L Magneto Syndicate, the Coventry-
based firm of David Morris and George Lister, which had supplied more than 60,000
magnetos during the war, mainly for aeroplanes. It now had a large order book from
the motor industry, producing 1,000 units per week. Smiths acquired 95 per cent of the
firm in July 1919, at a cost of £150,000 (2010: £5.4m), of which £30,000 represented
goodwill. Smiths retained the all-important personnel—especially the gifted electrical
inventor and engineer Ernest Ansley Watson—in an arrangement where key staff
received 10 per cent of the net profits.[54]

At the sign of the Bald-Headed Stag

Suffice it to say that they are the aristocrats of sparking plugs.

(Sydney Walton[55])

Gordon had his sights on another acquisition. Kenelm Lee Guinness, a distinguished
racing driver and future land speed record-holder, frustrated in the pre-war period
with the unreliability of sparking plugs, had patented his own design in 1913, with
improved mica insulation.[56] He and his racing friends had frequented the Bald-Headed
Stag in Putney, discussing engine improvements (see Plate 18). Trading under the name
KLG, Guinness established a small manufactory at the now disused pub, where

volumes reached 4,000–5,000 per week by 1914.[57] KLG developed a strong reputation for reliability, especially with plugs used for wartime aeroplanes. The business was incorporated as the Robinhood Engineering Works Ltd in 1916, its directors including Guinness, Louis Coatalen of Sunbeam racing fame, and the colourful and wealthy Noel van Raalte, who reportedly bankrolled the project, later becoming W. O. Bentley's first customer.[58] Demand for Robinhood's product was high, for example for Sopwith aircraft, and just before the conclusion of the war, the Air Ministry encouraged the production of KLG plugs under licence by Smiths. Gordon attempted to buy the firm outright, but was rebuffed by Guinness.[59] Some accounts wrongly suggest Smiths started manufacturing the plugs at this stage, but this is a myth. Instead, Gordon simply succeeded in negotiating the world selling rights.

In the midst of all this activity, Charles Percy Newman of Newman Hender was elected to the board.[60] Later described as 'a strong disciplinarian who would never accept any standard but the best—business was his life', he ran the engineering and brass foundry company in Gloucestershire, a link between the firms probably forged in earlier joint work on munitions.[61]

In May 1918, Gordon had started talking to Metallurgique, neighbours in Cricklewood, about acquiring their premises and these were finally acquired in September 1919.[62] Within months Gordon announced plans to convert the canteen at Central Works into assembly shops, moving catering to the newly acquired premises, and roofing in space between various buildings to create large stores.[63] Sales were now running at £1 million per annum, and reports of staff numbers jump markedly from 'about 2,000 hands' in mid-1919 to '3,000 hands' in February 1920 (see Plates 15, 16, and 17).[64] These were boom times, and with increased labour, the factory was now laid out to produce instruments at the weekly rates shown in Table 3.1.

Increased production demanded further investment, and more capital. Following the February 1919 fundraising, July saw a further new issue of shares, underwritten by Szarvasy's BFCC. At this stage, while *The Economist* was happy with dividend cover on the preference shares, it commented 'the ordinary shares may be regarded in the nature of a speculative industrial risk'.[65] Issued share capital increased from £450,000 to £800,000. Early 1920 saw the authorized capital increased again to allow for further issuance. With an increased dividend on both existing and these new preference shares, the market proved receptive for yet further issuance, underwritten once more by

Table 3.1 Weekly production rates by major product (1920)

Speedometers	3,000
Motor clocks	2,000
Gauges	1,000
Dynamo lighting sets	2,000
Carburettors	2,000
Mechanical horns	2,000

Source: Cann, 'Chronological Record', i. 100.

BFCC. The firm had now raised £1,200,000 in cash equity, much of it since the end of the war, a little over a year before. For the time being, things look set fair.

The wheels start to come off: 1920

> *No British industry has ever had to go overseas for critics.*
>
> (*The Life of Lord Nuffield*[66])

With the tide of post-war acquisition fever running high—an 'orgy of speculation' as Eichengreen calls it—the board succumbed to a recommendation from its solicitor, Clifford Turner, to acquire H. W. Smith of Lydbrook, a cable manufacturer, now in receivership after losing lucrative government contracts.[67] Gordon meanwhile continued to pursue the physical expansion of the Cricklewood site, and agreed a deal with Sir Samuel Waring to acquire the adjoining large assembly hall of the Nieuport & General Aircraft Company, for a mixture of cash and (mainly) equity.[68] After completion, Smiths' premises now extended from Cricklewood Broadway all the way back to Langton Road.

With hindsight, the motor industry was clearly on a treacherous footing. Many manufacturers had been drawn into wartime munitions production and this had led to broad wage inflation (and expectations), sustained by the strength of demand for engineering in the immediate post-war period. Labour and material costs were high, and the major benefits of mass production lay largely in the future. With Bank Rate increased to 7 per cent in April, and Chamberlain's June budget introducing corporation tax and increasing excess profits duty from 40 to 60 per cent, it became painfully apparent the wave of optimism of the last eighteen months had finally broken, as pre-war patterns of the flows of goods were re-established and manufacturing began to meet demand, while the loss of government contracts hit hard and the restriction of credit to dampen inflation began to bite. Wholesale prices, peaking in March 1920, were to halve over the next two years.[69] From peak to trough, manufacturing production fell by 22 per cent and GDP by 12 per cent, while unemployment shot up from 2.5 to 20 per cent. Though it may have been short-lived, the slump was ferocious.[70]

The bubble of demand for cars in the immediate aftermath of the Armistice now burst. Smiths had accumulated large levels of stock, but by mid-1920, its clients were requesting it to hold up deliveries, even under firm contracts. This was not the only worry. At the same time we find the first recorded trace of industrial action at Smiths— in May 1920, 1,400 of the Cricklewood staff walked out in support of the reinstatement of a shop steward who had been dismissed. Staff at other locations were threatening their support as well.[71] The strike was to last a whole month, and quite how it was resolved remains uncertain, although anecdotally Gordon was responsible for negotiating its end in a quiet chat with one of the pickets.[72]

Having raised substantial new equity, and having greatly expanded both premises and staffing levels, the market caravan had moved on. Nervousness about the firm's finances emerges in the May board minutes, and by September 1920, Gordon was looking to reduce costs. The Acton premises were the first to feel the axe, with production (presumably still airspeed indicators) moved to Cricklewood and the workshops closed.

By the end of September, standby financing had been arranged through Lloyds, yet again with the assistance of BFCC. Smiths could borrow on overdraft at base rate plus ½ per cent, depositing its title deeds with the bank. Judging from later correspondence, BFCC, or perhaps Szarvasy personally, added a further guarantee. All of this was in addition to financing Lloyds had provided to the recently acquired H. W. Smith of Lydbrook, and Smiths had backed this with its own guarantee—it was an acquisition already looking decidedly ill-judged.

Into the arms of the banks

> *The company's brief record affords one of the worst examples yet seen of the sequel to 'boom' finance.*
>
> (*The Times*[73])

Things were about to take a significant turn for the worse. One of Smiths' larger clients was Harper, Sons & Bean, a major car manufacturer which, like Smiths, had been a supplier of materiel. Its parent company had floated in late 1919, yet by the autumn of 1920 the car maker was insolvent, prompting the criticism quoted from *The Times*.[74] In receivership by October 1920, £475,000 was owed to trade creditors, and Smiths' share was significant. Harper's was not an isolated case—Morris Motors supplied 276 cars in September 1920, yet numbers declined each month, to just 74 cars in January 1921.[75]

It was standard practice for Smiths to provide supplier credit, by drawing usance bills of exchange on its clients.[76] Smiths could hold bills to maturity, but needing liquidity itself Smiths had discounted bills drawn on Harpers with the London County Westminster & Parrs Bank (today's NatWest, hereafter London County). Having endorsed the bills, Smiths were now on the hook, should Harper's fail to pay. Harper's insolvency placed everyone in a difficult position, and Smiths' solicitor, Clifford Turner, now in his element, was at the heart of negotiating a solution.[77] Another Harper Group company, British Motor Trading Corporation, had delivered a batch of Crossley cars to Smiths, presumably in lieu of Harper's payment, and Turner's solution involved Smiths acting as agent to sell the cars for the bank, in exchange for the bank agreeing to deliver the bills back to Smiths.

Despite agreeing this, by early 1921, London County was exposed to Smiths to the tune of £360,000 (2010: £12.5m). A further £25,000 was added to the Lloyds facility, making a total of £510,000 owed to just two banks. In an attempt to deal with the sudden ballooning of debt, an issue of £600,000 in debentures was authorized, maturing in twelve annual instalments commencing January 1923—priced to give a notional yield-to-maturity of 9½ per cent.[78] If the firm could get the issue away, it would provide much-needed breathing-space. Gordon wrote to shareholders twice, emphasizing the yield and the adequacy of the firm's assets, yet just 11 per cent were sold.[79] £520,000 of the debentures were instead issued to Lloyds and London County, to secure their advances, leaving the banks with a vice-like grip on the firm's assets.

Belt-tightening: 1921

> *The Board of Directors have decided that a reduction in salaries is necessary in order to place the Company on an economic basis.*
>
> (*Smiths Bulletin*, 104, 2 September 1921)

As it was for many firms, 1921 was thereafter dominated by a crisis in finances and the search for solutions. Various major changes were put in hand. Between February and March the firm moved its head office operation from Great Portland Street to Cricklewood, leaving what was described as 'surplus' (i.e. unsaleable) stock valued at £80,000 in the West End. Looking no doubt to reduce their reliance on the haemor-rhaging motor industry, effort was put into establishing a domestic clock business—presaging a major effort that was to be renewed the following decade—but this seems to have stalled.

In difficult times, sales staff come under additional pressure to sell more, and operations staff have to find cost savings and cuts. Tensions surfaced. Buckland (the sales manager) needled his colleagues about delays in speedometer production when sales were held up, leading to a defensive reaction from Gordon, who in turn queried why more lighting sets were not being sold, especially when more salesmen had been hired.[80] Gordon was adamant that ways must be found to produce cheaper products, particularly lighting sets.[81]

Cost-cutting involved looking at what operations could be closed and moved to Cricklewood, and the bold move of simply closing the factory for two weeks in August. Having acquired Nieuport's premises, Gordon was now proposing to move out again and to sublet the space, which was finally achieved the following April.[82] By October 1921, and echoing the opening months of the war seven years earlier, the decision was taken to reduce wages by 15 per cent, although under a formula by which they could rise again in response to performance.[83] A few months later the directors followed suit with a 50 per cent reduction in their fees. Still needing money, Gordon met with Clifford Turner and Szarvasy in December to see what chances there might be to issue more debentures, but was told there was no hope.

Hubert Thomas Marsh (1883–1935)

He was keenly interested in the constructive side of an accountant's life, and was well known for his work in factory costing and organisation, as well for his advice on reconstruction and amalgamation and general financial matters.

(Obituary, *The Accountant*[84])

An important feature of 1921 was the arrival of Hubert Marsh, chartered accountant. His firm—Whitehill & Whitehill of Birmingham—was employed by Percy Newman, and he may have introduced Marsh as another resource, independent of Wilson, Wright, the London auditors. Marsh attended board meetings from January 1921 and thereafter was crucial in guiding the firm through difficult waters. He was the only one in true command of the firm's figures, and Gordon, and therefore the board, relied heavily on him to explain what could and could not be done, and what they should be aiming for, particularly in terms of cash generation. Marsh's health was not good, and when he could not attend meetings, it is telling that finance matters were invariably held over. It would have been Marsh who encouraged a robust treatment of overdue receivables in the July 1921 year-end accounts, in which Smiths posted a loss of nearly £300,000, after writing off bad debts as a result of 'the failure of several big motor manufacturing companies'—an action *The Economist* felt showed 'wisdom and courage'.[85]

No end in sight

This is not a very pleasant picture, but with efficient management and the loyal support of shareholders it may be that the undertaking has passed through the worst of its difficulties.

(*The Economist*[86])

The Economist's optimism was misplaced. The *Financial Times* cast the government as Mr Micawber—hoping something would turn up—action finally emerging in the Geddes Committee on National Expenditure of 1921 and its infamous 'axe'.[87] Smiths was far from out of the woods. Board meetings were dominated by Marsh's relentless analysis. Each month brought losses, added to which the firm's loan to M-L Magneto had to be capitalized, owing to the subsidiary's own dire finances.[88] In April 1922, Marsh pointed out that, aside from such exceptional items, the firm was generating £1,500 per month less than the targeted figure Samuel had set in his last speech to shareholders—the banks would worry that operations were not covering interest commitments—partly because monthly royalties on KLG plugs were swallowing £1,000—an arrangement Gordon was fortunately to renegotiate by May.[89]

In June, Marsh delivered a detailed assessment.[90] Operating margins were improving slowly, but more cost-cutting was needed. He queried if foundry work could be outsourced and where gas, light, and power costs could be reduced. The figures for the year were boosted significantly by a total of £75,000 in refunds of excess profits duty which Marsh negotiated with the tax authorities—funds that he strongly urged the board to use as a reserve to cover future liabilities to the banks.[91] Another Marsh success was the settlement of an item referred to only as the 'Ministry claim'—presumably an amount to cover the cancellation of a munitions contract—which brought in a further £8,500.[92] Stock levels were being run down, but profitability was elusive.

Nervousness on the part of the banks expressed itself in the nomination by Lloyds (mediated by Szarvasy) of a new and ultimately highly important board member, Walter Henderson-Cleland MC, a solicitor who had enjoyed a distinguished war career.[93] He joined the board in April 1922 and soon began working with Gordon and Marsh on a potential merger of Smiths with C. A. Vandervell, the Acton-based car lighting manufacturer. CAV had a turnover of £50,000 per month and the proposal was that, with proper controls, substantial profits could be earned.[94] Months of negotiations took place but ultimately Smiths allowed the matter to die, though rewarding Henderson-Cleland with a small cash payment for his efforts.[95] Lucas was to acquire CAV in 1926.

If the board was being broadened with more outside talent, this was at the expense of the family. Szarvasy wrote to the board encouraging its reorganization but it was left to Marsh to spell out at the April meeting that family representation needed to reduce— the banks wanted to see more of an emphasis on professional management.[96] With Samuel and Gordon occupying senior roles, Reginald, the youngest, had to resign. G. W. Arnold, another of the old guard, and a veteran of constant international travel around the overseas offices, also stepped down.[97] Samuel, who had not been well—he suffered from neuritis—may also have felt similar pressures, as he began discussing his resignation as chairman in December—added to which Annie, his wife for nearly fifty years, had died at the end of October.[98]

On a more positive note, the board felt sufficiently confident by August 1922 to cancel the blanket 15 per cent reduction in wages, going further by putting in place a profit-related bonus scheme. An important long-term positive was the winning of substantial contracts from Morris, who was now pressing ahead with an aggressive strategy of price-cutting, on the back of pressuring his suppliers to cut their prices to the bones—the Morris Cowley's original price of £465 fell to £300 in late 1921, and then to £225 at the 1922 Motor Show—leading to considerable sales success.[99] As a business associate of Morris commented, 'basically, he was a buyer and a very acute buyer indeed. Anything he bought, he bought at a very keen price.'[100] Smiths supplied dynamos, 10,000 lighting sets, speedometers, and clocks as well, no doubt after spirited competition with other firms, such as Lucas.[101]

Moving forward into 1923, there were changes among some of the actors. 'Cotty' Cotterell, long-term company secretary, moved to become chief buyer, with Henry Warwick, the works accountant, stepping into his shoes.[102] Wilson, Wright resigned their appointment as auditors, for reasons unknown, but this paved the way for

Marsh's firm, Whitehill & Whitehill, to take their place—an appointment filled with conflicts of interest that would not survive modern inspection, but which probably seemed the most natural outcome at the time.[103]

The bankers take charge: 1923

> *Whilst there can be no objection in principle to a representative of the Bank being on your Board, it largely depends on who their deputy is.*
>
> (Szarvasy to Gordon Smith, 26 February 1923)[104]

In this era, British banks based their credit assessments on collateral and assets, not cash-generating ability. This explains the significant interest London County took in the firm's stock figure, no doubt concerned it might still contain valueless items. The bank even appointed independent accountants to monitor Smiths' figures, increasing Marsh's workload, since he now had to justify his figures to a third party.[105] But in February 1923 the bank was sufficiently happy with a recent stocktaking report to renew the overdraft facility, though reduced in limit once again, to £350,000, with the result the board also resolved to reduce the Lloyds facility to £150,000.

With these bank negotiations out of the way, and once Henderson-Cleland had checked with Szarvasy (and therefore Lloyds) that the move was supported, Percy Newman took up the chairmanship vacated by Samuel. A committee was immediately formed, of Newman, Henderson-Cleland, Gordon Smith, and Marsh the accountant, to consider a much-needed scheme of reconstruction of the firm's capital—again probably largely influenced by Szarvasy, whose later reputation rests on such reorganizations.[106]

Stock remained a key focus for London County, and the appointment of its own supervisor to oversee the stocktaking process created significant tension. The board minutes report anger and frustration at the alleged incompetence of the man involved, and eventually a satisfactory substitute was agreed: McRobie Turrell (formerly Harry Lawson's 'natty adjutant').[107] Turrell would probably have become a director—London County's nominee—but he died unexpectedly soon after. The bank's influence is clear from interesting correspondence between Szarvasy and Gordon Smith. As Szarvasy wrote:

> What you really want is some person who is well known and on friendly terms with the important motor companies and users of your accessories and who could make some use of his influence in bringing you nearer to customers with whom you are not in touch at present. If you discuss the matter along these lines with the Bank they might nominate somebody who would be really useful to you.[108]

The outcome of the stocktaking Turrell had overseen in the spring was the next major project—to print 20,000 copies of a catalogue of the excess stock. This would be circulated to every important garage, and all of May and June 1923's advertising budget was earmarked. The travelling salesmen had instructions to move stock at all costs and special sale displays were set up in Great Portland Street, Manchester, Glasgow, and Birmingham.[109]

The extended dance between the firm and its bankers continued from month to month. The firm wanted to retain maximum flexibility and liquidity, while London County in particular wanted debt reduction, reducing the overdraft by a further £10,000 to £340,000 in the autumn, though Marsh continued to argue, unsuccessfully, that the reserve from the refund of excess profits duty should remain a cushion to cover debt service, not used as a permanent reduction.[110]

Beginning to turn the corner: 1923–1924

Two of the outstanding features of general interest at the Motor Show, which opens this morning at Olympia, are low prices and improved design.

(*The Times*[111])

Autumn 1923 saw a measure of optimism emerging, especially after the October motor show when sales increased.[112] The Morris contract had been profitable, leading to bonuses and the promise of more if the value of the 1924 Morris contract came out at £100,000 or more—the only downside to large volumes with Morris being the need to finance a build-up of associated stock.[113]

But if things were looking up, a check came with the December election, in which Labour ended up forming its first (minority) government. The confused political situation led to Morris reducing his Smiths orders by one-third from 500 lighting sets per week to just 330.[114] Further, when Marsh presented the audited 1923 figures at the end of the year, bad debts and stock write-downs loomed large. After two years and losses of close to £550,000, the firm had finally made a profit, if only £7,000.[115]

Into 1924, and having lost one candidate, London County finally secured a nominee on the board in Sydney Dawson Begbie, managing director of Aster Engineering with a large works in Wembley, who joined in January. With a pedigree in engine-making, including wartime aero engines, Begbie had started producing luxury cars in 1922, buying magnetos from Smiths' subsidiary M-L. He now launched his Smiths career with a closer look at how practical economies could be made at Cricklewood.

The tone of board meetings in the first part of 1924 changed markedly from the previous two years. Marsh's reports showed favourable year-on-year data and welcome increases in sales, although the effects of the cutbacks in deliveries to Morris were keenly felt.[116] In May, more capital expenditure was approved (lathes, milling machines) but now both Newman and Begbie wanted more hands-on involvement in selection, as both had direct manufacturing experience.[117]

The McKenna duties

In our opinion, if the duty is abolished, this particular industry will be reduced to its pre-war level, and unemployment consequently increased.

(Gordon Smith, speech to Central Works, *The Times*[118])

From April a greater threat emerged, not only for Smiths but for the entire motor industry. In 1915, the Chancellor, Reginald McKenna, had introduced a 33⅓ per cent levy on luxury imported goods, including cars and clocks.[119] These 'McKenna duties' greatly benefited the UK car manufacturing industry, and by extension Smiths, depressing foreign competition. Labour had fought the election on tariffs and there was widespread concern the Chancellor would elect not to renew the duties in his first Budget. Agitation emerged at affected plants in various industries, and in April 2,000 Smiths workers assembled in the Cricklewood canteen to hear Gordon's speech in favour of retaining the duties—suggesting, dramatically, that should they be abolished 'from 70 to 80 per cent of the workers would be thrown out of employment'.[120]

The duties did indeed disappear from the end of July 1924 and there were immediate consequences. Morris reduced production at Cowley by 50 per cent to 600 cars per week, and discharged 1,300 employees.[121] As things turned out, while job losses occurred, the Jeremiahs were proved wrong—indeed the predicted demise of the industry was simple political posturing. With the change of government in 1925 the McKenna duties were reinstated but, judging from Smiths' results, it did not suffer and its figures improved throughout the year.

Decisive reorganization

Nibbling at the cherry, or rather at the pill, is no good at all. [It was better to] get rid of all the useless assets and to put capital on a proper earnings basis.

(*Financial Times*[122])

Smiths finally took action that spring to write down the firm's capital—something anticipated at the previous AGM—indeed the 1923 accounts carry the remarkable and bold warning in the balance sheet 'NOTE—the value of these Debts and Investments is considerably less than the amount stated'. Everyone had been on notice and action was necessary. Indeed, it was being pressed by London County at least. At the April AGM, in his chairman's speech, Newman started by mentioning the addition to the board of Begbie (London County's nominee) and continued to say that 'after careful consideration with *him* they had come to the definite conclusion that the time had arrived' for a 'drastic' but 'sound' 'reorganisation of capital'.[123] The meeting was tense and a disaffected shareholder, Mr W. H. Paterson, sought to have it deferred so the accounts could be investigated by a shareholders' committee. Clifford Turner, the nimble-footed solicitor, intervened—there was to be a later EGM to approve the restructuring and Turner suggested Newman's speech for that later meeting be brought forward. Paterson's complaint was that the shareholders did not know what assets were to written down and by how much.

Newman now gave specifics—covering write-downs in buildings, plant, stock, and, importantly, amounts invested in and due from subsidiaries, as an important element of the business model needed drastic change. It had been standard industry practice to export a 'skeleton vehicle', fitting accessories at the final destination and Smiths had formed foreign subsidiaries to supply the needed accessories—both their own and other factored products. In the early 1920s, policy had altered radically, with manufacturers now shipping fully fitted vehicles. In one sense, Smiths had not lost the business—it had merely become domestic—but they were saddled with useless foreign subsidiaries. Between further accumulated losses and necessary write-downs, the capital of the firm was reduced by more than £1 million—meaning the ordinary shareholders had lost some 85 per cent of the nominal value of their shares.

Change of guard

> *He had done his best . . . over three years which had been very anxious ones . . . and now that the reorganisation scheme was through and the Company in smoother water he tendered his resignation as Chairman.*

(C. P. Newman, *Minutes*[124])

Leaving aside the legacy of the past, the firm was certainly achieving unit sales growth, as Table 3.2 shows.

Table 3.2 Accessory sales, by category (1921–1924)

	1921–22	1922–23	1923–24
Speedometers	26,747	48,697	82,985
Clocks	9,782	30,946	68,187
Gauges (pressure)	5,346	18,307	19,020
Gauges (petrol tank)	3,679	4,395	10,422
Flexes	21,036	49,585	88,234
Drive gear box sets	3,569	20,513	44,694
Carburettors	7,643	22,503	44,648
Dynamos	1,998	6,024	4,772
Starters	589	4,590	4,369

Source: *Minutes* (24 July 1924).

The forecasts for 1924–5 saw at least 20 per cent increases possible in most of these lines, and up to 50 per cent in some. The after-sales side of the business was also expanding rapidly since the firm had instituted a popular repair and overhaul service that promised a forty-eight-hour turnaround, and space for all departments at Cricklewood was under pressure. With clients such as Austin's, Standard, and Bean all expected to increase their orders significantly for 1925, Gordon commissioned architect's drawings for factory additions, and by October work was under way.[125]

Smiths' fortunes were mixed in the second half of 1924. There was important new business—for example, an order for 20,000 sparking plugs from the Russian government—and the Morris contract continued to be valuable, earning bonuses for Rex Smith, by now chief engineer. But Morris also poached King, Smiths' carburettor man, prompting a meeting between Gordon and Morris to smooth over waters. Percy Newman, chairman since early 1923 and through difficult times, now felt things were on a more even keel, allowing him to concentrate on reviving his own firm, Newman Hender—he resigned in November, to be replaced by Henderson-Cleland, once the firm had completed the annual ritual of deferring repayment under its debentures. Crises still erupted—just before Christmas 1924 an emergency board meeting was called, as M-L Magneto had no cash and it was once again the accountant Marsh who rode to the rescue, negotiating a refinancing package with Lloyds, but things remained very tight. Within months Smiths had to purchase equipment needed by M-L, which it supplied on a hire-purchase basis.[126]

Back on a sound footing: 1925

They had brought the company from its depressed state until now they could see a prosperous time coming. As long as the board went on as they had done in the past, the company should prosper.

(Lord Dewar, vote of thanks, *The Times*[127])

Taking early advantage of a pioneering development in financial markets, 1925 opened with Smiths securing credit insurance through the Trade Indemnity Company to cover potential default by some of its main debtors—Harper, Sons & Bean, AC Cars, and Clyno Engineering. The insurer was a novel vehicle of Cuthbert Heath's (of Lloyds fame) and was unique as a private sector credit insurer, with some backing from the main insurance companies who acted as its reinsurers.[128]

If this sounded a cautious note, cash generation was nevertheless increasing, and London County therefore pressed for further permanent reductions in their exposure—£10,000 was agreed—and Smiths increased the amount set aside each month for debt service. Against this more positive backdrop, Gordon busied himself with negotiating an improved sales arrangement with Robinhood Engineering covering Smiths' sales of plugs.[129] At the same time, an agreement was signed with the Tavannes Watch Company in Switzerland, the firm supplying Smiths with escapements for their car clocks, which were otherwise fabricated entirely at Cricklewood—an arrangement that would lead to trouble.[130]

Growth was visible—not least in the numbers attending the annual sports day at the Dudden Lane sports ground in Neasden, where 1,500 turned up in July.[131] That month, forecasts for year-end profits suggested £20,000 would be achieved, and this activated commission payments for Gordon and Charles Nichols, after a fallow period. Further capital expenditure and yet more factory expansion were under discussion mid-year 'in view of the increased output in the motor trade as experienced by the increased demands upon our resources from Messr Morris Motors, Austin Motor Co., and several other customers'.[132]

It will not have escaped Smiths' notice that its major client, Morris, had a clear strategy of acquiring and controlling suppliers that were vital to his mass production operations. Perhaps hoping to anticipate Morris, Smiths acquired (for £4,000) the Johnson Motor Company of Aston, makers, and suppliers to Morris Commercial Motors, of the Maxfield tyre pump and the 'Thermet'—a valve fitted between cylinder head and radiator that opened only at a predetermined temperature. Mindful of preserving goodwill, the purchase agreement stipulated that Morris himself had to be aware of its terms and to be agreeable.[133] Francis (Frank) Hurn, who joined Smiths in 1919 after being de-mobbed from the RFC (and a future MD of the motor accessories business), had been made Midlands Manager at the Smiths depot in Birmingham in 1923, so he was a natural local choice, along with Charles Nichols, for the board of Johnson Motors.[134]

Cleaning out the Augean stables took time. The ill-advised purchase of H. W. Smith continued to haunt the firm and it was forced to pay out to Lloyds to discharge the guarantee it had issued for the subsidiary, though the overall relationship with the bank remained strong, supported by Szarvasy's BFCC and its guarantee of Smith's obligations, which ran through till March 1927.[135]

Overall, business was improving and Henderson-Cleland was able to deliver a relatively bullish speech at the December 1925 general meeting.[136] Speedometer sales had doubled and the firm was now producing 3,000 per week, while clock and carburettor sales had trebled and these three items represented the bulk of factory output. New lines were still being introduced—including a new powered windscreen wiper (still a relative novelty) and a cigar lighter—the latter now an anachronism but in 1925 clearly judged by Smiths (and the press) to be an important addition to the catalogue.

The General Strike

> It was resolved that the Board do tender their thanks and congratulations to Mr Gordon Smith and his staff for the manner of handling and the success attained in dealing with the situation arising from the General Strike.
>
> (*Minutes,* 27 May 1926)

Despite (perhaps even because of) continued progress on the development of the firm's sales and overall health, the banks continued to maintain pressure. As 1926 began,

London and County pressed for a further reduction of £15,000 in its facilities, and Begbie was asked to negotiate—although it ended up being Marsh, the accountant, as so often, who delivered, agreeing a smaller reduction, with Lloyds going pro rata.

The year is often best remembered for its general strike, in May, and the coal strike which rumbled on till November, though there is scant evidence of how workers at Smiths reacted to the broader TUC action that commenced near midnight on 3 May—certainly the firm was unionized and there will have been shop-floor support for the strike, but the chairman was later to comment on the 'loyalty' of the staff.[137] One analysis of the strike summarizes that, 'believing their privileged existence and their world to be threatened by the 1926 British General Strike, upper-class volunteers came out as strike breakers and transformed a potential working-class revolution into a nine-day May festival. Their behaviour was reminiscent of larks, rags, fancy dress, and leg-pulls.'[138] This phenomenon was perhaps echoed at Smiths, with surviving photographs showing several members of senior management rallying to the anti-strike cause—witness Rex Smith at the wheel of the No. 2 bus at Golders Green—part of a large group of white-collar amateurs who manned trains, buses, and trams, under the protection of the police, to maintain services. On 13 May, *The Times* launched a National Police Fund, in recognition of the role the police played, and Smiths voted to contribute 25 guineas at the board meeting on 27 May 'as some recognition of the services rendered by the police during the strike'—suggestive perhaps that the firm had benefited from a police presence in Cricklewood.

But otherwise the strike seems not to have disturbed the board, which at the 27 May meeting focused on reviewing patents for a wide range of accessories, several of which covered overseas markets. Expansion of the factory, repairs, upgrading, and the addition of more machine tools still continued, while the banks pressed as ever for debt reduction. As part of a regular cycle, a further amount had to be shaved off the London County balance, a pro rata amount with Lloyds, and the debenture holders were fobbed off for yet another year (although this was for the last time) in October.[139] Good news emerged in November when Marsh, the accountant, was able to report that M-L Magneto had finally reported a profit.

Deliverance from the banks: 1927

The generous return offered on these cumulative preference shares indicates the degree of risk involved.

(*The Economist*[140])

The firm entered 1927 on a different footing. Sales had increased each year since formation. It wielded significant market power—supplying 80 per cent of the market for its principal products. Profitability had returned, and was on an increasing trend. It had stripped out the vast bulk of its risky factoring business, and scaled back its overseas investments—though it now profitably exported its products again. Debt had steadily reduced and the confidence of the banks had been maintained—partly through the banks involving themselves so closely, with their nominated directors exercising a guiding influence alongside Gordon Smith, ensuring their interests were advanced. Ordinary shareholders will have been particularly cheered at the general meeting in January 1927 to find they were at last to receive a dividend. Indeed Henderson-Cleland could report positive changes in most items in the balance sheet, with creditors reduced alongside a reduction in debt; the book value of depreciated fixed assets now undervalued their true worth; and while stock had increased somewhat this was in support of a significantly increased turnover.

Importantly, though the balance sheet was still dominated by debt to the two banks, market circumstances had now changed and Smiths could finally restructure the balance sheet. Back in 1920, when Smiths' capital had been increased, Myers & Co. had acted as brokers. More recently, in early 1926 Myers underwrote a significant £1.5 million debenture issue for the Austin Motor Company—part of a series of motor industry related deals, and in January 1927 it was Smiths' turn, with Myers underwriting a new issue of £400,000 preference shares.[141] This successful placement produced sufficient funds to redeem the troublesome debentures, and to pay down bank debt, although Lloyds was happy to keep £50,000 on an unsecured overdraft basis, bringing to an end the need for guarantees arranged by Szarvasy. It was not cheaply raised money, given an underwriting commission of 3 per cent, plus £20,000 in expenses and up to £2,500 in brokerage fees—in total nearly 9 per cent of the issue—but it was equity, not debt.

The importance of being English

> *Lenoir is the only one who really understands the business.*
>
> (Gordon Smith[142])

By the mid-1920s, country of origin for manufactured items was important—a patriotic 'Buy British' campaign was reviving—one result being the Merchandise Marks Act (1926), updating the 1887 legislation. That Smiths was conscious of the need to manufacture domestically is borne out in a 1928 decision, with £3,000 'authorised to be spent on "Buy British" publicity, such sum to be divided pro rata between the Smith group of companies'.[143]

Turning back the clock to the early 1920s, a small competitor for Smiths was Rotax (Motor Accessories) Ltd, the vehicle of Herman and Eugene Aron, and later acquired by Lucas in 1926. It produced lighting equipment at Willesden Junction, with an agency for speedometers supplied by Jaeger, Paris. Frustrated by Rotax's lack of sales, Jaeger despatched Robert Lenoir to London in 1920 as a technical engineer, to fit its instruments and to advance its interests. Later a critically important figure within Smiths,

Lenoir started his career by qualifying at the watch school at Le Locle, in Switzerland, and was then severely wounded in the Great War, spending the rest of his life with bits of shrapnel floating around his body.[144]

The Arons transferred the Jaeger agency to a relative, Joseph Sidney Simmons, who ran the administration while Lenoir, as chief technician, established a footing for Jaeger through sheer hard work and regular factory visits to the major car manufacturers. He forged valuable relationships with chief engineers and head testers, as well as spending weekends at Brooklands getting close to racing legends Malcolm Campbell, Henry Segrave, and Kaye Don, persuading them to fit his instruments, the most important being the accurate 'type F' chronometric speedometer—which in various guises remained in production for thirty years.[145]

The UK agency was incorporated as Ed. Jaeger (London) Limited in 1924, and Francois Coatalen (brother to Louis, automobile engineer of Sunbeam fame) came onboard. With the acquisition of a small factory nearly opposite Rotax, the firm moved from assembly to production—Jaeger also understood the importance of 'British Made'. In Switzerland and France it duplicated jigs and press-tools to equip the London factory and specialists travelled to Britain to establish the business, including René LeCoultre who set up the service and repair side. In 1925, Ed. Jaeger started supplying Humber, which demanded British-made instruments, and it was also this year that Wilfrid Cann, Smiths' first biographer and an important source for this book, joined Ed. Jaeger. Business went well, and by 1927 was causing concern to its competitors—chiefly to Smiths. Jaeger had submitted a design to Austin's for test on their successful 7 hp car and Smiths' management was troubled—in addition to which 'the Smiths executives had always admired the styling of the Jaeger instrument and the excellence of its dial layout and printing'.[146] A possible approach by Jaeger to Lucas with a view to cooperation in the UK may also have caused concern.[147]

Gordon Smith and Ben Haviland, Cricklewood Central Works manager since 1921, visited Lenoir for a factory tour. They acted and, 'as a result of discussions lasting some months, it was announced in September, 1927 that S. Smith . . . had acquired a controlling [75 per cent] interest', at a cost of £75,000, plus £15,000 in shares. The new board comprised Henderson-Cleland and Gordon Smith, together with Gustave Delage from Jaeger. Lenoir became works manager—Gordon was heard to remark 'Lenoir is the only one who really understands the business'—with Simmons and Coatalen as sales manager and secretary respectively.[148]

In hot water with Swiss parts

> *The defendants pleaded guilty to the charges and admitted the escapement was foreign made.*
>
> (BHI *v.* S. Smith & Sons, *Horological Journal*[149])

Gordon Smith had an ulterior motive in acquiring control of this competitor, since it brought him not only Lenoir, a Swiss-trained horologist, but also closer links to Jaeger and

LeCoultre. In 1925, Smiths had concluded an agreement with the Tavannes Watch Company to supply certain clock parts, but in early 1927 Smiths had to attend Willesden Police Court to answer a summons 'for applying a false trade description to a motor clock and for selling the same contrary to the provisions of the Merchandise Marks Act'.[150]

Having started by importing complete Swiss clocks, Smiths now made all parts of the car clock save for its regulating heart, the escapement, which was still imported whole from Tavannes. The firm had the agreement of the Board of Overseas Trade and the SMMT that the resulting clock could be described as 'British Made', but a very different view was taken by William Edward Tucker of H. Williamson of Coventry, a firm we met in Chapter 2.[151] Samuel Smith had forced Williamson's to abandon speedometer making, in order to retain Smiths' custom. Williamson's had also lost a fierce battle involving foreign content in its watches, under the Merchandise Marks Act (1887), and, still aggrieved, Tucker pressed the British Horological Institute into issuing the summons over Smith's 'British' car clock.[152] Smiths' counsel argued his client's good faith in checking with trade bodies that 'British Made' would be acceptable, but this cut no mustard.

The penalty of £10 with 20 guineas costs meant little—of far greater consequence was the need to be seen to be wholly behind the 'Buy British' trend and to be making in Britain. In acquiring a controlling interest in Jaeger, Smiths not only acquired the manufacturer of a fine speedometer, but also moved closer to the solution of its escapement problem.

Discussions with LeCoultre and Delage about Smiths making escapements of its own followed mid-1928, and then in September the All British Escapement Company Limited (ABEC) was formed, with £14,000 in capital, owned by the same shareholders as Ed. Jaeger.[153] Gordon must have conceived a grand plan early on—since at the same time that he was acquiring control of Ed. Jaeger, he agreed to purchase 9½ acres of land on the North Circular Road, on the Brentwater Estate, at £800 per acre, a deal closed in November 1927.[154] This provided a site for the new factory that was soon being planned. At the same time, a contract was signed with ABEC, committing Smiths to purchases of escapements for eighteen years, giving the new firm a sound foundation.

Robinhood Engineering

Your 1928 Resolution—'Fit and Forget'—a Set of the Famous KLG Sparking Plugs.

(Advertisement, 1928)

There was another matter that occupied significant time in late 1927. The licensing agreement under which Smiths had sole overseas rights for the sale of KLG plugs, and a significant role in UK sales, would expire on 31 March 1928. Kenelm Lee Guinness, who rebuffed an approach in 1918, was now keen to sell his firm. Gordon could not let it go

1. Samuel Smith (1826–1875).

2. Samuel Smith (1850–1932).

3. The shop at 151–153 Newington Causeway (1897).

4. One of several shops on the Strand, at No. 6 Grand Hotel Buildings (*c.*1910).

5. Staff at No. 9 Strand (*c.*1905), including Charles Nichols, P.O. Dorer, and Charles Bennett (Roger Hurn's grandfather).

6. Smiths (white) vs. Nicole Nielsen (stripes). Reginald Smith (scarved), Gordon Smith to his left, Charles Nichols front row, third from left (1907).

7. Formerly home to the Association of Diamond Merchants, No. 68 Piccadilly (*c.*1920).

8. The first Smith & Sons speedometer, fitted to Edward VII's Mercedes (1904).

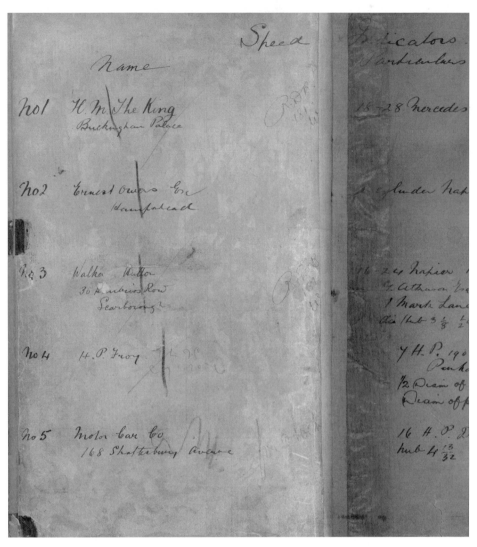

9. Speedometer sales ledger (1904–1905), showing the King as the first customer.

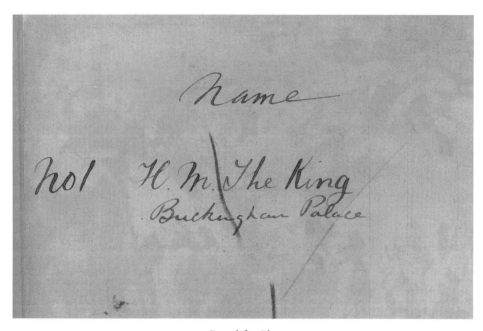

10. Detail for Plate 9.

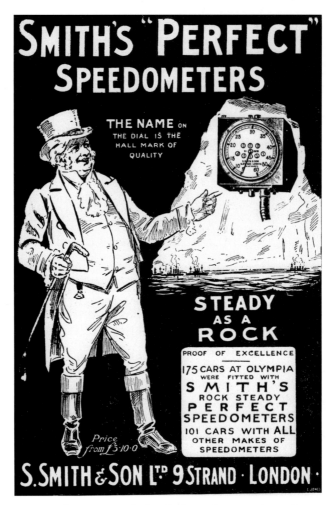

11. Advertisement for 'Perfect' speedometers (*c.*1908).

12. Captain Scott's pocket watch, supplied by Smiths.

13. The factory and headquarters at 179–185 Great Portland Street, 1913 onwards.

14. Munitions workers at Cricklewood (1916).

15. Cricklewood factory, press workshop, overseen by Bill Lewis, machine shop superintendent (*c*.1922).

16. Cricklewood machine shop, drilling operations (*c*.1920).

17. Works outing on the river (1919). Gordon Smith, Nichols, Barrett, Dorer, and Haviland all present.

18. Guinness (far left), Campbell, and Segrave in their Talbot Darracq cars at the Bald Headed Stag, the first KLG factory (c.1921).

elsewhere and he justified a purchase to the board on the following terms—half of Smiths' export sales were of KLG plugs, worth about £80,000 in turnover on which a reasonable profit was earned. It was increasingly valuable to have solid lines that were not dependent on other manufacturers and the commission arrangements for selling plugs via Smiths salesmen were profitable and subsidized the whole sales operation. Average profits over the last three years would, if continued, provide a 20 per cent return on the net purchase price.

Once again this was a transaction with Marsh the accountant at its heart, conducting detailed due diligence and negotiating alongside Gordon Smith. The purchase price was £276,000, split 50 per cent on completion, 25 per cent via six-month bills and the balance in twelve-month bills. Lloyds provided a further £125,000 in financing, on top of its £50,000 unsecured facility, against the pledge of shares in both M-L Magneto and Robinhood Engineering. Gordon argued Smiths could pay down debt by stripping £50,000 in liquidity out of Robinhood itself, and placing further preference shares—which Myers & Co. soon achieved. The minutes record substantial discussion—largely because the goodwill being acquired was some £121,000 or 44 per cent of the price. Yet this was much reduced from the figure in the opening negotiations and one senses it was Marsh once more who was instrumental in securing Gordon a more favourable deal.

Capital raising and financial outcomes: 1914–1928

> *I would point out that at the issue price of 95% the Debentures yield £8-18-0% and adding the profit upon redemption £9–10–0%. There is also ample security of capital.*

> (Gordon Smith to shareholders, 1921)

The path on which Smiths' capital structure evolved was anything but inevitable. The flotation was probably expected to raise sufficient funds to last for several years, and to see the continued development of motor accessory manufacture in the West End. Having initially sold half the equity to the market in 1914, the rapid expansion necessitated by munitions work saw ownership of the firm rapidly pass to external investors. With the post-war slump, everyone, the Smiths included, lost nearly their entire investment (see Table 3.3).

Turning to the accounts, turnover figures are witness to the wartime expansion, with sales of £118,000 in 1915 rising to near £900,000 in 1918. Profitability did not quite chart the same path, only doubling from £25,000 in 1915 to £49,000 for 1918. Profits doubled again to £98,000 in 1920, but after the Lord Mayor's show came the muck cart of two years of losses totalling £550,000. The 1922 annual report recorded the lowest point to which Smiths' fortunes fell in the 1920s. The last six months of the financial year saw

Table 3.3 S. Smith & Sons (Motor Accessories) new issues and restructuring (1914–1928)

Year	Arranger	Equity raised
1914 (IPO)	S. Smith & Son	£50,000 (plus £50,000 issued in kind) ordinary
1915	BFCC	£100,000 ordinary
1916	BFCC	£100,000 ordinary
1919	BFCC	£150,000 ordinary
1919	BFCC	£350,000 (200,000 ordinary, 150,000 preferred))
1920	BFCC	£400,000 (200,000 ordinary, 200,000 preferred)
1924		Existing £1.2m equity written down 85 per cent and exchanged for £192,000 new shares (42,000 ordinary, 150,000 preferred)
1927	Myers	£400,000 preferred
1928	Myers	£100,000 preferred

Source: Prospectuses.

the firm return to gross operating profit, but the net figures were dominated by stock write-downs, earlier trading losses, losses on overseas branches, and cancelled contracts amounting to some £220,000.

The return to profitability came in 1923, at a modest £7,000, followed by healthy annual increases, rising to above £100,000 in 1927. The experience of the early 1920s had been painful and it was reflected in the emergence of an emerging conservatism going forward—from 1926 the accounts show significant 'general' reserves being accumulated, rising to £175,000 by the end of 1928.

A firm footing is established

> *It is not always the fastest that wins the Waterloo Cup, the famous 'blue ribbon' of English coursing, for a number of other points, including the cleverness displayed in making turns, influences the decision of the judges.*
>
> (*The Bradford Era*[155])

By 1927 and 1928, the firm had turned the corner, profitable and paying dividends on all classes of shares. The burden of debt had finally been trimmed and replaced with equity, while unprofitable business lines and assets had been written down or stripped out. The firm now manufactured, rather than acting as an agent or factor, and enjoyed a commanding market share, with sales still increasing, not only in motor accessories, but in other fields as well, while the threat of competitors acquiring KLG or Jaeger had been neutralized.

Though Gordon Smith was a natural leader, he had not acted alone, and had been supported by a close circle, both executive and non-executive—notably by Marsh, the accountant. Indeed, without Marsh, it is doubtful whether the firm would have survived the downturn of the early 1920s, which marked the end for so many other firms. Gordon had also now gathered together an effective team at Cricklewood, combining aggressive sales activity, headed by Nichols, and an inventive pool of talent, constantly developing new and better products, supporting an effective volume production facility.

Samuel's health meanwhile became increasingly frail and the champion of the old business began to fade—the jewellery venture in Siam failed, and the Trafalgar Square shop just ticked over. The business had transformed radically from the days of hoarding jet and running a large and valuable stock. As other jewellers found, 'in the uncertain financial climate of the twenties and thirties [this was] a burden rather than a strength', with both values and fashions changing—the trade was now dominated by the cheap jewellery chains, such as H. Samuel and Bravingtons.[156] Thus, leadership passed to Gordon, now in his forties, and settling into his stride, with ideas forming for a changed strategy and business mix, though motor accessories provided the bedrock, given the continued growth of the market—note the doubling in size of the number of vehicles in the UK from 1925 to 1930 (see Figure 3.1). Persistence was paying off, not just commercially but in his hobbies too (see Plate 19). Rugby days behind him, but keen on sport as ever, the decade brought him marked success with his greyhounds in the Waterloo Cup, first with Cushy Job in 1924 and then Golden Seal in 1927. Gordon Smith was a determined man, both in business and leisure. Walter D'Eye later remembered him taking the Waterloo Cup along to the showroom in Great Portland St, where the staff drank champagne from it.[157]

Notes

1. Alan Booth, 'Corporatism, Capitalism and Depression in Twentieth-Century Britain', *British Journal of Sociology*, 33/2 (June 1982), 208.
2. Roy Close, 'A Short History of Newman Hender', *Journal of the Gloucestershire Society for Industrial Archaeology* (1994), 13; C. P. Newman eventually nursed the firm to recovery out of receivership.
3. Neil Buxton, 'The Role of the "New" Industries in Britain during the 1930s: A Reinterpretation', *Business History Review*, 49/2 (1975), 208, 213.
4. 21 July 1914, 7.
5. Prospectus, *S. Smith & Sons (Motor Accessories) Limited—£50,000 ordinary shares* (London: 1914).
6. *Financial Times* (20 July 1914), 7.
7. The business was transferred as of 31 Mar. Oversubscription detailed in a press clipping of 22 July, 'S, Smith & Son (Motor Accessories) Limited', *Loan and Company Prospectuses–Stock Exchange (1914)*, Guildhall Library.
8. *The Economist* (25 July 1914), 183.
9. *Financial Times* (21 July 1914), 6.
10. 'A Brief History', 13.
11. For the context, see Richard Roberts, *Saving the City: The Great Financial Crisis of 1914* (Oxford: OUP, 2013), passim.
12. *Minutes* (17 Nov. 1914, 16 Mar. 1915).

13. *Minutes* (20 Oct. 1914).
14. *Report of the Directors* (1915), *Historical Journal,* 48/4 (2005) (1915); *Minutes* (20 Oct., 17 Nov. 1914); *Financial Times* (10 Sept. 1915), 3.
15. *Minutes* (17 Nov. 1915, 2 May 1916).
16. Patent GB19,860 (1913); *Minutes* (17 Nov. 1914).
17. Priced at £5 4s per 100, Contract 7/4839 of 8 Dec. 1914 per TNA: MUN 4/5256.
18. Cann, 'Chronological Record', i. 83.
19. *PIVOT* (June 1944), 10–11.
20. *Minutes* (16 Mar. 1915).
21. *Minutes* (29 Mar. 1915), though note the 1915 *Report of the Directors* which suggests the orders came at the end of 1914. S. Smith & Sons, *Prospectus, 100,000 ordinary shares* (Aug. 1915), 2; *PIVOT* (Aug. 1946), 3.
22. *Minutes* (19, 22 Apr., 30 Sept. 1915).
23. *The Commercial Motor* (3 Dec. 1914), 251.
24. Details of Cyril's war rely heavily on the research of his great-nephew Graham Smith, and Aurel Sercu, battlefield researcher.
25. *GB105,468* (1916).
26. TNA: ADM 339/3/1537.
27. Letter, Gordon Smith to Admiralty (29 Dec. 1916), TNA: WO 339/78698.
28. Thomas Owen Marden, *A Short History of the 6th Division, Aug. 1914–March 1919* (London: Hugh Rees, 1920), 18–19.
29. *Minutes* (8 Feb. 1915); GB2729 (1915).
30. TNA: PRO ADM 339/3/1537.
31. Marden, *6th Division*, 19.
32. *Minutes* (25 Apr. 1916); no patent was secured.
33. *London Gazette* (7 Apr. 1916), 3691.
34. O'Moore Creagh and E. M. Humphris, *The Distinguished Service Order, 1886–1923* (London: J. B. Hayward, 1978), 342.
35. Letter, Bradby to Smith (10 Nov. 1916), TNA WO 339/78698.
36. *Minutes* (13 Aug. 1915).
37. For the importance of Szarvasy to Turner, see Judy Slinn, *Clifford Chance: Its Origins and Development* (Cambridge: Granta, 1993), 105–6.
38. See 'Szarvasy, Frederick Alexander (1875–1948)', *DBB*, v. 427–8.
39. *Financial Times* (9 Sept. 1915), 2.
40. Based on a 1917 return, TNA: BT 31/23831/148530.
41. *Minutes* (8 Sept. 1915).
42. *Minutes* (30 Sept., 19 Oct. 1915, 26 Jan. 1916).
43. *Roadcraft* (Nov. 1920), 95–7.
44. By the early 1920s, there were reports on cricket, tennis, netball, swimming—even a concert party. See *Roadcraft* (1920), 'athletics supplement', 8.
45. *Minutes* (5 July 1916).
46. See e.g. patent GB111,308 (1917).
47. Cann, 'Chronological Record', i. 91; TNA: ACC/1047/28.
48. Contract 7/5294 (10 Mar. 1915) TNA: MUN 4/5256; *The Times* (21 Dec. 1918), 14.
49. Walton, 'A Brief History', 14. This wire rope may actually have been from H. W. Smith, a firm only acquired post-war.
50. Cann, 'Chronological Record', i. 46, 90. Presumably a speedometer.

51. *Prospectus*, S. Smith & Son (Siam) Limited (Nov. 1917), TNA: BT 31/23831/148530.
52. 21 Dec. 1918, 857.
53. *The Economist* (1 Mar. 1919), 380.
54. *Minutes* (18 July 1919).
55. 'A Brief History', 16.
56. GB24165 (1913), the second of over thirty international patents to his name.
57. For a popular history of the firm, see Chris Ellis, *K.L.G.: From Cars to Concorde: The Story of the Famous Smiths Industries K.L.G. Site in Putney Vale* (Surbiton: Kristall, 1989).
58. This team offered an explosive cocktail of racing circuit strength, judging from the reported thrashing meted out to Coatalen by van Raalte when he discovered his wife's adultery with the Sunbeam engineer: *The Times* (9 Nov. 1920), 20.
59. *PIVOT* (Nov. 1946), 1.
60. *Minutes* (14 July 1919).
61. Close, 'Newman Hender', 16.
62. *Minutes* (3 Sept. 1919).
63. *Minutes* (9 Jan. 1920).
64. *Prospectuses* (29 July 1919, 17 Feb. 1920).
65. *The Economist* (26 July 1919), 142.
66. P. W. S. Andrews and E. Brunner, *Life of Lord Nuffield* (Oxford: Blackwell, 1955), 96.
67. Barry Eichengreen, 'The British Economy between the Wars', in R. Floud and P. Johnson, *The Economic History of Britain since 1700* (Cambridge: CUP, 2004), 323.
68. *Minutes* (7 July 1920) and *The Times* (1 Jan. 1921), 17.
69. W. Arthur Lewis, *Economic Survey 1919–1939* (London: Allen & Unwin, 1949), 19–20.
70. Richard Roberts et al., *Sharpening the Axe* (London: Lombard Street Research, 2010), 4–5.
71. *The Times* (7 May 1920), 9.
72. *The Times* (1 Jan. 1921), 17. Gordon's role is reported in Pam and Peter Wotton, *Sir Allan, Smiths & SEC* (self-published), 17, very probably relying on notes from Dennis Barrett.
73. 20 July 1921, 17.
74. *The Times* (20 July 1921), 17.
75. Geoffrey Evans, *Time, Time and Time Again* (Barry: Quinto, 2008), 99.
76. i.e. the client (the drawee) is offered deferred payment terms, confirming its payment obligation under a deferred IOU (the bill), held by the drawer (Smiths in this case).
77. *Minutes* (9 Dec. 1920).
78. Bank Rate was 7%, falling to 6½% in Apr.
79. Circular letters, A. Gordon Smith to shareholders, 19 Mar. and 2 Apr. 1921. SMAA.
80. *Minutes* (1 July 1921).
81. *Minutes* (21 June 1921).
82. *Minutes* (9 Dec.r 1921, 6 Apr. 1922).
83. *Minutes* (11 Oct. 1921).
84. 23 Feb. 1935, 263.
85. *The Economist* (31 Dec. 1921), 1155.
86. 31 Dec. 1921, 1155.
87. *Financial Times* (19 Aug. 1921), 8; Roberts et al., *Sharpening the Axe*, 4–6.
88. *Minutes* (1 Feb., 23 Mar. 1922).
89. *Minutes* (1 Feb. and 2 May 1922).
90. Marsh to the directors (27 June 1922), filed in *Minute Book B* (1917–24), at 221. SMMA.
91. *Minutes* (29 June 1922).

92. *Minutes* (5 Sept. 1922).

93. *Minutes* (6 Apr. 1922).

94. *Minutes* and *Report* (13 July 1922).

95. *Minutes* (18 Jan. 1923).

96. *Minutes* (6 Apr. 1922).

97. *Minutes* (14 Nov. 1922).

98. His neuritis is mentioned in a report of an AGM, *The Times* (1 Jan. 1921), 17.

99. Peter Thorold, *The Motoring Age: The Automobile and Britain 1896–1939* (London: Profile, 2003), 186.

100. Evans, *Time Again*, 113.

101. *Minutes* (29 June, 12 Oct. 1922).

102. *Minutes* (29 Nov. 1922, 16 Aug. 1923); Cann, 'Chronological Record', i. 108.

103. Wilson, Wright to Samuel Smith (25 Jan. 1923), filed in *Minute Book B* (1917–24), at 258.

104. Szarvasy to Gordon Smith (26 Feb. 1923), filed in *Minute Book B* (1917–24), at p. 267–9.

105. Absorbed by Touche, Ross in 1963.

106. *Minutes* (8 Feb. 1923).

107. Turrell was an insurance consultant and engineer, sponsor of Accles-Turrell Autocars in 1900, after working for Lawson at the Coventry Motor Co. *The Flying Lady* (Mar./Apr. 2004), 7268; Piers Brendon, *The Motoring Century: The Story of the RAC* (London: Bloomsbury, 1997), 28.

108. Szarvasy to Gordon Smith (26 Feb. 1923).

109. *Minutes* (7 June 1923).

110. Marsh to the board (10 Aug. 1923); correspondence between Smiths and London County (Aug.–Sept. 1923), filed in *Minute Book B (1917–24)*, at 317.

111. 2 Nov. 1923, 17.

112. *Minutes* (8 Nov. 1923).

113. *Minutes* (27 Sept., 22 Nov. 1923).

114. *Minutes* (18 Dec. 1923).

115. *Minutes* (18 Dec. 1923).

116. *Minutes* (17 Mar. 1924).

117. *Minutes* (1 May 1924).

118. 25 Apr. 1924, 7.

119. Also motor-cycles, watches, musical instruments, and 'kinematograph films'.

120. Gordon Smith, speech to Central Works, *The Times* (25 Apr. 1924), 7.

121. *Manchester Guardian* (5 Aug. 1924), 3.

122. 27 Mar. 1924, 4.

123. *Financial Times* (3 Apr. 1924). 2; emphasis added.

124. 20 Nov. 1924.

125. *Minutes* (24 July 1924).

126. *Minutes* (18 Dec. 1924, 2 July 1925).

127. 11 Dec. 1925, 24.

128. Ethel Dietrich, 'British Export Credit Insurance', *American Economic Review* (June 1935), 241.

129. *Minutes* (2 Apr. 1925).

130. The escapement is the delicate part (the 'beating heart') of a watch or clock mechanism that regulates the 'escape' of energy from the spring or weight.

131. *Commercial Motor* (21 July 1925), 9.

132. *Minutes* (23 July 1925).

133. *Purchase agreement* (29 Sept. 1925), filed in *Minute Book C* (1924–33), 105–6. SMMA.

134. Cann, 'Chronological Record', i. 96, 123; *Minutes* (29 Oct. 1925).

135. It is possible the guarantee was from Szarvasy in person; see, in particular, *Minutes* (10 Sept. 1925).

136. *The Times* (11 Dec. 1925), 24.

137. *The Times* (21 Jan. 1927), 22.

138. Rachelle Saltzman, 'Folklore as Politics in Great Britain: Working-Class Critiques of Upper-Class Strike Breakers in the 1926 General Strike', *Anthropological Quarterly*, 67/3 (1994), 105.

139. *Minutes* (16 Sept. 1926); *Notice to debenture holders* (21 Oct. 1926). SMMA.

140. 22 Jan. 1927, 165.

141. *The Times* (18 Jan. 1926), 21; cumulative preference shares, with a 7½% dividend. Myers did have (undisclosed) sub-underwriters. *Prospectus* (20 Jan. 1927).

142. Material on Lenoir and Jaeger generally relies on Wilfrid Cann, 'Robert Lenoir 1898–1979', unpublished manuscript (1980).

143. *Minutes* (15 Nov. 1928).

144. Cann, 'Lenoir', 10.

145. Cann, 'Lenoir', 12.

146. Robert Lenoir and Wilfrid Cann, 'The Introduction of Jaeger Speedometers and Clocks into Britain, 1920', unpublished manuscript (1976), 6.

147. Monopolies Commission, *Report on the Supply of Electrical Equipment for Mechanically Propelled Land Vehicles*, HC 21, 1963–4, 88–9.

148. Cann, 'Lenoir', 15.

149. Mar. 1927, 153.

150. *Horological Journal* (Mar. 1927), 153.

151. *Horological Journal* (Apr. 1927), 162.

152. *The Times* (14 Nov. 1900), 14; *Horological Journal* (Jan. 1948), 22–5.

153. *Minutes* (27 July 1927) and Lenoir and Cann, 'Introduction of Jaeger', 7.

154. *Minutes* (29 Sept., 10 Nov. 1927).

155. 15 Mar. 1927, 9.

156. Gere and Culme, *Garrard*, 51.

157. *Smiths News* (Mar./Apr. 1967), 4.

....

1929–1939

A Decade of Diversification

....

There was a limit to the number of new devices that could be fitted to cars.
It was necessary, therefore, to seek new opportunities for expansion.

(*Financial Times*[1])

RAMSAY MACDONALD's Labour government of 1929 arrived in power on a euphoric wave, but in the wake of the October stock market crash in New York and the subsequent economic collapse, the UK economy went into decline, with demand falling and unemployment rising. For Smiths' main client industry, vehicle manufacture, it was time for a further shake out. Large numbers of small and specialist manufacturers were under pressure, given the growing market power of Morris and Austin, which now produced two-thirds of all UK vehicles. Overall UK production dipped until 1931, then turned upwards towards strong growth to 1937 (see Figure 4.1). The decade witnessed the continued struggle between road and rail, in which rail shareholders suffered as commercial and private vehicles secured strong traffic gains (despite a degree of regulatory protection for the rail industry). With the total sales value of vehicles doubling from 1924 to 1935, the cost of living-adjusted index of car prices decreasing, and disposable income increasing, the motor industry benefited, and Smiths with it.

Smiths had ended the 1920s having reinvented itself once again. With rebuilt finances, Gordon Smith was in a position to engineer a significant restructuring, focusing the motor business on core activities, and building entirely new business lines—notably in the clock industry, in which Smiths led the way in revitalizing a moribund sector—astonishingly by the mid-1930s Smiths was producing half the clocks manufactured in the UK. By contrast with its motor accessory business, it is notable that Smiths effectively created a new industry in which it became the dominant top-level manufacturer, not simply a component maker.

The navigational instrument business was greatly boosted, partly through acquisition, and better integrated into Smiths' mass-production empire, while new wholesale distribution channels were added. The 1930s were characterized at Smiths by continuous in-house technical development, reflected in hundreds of patents acquired each year. Zeitlin has described both the resistance and scepticism that greeted the post-war

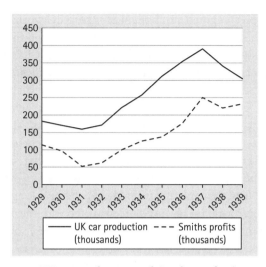

FIGURE 4.1 UK car production and Smiths profits (1929–1939).
Sources: SMMT; Smiths accounts and Ackrill,
Manufacturing Industry since 1870

'Americanization' drive in industry—yet even before the war Smiths formed part of a minority of British industrial firms that by contrast welcomed innovation derived from contact with the US, in fact-finding and observation missions followed by the introduction of latest (and imported) factory practice.[2]

Technological advances in the UK in turn mirrored a backdrop of rapid social change, where growing car ownership and the completion of the national electricity grid formed two important elements shaping an increasingly modern consumer society that wanted Smiths products. The firm continued to foster strong loyalty with a host of staff benefits, not least the relatively early introduction of a pension scheme. The firm had survived through tough times—surely there were good times ahead? From an awareness of aggressive trade practices (e.g. dumping aimed at hampering UK precision engineering) Gordon Smith appreciated the direction of German policy and the increasing likelihood of conflict—influencing work, from 1936, on preparing the staff and factories for war.

It was a record time

> *A group of sportsmen has made it possible for England to construct some £18,000 worth of motor car for some thirty seconds' furious action . . . at Daytona, in Florida. Surely this is Romance in its highest form.*
>
> (*Illustrated London News*[3])

1929 started well for Gordon Smith. Despite betting of 6–1 against his entry, he won the Waterloo Cup for the third time in March with Golden Surprise.[4] This followed only a few days after Henry Segrave established a new land speed record in *Golden*

Arrow—a 900hp Napier-engined car, built at Smiths' KLG works at Putney Vale, and fitted, of course, with KLG sparking plugs. Segrave was to cap this over the following months with a series of international trophies piloting Sir Charles Wakefield's *Miss England* speedboat—again using KLG plugs. Running a dedicated race team, Smiths capitalized on all these events and used them in regular advertising, cementing in the public mind an association with record flights and other achievements. Another group company that enjoyed good publicity in 1929 was M-L Magneto, whose products were fitted to the top machines in three different classes of the RAC's Motorcycle Tourist Trophy on the Isle of Man in June. That same month, Bentley triumphantly took the top four places in the 24–hour Le Mans race, sporting Smiths instruments, but the firm was unhappy that, despite being a long-standing customer, Smiths had never reciprocated—an omission corrected with the purchase of a 4½ litre model for Gordon Smith at a special price of £1,200 (2010: £57,000).[5]

The year had also kicked off with a further fundraising exercise, in which £62,000 of equity was added, £10,000 being allocated to an extension of the MA1 machine shop at Cricklewood, and £5,000 spent to acquire a windscreen wiper patent from Gordon Smith and his principal technician P. O. Dorer (2010: £240,000). Patent purchases from members of the executive were relatively common in this period, before employment agreements routinely ceded intellectual property rights to the employer—and the sums involved were not negligible.

Smiths could now claim that 'the main products of this company and its subsidiaries—i.e. speedometers and clocks—are now fitted as standard to over 95 per cent of the British-made motor-cars and commercial vehicles'.[6] Other accessories were fitted to a lesser degree, but it was clear that the market was nearly saturated with Smiths instruments—without an increase in general car sales, further motor accessory growth was limited unless new lines could be developed, the three most promising areas as the 1920s drew to a close being thermostatic radiator valves, electric petrol gauges, and jacking systems—the latter now largely forgotten in a world unused to punctures.[7] But Smiths was also looking further afield at how it could develop non-motor instrument business, and in 1929 it concluded an agency agreement with Henry Hughes & Co., a firm with roots in the early nineteenth century and justifiably famous for its nautical instruments. It had developed a recording echo sounder in 1923 and had extended its nautical and navigational business to include items such as early aircraft compasses—all natural extensions of Smiths' interest in instrumentation. This was just one strand in Gordon Smith's plans for the future.

The elimination of competition

> *The results of this sale will enable both firms to concentrate their efforts on those lines in which they have specialised for many years.*
>
> (*The Economist*[8])

While the escapement and Jaeger instrument business was being developed in 1930, the motor side of the group was undergoing change, against a backdrop of strongly mixed signals from the economy. Confidence had been weak since the Wall Street Crash the previous October, and economic activity was suffering, with UK unemployment rising from 1.5m to 2m between March and August 1930. Motor-car sales had remained strong until mid-year, but 'during June and July there had a pronounced falling off in the motor industry'.[9] Since March, Gordon Smith, Nichols, and Henderson-Cleland had been conducting detailed negotiations with a competitor, Joseph Lucas Ltd of Birmingham, to sell the M-L Magneto subsidiary and all of Smiths' lighting, starting, and ignition department, in exchange for Lucas shares, but crucially also to agree a non-competition agreement.[10]

The deal was agreed and concluded in May 1930, with the transfer to Lucas of all stock, plant, and goodwill in M-L in exchange for 31,000 Lucas shares, which were trading at around £3 15s at the time, valuing the deal at £116,250, an apparent premium of around 40 per cent to M-L's book value.[11] But the rationale for this deal was far from a simple financial calculation—it had a strong strategic element as well.

When Smiths had acquired Ed. Jaeger, it removed the threat of Lucas forming a competitive association with a highly reputable speedometer manufacturer. Smiths was heavily dominant in most motor accessories, and to preserve that position it was prudent to remove competition where possible. It was clear to Smiths that it did much better in instruments than in magnetos and lighting, the business that Lucas was interested to acquire. With the mutual agreements signed in May 1930, Lucas and Smiths undertook not to manufacture a range of goods specified on agreed schedules, reserving market territory for themselves, and arranged the supply of goods to each other at agreed prices which still provided significant profit margins—for example, the Lucas price to Smiths for batteries was the retail price list less 62½ per cent.[12]

More than thirty years later, Lucas pooh-poohed the arrangements to the Monopolies Commission, but, as the report points out, Smiths' records make clear 'negotiations had been proceeding with Joseph Lucas for some considerable while in order to remove competition between the companies'.[13] All in all, from Smiths' point of view, it was a neat move, offering a distant parallel with another transaction with Lucas in 1983. It was also personally rewarding, as 2,775 of the Lucas shares in the transaction were transferred to Gordon Smith, Nichols, and Henderson Cleland in recognition of their role in negotiating the deal—shares with a market value of £10,400 (2010: £513,000), of which Gordon took two-thirds.

Revival of an ancient craft

> In making those arrangements, the directors believed they had laid the foundation of a new industry in this country—clock-making on a competitive basis.
>
> (Financial Times[14])

With the M-L sale, Smiths had streamlined and reorganized the motor side of the business, but since 1927–8 another important strategy had been under implementation—a strategy that Robert Lenoir remembered Gordon explaining early on—to revive a flagging industry, in British clockmaking.[15] The formation of ABEC and closer ties with Jaeger, though prompted by the need to manufacture entirely British products, had wider possibilities. The *Financial Times* reported in 1930 that approaching 90 per cent of clocks sold in the domestic UK market were manufactured overseas, while Board of Trade figures showed that more than 3 million clocks, and over 1 million mechanisms, were imported each year, of which 80–90 per cent came from Germany.[16] Smiths' experience with car clocks meant it knew how to mass produce; it was taking serious steps to make its product entirely British; it had both technical know-how and access to further expertise through industry contacts; and it had long experience in marketing and selling. If it could dominate the motor accessories market, could it not do the same in clocks, at prices sufficiently keen to meet competition from German imports? With many years of machine shop experience in producing the wheels and plates that formed the other components of a clock, Smiths were on the way to domestic production of entire clock movements, which, suitably cased, could be destined for the home as well as the car dashboard.

Chronos Works

> *We don't let the girls catch cold here. If anyone sneezed the whole output would be blown out the window!.*
>
> (Harold Buckland, *Chronos*[17]–see Plate 38)

New factory space was needed, and the major development under way at year-end 1929 was the expansion and rehousing of the Jaeger subsidiary, to which Smiths granted a building lease for 48,500 ft² (4,500m²) of the North Circular site Gordon Smith had secured in late 1927. To achieve the best design, Robert Lenoir took Smiths' architect, Samuel A. S. Yeo, to Switzerland to study factory layouts and to consult with J. D. LeCoultre and his staff.[18] With financing arranged by Ed. Jaeger, work commenced in late 1929, with the first parts of the factory complete by April 1930, into which Jaeger moved, together with the A. T. Speedometer Co. Ltd, a recent acquisition.[19] Administration, management, and despatch were housed in the range fronting onto the North Circular and speedometer manufacture occupied the west wing of the newly named Chronos Works (see Plate 20).

With the factory occupied, the decision was taken for Jaeger to build a further wing on the east side, and to lease this to ABEC, the escapement manufacturer. Orders were placed for specialist machinery through LeCoultre, and ABEC arranged 'the temporary transfer of Staff in this country to Switzerland for the purposes of getting training in escapement manufacture'.[20] The outcome was interesting for both sides, since Lenoir realized he could not distil a lifetime's experience into a short visit by his 'pool of unskilled and semi-skilled labour' from London, and thus 'it was useless for the tooling to be exact duplicates':

> The assembly operations usually carried out by highly skilled watchmakers were split into simple routines with accurate jigs. The more complicated ones, such as hairspring vibrating, were made automatic through the use of a photocell.[21]

Lenoir's approach worked, and when ABEC commenced operation in late 1931, it was essentially a unique operation in the UK that could 'produce escapements at a price comparable with those of Switzerland by using entirely different methods of assembly'—all of this a far cry from the sound and fury of a traditional machine shop—ABEC's assembly room was dazzlingly bright, with windows on three sides, and, to reduce dust, it had flooring of 'closely laid oak planks polished and waxed daily', while the staff were issued with 'house slippers'.[22] Morale would have been high, in a new factory, with new equipment, added to which Gordon could proudly announce to the press that, even before starting production, ABEC had secured an order for 20,000 escapements from the Horstmann Gear Company for its timeswitches.[23]

Greenwich Time—from the mains

> *The Board has wisely sought new opportunities for expansion. Its choice is likely to be attended with far-reaching consequences to the future of British trade and employment.*
>
> (*Financial Times*[24])

Remarkably, Gordon Smith was attempting to develop an entirely new industry against a backdrop of national crisis. With the publication of the mid-1931 report from the Committee for National Expenditure, confidence collapsed and speculative attacks on sterling increased, leading to the abandonment of the gold standard in September. In August, differing views within the Cabinet on the methodology for balancing the budget had led to resignation of the Labour government—replaced by a new 'national' government, still with MacDonald at its head, but now heavily shored up by Conservative representation.

Just as this was unfolding, the results of several years' work at Smiths came to fruition. Alongside the effort to (re)create a traditional (mechanical) clock business, there were other important developments happening in parallel. Since the passing of the Electricity Supply Act (1926), the CEGB had been constructing the new national grid, and a feature was tight frequency control for the alternating current mains. This allowed the creation of a new type of clock that could derive its timebase from that accurate mains frequency, rather than an onboard oscillator such as a pendulum or balance wheel. Just half a million houses had an electric supply in 1919, but from 1926 numbers increased rapidly, reaching 8 million in 1938 (two-thirds of the housing stock).[25] Things had happened faster in the United States where 29 million people were using clocks driven by the mains by 1925.[26] In the UK, the *Watch and Clockmaker* introduced a regular feature, showing national maps, gradually charting the spread of the grid and uniform frequency—and therefore time. From 1927, Everett Edgcumbe started offering synchronous (mains-driven) clocks in the UK, initially with adapted motors imported from the US, but the market remained small until the early 1930s, when the clock trade woke up with a start to discover there was a new product, pushed hard by Smiths, which might represent a threat to their livelihood.

Here was a clock with no delicate escapement—it simply plugged in, the hands were set, and away it went, potentially for many years, with no hint of the service necessary for traditional clocks. *The Times* noted that 'clocks are now on the market which . . . require no winding or attention, they will work in any position, and are independent of temperature and climatic conditions', added to which 'they will run 500 hours or more for the cost of one unit of electricity, and are cheap to buy'— though we might now question 'cheap'.[27] Without the need for specialist intermediaries, electricity supply companies and general retailers started offering clocks, prompting an outcry from the protectionist clockmakers.[28] Whether it was Gordon Smith that saw the potential, or perhaps the gifted inventors around him, Smiths committed itself heavily to this new product. The situation resembled that of the speedometer in 1904, in that, though Smiths were not the first on the scene, it rapidly positioned itself to produce a robust and successful device on a scale that dwarfed the rest of the market.

Though M-L had gone to Lucas, it is clear that its technical director maintained his independence. Dr Ernest Ansley Watson (OBE for outstanding work on Great War aero-engine magnetos) would be named on more than 100 patents between 1911 and 1948, but not always jointly with his employer. Smiths were still able to consult him and by late 1930 he was engaged on the design of a suitable synchronous clock motor, for which the patent was lodged in January 1931, and assigned to Smiths in February.[29] This fundamental design was to serve Smiths for many years, but two filings for important improvements were made within months, one by Gordon Smith in September which formed the production patent.[30] Crucially, given Smiths' methods, it states:

> By the construction and arrangement above described, the assembling of the parts of the clock can be effected in a very simple and expeditious manner which is *well adapted to the requirements of large scale production*.[31]

As the country went to the polls in October 1931, clock production commenced, and in December the *Watch and Clockmaker* ran a highly positive illustrated feature on Smiths, describing both the emergence of entirely domestically produced escapements for mechanical clocks at the Chronos factory and the new electric clocks at Cricklewood—production of the latter running at 1,000 clocks per week.[32] An all new British alarm clock was also on offer—a first—as well as mechanical clocks that met French and German competition head on. At the Smiths general meeting in December it was revealed:

Arrangements had been made for the marketing of the [electric] clocks through the electric supply companies, large electrical dealers, jewellers, clockmakers, and the large stores, backed up by an intensive selling organization of their own.[33]

It was effective, with production of synchronous clocks rising to 4,000 per week in January in order to meet demand. By July 1932, Smiths was claiming sales of 15,000 per month, against a backdrop of continued declines in motor industry sales—so as the old business remained in the doldrums, new avenues appeared fruitful.[34] Smiths had single-handedly revived the clockmaking industry, in a new and modern guise—the rapid growth of the synchronous clock industry is apparent in Figure 4.2.

Other decisions taken earlier in the year were to change the name of Ed. Jaeger to British Jaeger Instruments Ltd, and also to incorporate Smiths English Clocks Ltd (SEC), and its subsidiary Synchronous Electric Clocks Ltd, probably formed to supply other clock companies with synchronous movements—there were to be many of these, since Smiths realized that it benefited them to increase the overall size of the market, so while Garrards (the Crown jewellers) and Synchronome (among many others) sold clocks under their own brands, the movements actually used Watson's motor, produced at Cricklewood.[35] Smiths was now establishing in clocks the sort of market power it enjoyed in motor accessories. At SEC, two names now emerged as front-runners—Dennis Barrett and Rex Smith, Gordon's nephew, who had made a great success in sales of motorcycle speedometers. These two were to be Gordon's key generals in the division, entrusted with leading the charge for the enlarged clock business. Barrett clearly allied himself closely to his mentor—'he was very useful to Gordon. He would carry a pair of collapsible scissors in his pocket, and if he saw an article in a magazine or anything that might prove useful, he would cut it out and keep it in a commonplace book, perhaps to help with a speech. He would dot the i's and cross the t's for Gordon.'[36]

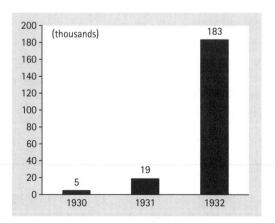

FIGURE 4.2 UK output of synchronous electric clocks (1930–1932).

Source: *BCM* (1933)

Acquisitions and 'Empire'

Experts concentrate—Richard's attention is concentrated on clocks all clocks and nothing but clocks, and clock service.

(Advertisement, 1932[37])

Smiths had been considering how best to place its products in the market. In early 1931, Gordon Smith was in negotiation with a significant London clock wholesaler, Richard & Co., with a view to taking control and using it as sole distributor to the trade. The firm, which already acted as concessionaires to Smiths, was controlled by Ernest A. Richard and his family, and had a close relationship with H. Williamson of Coventry—the manufacturer behind the legal action against Smiths in 1927.[38] Richard & Co. was managed by John Henry Seager, a veteran Williamson's man—whom we have met before—it was he who described the basement of 9 Strand as 'an Aladdin's cave' in Chapter 2. Smiths took control in November 1931, later increasing its holding in 1933.[39]

If Gordon Smith had been upset at being prosecuted in 1927 under the Merchandise Marks Act at Williamson's instigation, vengeance was served in the rapid failure of the Coventry firm, in voluntary receivership in August 1931, and being liquidated within months—makers of spring-driven British clocks struggled to cope with the tide of cheap German imports. Williamson's had a Coventry subsidiary, English Clock and Watch Manufacturers (ECWM), producing domestic clocks, but also an electrically rewound car clock, under the 'Empire' brand, designed by Harry Norman Walford, a gifted engineer, and this met the criticism that Smiths' existing car clocks required regular hand-winding.[40] Gordon Smith and Marsh were authorized to investigate acquiring ECWM from the liquidators, submitting a final bid in March 1932. The transaction was finally agreed mid-year, bringing both the well-known brands 'Empire' and 'Astral' into the fold. The dismantling of the Williamson empire continued with the receivers' sale of stock to Bravingtons, the high street jeweller, and the departure of key staff—such as Charles Tucker who formed Tucker, Nunn & Co. at 108 Hatton Garden in late 1932 with George Nunn, a Williamson's travelling salesman. Smiths picked over the carcase and, despite controlling Richard & Co., chose to form yet another wholesale outlet, acquiring the goodwill and forming a revived Williamson Clock Company, based on Farringdon Road, transferring J. H. Seager from Richard & Co. to manage it.[41] Captive control of well-known brands in both manufacturing and wholesaling formed important threads in Smiths' strategy.

The British Clock Manufacturers' Association

Nothing more unobtrusive in the way of industrial enterprise can be imagined than the way the English Clock Manufacturing Industry has quietly come into being and forged ahead.

(*The British Clock Manufacturer*[42])

While Smiths had geared up production of synchronous clocks from October 1931, so had other firms—all expecting to develop a large market, but a market each firm was keen to capture for itself. A letter discovered in Ferranti's archives, sent by Everett Edgcumbe, is intriguing:

> [It] asked for some agreement to be made over a minimum price. They stated that they produced their lowest priced clock at 40 shillings and had observed that Smiths then dropped theirs to 35 shillings and now Ferranti dropped theirs to 30 shillings. They needed to stop the vicious process now to maintain any margin of profit.[43]

Gordon Smith was working hard on ensuring success both for Smiths and for the wider market, and to draw together the interests of his fellow manufacturers (and prevent damaging competition), he was instrumental in establishing the British Clock Manufacturers' Association (BCMA), which held its inaugural meeting on 17 February 1932.[44] As its first chairman, he brought together Smiths, British Sangamo, Everett Edgcumbe, Ferranti, Garrard, Rotherham's, and others, using the association to campaign for support of the industry, particularly from the Board of Trade. The association had an international role as well, and unsurprisingly it was Dennis Barrett of SEC that travelled to represent the BCMA at the Ottawa conference later in the year. Back in March 1932, all the BCMA members had stands at the British Industries Fair, and Gordon relived his folklore triumphs of 1904 and sales to Edward VII, since the press photographed Queen Mary, the Prince of Wales, the Duke and Duchess of York, and Princess Mary gathered on the Smiths stand—indeed several of the party purchased clocks—a valuable endorsement indeed.[45]

There was a considerable focus on building the clock side of the business—ABEC's operation required both more capital and space, for increased production, and British Jaeger arranged a further extension at the Chronos Works in 1933.[46] On the publicity side, the firm introduced a range of painted vans that toured the country with 'a very bold display of synchronous clocks', carrying a big clock on the roof, 'attracting very considerable attention... doing good work in popularising the idea of synchronous time' (see Plates 22 and 24).[47] If the public needed educating, so did both the trade and government. In February 1933, the *Watch and Clockmaker* and *Goldsmiths Journal* carried a new 74-page supplement (twice the size of the main journals), called *The British Clock Manufacturer*, which became an annual feature. The first edition, running to 10,000 copies, was widely distributed, both domestically and internationally, attracting the attention of MPs.[48] It led with the headline 'Remarkable Growth of the British Clock Industry' and Gordon's new BCMA featured heavily—indeed it is likely the bulk of the editorial reflects his detailed input—and between features on the firm and its own advertisements, Smiths accounted for 13 pages (17.5 per cent), added to which it was providing escapements and motors to some of the other firms featured. The remarkable growth in the mechanical clock industry is clear from Figure 4.3, almost entirely attributable to Smiths. It was claimed £3.5 million of capital had been raised in the UK clockmaking industry over four years, involving 15,800 employees. Starting from a very low base, clock production had risen to over 800,000 units in 1932, with an estimate it could rise to 2.5 million per annum, all against a backdrop of desperate dumping of foreign clocks by firms, particularly in Germany, vastly below cost—all

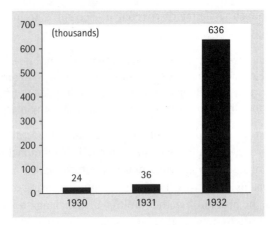

FIGURE 4.3 UK output of mechanical clocks (1930–1932).

Source: *BCM* (1933)

data taken up by Leo Amery in the Commons, arguing powerfully against a change in tariffs on German imports.[49] German policy was to hamper the development of a UK clockmaking industry that could be turned to military purposes if needed, and Germany was not the only threat—the BCMA was also aware of Seikosha in Japan, already producing a million clocks per year, with just 2,000 staff.[50]

The success of the synchronous business did not mean Smiths ignored mechanical clocks. Another well-organized and 'competitive business' was the Enfield Clock Company, formed in 1929 by Carl Schatz and several fellow Germans who had imported their successful mass-production model, together with a group of workers. Though it thrived, the continued competition from imported (and ever cheaper) German clocks must have been galling, and the owners were open to an approach from Smiths in mid-1933, under which two-thirds of the firm was acquired, though the managers (Schatz, Roles, and Baxter) remained in place, receiving a percentage of the profits.[51]

The clock business was not the only division to receive attention. Since the Great War, Smiths had slowly been developing an aviation instrument business, but the product range was still relatively simple. This changed in early 1932, for while the motor business remained depressed, aviation made a significant step forward, with the signing in February of a licence agreement with two eminent technicians from the Royal Aircraft Establishment at Farnborough, Philip A. Cooke and Frederick W. Meredith, to manufacture 'gyroscopic systems for controlling dirigible objects such as aeroplanes'—this was the 'two-axis autopilot' and the beginnings of a more sophisticated enterprise.[52] Smiths rapidly set about exploring international possibilities and in June sought foreign patents for the device in seven countries.[53]

The baton passes

A well-known figure in the clock, watch and jewellery trade passed away on Christmas Day last.

(*Watch and Clockmaker*[54])

From August to October 1932, the firm saw 'a considerable increase in business' on the back of 'a definite improvement in the motor industry'.[55] But the same could not be said of Samuel Smith, whose health was failing—he attended just one board meeting in 1932, on 9 June, but this was to be his last. In November, Gordon started breaking up Smith & Sons (1929) Ltd, the vehicle in which Samuel's remaining jewellery businesses were held, and for which he was a trustee.[56] On the basis that it was 'dangerous for a name so similar to this Company to get into other hands', Smiths purchased the name, goodwill, and trademarks for £2,000—an intriguing outcome in retrospect. Bravingtons took over the Trafalgar Square premises, continuing the business in their own name. Bringing to an end the link with the diamond merchants opened on the Strand in 1872, Samuel died at the Hydro in Richmond on Christmas Day 1932, and was buried at Aldingbourne four days later, where Annie had been buried ten years earlier, close to Gordon's house. The housekeeping that had been obvious in recent months was clearly extensive—Samuel had been a wealthy man, yet his estate amounted to just £124 0s 4d. With the departure of a Smith generation from the board, it was time for the next to rise, and Gordon's son Ralph was co-opted in January 1933.

Improving long-term prospects

The board feels assured, from the fact that the staff can now look forward to security in their old age, that the good will of our workers towards their employers will be intensified.

(Chairman's speech, 1933 AGM)

Significant effort was put into diversifying Smiths' business in the early 1930s, but the motor business remained dominant and the major source of income and cash flow, though this had been a period of austerity in which car sales, especially luxury models with lots of instruments and accessories, were depressed. Some respite occurred with the move off the gold standard in late 1931, and the resulting boost to exports from cheaper sterling. As a response to the prevailing negative sentiment that year, a blanket reduction of 5 per cent in wages and salaries (even for directors) had been introduced.[57] By 1933, the market had definitely turned, with advancing motor sales feeding through to increased sales at Smiths. This improvement came too late for North & Sons in Watford, the firm that had supplied Smiths with speedometers in the 1904–12 period. It had limped on, with a few clients for instruments, but was liquidated in late 1933. Smiths regarded 'this business and property . . . only of break-up and nuisance value' but it was sufficiently important both to Smiths and Lucas, cooperating closely again, to agree to share profits and losses from acquiring the residual assets and breaking up the firm between them. At Smiths, British Jaeger took over speedometer orders, special tools, and stocks.[58]

In late 1933, this improved situation and a greater cushion led to various decisions, the most significant being to create an employee pension scheme, and the approval of a £30,000 (2010: £1.66m) transfer from reserves to provide initial funds, together with an assessment that a further £4,000–5,000 would be needed each year.[59] This decision placed Smiths relatively early among industrial companies—earlier than ICI for example—to put in place a pension scheme. To put the initial £30,000 in context, this represented about one-third to a half of annual profits, and 10 per cent of the reserve fund accumulated since 1926. Gordon was authorized to negotiate with Prudential Assurance and over the following six months a scheme was worked up and then offered to the workforce. It had a favourable initial reception, with 305 men and 54 women applying to join at the outset.[60] Another fillip for the workforce would have been the removal of the 5 per cent reduction in wages and salaries, dating back to 1931. For years Gordon had worked on building camaraderie and team spirit with the provision of sports facilities and outings—this new effort was significantly more serious and formed part of the broader 'general arrangements for the comfort and work of the employees' which met with the 'cordial approval' of the Duke of Kent, Inspector of Factories.[61]

1934 was a year of general expansion and consolidation, with further equity raised for the main company. Profits had nearly halved from 1930 to 1931 (see Figure 4.1), but on a strong rising trend recovered by 1933, rising through till 1937. The French operations were restructured, with Kirby Smith (an earlier investment) wound up and a new KLG subsidiary formed, two-thirds owned by Smiths, the remainder by long-standing French partners.[62] Gordon travelled to the US on a marketing and fact-finding trip mid-year, while in the UK, a new KLG plug, priced at 5 shillings, was selling well—the firm could proclaim further success, with all the British participants in an air race to Melbourne using KLG plugs and Smiths instruments.[63] A new line in vehicle heating and ventilation systems showed promise (though known irreverently as 'fug-stirrers'), as did a revised version of the Jackall hydraulic car-jacking system, priced to 'enable every motor-car owner to have his car fitted with it', echoing a time when owners might expect regularly to use a jack.[64] The chronometric speedometer sold well, but was an expensive instrument and a cheaper alternative was introduced, using magnetic coupling to a Jaeger design. Tooling came from Paris, but the fourth wing at Chronos Works was required to house it, creating a courtyard, with a central fountain and deep pond containing huge goldfish—the commissionaire was allowed 6d per week for ant eggs to feed them.[65]

The clock division produced the first of its 19-ligne 'Calotte' clocks—8-day travelling clocks—a first for a British manufacturer, and again a line that was to be mass produced in vast numbers. A further development, utilizing escapements from ABEC, was the 'Batriclock', taking Harry Norman Walford's battery-powered 'Empire' car clock technology from ECWM and employing it in a new small domestic clock, capturing sales where the national grid was not yet in place. In the autumn, there was some rationalization of factory sites, with the surrender of ECWM's lease of its Coventry works, and the move of the operation to the Langton Road site in Cricklewood—increasing the role of Walford in Smiths' clock business.[66]

Successfully exporting volume production experience from motor accessories into an industry the company had rapidly led, by now Smiths could claim to produce more than half of all clocks produced in the UK, led by dominance in the synchronous clock market, and Gordon's BCMA could claim nineteen members—'practically the whole industry'—while he joined the clock establishment, being raised to the livery of the Worshipful Company of Clockmakers in January 1934.[67]

Riding the wave

> World's Land Speed Record again broken on KLG sparking plugs by Sir Malcolm Campbell. This is the sixth consecutive Land Speed Record to be broken on KLGs.
>
> (The Times, 1935)[68]

KLG and Smiths basked in the glory of records broken in 1934 and 1935, as Sir Malcolm Campbell raised the land speed record several times, finally to above 300mph in his *Blue Bird*, while the Italian Macchi MC 72 established a new seaplane speed record—both used KLGs, and Campbell also used Smiths' instruments. In the same year, the King's Air Cup Race was won for the fourteenth successive time on KLG plugs (see Plate 27).[69]

If the customers were confident of the products, so was the City in the prospects for the firm. Since the early 1930s, the shares had gradually been ticking up. In 1934, shareholders took up an offer of the 1s deferred ordinary shares at 3s, leading to a £53,000 balance on the share premium account, but this placement had been at a marked discount to the market price of perhaps 8–9s. By early 1935, the £1 preferred shares had risen to some 65s from around 15s five years earlier. In February 1935, an outright bid was received from Helbert, Wagg for 50,000 in £1 preferred ordinary shares and 280,000 of the 1s deferred ordinary shares at market prices.[70] Unsurprisingly, the board considered market pricing for a bid in size as 'favourable'—Clifford Turner's advice was that 'the time for and the method of the issue of these shares was opportune' and Smiths therefore accepted, giving rise to a further £200,000 in share premium.[71] The shares were largely placed with Pearl Assurance and other institutions, but also, as was customary, with a range of favoured Helbert, Wagg clients, prominent in society, such as Lord Sandon and Sir Max Bonn.[72] Gordon's pivotal role in negotiating with Gordon Munro at Helbert, Wagg emerges with the board congratulating 'the Managing Director on the excellent terms which he had obtained'—so much so that 'it was resolved that a sum of £2000 [2010: £108,000] be paid to the Managing Director as a recognition of the very special services he had rendered . . . and to enable him to reimburse himself in respect of the considerable expense he had incurred'.[73]

But the triumph of raising money on good terms was tinged with tragedy. Hubert Marsh, the accountant, never in the best of health, had not attended a board meeting since November. A week after Helbert, Wagg's approach, Marsh died after a short illness.[74] He had been vital to Smiths' slow recovery from the crash of the early 1920s and Gordon and the board had relied heavily on him to steer the finances of the company for nearly fifteen years, so in recognition they voted £1,200 to be paid to Marsh's partner, Jackson, to be used for the benefit of Marsh's widow and daughter.[75] Illness struck closer to home as well—Gordon's brother Reginald was ill from January onwards, and in July the board voted to keep him on full pay for a further three months—which ended up being prolonged for more than two years.[76]

As ever, hand-in-hand with increasing sales and production came the need for more factory and office space, though not in the West End, where the second, fourth, and fifth floors of the Great Portland Street building were sublet.[77] At Cricklewood, Heaton Tabb, a furniture manufacture, had sublet the Langton Road works for several years, but in 1934 Gordon had managed to buy them out of their lease, providing space into which to move Smiths English Clocks (SEC), which could no longer be accommodated in the main Central Works building. From 1935, SEC was kept quite separate, with its own plant and stock, succeeding in increasing sales by 40 per cent during the year—probably reflecting the fact the market for synchronous clocks was far from being saturated.[78] Plans were drawn up in early 1935 for both a new office block in the south-east corner of the Cricklewood site, and for a new factory building down the Waterloo Road side of the sports ground at the North Circular site, and though the office was delayed, by mid-1935 the new factory was under way.

The components of the former H. Williamson group continued to gravitate towards Smiths—on the distribution side, there were rearrangements that brought Tucker, Nunn & Co. into the Smiths group in a series of complicated share and asset swaps, effectively merging it with the Williamson Clock Co. subsidiary, to form Tucker, Nunn & Williamson.[79] Smiths now had this and Richard & Co. as two captive wholesale distribution businesses—a difference between the two being that Richard & Co. continued to deal in foreign clocks, as well as domestic—if clocks were continuing to be imported, Smiths wanted somewhere to earn a margin on these as well. Richard & Co.'s business continued to expand, leading to a move from its long-time premises in Aldersgate Street to larger showrooms in Goswell Road at the end of the year.[80]

Henry Hughes

> The ship chandler's on Poverty Corner gave wings to the imagination of the boy who passed it every day.
>
> (H. M. Tomlinson, Fathom[81])

Smiths had operated with Henry Hughes & Co. on an agency basis since 1929, but early in 1935 Gordon sought approval from the board to negotiate taking a controlling stake.

He was authorized to spend up to £22,000 to seal a deal and this was duly completed in May.[82] This provided a captive manufacturing capacity for a wide variety of nautical and navigational instruments, including a depth-sounder, used to spectacular effect within months, when the crew of the SS *Ophir* located the wreck of the *Lusitania* in October 1935.[83] Control of Henry Hughes also allowed Smiths to develop further their aeroplane instrumentation business—and the importance placed on this is evidenced by the purchase in early 1936 of an aeroplane—a De Havilland Dragon, G-ADOS, used for demonstrating the firm's aviation products.[84] *Flight* reported extensively on 'a Real Flying Showroom'—a phrase picked up in subsequent advertisements—detailing over fifty instruments that were installed, the most important being the three-axis auto-pilot.[85] The plane travelled extensively, first to Scandinavia and the Baltics, but apparently later took in Italy, Yugoslavia, Turkey, and Germany, where in 1937 the Mk 1A autopilot was demonstrated to Siemens—something probably regretted in retrospect.[86]

With the acquisition of Henry Hughes, the group was now more formally arranged with three principal divisions: (i) Motor—comprising S. Smith and Sons (Motor Accessories), British Jaeger Instruments, and KLG Sparking Plugs; (ii) Aviation—comprising Smiths Aircraft Instruments and Henry Hughes; (iii) Clocks—comprising All-British Escapement Company, English Clock and Watch Company, Enfield, Synchronous Electric Clocks, and Smiths English Clocks—the clocks division being consolidated under a single holding company.[87] As 1935 drew to a close, and the programme of diversification had been under way for over five years, Henderson-Cleland could tell shareholders 'the turnover of the Smith Group of subsidiaries is now approaching that of the parent company, and is making a valuable contribution to profits'.[88]

Mass advertising and bijou movements

> *An industry the activity of which is geared to two of the most prosperous manufacturing trades in the country—motor cars and aircraft—can be counted upon to return big profits in present circumstances.*
>
> (*Financial Times*[89])

The firm restructured its balance sheet significantly in 1936, as well as raising significant new funds for physical expansion. The subsidiaries had to date been financed with loans from the parent, and were now put on a permanent footing with the conversion of these debts to equity. A total of £107,000 (2010: £5.7m) was spent on factory expansion, partly on the Henry Hughes 'Husun Works' at Barkingside, but mainly at the North Circular site, where a substantial new factory (known as MA2) was completed down the Waterloo Road side of the sports ground—to which Smiths English Clocks and the aviation instruments business moved, from Cricklewood (see Plate 21). Before it was even complete, the board had resolved to build a third factory on the site, plus a large canteen, while at Cricklewood the firm started considering a new office block on the Edgware Road frontage.[90] With much praise from the board, it also renewed the service agreement of Ben Haviland, Cricklewood works manager, who had clocked up twenty-one years of service.[91]

The newly consolidated clocks division estimated that in 1936 its sales of domestically made clocks had equalled half the value of total UK imported clocks, a position achieved within a short space of years. Interestingly, it was not jewellers that were selling the mains-driven clocks—Dennis Barrett claimed 'electricians are selling 75 per cent of all synchronous clocks sold in this country'—but Smiths still valued the wholesale clock trade: 'we are prepared to send a technical instructor to any jeweller . . . to give a course of instruction on synchronous clocks. This . . . has now been given to about 500 jewellers'.[92] Rex Smith became sales director at SEC in 1936, and will have masterminded the large commitment to advertising to support the wholesale trade— the trade notices claimed '30 million advertisements for Smiths electric clocks will bring you customers this winter', a figure presumably calculated from the circulation figures for various newspapers and the publicity for the Ideal Home Exhibition.[93] Tying the BCMA closer to the trade was also achieved with its move to the premises of the British Horological Institute, and the appointment of a joint secretary for both organizations— Frank Bowlam Cowen—perhaps by fleet footwork behind the scenes from Gordon.[94] At ABEC, which had started work in late 1931, they could report making their first millionth escapement, and in some corporate housekeeping, Smiths paid £10,000 (2010: £530,000) to buy out the personal interests of Gordon, P. O. Dorer, and E. A. Watson in the synchronous patents held by Synchronous Electric Clocks Limited.[95] It was also the year in which Smiths introduced a new and updated synchronous motor for its clocks—named the 'Bijou'—which was to become very successful as an industry standard, both in-house and for many other firms, for more than two decades.[96]

On the motor side, the firm benefited from increased overall car sales, but sparking plugs also sold well on the back of increased aircraft orders. As a result, net profits continued on their rising trend. But though cash flow was not under pressure, the expansion of the factories was not complete and Smiths wanted to build further reserves, leading to a decision to launch another equity-raising exercise in mid-year. It would not be possible to achieve the sort of pricing of the Helbert, Wagg deal a year earlier but the shares had continued to perform well. An offer of both classes of share was launched at a discount, and a total of £195,000 was raised in the second half of the year.[97] This was in part raised to cover the tender, accepted in June, from William Moss of Loughborough for the construction of a new head office on the Edgware Road frontage of the Cricklewood site, to be completed by mid-1937.[98]

Territorial ambition

> The prospects of the company are good—better than at any time since I have been associated with it.
>
> (Gordon Smith, 1936 AGM)

While so much of the news was positive, 1936 was also the year in which we can see Smiths beginning its long-term planning for war, although it is easily imagined that

Gordon and his colleagues had begun thinking strategically in this direction earlier, or had been encouraged to do so—a small hint being £10,000 in expenditure on plant approved in January 1936 to support a contract for the Admiralty.[99] This was a year in which there were also renewed appeals for volunteers to join the Territorial Army, with government encouragement to companies not to penalize employees and to provide assistance to volunteers joining the annual camp of their unit.[100] In June, Smiths decided to grant a week's holiday (with pay) to Territorial volunteers. Fifty-four employees joined up to form a complete section to operate searchlights and sound locators, in B Company of the 36th (Middlesex) Anti-Aircraft Battalion, RE (TA), and Gordon threw Smiths behind the local recruiting effort, taking the chair of the local Employer's Territorial Recruiting Committee, installing Dennis Barrett of SEC as secretary. The following year Gordon published a booklet to encourage other local employers, by showing what had been achieved.[101]

Forward on all fronts

Once again my faith in Smith's Instruments and K.L.G. Plugs justified.
(Cable from Jean Batten, completing London to
New Zealand flight, SMAA[102])

KLG was working hard on the development of a new sparking plug that would revolutionize performance. Back in 1935 it had acquired a licence from Robert Bosch to manufacture plugs using a new ceramic compound and could therefore benefit from the 'patents and secret processes' for 'Corundite'.[103] Development work in 1936 led to a first design of a plug with the new insulator in early 1937, and with plant installed for turning out the new design 'in large quantities' it was adopted as the standard plug for Rolls Royce and Bentley cars during the year, and at wider level the firm could claim that the air, land, and water speed records as well as the altitude record had all been attained by machines using KLG plugs.[104]

Continued research and product development was a strong theme, with many patents and licences acquired across all divisions, and early in 1937 Gordon led a team of senior staff to the US on a fact-finding mission, looking at latest factory methods and operational practice, returning with a significant amount of data.[105] Similar trips were made to Germany, France, and Italy. When the annual staff dinner was held at the Hyde Park Hotel in May, where service awards were usually given, a gold wristwatch was presented to Dr Ernest Watson (Lucas's senior engineer) 'for many services, one of which was most outstanding, that of compiling the report of those gentlemen who went to America. This report consisted of 85 pages of highly technical matter.'[106] Another important award was a gold cigarette case for Frank 'Cottie' Cotterell for forty years' service.

Elsewhere on the motor side, the jacking business was expanded and consolidated further with the acquisition of Sessions Holdings in February (financed with the help of Lionel Fraser at Helbert, Wagg), and the agreement in May to acquire the patents and goodwill of Stevenson Jacks—so Henderson Cleland could claim at year-end Smiths 'are now able to offer jacking systems, more or less automatic, at all prices to suit all makes of cars'—indeed Smiths systems were 'fitted as standard equipment to more than 30 makes of cars'.[107]

Smiths already had a licencing agreement with Bendix of the US that allowed for the production of various aviation instruments, but in 1937 it introduced a new range of aircraft instruments that were to become standardized on very large numbers of aircraft.[108] In order for aircraft instrument panels to show the position of control surfaces (ailerons, flaps, etc.), the undercarriage, and other critical factors (fuel levels), together with fault-recognition, the firm had developed its 'Desynn' brand of remote monitoring equipment, which rapidly became widely standardized.[109] The aircraft instrumentation business had good support from the civil sector but Air Ministry contracts were now sizeable as defence preparation increased, added to which Smiths secured supply contracts with various foreign governments. With a product range from 'an automatic pilot costing some hundreds of pounds to the smaller navigating instruments', Henderson-Cleland told the shareholders in November 1937 of an ambition 'to consolidate our position as the leading manufacturer of aircraft instruments in the world', an effort coordinated by a new management committee for the aircraft section on which both Gordon and Ralph sat.[110]

The clock division continued to expand its operations—with selling coordinated through SEC and the various manufacturing subsidiaries 'now in a position to supply every make of clock previously imported from abroad. (Applause).' Looking forward once more to distant gathering clouds, Henderson-Cleland described the work of the division 'as "vital" advisedly, because in time of emergency it is essential that this country should have factories capable of making the delicate clockwork mechanisms required for the many devices used in the Services. (Applause)'. The threat, in many forms, from overseas clock industries, was really centred in Germany, though this was rarely expressed explicitly. Complaints were more generally worded—as when Gordon commented: 'the foreigner is still able to undersell us, partly owing to the fact that he is granted an export subsidy which nullifies the McKenna duties'.[111]

In early 1937, Smiths increased its stake in the Enfield Clock Company, purchasing half of Carl Schatz's residual stake, and the clock division's range was further extended in November with a controlling stake in Reginald Bailey and Thomas Johnstone's Synchro-Time systems, adding time recorders, turret clocks, advertising, and other public clocks.[112] Just before the end of the year Pullars Electric of Brighton, an instrument manufacturer, was also acquired in the clock division.[113] A long-standing brand was born that year, with the running together of 'synchronous electric' into Sectric—under which synchronous clocks were henceforward sold.[114] In the past, advertisements had featured a character called 'Mr Smith-Electric', but he was replaced in 1937 by 'Mr Sectric', who revealed substantial inflation in the figures from the previous year with the announcement to the trade that '60 million Sectric clock advertisements . . . will be in circulation in the next twelve months'.[115] Smiths continued to benefit from royal endorsement as well—at the British Industries Fair 'the Duchess of Kent chose three Chronos clocks, one a very beautiful production in lavender blue, and the Princess Royal had to two of our productions'. As Smiths noted—'two gracious gestures of encouragement to an important British industry'.[116]

The equity raised in the latter months of 1936 was deployed partly in the continued expansion of the firm's buildings, with further factory space at the Waterloo Road site, as well as the completion of a large canteen and social club on the south side of the site, placing the final touches on a remarkable sports ground, which had its baptism with the annual sports day in July 1937, where 250 employees competed in front of a crowd of 4,000—evidence of how important these days were.[117] The firm also moved into its new and modern headquarters building that month, at 317 Edgware Road, where it was to remain until 1981 (see Plates 25 and 26). Despite capital expenditure, the firm's position was strong, a substantial reserve of £650,000 (2010: £32.7m) being created by combining the general reserve and share premium accounts, while a further £25,000 was allocated to a research fund. Continuing a run of record years, net profit advanced 40 per cent, despite significant reserves now being made for Chamberlain's new 'national defence contribution', intended to operate as an excess profits tax, largely aimed (ineffectively) at firms that had benefited from the governments rearmament spending programme.[118]

Gordon was in the newspapers again in 1937, with the report of his appointment as a Deputy Lieutenant for Middlesex in April, probably linked to his support for the Territorial Army.[119] Away from the works, Gordon had also moved on from greyhounds, elevating the stakes with racehorses—his first horse, Fearless Fox, bought 'for rather more than 600 guineas', placed in the St Leger in September 1936, but then went on to win the Ascot Gold Vase in June 1937, and then the Goodwood Cup in July. *The Times* commented 'no one will grudge Mr Smith his success, for he is the best type of owner, who always seems to be amused at his success, and can also laugh at his failures, luckily so far few and far between'.[120]

Thorough preparation and training

> *Mr Haviland . . . appealed for the co-operation of all members of staff, not with the object of getting anyone panicky, but for the sole purpose of tackling the problem in a sensible manner.*
>
> ('A.R.P.', *Home Journal*, October 1938)

Preparing for an unknown future, but where the risk of war was certainly growing, Smiths understood it was not simply a question of building factories and installing plant—skilled and trained staff were equally vital. Foreshadowing foreign competition that would emerge over the next few decades, the UK clock industry knew significant investment was being made overseas in training—for example, it had been reported that Russia was training 200 people per year in watchmaking school and producing several million clocks per annum.[121] This gave rise to an initiative at Smiths that would have long-term benefits—the creation of an in-house technical school. Nominated by J. D. LeCoultre, Professor Pierre Indermuehle arrived from Switzerland in June 1938 at the new MA2 building on Waterloo Road, becoming its first principal, assisted by Jean Bader, a former student.

It was not only expertise that had to be imported from Switzerland. Despite the huge emphasis on selling English-made products, there were still components and machinery that could only be sourced from the Continent. In the case of delicate hairsprings for escapements, these had been supplied for years by Carl Haas, 'a German with a factory in the Black Forest', and by mid-1938 Smiths had started negotiating arrangements to form a hairspring manufacturer in the UK, perhaps jointly with Haas, with whom material and equipment supply discussions continued into the following year.[122]

With Territorial Army posters emerging across the country—'Safeguard Your Liberties!'—Gordon continued to stress the importance of recruitment. On 21 March he held a lunch at the Trocadero in Piccadilly (a favourite haunt of his father Samuel) 'for the purpose of inaugurating and concentrating interest on a County-wide territorial recruiting drive', with Lord Rochdale (Lord Lieutenant of Middlesex) and General Sir Walter Kirke (head of the TA) present.[123] The resulting two-week drive saw touring loudspeaker vans, recruiters at every cinema, and street parades of searchlights and guns. Back at Waterloo Road, the summer of 1938 saw work on the edge of the MA2 sports ground to create temporary air-raid shelters, largely from sandbags, and Air Raid Precautions (ARP) became a new added feature in the house journal, running to several pages, showing off the firm's preparation of its grounds, and the creation of an Auxiliary Fire Brigade and First Aid Corps.[124] Committees were established to consider decontamination, duplication of records, and the evacuation of employees.

F. W. Meredith, co-inventor of the autopilot ('George') which the firm had produced since 1932, joined from the Royal Aircraft Establishment, bolstering the design and engineering capacity of the aviation division—eight patent applications in his name (jointly with Smiths) were applied for in 1938 alone. The division's assets were enhanced further by the delivery mid-year of a new aircraft—this time a Percival Vega Gull (G–AFIE)—used for testing and demonstrating new designs for aircraft constructors and operators.[125] Another boost came from the extended technical visit to the division by J. Ottley of the Pioneer Aviation Instrument Co. of New York—probably arranged following Gordon's last US trip.[126]

The motor division had now assembled several different jack manufacturing subsidiaries and had the most comprehensive range on the market, but in mid-1938 a major consolidation and share swap exercise was concluded to move all the assets into a single company—Smiths Jacking Systems Ltd—simplifying matters for its trade customers. But the car market was nevertheless soft, leading to a fall in motor accessory sales, and hitting profits (see Figure 4.1).

Further consolidation took place at the end of the year in the wholesale distribution network on the clock side, following a recommendation from Gordon mid-year.[127] Richard & Co. was amalgamated with Tucker, Nunn & Williamson, with the minority shareholders bought out, to form Richard & Tucker Nunn, of 108 Hatton Garden, a feature being that it would 'sell British clocks only'.[128] However, Ernest Richard had a good and long-standing business importing French clocks which were sold mainly to Marks & Spencers and other stores, so this business was transferred into a new vehicle—the French Clock House—funded by Smiths and run by Richard—as the board noted, 'the reason for this amalgamation is to dissociate Smiths name as far as possible from the sale of foreign clocks'.[129] Further simplification came at English Clock and Watch Manufacturers, which had been producing electric car clocks for some time—this was simply absorbed into Smith & Sons (Motor Accessories).[130]

Overall, 1938 was a year of consolidation and preparation, though with significant emphasis still on technical development, particularly in aviation instruments. By this stage, Gordon was probably already spending some time discussing war preparation with officials and mid-year he retired as chairman at the sixth AGM of the British Clock Makers Association, blaming pressure on his time from other quarters—this despite the BCMA being Gordon's pet organisation, with practically one-quarter of its membership drawn from Smiths group companies. The association played its own part in ensuring Britain developed necessary technical abilities to support rearmament—the *Watch and Clockmaker* noted '"prolonged and highly confidential" negotiations carried on by Mr Smith with government departments'.[131] But there was still a little time to spend at the track, and Gordon will have been cheered to watch Lovely Mermaid win the Ladies' Nursery Stakes at Newmarket in October.[132]

Into the shadows

> *The managing director was authorised to look out for sites for a further factory more remote from London and report to the Board at a later date.*
>
> (*Minutes*, 19 January 1939)

In mid-January 1939, Gordon and his son Ralph met Sir Archibald Rowland, permanent secretary at the Air Ministry.[133] Rowland emphasized the vital importance of Smiths' aviation instrument operation and its vulnerability at Waterloo Road, added to which there was the uncertainty over the supply of hairsprings from Germany and jewels from Switzerland.

Nominally, the location of shadow factories depended on 'distances from German bases [which] determined a boundary from Bristol in South West England to Falkirk in Scotland, excluding the eastern part of Britain', but in practice they were built within this.[134] Folklore at Smiths suggested proximity to a major racecourse was an important criterion for Gordon, but whatever the reality, Ralph, Warwick the company secretary, and an estate agent, made many trips to the West Country where they finally identified a 308 acre site at Kayte Farm, Bishop's Cleeve, near Cheltenham, which the board approved, purchasing for up to £25,000 (2010: £1.2m) early in April.[135] Later that month, the board authorized Henderson-Cleland and Gordon 'to negotiate for such other pieces of additional lands at Cheltenham as may be deemed necessary by them', leading to the purchase of Cleeve Grange, a Gothic-style stone mansion, close by.

In June, Henderson-Cleland and Gordon were detailed to investigate how to finance the development of the Cheltenham site into a new factory complex—the probable cost being estimated at up to £250,000 (2010: £12m), with a further £15,000–30,000 estimated for local services. Given that matters were urgent, the decision was taken to award a contract to Sir Robert McAlpine & Sons, on a cost-plus basis, to build an office block, two factory blocks, a canteen, and necessary roadworks.[136]

On 3 July, S. Smith & Sons (Cheltenham) was formed, wholly owned by the motor accessories company, and £50,000 was advanced from London for plant and machinery purchases—'in addition to Plant which the Government are buying for us'.[137] The bulk of the financing for Cheltenham was raised externally from various assurance companies through Helbert, Wagg, by way of a private placement of £250,000 in guaranteed loan notes, paying a coupon of 4½ per cent, issued by the Cheltenham subsidiary, and guaranteed by Smiths (MA).[138]

Earlier in the year, a reorganization was completed at the Enfield Clock Co., where Walford, formerly running ECWM—now absorbed into Smiths (MA)—was made general manager, and a new product line launched under the brand 'Empire'—'a name with which Mr Walford has for a long time been closely associated'.[139] The stepping up of war-related preparation was visible in the signing of a licence agreement with the Secretary of State for Air relating to bombsights which would be made by Henry Hughes, and an agreement with Carl Haas in Germany, after a year of discussions, relating to machinery for producing hairsprings—the final delivery of which was also destined to pass into Smiths' folklore.[140]

The summer of 1939 saw the marking of several important milestones. It was the twenty-fifth anniversary of the formation and flotation of S. Smith & Sons (MA) Ltd, but this also meant that Gordon had served twenty-five years as managing director, and a large celebratory banquet was planned months in advance for late June, at the Savoy Hotel. It was to be a double celebration as matters turned out, with Gordon awarded a knighthood in the King's birthday honours list in early June, 'for political and public services'.[141]

The close of another era

Fortunately our principal products are as necessary in war as in peace.

(Chairman's speech, 1939 AGM)

It is clear Gordon Smith did not want the company to be caught out again as it had been in the early 1920s—overly dependent on a single industry—so his foremost priority was diversification. He was fortunate that Smiths could transfer existing skills and know-how into other sectors—clocks and navigation instruments—and then mass-produce robust goods of good quality, surprising numbers of which survive to this day. Despite a backdrop of rising unemployment, economic uncertainties, devaluation of sterling, and national government, the 1930s were also a decade of increasing affluence, mobility and comfort for many. Whether it was in the home or on the dashboard of cars parked outside, Smiths enjoyed growing demand for its products— detailed in chrome, sans serif fonts, and housed in Art Deco casings, all that was modern. Increasing sales and profits, and investors willing to buy shares, propelled continued growth in the motor accessories business, but also allowed Gordon to play a leading role in creating a new British clock industry, and marine and aviation instruments were an ideal business fit, with a national commitment to rearmament appearing mid-decade. A further theme was constant technical advance and Smiths continued to build a remarkable team of innovators and inventors—part of a workforce that had grown to 8,000 by 1939.[142] The company could not be perfectly prepared for war at the end of 1939, but it had laid many valuable foundations for difficult times ahead.

Notes

1. 4 Dec. 1931, 4.
2. Jonathan Zeitlin, 'Americanization and its Limits: Theory and Practice in the Reconstruction of Britain's Engineering Industries, 1945–55', *Business and Economic History*, 24/1 (1995), 277–86, passim.
3. 19 Jan. 1929, 93.
4. *The Times* (16 Mar. 1929), 5.
5. *Minutes* (31 May 1929).
6. *Financial Times* (6 Dec. 1929), 5.
7. Smiths had patent GB332, 314 (1929) for a liquid level gauge, jointly with Ernest Ansley Watson of M-L.
8. 21 July 1930, 1419.
9. *Financial Times* (12 Dec. 1930), 7.
10. *Minutes* (1 Apr. 1930).
11. Based on investment in subsidiaries in the 1930/1 accounts.
12. Monopolies Commission, *Report on the Supply of Electrical Equipment for Mechanically Propelled Land Vehicles*, HC 21, 1963–4, 89.
13. *Minutes* (1 Apr. 1930), quoted also in Monopolies *Report*, HC 21, 30.
14. 12 Dec. 1930, 22.
15. Cann, 'Lenoir', 18.
16. *Financial Times* (12 Dec. 1930), 22; *The British Clock Manufacturer* (Feb. 1933), supplement to *Watch and Clockmaker*, 4 (hereafter *BCM*).
17. Cann, 'Lenoir', 20–1.
18. Lenoir and Cann, 'Introduction of Jaeger', 7; Cann, 'Lenoir', 15–16.

19. Auto Tempo (AT) had German parentage, resulting in confiscation in the Great War. Ownership passed to Smiths, then to S. D. McKellen in 1920, thence back to Ed. Jaeger in 1928.

20. *Minutes* (24 Apr. 1930).

21. Lenoir and Cann, 'Introduction of Jaeger', 7; Cann, 'Lenoir', 16.

22. *Watch and Clockmaker* (15 Dec. 1931), 335 (hereafter *WCM*); Lenoir and Cann, 'Introduction of Jaeger', 8.

23. *WCM* (Mar. 1931), 14.

24. 4 Dec. 1931, 4.

25. Leslie Hannah, *Electricity Before Nationalisation* (London: Macmillan, 1979), 188–9.

26. Robert H. A. Miles, *Synchronome: Masters of Electrical Timekeeping* (Ticehurst: AHS, 2011), 208.

27. *The Times* (27 Nov. 1931), 9.

28. *WCM* (1931–3), passim.

29. GB366,710 (1932); *Minutes* (26 Feb. 1931).

30. GB374,713 (1932).

31. Emphasis added: Pam and Peter Wotton, *Birth of the Synchronous Motor Clock* (self-published), i. 26–7.

32. *WCM* (15 Dec. 1931), 334–5.

33. *Financial Times* (4 Dec. 1931), 8.

34. *WCM* (15 July 1932), 137.

35. *Minutes* (26 Mar. 1931); SEC was registered 14 Feb. 1931. See *WCM* (Apr. 1931), 63.

36. Graham Smith, interview (29 Aug. 2012).

37. *WCM* (Sept. 1932). 200.

38. *WCM* (15 Feb. 1930) 585.

39. *Minutes* (4 May 1933).

40. Probably under GB296,150, (1927) by ECWM and Harry Norman Walford.

41. *WCM* (15 Dec. 1932), 305.

42. 15 Feb. 1933, 1.

43. Mark Lines, *Ferranti Synchronous Electric Clocks* (Milton Keynes: Zazzoo, 2012), 36.

44. *WCM* (15 Mar. 1932), 27.

45. *WCM* (10 Apr. 1933), 181.

46. *Minutes* (4 Apr., 8 June 1933).

47. *WCM* (Nov. 1932), 278.

48. *BCM* (Feb. 1934), 7. Copies went as far as North Borneo and Iraq.

49. *HC Deb* (1 May 1933), vol. 277, cc. 519–645.

50. *BCM* (Feb. 1933), 1–5.

51. *Minutes* (20 July 1933). The deal also involved £12k in loans from Smiths, to be repaid as a percentage of profits.

52. *Minutes* (25 Feb. 1932). Meredith and Clark held important patents, GB365,186–9 of 1925.

53. *Minutes* (9 June 1932).

54. 15 Feb. 1932, 15.

55. *The Times* (23 Nov. 1932), 20.

56. *Minutes* (7 Nov. 1932). No files exist in the BT31 series—the document destruction policy has done its work. Samuel had resigned from S. Smith & Son in 1929, and winding up commenced in 1930, TNA BT 31/16170/61326. The Association of Diamond Merchants was wound up in 1931, TNA BT 31/16170/61327.

57. *Minutes* (23 July 1931).
58. *Minutes* (20 July, 2 Nov. 1933, 14 June 1934).
59. *Minutes* (2 Nov. 1933, 1 Feb. 1934).
60. *Minutes* (26 Apr. 1934).
61. *WCM* (10 Aug. 1933), 181.
62. *Minutes* (21 Mar. 1934).
63. *Financial Times* (15 Nov. 1934), 4.
64. *Minutes* (3 July 1934); *Financial Times* (15 Nov. 1934), 4.
65. Cann, 'Lenoir', 20.
66. *Minutes* (1 Feb. 1934).
67. *Financial Times* (15 Nov. 1934), 4; *BCM* (Feb. 1934), 6.
68. 4 Sept. 1935, 8.
69. *The Times* (22 Nov. 1935), 4.
70. *Minutes* (7 Feb. 1935); Helbert, Wagg to AGS (5 Feb. 1935), Schroder Archive, SH851.
71. *Minutes* (7 Feb. 1935).
72. 'Final placing list' (11 Feb. 1935), Schroder Archive, SH851.
73. *Minutes* (2 May 1935).
74. *The Accountant* (23 Feb. 1935), 263.
75. *Minutes* (30 May 1935).
76. *Minutes* (4 Feb. 1937).
77. *Minutes* (20 Aug. 1935, 27 Feb. 1936).
78. *Financial Times* (22 Nov. 1935), 4.
79. The Williamson Clock Co. received shares in Tucker, Nunn, in exchange for the bulk of the assets, liabilities, and goodwill in Williamson's. Smiths acquired from Richard & Co. its shares in Williamson's. *Minutes* (20 Aug. 1935).
80. *Minutes* (19 Dec. 1935); *WCM* (Dec. 1935), 368.
81. Autumn 1951, 3.
82. *Minutes* (11 Apr., 30 May 1935).
83. *New Scientist* (13 Feb. 1958), 46.
84. *Minutes* (21 Nov. 1935); Wilfrid M. Cann, 'Smiths Industries Limited: A Chronological Record' (London: Smiths, 1962, revised 1967/8), ii. 141.
85. *Flight* (30 Apr. 1936), 463.
86. *Smiths Industries at Cheltenham: The Story of Fifty Years at Bishop's Cleeve 1940–1990* (Surbiton: Kristall, 1990), 77–9.
87. S. Smith & Son (1934) Ltd.
88. *Financial Times* (22 Nov. 1935), 4.
89. 18 Nov. 1936, 6.
90. *Minutes* (6 Mar., 4 and 9 June 1936).
91. *Minutes* (15 Oct. 1936).
92. *WCM* (Oct. 1936), 279.
93. Cann, 'Lenoir', 18; *WCM* (Nov. 1936), 312–13.
94. *WCM* (Feb. 1936), 416.
95. Under an agreement of 20 July 1932. See *Minutes* (27 Feb. 1936).
96. *WCM* (Nov. 1936), 316.
97. Subscriptions spanned the year-end so the effect was seen across two sets of accounts: 1936 and 1937.
98. *Minutes* (9 June 1936).

99. *Minutes* (30 Jan. 1936).

100. See e.g. *HC Deb* (15 July 1936), vol. 314, cc. 2049–50.

101. *The Times* (20 Aug. 1937), 15.

102. *Smith's Home Journal* (Feb. 1937), 13. Batten's flight took eleven days, using a Husun compass.

103. *Financial Times* (19 Nov. 1937), 4.

104. The licence was acquired in Aug. 1935. See *Minutes* (20 Aug. 1935); Cann, 'Chronological Record', ii. 138. 1,000 shares in KLG were transferred to Bosch. See *Minutes* (14 Jan. 1937).

105. *Minutes* (14 Jan. 1937). The RMS *Berengaria* manifest includes Eric Moss, Arthur Hughes, Hugh Samuelson, Dr Watson, Ben Haviland, Gordon, Bea, and their daughter Muriel.

106. *Smiths Home Journal* (June 1937), 1; *Minutes* (1 July 1937).

107. Lionel Fraser to R. Gordon Smith, Schroder Archive, SH851; *Financial Times* (19 Nov. 1937), 4.

108. Agreement on reciprocal use of patents—see *Minutes* (15 Oct. 1936).

109. *Flight* (27 Apr. 1939), 442.

110. *Minutes* (7 Oct. 1937); *Financial Times* (19 Nov. 1937), 4.

111. *BCM* (Feb. 1937), 3.

112. *Minutes* (22 Feb. 1937). The consideration was £1 10s per share, less than paid for the initial stake in 1933. Schatz retained a repurchase right. For Synchro, see Martin Ridout, *English Clock Systems Limited*, AHS EHG technical paper, 68 (2005).

113. *Minutes* (4 Nov. 1937); Cann, 'Chronological Record', ii. 143.

114. *Smith's Home Journal* (June 1937), 3.

115. *WCM* (July 1937), 164.

116. *Smith's Home Journal* (June 1937), 13.

117. *Smith's Home Journal* (Aug. 1937), 10–17.

118. See e.g. Robert Shay, 'Chamberlain's Folly: The National Defence Contribution of 1937', *Albion*, 7/4 (1975), 317–27.

119. *The Times* (29 Apr. 1937), 19.

120. *The Times* (30 July 1937), 6.

121. *WCM* (Aug. 1936), 185.

122. Cann, 'Lenoir', 23; *Minutes* (21 July 1938).

123. *Smiths Home Journal* (Apr. 1938), 50.

124. *Smiths Home Journal* (Oct. 1938), 18–19.

125. *Smiths Home Journal* (Oct. 1938), 20–1.

126. *Smiths Home Journal* (Oct. 1938), 21.

127. *Minutes* (21 July 1938).

128. *Minutes* (29 Nov. 1938).

129. *Minutes* (29 Nov. 1938).

130. *Minutes* (3 Nov. 1938).

131. *WCM* (Aug. 1938), 172.

132. *The Times* (27 Oct. 1938), 5.

133. *Smiths at Cheltenham*, 19; *Minutes* (19 Jan. 1939).

134. Stephen E. Little and Margaret Grieco, 'Shadow Factories, Shallow Skills? An Analysis of Work Organisation in the Aircraft Industry in the Second World War', *Labor History*, 52/2 (May 2011), 197.

135. *Minutes* (6 Apr. 1939).

136. *Minutes* (1 June 1939).
137. *Minutes* (6 July 1939).
138. The issue was sold at a price of 99% of face value. See *S. Smith & Son (Cheltenham) Ltd Minutes* (21 July 1939) (hereafter *Cheltenham Minutes*). The investors were Pearl Assurance, Provident Mutual, Royal National Pension, Gresham Life, and Legal & General.
139. *WCM* (Feb. 1939), 5.
140. Bombsights under patents GB521,737–9 by Edward Cecil Hornsley, applied for 1929–30; *Minutes* (2 Mar. and 6 Apr. 1939). Henry Hughes worked with E. R. Watts of Camberwell on the bombsights.
141. *The Times* (8 June 1939), 10.
142. Cann, 'Chronological Record', ii. 148.

CHAPTER 5

....

1939–1945

The War Factory

....

*Since the outbreak of war, the company's resources have been reorganised,
and the factories are now fully employed on national work.*

(Chairman's speech, 1939)

WE have seen that Smiths was sensitive to the move towards rearmament and the preparation for war from 1936 onwards. The strong focus in rearmament lay in the aircraft industry, but the motor industry formed a natural target for Lord Weir to draw into his 'shadow' scheme to boost aero-engine production, and Smiths will have followed the reaction of its clients, particularly Lord Nuffield of Morris, with close interest—would changes in the motor assemblers' business result in changes for Smiths? But by now Smiths had also strongly developed its aircraft instrument business and was therefore already directly and deeply involved in component supply for the strengthening armed forces. With the escalation of preparation from 1938 onwards, it would be drawn into the shadow programme as well.

Smiths had developed into a stable and profitable concern through the 1930s. It had diversified away from its dependence on the motor industry—still its largest market—and could now leverage broader expertise in instrumentation and measuring equipment, coupled with mass-production techniques, across several sectors. It provided high-value autopilots and technical equipment for aircraft and ships at one end of the scale, but at the other could fill strong demand for the latest in timekeeping technology. Despite the humble nature of the speedometer or the synchronous clock, much of what Smiths did can be regarded as the current 'hi-tech'—unsurprisingly it devoted considerable resources to securing the best people and to continued research and development, constantly lodging or acquiring patents, both at home and abroad. All this led naturally to a deep engagement in the war effort from 1939 onwards, and engendered a further stage in its long-term evolution. David Edgerton argues the aeroplane lies at the heart of the British 'warfare state', with vast resources committed to military aviation.[1] In terms of aviation instruments and sparking plugs during the Second World War, Smiths contributed more to this effort than any other British firm.

The phoney war

Throughout this history of the Smiths of England...what better fruit could have been produced than the tangible weapons which have helped the survival of our great nation?

(Sydney Walton[2])

With the declaration of war with Germany in September 1939, there would have been reminders for Gordon Smith and his colleagues of the summer of 1914, but also marked differences. Part of the senior management team (for example, Charles Nichols on sales and Ben Haviland running the MA1 Cricklewood works) had been through the previous conflict, which had seen Smiths' first major expansion, from a few hundred workers to a few thousand. In 1914 the management had little or no idea of what was coming. This time it was different, and although Britain's rearmament was slow to start, Gordon Smith was among those who saw a need for early preparation—witness his strong support for the Territorial Army both in and outside the company. Smiths had been drawn into munitions production in the Great War on the basis of a small-scale speedometer and carburettor plant in the West End. With the large-scale Cricklewood factories that resulted, and after the wobble of the early 1920s, the emerging Smiths empire of motor accessories, clocks, aircraft instruments, and marine equipment was a natural fit for the military-industrial complex being assembled in the late 1930s. For example, the precision instrument facilities at Chronos Works lent themselves naturally to fuze manufacture, and following successful tests at Shoeburyness, the works received a contract to tool up and produce the type 206 anti-aircraft mechanical time fuze. Smiths' shadow factory programme extended to KLG, which was producing sparking plugs at a high rate for Rolls Royce Merlin engines, and a further factory was soon under way at Treforest in south Wales, completed by the end of the year and in operation in early 1940, under the management of S. E. Burlington.[3] This doubled KLG's capacity.

Robert Lenoir had been works manager at Chronos Works throughout the 1930s, but his time was now increasingly taken up with the new Cheltenham factory and preparation for war. Discussions with Carl Haas GmbH in Schramberg from the previous year led to an agreement for the supply of machinery for making hairsprings, and July 1939 saw Lenoir in Basle working on expediting the despatch of machine tools being sourced from Germany via Switzerland.[4] Interestingly the final consignment did not leave the Haas works until after Britain had formally declared war and there is a suggestion Dennis Barrett of SEC had to travel to Dieppe and with Royal Navy assistance load some of the machinery onboard ship in order to bring it finally to England, with another consignment left in a railway siding for the rest of the war.[5] The Haas equipment was destined for Cleeve Grange, the country house close to the Cheltenham site, where W. T. Kelly took charge of hairspring manufacture, the first results emerging by the end of 1940.[6] In a similar vein, KLG had placed orders with

Robert Bosch for vital equipment in the summer of 1939, and the contract was honoured in the autumn, involving deliveries via neutral Sweden, implying some significant and subtle manoeuvring by the authorities, behind the scenes.[7]

With war declared on Sunday 3 September, the board met the following Thursday. Gordon Smith—actually now confusingly Sir Allan Gordon-Smith, after changing his name by deed poll on 17 August—reported on progress at Cricklewood, where it is clear that 'governmental requirements' were already being met, with production adjusted accordingly.[8] The board also had to consider immediately the fact that male staff were already being enlisted and policy was formulated for making a gratuitous payment of a further month's wages, in addition to recognizing continuous service for those enrolled in the pension scheme.[9] There were new arrivals as well—among them Eddy Downey, the 16-year-old son of a Hammersmith butcher, who had heard war announced on the radio while encamped with the Sea Scouts at Greenwich.[10] His uncle, Ted Pitman, chief buyer at MA1, encouraged him to apply to Smiths as an apprentice, and he joined in November 1939, spending six weeks on a rotation around the drilling section, then onto lathes, first in the small machine gang, then on larger capstans, followed by the press shop, grinding section, and then the toolroom for those boys selected for their aptitude. From there, again on a selective basis, apprentices would move to various assembly sections, finishing off in heat treatment, plating, and spraying.

Factory construction and recruitment were key issues. From Gordon's reports to the board it is clear he was regularly in touch with governmental departments, and in November reported instructions from the Admiralty for the construction and equipping of a new factory at Elstree to expand the manufacture of the type 206 fuze, the building contract being issued to John Laing a few months later.[11] Down at Cheltenham, progress was being made with the factories and key staff were moved from London to oversee equipment installation (e.g. machine tools from SAFAG in Bienne for making precision cutters—Britain was and would remain chronically short of machine tools), with Ben Haviland transferring from Cricklewood to become the works manager, assisted by W. E. Watson. Haviland was to remain at Cheltenham for twenty years—an extrovert figure, somewhat 'in the mould of Allan Gordon-Smith, knew every corner of the business. No one would move a finger without checking with him.'[12] Interestingly, Eddy Downey recalled murmurings that Haviland sourced Cheltenham transferees from MA2 on Waterloo Road, rather than disturbing his precious crack squad of engineers at MA1 in Cricklewood, but whatever their origins there was little accommodation available, and the temporary solution was found with a caravan supplier on the Kingston Bypass who provided upwards of fifty caravans at 30s–50s per week per van, installed in the grounds at Cleeve Grange—there may have been two hundred caravans at one point. It was a particularly hard winter, and folk memory recalls that on Christmas morning, after a particularly hard frost, some people found themselves frozen to their beds.[13] In the spring, the firm began a programme of more than twenty-five house purchases in Cheltenham that was to continue over several months, making a more permanent solution to the accommodation issue, while recruitment of local staff was stepped up, taking unskilled farm labour and providing training, and also importing watchmakers from across the country.[14]

Smuggling, but diplomatically

The position with regard to jewels is complex . . . the Commercial Coun-
sellor in Berne executed these orders.

(Edwards (PS17), Ministry of Aircraft Production[15])

Shortage of precision machine-tools and an over-reliance on German hairsprings had not been Smiths' only weaknesses in relation to foreign imports. Smiths and other precision instrument manufacturers were reliant on the import of the jewels needed for fine bearings—and about 95 per cent of these came from Switzerland.[16] It was only early in 1940 that any response began to emerge, with the import of necessary machinery (probably from Gianque & Haesler of Le Locle) but the raw material for synthetic jewel production—aluminium oxide—was also needed.[17] Here Lenoir could help again and through his network made contact with the Baikowksi factory in Annecy, which specialized in the jewel-making process. Gordon Smith and Lenoir flew to Paris in a military plane on 4 May 1940, reportedly hedge-hopping most of the way, for a series of meetings, certainly with J. D. LeCoultre, but also probably with Max Baikowski, to agree the supply of a large quantity of aluminium oxide. This was immediately shipped and stored at the Ministry of Aircraft Production (MAP) head-quarters, partly to be used at Avon House Works in Warwick later in the war for the development of a synthetic jewel production capacity.[18] Trips overseas such as this probably unnerved Gordon-Smith's fellow directors, especially given that Germany commenced its invasion of France a week later, and perhaps unsurprisingly they resolved to put in place a £60,000 life insurance policy on the occasion of each journey (2010: £2.9m).[19] On another overseas trip, years later, probably around 1952, Rex Smith and his family visited Annecy, where Graham Smith recalls Max Baikowksi, by now visibly a very prosperous man, treating his good friends from Smiths of England to a wonderful celebratory lunch, recalling past adventures.[20]

With the fall of France in mid-1940, supplies of finished jewels from Switzerland ceased, as the standard supply channels were blocked. Two outcomes were (i) the establishment of a specialist jewel advisory committee, organized by MAP's Emergency Powers Committee, on which Lenoir and E. B. Moss of Smiths sat, and (ii) in Switzerland the more hazardous development of unofficial smuggling channels by the commercial attaché in Berne—John Lomax—who recalled 'jewel-bearings are minute in size but high in value and light for their bulk: they called for the safest routes, and we never lost a consignment'.[21] Ted Pitman of MA1 explained years later to his nephew that he had been sent to a tailor for the fitting of a bespoke suit, which he wore for the flight to Lisbon, and thence to Switzerland, where the suit was carefully and secretly packed with a huge quantity of watch jewels. Returning via Lisbon, he handed over the suit, thus replenishing jewel supplies in the UK.[22] He may have been one of several to make such trips, and it is clear that John Lomax, the diplomatic smuggler, must also have devoted appreciable time to the sourcing of jewels at the Swiss end, given his autobiography, written twenty years later, reveals close detail of the manufacturing process, drawn from personal knowledge.[23]

And they're off, at Cheltenham

> *In the orchestra at the Cheltenham Town Hall, they had one chap who used to play the 'Post Horn Gallop' on a trumpet about a metre long—it used to bring the house down.*

> (Eddy Downey, 2013)

Construction of the shadow complex at Cheltenham moved forward and May 1940 saw the first factory—CH1—in operation, involving a precision machine shop, and the production of a wide variety of aircraft instruments, and eventually the machinery for producing ball races for autopilots, as well as the end products (see Plates 31 and 32).[24] CH2 followed within months, at first housing both the school and the finer work, including the production—transferred over from CH1—of 8-day centre-second aircraft clocks to a LeCoultre pattern, also made at Chronos Works.[25] It was here that a group of ten Swiss watchmakers worked, and the equipment included a range of smaller automatic Swiss machines, using single-point tools and cam-directed slides to produce accurate small-scale components in batches.[26]

Between the two main works structures were two further buildings, housing the canteen and a heat treatment department. Everything was single-storey, making it easier to hide, with dummy hedges, roads, and 'wire netting supported all round by telegraph poles . . . angled down to the ground . . . then covered with chicken feathers which were painted in "natural colours"'.[27] A dummy stream was even painted over the top, following the course of the real one below.

For all the Swiss machinery and hard work, preparation had not started early enough—the Air Ministry was expecting 20,000 clocks in April 1940, but Smiths had to revise the delivery date to September. The firm was relying on the combined efforts of Chronos Works and Cheltenham but even this revised date was badly missed, with deliveries finally being made between January and June 1941, perhaps owing to difficulties with the supply of both jewels and hairsprings.[28]

With the expansion of Cheltenham and the growing need for permanent and local housing solutions, Smiths laid plans in the spring of 1940 to work with the 1933 Housing Society for the building of fifty houses, off Gay Lane, in Bishop's Cleeve, negotiating with Structural Contractors for the building work.[29] However, this arrangement was modified and in July the Air Ministry agreed a deal with Ralph Gordon Smith under which the ministry took over the scheme for the Meadoway Estate, which later developed into the Bishop's Cleeve Housing Association.[30]

June 1940 saw the transfer of Professor Indermuehle's school from London to Cheltenham, and the apprentices were at first put to work in helping to install machinery.[31] It was not only machinery that had been imported from Swiss firms—a sizeable team of Swiss technicians had arrived as well, and they were busy not only installing precision machinery but also manufacturing the parts that could not be supplied—leading to part of CH1 being known as the 'Swiss toolroom'.[32] The apprentices were thrown in at the deep end, not just using machinery, but helping to manufacture it in the first place.

Darkening skies: Smiths under attack

> *The Managing Director reported that he had been approached by the Mayor of Willesden to contribute to a local fund for the purpose of purchasing one aeroplane.*
>
> (*Minutes,* 1 August 1940)

Summer 1940 saw the Battle of Britain waged overhead, increasing the demands on Smiths, not only for new instruments but also for the rapid repair and refurbishment of existing parts. Following a survey of 'a bewildering acreage of damaged instruments' at Kidbrooke, and under instruction from the Air Ministry, a major department had developed under George E. Hester, the service manager, based in a warehouse at Cricklewood, adjoining the in-house fire brigade's office.[33] Over time, Hester's team would repair not only Smiths instruments, but those of forty-six other British and American manufacturers, reaching a record of 2,800 instruments repaired in one week alone, and half a million in total.[34]

It was time for a life-changing posting for Frank Hurn, Midlands manager in Birmingham, whose career would later lead him to senior management of Smiths. He had evacuated his wife and two sons (one of them a future chairman) to Clevedon in Somerset at the beginning of the war, but he was now moved to London to assist Charles Nichols in the motor division. Mike Hurn recalls 'Mother said that if Dad was going to be in London we would all go there together and share the danger.'[35] The Luftwaffe showed its appreciation of the family's arrival in London with a stick of bombs dropped along the roadway outside on their first night in residence, in August.

Autumn 1940 saw the Blitz break out over London, and unsurprisingly, Smiths caught some of the action. On 28 August, an oil bomb destroyed Hester's recently established repair shop—and only prompt action by the company's fire brigade and the national service 'prevented the blaze jumping the yard to involve the main machine shops'.[36] The leadership shown that night by Len Potter, the company's chief fire officer, contributed to his George Medal.[37] Hester was immediately working on plans for reconstruction and a tender from William Moss & Sons—builders of the main office block at 317 Edgware Road—was accepted in September.[38] Despite the Air Ministry invoking the shadow factory principle, and suggesting a Government Instrument Repair Department at Cheltenham, Hester remained in Cricklewood. Handley Page had leased the building adjoining Smiths from Stoll Picture Productions in September 1939, but the Air Ministry stepped in and installed Smiths, providing Hester with space for a new instrument repair workshop, which was to remain till the end of the war.[39] Chronos did not escape entirely, also being hit, but on this occasion the bomb did not go off. The same thing happened back at Cricklewood where a delayed action bomb and two further HE bombs fell. Despite the risk, Potter spent hours with volunteers building a sandbag wall 'to reduce the effect of the explosion had the bomb gone off'.[40]

Both MA1 (Cricklewood) and MA2 (Waterloo Road) now had large air-raid shelters—at MA2 they were built into the athletics ground, while at MA1 they were in the north-west corner of the site, built into the railway embankment on the perimeter—for which privilege Smiths paid the LMS railway company rent. Factory air-raid shelters were typically large and were therefore also often used to house additional equipment. When Eddy Downey had proved his ability in the main machine shop at MA1, he was paid an extra farthing per hour to work as an 'assistant-setter', ensuring the correct setting of the cutting tools and their stops on a bank of five Schaublin 70 lathes, housed in the shelters—operated by five girls who didn't get their bonuses if the machines were incorrectly set and the output was wrong—'they soon marked my cards. There I was, at the age of seventeen and a bit [laughter], with five very, very lusty females, in an air-raid shelter [laughter], a couple of hundred yards from any authority [laughter] I won't dwell on it, but the girls were a lot more mischievous than I was.'[41]

To diversify the range of production sites against the backdrop of repeated raids, clock escapement and gauge movement assembly at Chronos Works was duplicated at Ben Haviland's old home, The Pine House at Bushey. He had given it up to move to Cheltenham—while another house was also rented in Bushey for use by the directors and senior staff as a hostel.[42] Further duplication was organized for fighting vehicle speedometer and tachometer assembly in premises at Mollison Way, Edgware. At Treforest in Wales, KLG was similarly matching its London operation's output, and in common with other factories, the Putney Vale main factory was camouflaged from mid-1940.[43] Though it was never hit, captured documents show that detailed target photographs were issued to Luftwaffe crews, and at least one high explosive bomb landed remarkably close.[44]

Another local development from the Blitz was prompted by a raid in early September.[45] Charles Nichols arrived at Cricklewood on a Saturday morning to find a dishevelled and distraught employee—her home destroyed in the previous night's raids, she was left only with the clothes she wore. Handing over a note from his wallet to tide her over the weekend, Nichols was much troubled and on Monday he secured gifts from his colleagues sufficient to establish the 'War Time Hard Luck Fund', which had two initial advisers—H. Blaise to cover MA1 and William Cann at Chronos and

MA2. Additional funds came from Sports Club contributions and employees, while the company provided £2,500, plus match-funding of staff contributions, and arranged the rental of four flats in Neasden and Dollis Hill 'for temporary accommodation of those who have to evacuate their own homes owing to bombing'.[46] As Cann records of his own experience:

> Perhaps the most valuable assistance rendered was completing the Government claim forms to ensure compensation for material losses due to enemy action. The Advisor to MA2 and Chronos Works dealt with 373 cases out of some 2,500 people, visited hospitals, mortuaries, funerals, at one of which 37 coffins were interred in a common grave.[47]

The entire workforce was of course strongly motivated to support the war effort. Savings in 2½ per cent war loan stock were encouraged, with the firm buying blocks for its own account but also topping up staff purchases with an extra certificate for each twenty subscribed. Another notable exercise by the workforce was the raising of £6,640 (2010: £256,000) to present 'Lord Beaverbrook with a Spitfire', dubbed 'Smithfire'. Gordon-Smith made the point to shareholders 'that all this was subscribed by individual members of the firm and no contribution was made by the company'.[48]

Sir Allan goes to war: 1940

> *You did so much, in stormy days, to build up the Ministry and make it an effective instrument supplying the R.A.F. in the battle-front.*
>
> (Beaverbrook to Gordon-Smith[49])

In mid-May 1940, the Air Ministry's procurement responsibilities were transferred to the newly formed MAP, headed by the controversial figure of Lord Beaverbrook. At the end of the month, Gordon-Smith was appointed to MAP's Emergency Powers Committee, cementing the association between Smiths and the key government body which was to provide it with so much work.[50] It is worth emphasizing that, though Gordon-Smith reportedly gave 'a great deal of his time to the Ministry', he remained managing director of Smiths throughout the war and it was extremely rare for him to miss a board meeting. In this context it is interesting to consider a description which no doubt stems from observations by Dennis Barrett of SEC when interviewed for a book on business enterprise in the late 1950s: 'His instinctive judgements were moderated and tested by others whose minds were more analytical and critical than his; but there was no doubt during Gordon-Smith's lifetime as to who led the firm.'[51]

His contribution to the war effort outside the firm was nevertheless not going unnoticed and in January 1941 he was made a Knight Commander of the British Empire.[52] Mid-year, his responsibilities enlarged yet further, with the reorganization of MAP that followed on the arrival of John Moore-Brabazon as minister, replacing

Beaverbrook. Under Sir Archibald Rowland as permanent secretary, Gordon-Smith now 'had a wide field of responsibility for factory construction—itself an organisation of five directorates—emergency services, the area organisation, and factory defence'.[53] From June 1942 he served on the Central Committee, which handled coordination of MAP's regional boards, soon graduating to be Deputy Controller of Construction and Regional Services. He was elected to the Aircraft Supply Council in January 1943—a position in which he would be deploying knowledge and experience gained over twenty-five years in running a firm with several thousand workers engaged in volume-production light engineering.[54]

In and finally out of the Blitz: 1941

I remember on one occasion I went to sleep with the oil heater left on. It caused condensation which ran down the walls and froze my hair to the wall of the caravan.

(Eddy Downey, 2013)

City-dwellers had weathered months of night-time raids by early 1941—London had been bombed every night from 7 September to 3 November 1940 and there were many more raids to come before the worst was passed. But in February 1941, Eddy Downey and fellow MA1 colleague Doug Maskell were removed from London and transferred to the school in Cheltenham, where Eddy would stay until August 1943, gaining an Ordinary National Certificate before being transferred back to Cricklewood. Progress was highly accelerated for these wartime trainees, who rapidly graduated to precision tool manufacture, copying and supplementing the fine Swiss machinery in use in CH1 and CH2—for example, Eddy helped to make a pivot polisher—demonstrating skills that would normally take many more years to develop.[55] Like others before, he was housed in a caravan for a few weeks, but its obvious discomforts—frozen hair included—encouraged him to find local digs, and around this time in early 1941 some staff and families also moved into the first ten houses on the new Meadoway Estate.[56]

Back in London, as the Blitz was nearing its end, the largest raid of the whole war occurred overnight on 9 May 1941, probably witnessed from the Cricklewood MA1 Control Tower by T. S. Osbaldeston, who put out charting information on enemy aircraft positions to the air defence network, and kept up a commentary for seventy local factories, using a Tannoy system—later in the war relaying the positions of V-1 flying bombs, urging workers to 'Keep down, keep down—just a little longer'.[57] The May 1941 raid left the original site of Samuel Smith's jewellery shop on Newington Causeway destroyed, but also by coincidence united two companies in adversity. Henry Hughes's London shop at 59 Fenchurch Street, EC3, was destroyed, but so was that of Kelvin, Bottomley & Baird at 11 Billiter Street, EC3, a firm to which Smiths had been growing closer—indeed Mr King of Kelvins had recently been invited to join the board of Henry Hughes.[58] Finding themselves both without premises, the two chose to join forces, opening a joint office at 107 Fenchurch Street, which in turn led to the formation of Marine Instruments Limited, to distribute and service the marine instruments of both firms—a precursor of greater cooperation to come.[59]

First post-war planning: 1942

The only way we can see of keeping engaged after the war the factories [and] particularly trained labour at present employed...mainly on instruments for aircraft, tanks and ships, is by producing clocks and watches.

(Barrett to Sir Samuel Beale)

In 1942—surprisingly early, given the state of the war—and against the backdrop of the work being done that would lead to the Beveridge Report in December that year, serious consideration started being given to planning for post-war industrial redevelopment. The clock and watch industry, though small, was a candidate for consideration, given that its new champions (Smiths and fellow members of the British Clockmakers Association, the BCMA) wanted to see their industry supported and promoted, while the government had become acutely conscious of the need for fine detail precision engineering as part of its military and defence requirements. Where Germany had planned well in advance, it was clear the UK had been ill-prepared. To a degree Smiths was therefore pushing on an open door in advocating the continued support of the industry in a future post-war environment, where clockmaking companies and plant would form part of a notional reserve capacity in precision defence manufacture. The experience of having to smuggle both machine tools and finished timekeeping products from Switzerland should not be repeated.

In August 1942, a meeting at the Board of Trade, chaired by Sir Samuel Beale, received representations from the Clockmakers Export Group (chaired by Dennis Barrett of Smiths) and its parent the BCMA. The clockmakers emphasized the history of international (particularly German) investment in, and government protection of, overseas clockmaking industries, which had hampered any similar development in Britain, essentially as a result of large-scale dumping of cheap foreign clocks in markets such as Britain. Barrett had witnessed German determination at first hand on visits to Germany in the 1930s, discovering that, if the 40 per cent German government subsidy to its clockmakers were not sufficient, it would be increased.[60] Now that Britain had developed onshore capacity as part of the war effort, it was argued this needed to be nurtured in the post-war period, with a degree of protection, probably through import quotas. If manufacturing volumes could be increased, with commensurate cost-savings and reduced unit pricing, this would lead to useful employment, export earnings (for example, it was argued strip steel valued at £50 could yield £5,780 of export business), and an industry with tooling that lent itself to defence manufacture at short notice.[61] Barrett followed up with further memoranda detailing potential quantities of raw materials, finished products, and employment statistics. Part of his pitch was drawn from Smiths' experience in acquiring the United Kingdom Clock Co. in mid-1941, and then turning the premises over to the development of inexpensive alarm clocks, for which it was argued there was long-term demand—added to which, local production would reduce foreign exchange outflows.[62]

The long struggle of the middle years: 1942–1944

From eight in the morning till eight at night, life is taken off one's own hands completely and absolutely.

(Mass Observation[63])

In 1980, when Wilfrid Cann came to write up the life of Robert Lenoir, based on fifty-five years of close friendship and access to his papers, the result was a chronologically based account, filled with excellent detail—yet the period 1942–5 is largely summed up in a single sentence—'The war years passed slowly, each one packed tight with concentrated effort, leaving little time for home life let alone recreation.'[64] Nevertheless, occasional high points included the children's tea parties at Christmas, a long-standing tradition started in 1920, held in the Cricklewood canteen, where Santa would arrive by sleigh, on a well-decorated electric flat truck—'For some weeks prior to this event the same canteen was used over weekends as a workshop to make toys for Santa to hand out to us well-impressed children.'[65]

Over time, the anti-aircraft battery perched atop 317 Edgware Road saw less action and the nightly peril of the Blitz passed as Hitler chose to focus his forces elsewhere, noticeably against Russia, but there was to be a long period before sentiment moved to a strong feeling that an Allied victory would emerge—a period in which the shadow factories and their employees simply knuckled down. From January 1943, unmarried women and married women with no children were conscripted, through to the age of 45. Mass Observation reports—such as *War Factory*—highlighted both the drudgery and monotony of mass-production munitions work, where individual components seemed in themselves to mean little to the operatives. *War Factory* drew on observations in a remote MAP aircraft components factory, which, like Smiths, had a predominantly female workforce. Their poor opinion of their male comrades, usually in higher paid positions of more authority, was obvious, yet generally whispered.[66] Smiths on the other hand had *PIVOT* magazine, and the regular feature 'Our Post Bag' gave the workforce a voice—an opportunity taken up regularly by one forthright correspondent, signing herself 'Pussy'. She would take male (sexist) contributors to task, and in an exchange across many editions must have raised an eyebrow or two with her contributions:

Mothers, sweethearts, sisters, daughters ... are suffering untold agonies as the result of this mad man-made conflict ... if one could only believe that one day the co-operation of the sexes would reach fructescence then there would be every hope of a brave new world.[67]

But the current world was Orwellian, the sense of being lost within one vast machine further emphasized when day and night shifts were introduced, leading to constant production—as Cann noted, 'this was the pattern of life till the end of the war'.[68]

He also commented that 'strict censorship prohibited the publication of company news, production or achievements likely to be useful to the enemy', and detail of the company's operations becomes harder to find. Slowly, over the middle years of the war, Smiths gradually formed or invested in additional specialist group companies, expanding the product range in a series of complementary steps. The hairspring operation at Cheltenham was incorporated as British Precision Springs alongside Clock Components Limited (both around March 1942), while a stake in Furzehill Laboratories, purchased from its owners—John and Barbara Reyner—boosted the range of electronic aviation instruments in October 1942.[69] The cooperation with Kelvin, Bottomley & Baird, at this stage still only through a joint sales operation at 107 Fenchurch Street, was enhanced by Ralph Gordon-Smith's election to its board in March 1943.[70] For some time, Smiths had used 'unbreakable' and flexible tube, especially for applications involving petrol, made by the Petro-Flex Tubing Company of Watford—this too was brought into the fold with an outright acquisition (financed through shares placed by Helbert, Wagg) in April 1944, followed by David Harcourt of Linkula Works, Birmingham, pressure gauge manufacturers, purchased for £40,000 in June 1944.[71]

Memories of an apprentice

> *His assistant, called Bader, kept a little black book*
> *And in it the names of latecomers he took,*
> *And if you were late, you were sure to find*
> *That his anger increased with the square of the time.*

(Early school song, Cheltenham)

Down at Cheltenham, Eddy Downey was working through his apprenticeship at Professor Indermuehle's school, now moved to a new building, CH3. Memories of Indermuehle's stern assistant, Jean Bader—a disciplinarian referred to as the 'Nazi' by the apprentices—are mingled with fond recollection of some of the freedoms away from London—the bar at Cheltenham town hall on a Sunday night, perhaps, following a recital by Dame Myra Hess. Chris Ellis's compilations of recollections of wartime life in Cheltenham by Smiths' staff paint a picture of tiring routine—for example, the Bishop's Cleeve site formed its own Home Guard unit (H Company) and manned its own fire brigade, and many staff would spend one night in five, or one weekend in four, involved in these activities, or as volunteer ambulance drivers. Local transport was a difficulty, and an early solution was to issue bicycles to the workforce. Later, a local bus route was added, but with the last service at 21.30, this did little to enlarge the workers' social lives in Bishop's Cleeve when the six cinemas and Saturday night dances were in Cheltenham. Eddy recalls ignoring the service in any case—'we boys couldn't care less about the buses—we had much more fun on our bikes. We had a crocodile of twenty four. Everybody stand aside! The school was coming!'[72]

Apprentices received a voucher each six weeks for a weekend train fare to London, but enterprisingly these were sometimes sold to others more desperate to make the journey. Some workers even cycled home to London on their weekends off—Eddy would leave the school at midday on Saturday and set off on his bike to his parents' home in Hammersmith. He stopped only for a coffee and meat pie about half way. His mother would start running a bath at 5.30 p.m., and it was always steaming hot when he arrived, always before 5.45 p.m.—a journey made nearly twenty times during his stay at Cheltenham. The return journey was made from midnight on a Sunday night, with a short sleep before work.

In the run-up to departure for London in February 1943, he recalls the excellent tuition of Harry Gyoury, the former toolroom foreman from MA2 in London, brought down to Cheltenham to provide experience from the shop-floor—'he was the chap who taught me an awful lot about life in engineering'. A rather different authority figure was Queen Mary, whom Eddy recalls making a visit in early 1943, firmly resisting the boundaries of the guided tour, marked out in tramlines on the factory floor, and wandering wherever she pleased.

Returning to London with his ONC, Eddy was posted to P. O. Dorer's design office at Cricklewood, now located on an upper floor of the old Nieuport building on Langton Road. Technically, his apprenticeship was not complete, and despite being proud to recruit the top apprentice passing out of Cheltenham, Dorer was not prepared to have anyone on his staff 'on the clock'—paid hourly—and thus Eddy joined the staff on a salaried basis. But this was to last just a year, as the call came in February 1944 for him to join the 'Bevin Boys', working in the Warsop Main Colliery—arriving in 'Grade I' health, though that was not to last.

He recalls that before he left for Warsop there was an awareness in Smiths of a build-up towards what would turn out to be Operation Overlord—the factories were turning out more instruments and equipment than ever before. The Battle of the Atlantic had largely been won, and Kelvins had contributed with the provision of anti-submarine detection (ASDIC) equipment. Bomber Command's massive raids were flown with aircraft populated with Smiths instruments and driven by engines containing KLG sparking plugs—contemporary Smiths and KLG advertising showed the massed styl-ized silhouettes of RAF bombers against the night sky, and for the last eighteen months of the war virtually all the resources of KLG were devoted to producing plugs for the Rolls Royce Merlin engines of the RAF—250,000 in the month of June 1944 alone.[73] Late that year the Society of British Aircraft Constructors issued a report on the technical supremacy of the KLG plug, capitalizing on recent praise from Roosevelt, who had

19. Gordon Smith, victorious with Golden Seal, Waterloo Cup (1927).

20. Chronos Works, built 1929–1934 (*c.*1936).

21. MA2, Waterloo Road, home to SEC from 1936 (*c.*1965).

22. Vans promoting the new synchronous clocks toured the country from 1932.

23. Advertisement for Bluecol anti-freeze (mid-1930s).

24. Giant synchronous clock, Hendon Aerodrome (*c*.1935).

25. Head office (1937–1981), 317 Edgware Road.

26. Cricklewood complex (mid-1960s).

27. KLG factory, Putney Vale, built 1937–1938, on the site of the Bald Headed Stag.

28. Sir Allan Gordon-Smith (1881–1951).

29. Charles Nichols (1884–1962).

30. Robert Lenoir (1898–1979) describing watch assembly to the King, Cheltenham (1944).

31. The Cheltenham factory complex (*c.*1959).

32. CH1 at Cheltenham (*c.*1959).

33. Allan Gordon-Smith and Stafford Cripps (*c.*1944).

34. Ystradgynlais complex (*c*.1953). The Enfield factory is in the foreground, and Anglo-Celtic to the rear.

35. Assembly of the SEP1 automatic pilot (*c*.1950).

36. Witney factory complex (late 1950s).

37. Witney—main administration block.

THE GIRL WHO SNEEZED IN THE WATCH ASSEMBLY

38. *PIVOT* cartoon, 'the girl who sneezed in the watch assembly', Sydney Walton (July 1957).

39. From left, Harold Buckland, Stanley Burlington, Rex Smith, Dennis Barrett, Allan Gordon-Smith, Frank Hurn, Charles Nichols, and Ralph Gordon-Smith (late 1940s).

commented that 'since 1943 virtually every U.S. *Flying Fortress* has taken off from British bases with these plugs . . . it would be impossible to estimate how many thousand United States bomber crews may since then have owed their lives to these spark plugs.'[74]

To provide more capacity for Smiths to manufacture Desynn meters and aircraft instruments, and against the emerging threat of V-1 flying bombs, MAP requisitioned factory space at the Carfin Trading Estate, seventeen miles south-east of Glasgow, thus relieving some pressure on the London and Cheltenham plants. A small group of Scottish women travelled south to train in fine coil-winding and other skilled tasks, and on their return to Scotland, around August 1944, formed the nucleus of a new workforce. Initially parts were sent from London for assembly, until Carfin began its own component manufacture, as well as dial finishing and luminizing, which 'as for coil-winding, called for extreme patience both from the workers and instructors'.[75]

Sir Stafford Cripps was now running MAP, and in February 1944 acted as guest of honour at the opening of an exhibition in the showroom in Cricklewood—on 'The Smiths of England'—a chance to showcase the firm's products, with a strong role in lifting the spirits of the workforce, who needed to see how their individual efforts formed part of the wider war effort. A machine tool of Eddy Downey's was one of many exhibits, but the most memorable feature was effectively a flight simulator in which a visitor could be 'flown' by bomber in a 'trip over Berlin', complete with realistic sound effects through headphones.[76] If the workforce understood their present roles, both management and various ministries were now seriously beginning to consider what would follow the eventual cessation of hostilities.

Divisions for the future battlefields: 1944 reorganization

The business has now been segregated into four different divisions . . . this, in the opinion of the board, represents a big step forward and considerably simplifies the problem of post-war planning and management.

(Chairman's speech, 1944)

When Dennis Barrett addressed the Board of Trade in August 1942 on the post-war future of the clock industry, the end of the war was not yet in sight. The momentum in the lobbying by the BCMA for preferential tariff treatment and general arrangements to support the industry seems then to have been lost for a time. But a year and a half later, as 1944 opened, Smiths began thinking ahead again, in earnest, as optimism slowly began to emerge.

In March 1944, with the firm now increased in size significantly since the 1930s, a corporate restructuring was agreed, to divide activities more formally between divisions—a distant echo of Samuel Smith's division of his businesses into four separate companies, back in 1899. In April and May new companies were formed, and the original Smiths motor accessories company changed its name to S. Smith & Son

(England) Limited, cementing its formal role as holding company, with three new subsidiaries (to add to the existing Smiths English Clocks):

- Smiths Motor Accessories
- Smiths Aircraft Instruments
- Smiths Industrial Instruments

This provided a modern multi-divisional structure with four main operating divisions, now clearly segregated, with Allan Gordon-Smith, his son Ralph, and Charles Nichols common to all boards. The management hierarchies within each division were formalized, with key lieutenants appointed more specifically. So, for example, Frank Hurn and Harold Buckland joined the boards of both Motor Accessories and Industrial Instruments, while Charles Molyneux Carington MC ('the Major'), who had run KLG since 1927, joined the Motor Accessories board, as did Ben Haviland.

Further refinements saw the sale back to E. A. Richard of the firm's stake in the French Clock House company in June, and then a small share transfer between Henry Hughes and Kelvin, Bottomley & Baird in September, which linked the two firms more closely, although further amalgamation would not occur for several more years.[77]

Plans for post-war reconstruction

The clock industry is a source of skilled labour for light engineering work, capable of setting up automatics, and semi-skilled labour for machine loading, light precision pressing and so on.

(Board of Trade, 1944)

Board of Trade papers show that from August 1944 onwards the government was actively looking at the role the clock and watch industry could play in post-war reconstruction.[78] Smiths took a lead in articulating both the value of the industry, and its requirements for support in the form of 'protection from foreign competition'. The argument had two pillars: '(a) the value of the industry to our post-war economy, and (b) the value of the industry as a source of war potential'.[79] The argument was familiar—considerable effort had been put into re-establishing the clock industry in the 1930s, against significant and strategic competition from Germany. It would now be possible to continue its expansion, increase employment, and create export earnings, if wartime resources could be redirected into the production of a range of products, including simple alarm clocks, and if imports of clocks could be restricted for some period, either through tariffs or quotas. Watch manufacturing was a different story—it was only the dependence on Switzerland that continued into the first years of the war that had prompted the channelling of new resources into the field. Smiths at Cheltenham had received £100,000 from MAP for watchmaking equipment alone—yet 'even now, after more than four years, we cannot meet the requirements of the Services'. Despite a variety of problems foreseen in training labour, jewel production, and indeed from the expected resumption of Swiss competition following the end of the war, the assessment was that 'the establishment of English watch-making is of far greater economic value than the clock-making industry and it seems well worth while preparing a concrete scheme for its expansion'. Thus plans started being formulated for a new industry that would provide everything from high-grade wristwatches to humble bedside alarms.

These plans had their foundations in the wartime achievements of the group's chief horological engineer, Robert Lenoir, whom Gordon-Smith had cannily acquired with Ed. Jaeger back in the late 1920s. In addition to his role in devising pure materiel in the form of fuzes and the like, Lenoir was chiefly responsible for Smiths' development and manufacture of an impressive array of watches and clocks for the forces. These included:[80]

- small 8-day centre-seconds movements for the RAF—1,800 per week;
- pocket watch for the army;
- centre-seconds wristwatch for both army and navy (assembly);
- stop-watches for anti-aircraft battery control and fire control on battleships—2,000 per week.

A high point for both Lenoir and the whole factory complex came on 19 July 1944, when he and Allan Gordon-Smith had the chance to give George VI and Elizabeth a tour of the Cheltenham site, presenting the King with a Smiths wristwatch, and providing a detailed explanation of watch assembly, maintaining a tradition of supplying Smiths' instruments to the royal family (see Plate 30).

Lenoir was not only responsible for the finer points of design and manufacture. He immersed himself fully in the job of arranging the manufacture of raw materials, such as steel and brass rods and strips used in the automatic presses, jigs, lathes—setting specification standards that would apply for many years after the war.

From plans to action: 1944–1945

> *For some time past we have given the future policy of the companies most serious consideration.*
>
> (Chairman's speech, 1944 AGM)

Allan Gordon-Smith was able to devote more time to Smiths' role in these plans from October 1944, with his retirement from MAP, receiving flattering tributes from Beaverbrook, his first minister; from the highly influential Sir Percy Mills, Controller General of Machine Tools; and from Sir Stafford Cripps, who would continue to be a close ally, and whose letter of thanks acknowledged the appropriateness of Gordon-

Smith's return to his firm 'to establish a flourishing and expanding industry to the great benefit of our country'.[81] Just a few months later, Cripps visited the Carfin site in Scotland, in part because the factory was producing aircraft instruments for MAP, but also to emphasize the need for light industry in the region and to encourage Allan Gordon-Smith's plans for the plant's peacetime employment (see Plate 33).[82]

Gordon-Smith was already focusing heavily on new plans for Smiths before he left MAP—at the September 1944 board meeting he reported on negotiations to acquire a number of further premises: from the Pullmans Spring-Filled Company on the North Circular; from Vactric on Waterloo Road, to provide SEC with space for casing-up, warehousing, despatch, and sales; at Elstree, where he expected to lease the existing Smiths fuze factory back from the Admiralty, plus further land adjoining it; and at Cricklewood, where the firm occupied the Stolls building on behalf of MAP, but hoped to take an assignment of the lease—a hope later fulfilled.[83] Gordon-Smith had joined the board of Electrical and Musical Industries (EMI) in 1942—further research might reveal this was in relation to his work for MAP, since EMI's laboratories were at that time heavily engaged in the development of H2S radar—but now he was in a position to combine the potential peacetime interests of EMI and Smiths with a plan to manufacture car radios, and reported to the Smiths board his discussions to date. Finally, a plan was outlined for acquiring a larger stake in Kelvin, Bottomley & Baird, through offering a further share exchange, to which the board agreed, and an offer was communicated accordingly.[84]

In November, ideas for the expansion of the UK clock and watch industry became more concrete with the identification of a site about thirty-five miles north-west of the Treforest KLG shadow factory, on the Ynis-Cedwyn estate at Ystradgynlais. Reportedly, Dennis Barrett succeeded in extending the area designated by Hugh Dalton's staff for post-war development by a mile into Breconshire to encompass his chosen site.[85] In early December 1944 the estate trustees granted Smiths an option to buy the main estate house and the adjoining Home Farm.[86] Having discussed matters with the Board of Trade, Smiths exercised the option soon after, purchasing the freehold for £12,000 in March 1945, though on the understanding that the government would fund the construction of new factory space of some 100,000 square feet in area (9,300m²), to be rented by Smiths on a long-term basis (see Plate 34).[87]

One of the long-term uncertainties throughout the war had been home-grown synthetic watch jewel production. Despite a supply of aluminium oxide, arranged with the help of Robert Lenoir, MAP had failed to advance production and quality was abysmal.[88] In addition to attempts to improve production at two existing small concerns, there had also been an effort to establish an entirely new manufactory on a larger scale, at Avon House Works, in Warwick, another shadow factory, built in 1943–4.[89] MAP had subcontracted the management of this to Joseph Lucas, but it appears MAP also coopted Robert Lenoir some time in 1944 to assist.[90] MAP then asked Smiths to take over completely in February 1945.[91] In this way, Smiths took control of the production of synthetic jewels, providing neat vertical integration with its plans to build the new watchmaking plant at Ystradgynlais and its existing watch production at Cheltenham, where it exercised an option, dating back to 1943, to acquire from MAP watchmaking plant worth £110,000 which the government had initially financed.[92]

Towards victory in Europe: 1945

The managing director reported on the results of his visit to France and Switzerland.

(*Minutes,* 10 March 1945)

Allan Gordon-Smith was distinctly busy in the opening months of 1945, and one focus of his attention was achieving outright ownership of various subsidiaries in which Smiths only had a controlling stake. At the March 1945 board meeting, further group reorganization was agreed, and having reported on negotiations he had undertaken on his recent trip overseas, he secured a mandate to buy out the French outside interests in British Jaeger Instruments and ABEC from Gustav Delage and SAPIC (the Jaeger/LeCoultre holding company). All outside interests in Henry Hughes were also now acquired, and through a share exchange a 32.5 per cent holding in Kelvin, Bottomley & Baird was secured.[93] Authority was also given for the formation of Radiomobile, to be owned jointly with HMV, part of EMI, each party contributing £5,000 in initial capital and four directors, Allan Gordon-Smith taking the chair, supported by Ralph Gordon-Smith, Charles Nichols, and Frank Hurn.

The agenda before the board that March was unusually full, including the introduction and election of Charles Carington of KLG, who, together with Allan Gordon-Smith and E. B. Moss, travelled to the United States for a month shortly afterwards. Moss was now placed in charge of the engineering lab in MA4 on the Waterloo Road site, with a team of four senior design engineers, each with their own specialist sections. One was headed by Wilfred Owen Davis, a brilliant theoretician in gear theory, and it was his team that Eddy Downey joined in April 1945—returning to Smiths having been invalided out of Warsop mine with rheumatic fever—a month before VE Day, Tuesday 8 May.[94] Two days later the main Smiths board met once again to consider the future. Launching the firm forwards on full throttle from the outset, Allan Gordon-Smith outlined a budget for immediate expenditure of £600,000 on plant and premises, which included purchases of the Vactric Works, next to MA2, and new plant at Ystradgynlais, Carfin, and Cheltenham.

Finance, tax, and excess profits

I should like to point out here that, in addition to the great effort the group has made in regard to the supply of war materials, it has contributed no less than two million pounds in excess profits tax.

(Chairman's speech, 1946)

The wartime figures for Smiths are deceptive, since the figures are so heavily skewed by national defence contributions, taxes, and the gearing of the company's efforts to war-related activities. Overall, there is no doubt that the war was profitable for the firm, and that its activities were strongly cash-generating, but the machinery of relieving companies of cash to fund central government budgets was severe. Excess profits tax, on broadly similar lines to the system that applied in the Great War, rapidly rose from 60 per cent to 100 per cent, meaning that, to the extent a firm increased its profitability above a pre-war 'standard', there was no purely fiscal incentive for growing a business. To a degree there was a patriotic counter to this seemingly soul-destroying taxation burden, but Smiths in common with many other companies publicly pointed to what was argued to be an inbuilt unfairness in the taxation system—for example, that depreciation on plant was only allowable at rates that bore no relation to the useful life of fixed assets. The skewed nature of the figures is easily seen in the accounts for 1944–5, where the consolidated post-tax profit each year approached £200,000, yet the tax burden was in the range £700,000–900,000, and as Allan Gordon-Smith revealed, the group contributed £2 million in excess profits tax during the wartime period, broadly comparable to its net assets at the end of hostilities.

In this regard, Smiths' accounts reflect the norm for the period—to the extent a business had its production geared to the war effort, in munitions, aircraft production, etc., cash generation would be large, with relatively limited net profits. But in Smiths' case there is once more a revealing insight gained into personal outcomes, this time as a result of a challenge from the tax inspector with regard to directors' remuneration for the opening years of the war. At the end of 1943, when a settlement of excess profits tax was negotiated, the inspector disallowed part of the directors' remuneration as a deduction in the figures for the two years ending August 1941—leading to downward adjustments amounting to £7,500 for 1940 and £15,000 for 1941. Allan Gordon-Smith had voluntarily reduced his commission for the year ending August 1942 to a level of £20,000 (2010: £727,000), and as a result the full deductions for directors' remuneration that year were allowed to stand, but the adjustments for 1940–1 probably stemmed from an assessment that his annual commission payments were excessive—and in context they were indeed notable, at £31,308 in 1940 (2010: £1.33m) and £36,377 in 1941 (2010: £1.41m).[95]

But such figures were necessary, given the lifestyle Gordon-Smith led, even in wartime. When not staying at St Ermin's Hotel in London to be close to MAP, he lived with his wife Bea at Cowfold, Sussex, in Walhurst Manor, a remarkable Elizabethan house notable for its billiard-room covered in mounted stags' heads from the annual shoot in Scotland, and fine stabling for the horses—among them Navigator's Delight for which Gordon-Smith paid 2,700 guineas at Newmarket in January 1945.[96] Such outgoings made significant demands on his purse, not least as he was supported by his butler, Mrs Telford the housekeeper, Emily the cook, Alice the senior parlour maid who looked after two junior maids, Walter ('Wally') Wallington (one of two chauffeurs), two gardeners, a groom, and a stable lad—all of whom are remembered with affection by Graham Smith, Gordon-Smith's great nephew, who spent many happy days there.[97]

A catalogue of heroic achievements

The time has come when I am at liberty to disclose the tremendous part that your group of companies has played in connection with the vital equipment for our Forces.

(Chairman's speech, 1946)

Henderson-Cleland, originally brought into the firm to protect Lloyds Bank's interests, saw the war through as chairman, a post he held for twenty-one years, but he died suddenly at the age of 67 in August 1945.[98] Taking the opportunity to restructure the board slightly, and retiring Sydney Begbie, also after twenty-one years' service, it was Allan Gordon-Smith, stepping into his shoes as chairman, who addressed the shareholders from the chair for the first time in January 1946, and it was natural that he should pay a tribute to his predecessor, but then largely dwell on the significant wartime achievements of the group.[99] In the motor accessories division, 1.25 million speedometers and mileage recorders had been supplied for fighting vehicles of all sorts, for use in extreme conditions, added to which 5 million other vehicle instruments had been delivered (pressure gauges, thermometers, liquid level gauges, etc.). Hundreds of thousands of specialized jacking tools had been provided. In the aircraft division, over 10 million aircraft instruments and mechanisms were manufactured—ranging from complicated automatic pilots, through altimeters, rate of climb indicators, pressure and boost gauges, to thermometers, clocks, and watches. KLG produced over 12 million sparking plugs for aircraft—more than any other manufacturer. In the clocks division, 4 million clocks and escapements were made, while British Precision Springs produced 24 million hairsprings, with hundreds of thousands shipped to Russia and the United States. At Henry Hughes and Kelvin, Bottomley & Baird, the same sort of numbers of highly specialized marine and aviation instruments were both manufactured and repaired—including parts of the anti-submarine detection equipment that played a vital role in the Battle of the Atlantic.

Towards reconstruction

I think that the post-war possibilities of Smiths, covering as the company does so many different fields, are very great. One got an impression of strength coupled with conservatism.

(Lionel Fraser; Helbert, Wagg file note[100])

On balance—though some of its individual staff members were killed or maimed, lost their homes or loved ones, and everyone had to endure significant hardship—Smiths had a good war. It suffered no devastating losses from aerial bombardment, and indeed recovered remarkably positively from the most serious incident at Cricklewood in 1940.

It had the financial resources to fund its expansion and growth, whether in personnel or new factories, in Cheltenham, Elstree, Carfin, and elsewhere, and successfully avoided the pitfalls of overextending itself with a large debt burden that would be unsustainable in the post-war period. Robert North's business at Watford, which Allan Gordon-Smith knew intimately from the early speedometer days, had done precisely that during the Great War, and failed later under a mountain of debt-service obligations and the failure to replace government war contracts—it was a lesson well learned by Smiths, but a situation which caught out some contemporaries in the years following the Second World War. For example, its customer in north-west London, Synchronome, the clock manufacturer, expanded ten-fold to handle Admiralty work, and then struggled to survive post-1945. Instead, Smiths financed its factory expansion and fitting out either with its own strong cash-flow or with the direct help of the government—essentially MAP—which requisitioned space, provided machine tools, and even raw materials. Overall, Smiths ended up with better equipped factories, and a large and highly trained professional staff and general workforce, from product design, through mass production, to final precision manufacture.

Allan Gordon-Smith's network of relationships was always important both to him and Smiths. It will have been of enormous benefit, when he was seconded to MAP, that he enjoyed such good relationships with both Beaverbrook and Stafford Cripps who ran the ministry that was the single most important client for the firm. More fortunate still, the fact that Stafford Cripps would move on to be first post-war president of the Board of Trade placed Smiths in an excellent position, as the machinery of wartime production started to be redirected towards peacetime use. Unsurprisingly, however, a whole new range of challenges were nevertheless to emerge.

Notes

1. David Edgerton, *Warfare State: Britain, 1920–1970* (Cambridge: CUP, 2006), and his other works on the aeroplane and Britain's 'war machine'.
2. 'A Brief History', 23.
3. Ellis, *K.L.G.*, 49.
4. Cann, *Lenoir*, 24.
5. Frank Edwards, 'Military Timepieces', *Horological Journal* (July 1994), 453–7. Cann, 'Chronological Record', ii. 148. Another account has some machinery sunk in Boulogne harbour; *Smiths News* (May/June 1970), 2.
6. Eddy Downey, interview (18 Mar. 2013); Cann, 'Chronological Record', ii. 148.
7. Ellis, *K.L.G.*, 53.
8. *Minutes* (7 Sept. 1939); *London Gazette* (12 Sept. 1939), 6222.
9. *Minutes* (7 Sept. 1939, 14 Mar. 1940).
10. Downey, interview (2013).
11. *Minutes* (9 Nov. 1939).
12. Graham Smith, interview (2013).

13. Ellis, *Smiths at Cheltenham*, 24–5; Cann, 'Chronological Record', ii. 149. Cann has 'nearly 200 caravans'.

14. Ellis, *Smiths at Cheltenham*, 25; *Minutes* (1940), passim.

15. TNA: AVIA/637, *Minute 99*.

16. Neville Wylie, 'British Smuggling Operations from Switzerland, 1940–1944', *Historical Journal*, 48/4 (2005), 1086.

17. Machinery referenced in cypher telegram to Kelly (12 July 1940), TNA: AVIA/637, T.630/Z

18. Cann, 'Lenoir', 21–4. The LeCoultre meeting was to discuss manufacture of the 206 fuze at Sentier, not progressed.

19. *Minutes* (14 Dec. 1939).

20. Graham Smith, interview (2013).

21. 'The Manufacture of Jewels in the United Kingdom' (25 Oct. 1940), TNA: AVIA 15/740; John Lomax, *The Diplomatic Smuggler* (London: Arthur Barker, 1965), 145.

22. Downey, interview (2013).

23. Lomax, *Diplomatic Smuggler*, 132–3.

24. Ellis, *Smiths at Cheltenham*, 32.

25. Ellis, *Smiths at Cheltenham,* 25.

26. Downey, interview (2013).

27. Ellis, *Smiths at Cheltenham*, 27; Cann, 'Chronological Record', ii. 151.

28. Wylie, 'British Smuggling', 1081.

29. *Cheltenham Minutes* (27 June 1940).

30. *Cheltenham Minutes* (1 Aug. 1940).

31. *School Digest* (Easter 1951), 4.

32. Downey, interview (2013).

33. *PIVOT* (Aug. 1946), 4–5.

34. Cann, 'Chronological Record', ii. 151.

35. Personal communication (Mar. 2013).

36. Cann, 'Chronological Record', ii. 151.

37. *London Gazette* (3 Jan. 1941), 47; biography in *PIVOT* (Feb. 1946), 2. Potter was a critical figure in the ARP and fire service in the local area. Obituary in *Smiths News* (Oct./Nov. 1966), 4.

38. *Minutes* (26 Sept. 1939).

39. TNA: BT 177/1122.

40. *London Gazette* (3 Jan. 1941), 47.

41. Downey, interview (2013).

42. Cann, 'Chronological Record', ii. 151; *Minutes* (23 Jan. 1941).

43. Ellis, *K.L.G.*, 49.

44. Ellis, *K.L.G.*, 54; see www.bombsight.org.

45. Cann, 'Chronological Record', ii. 153–4. Drawn from Cann's own record and assumed accurate.

46. *Minutes* (24 Oct. 1940, 27 Mar. 1941).

47. Cann, 'Chronological Record', ii. 153.

48. *Financial Times* (2 Jan. 1941), 4.

49. Quoted in Cann, 'Chronological Record', ii. 163.

50. *Daily Telegraph* cuttings file on AGS (28 May 1940); *Minutes* (1 Aug. 1941).

51. Ronald S. Edwards and Harry Townsend, *Business Enterprise: Its Growth and Organisation* (London: Macmillan, 1958), 38.

52. *Daily Telegraph* AGS file (28 May 1940).

53. J. D. Scott and Richard Hughes, *The Administration of War Production* (London: HMSO, 1955), 299.

54. *Daily Telegraph* AGS file (6 June 1942); *Financial Times* (2 Jan. 1942), 4; Scott and Hughes, *Administration of War Production*, 85.

55. Downey, interview (2013).

56. Ellis, *Smiths at Cheltenham*, 28.

57. *PIVOT* (Feb. 1946), 24; See Richard Collier, *The City that Wouldn't Die* (London: Dutton, 1959); Gavin Mortimer, *The Longest Night: Voices from the London Blitz* (London: Weidenfeld & Nicolson, 2005).

58. *Minutes* (27 Mar. 1941).

59. Cann, 'Chronological Record', ii. 155.

60. TNA: BT BT 64/84, 'Memorandum on post war matters' (25 Aug. 1942), 2.

61. TNA: BT 64/84, 'Notes of a meeting' (25 Aug. 1942).

62. *Minutes* (17 July 1941); TNA: BT BT 64/84, 'Memorandum on post war matters' (25 Aug. 1942), 3.

63. Mass Observation, *War Factory: A Report* (London: Gollancz, 1943), 47.

64. Cann, 'Lenoir', 27.

65. Peter Graham, 'Reflections on a life influenced by Smiths', kindly communicated to the author (Mar. 2013). Ben Haviland started the parties, with Bill Lewis as MC, *PIVOT* (May 1950), 2.

66. *War Factory*, 63–73.

67. *PIVOT* (Nov. 1943), 7.

68. Cann, 'Chronological Record', ii. 157.

69. *Minutes* (26 Mar. 1942, 1 Oct. 1942).

70. *Minutes* (4 Mar. 1943).

71. Helbert, Wagg to Smiths (13 Apr. 1944), Schroder Archive, SH270; *Minutes* (27 Jan., 25 Apr., 8 June 1944). The firm's history appears in *PIVOT* (Aug. 1947), 22–3.

72. Downey, interview (2013).

73. Ellis, *K.L.G.*, 49; Cann, 'Chronological Record', ii. 162.

74. Society of British Aircraft Constructors, *A British Technical Triumph* (14 Dec. 1944), 2.

75. R. K. Humphreys, 'The Story of Carfin', *PIVOT* (Sept. 1945), 12.

76. Cann, 'Chronological Record', ii. 162.

77. *Minutes* (28 Sept. 1944).

78. TNA: BT 96/225, passim.

79. TNA: BT 96/225, 'Some notes on the post war position of the clock and watch industry'.

80. Cann, 'Lenoir', 26.

81. Cripps to Gordon-Smith (6 Oct. 1944). SMAA.

82. Visit on 10 Feb. 1945, *PIVOT* (Apr. 1945), 18.

83. TNA: BT 177/1122.

84. *Minutes* (28 Sept. 1944).

85. For an account, see Geoffrey Evans, *Time, Time and Time Again* (Barry: Quinto, 2008), 14–15, but note the BOT files at Kew offer important further insights and detail.

86. *Minutes* (7 Dec. 1944).

87. *Minutes* (28 Dec. 1944, 20 Mar. 1945); Barrett to Sadler Forster (19 Feb. 1948), TNA: BT 177/1122.

88. Wylie, 'British Smuggling', 1087.

89. Arthur Astrop, 'Avon House Works', *Retort! Bulletin of the WIAS* (Summer 1998), 3–10.
90. Wylie, 'British Smuggling', 26.
91. *Minutes* (1 Feb., 20 Mar. 1945).
92. *Agreement* (25 June 1943), referred to in *Minutes* (20 May 1945).
93. *Minutes* (20 Mar. 1945).
94. Davis wrote the definitive *Gears for Small Mechanisms* (London: NAG, 1953).
95. *Minutes* (30 Dec. 1943).
96. *Daily Telegraph* AGS file (24 Jan. 1945).
97. Graham Smith, interview (2013).
98. *Minutes* (17 Dec. 1945); Begbie died mid-1947, *Minutes* (25 June 1947).
99. MHB to Munro (9 Nov. 1945), Schroder Archive, SH851.
100. Lionel Fraser, meeting note (7 Feb. 1945), Schroder Archive, SH851.

....

1945–1959

From Austerity to Prosperity

....

I remember vividly on Friday nights in Coventry we would go down the lines,
collect rejects, take them back to London to be re-worked over the weekend, to
be delivered back to the lines on Monday—that's how short supplies were.

(John Thompson[1])

FOR Smiths, the fifteen or so years after the Second World War can be divided into two distinct periods: the first (1945–50) was chiefly characterized by the fruit of close relationships between the right-leaning senior management and key ministers in the Labour government—focused on (re)building industry and employment in development areas, and ensuring the solid creation of precision engineering capacity that could support defence needs. The second period (the 1950s), with a Conservative government in power, saw the gradual dismantling of tariffs and protections, doing the clock and watch businesses no favours, while the rapidly increasing standards of living kept the motor division buoyant. The precision engineering that most closely tied the firm to the defence of the nation moved away from horology and towards aviation and marine technology. Smiths expanded its manufacturing capacity and workforce dramatically over the period, striving for more output and efficiency, as well as increased exports. It relied in part on new ideas for improved volume production, developed following study of US factories and methods, but despite innovation, it nevertheless had to deal with serious shortages in materials, labour, and housing. It also had to cope with the early death of Allan Gordon-Smith, and therefore the significant loss of a major controlling mind.

In motor accessories, Smiths' fortunes broadly tracked the motor industry (shown in Figure 6.1). Apart from a couple of short-term slumps, the whole period was characterized by increasing standards of living and wider car ownership. Smiths had early on achieved significant market power, and under the leadership of Frank Hurn who pushed for continued investment, particularly in ventilation and heating technology, succeeded in holding market share. In the absence of worrying foreign competition, the firm stood to make good money, and it understood volume production well. But a more militant labour environment putting pressure on wage costs would offer one among several challenges.

The performance of aviation is harder to quantify. With George Potter of Kelvin & Hughes (a marine man) nominally in charge, it did not have a champion like Hurn or

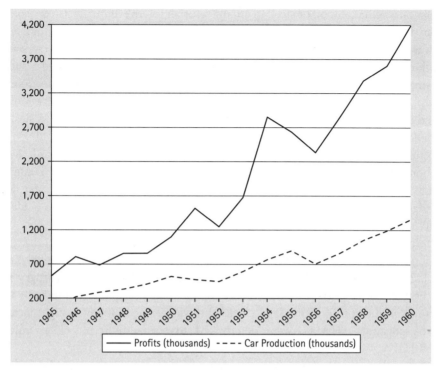

FIGURE 6.1 Smiths' profits vs. UK car production (1945–1960).
Source: annual accounts; SMMT

Barrett, and its activities were obscured by both the board's focus on motors and clocks, and the nature of its government work. Research and development featured heavily, and a transition occurred from offering individual instruments to complete and integrated flying systems. Aviation effectively replaced horology as the natural target for government backing, as defence technology requirements evolved from pure precision engineering to a combination of electronics and engineering, in both aviation and marine. The significant growth in civil air travel in the period provided a further boost. Defence budgets could certainly be relied upon not to disappear, but their overall size was at risk of policy change.

Instruments of policy

> *If we had had a considerable watch and clock industry earlier, not only should we have avoided the risks which are inseparable in such circumstances from dependence on overseas sources, but we should have had a reservoir from which we should have drawn machine tools, skilled labour and management well suited to the manufacture of many of those precision instruments upon which war so much depends to-day.*
>
> (Stafford Cripps[2])

After VE Day in May 1945, *PIVOT* recorded the return of Smiths workers who had been enlisted and in service all over the world, coming back to a country beset by shortages, whether of food or steel. In all, 107 returnees were eventually listed—some of whom had endured horrific conditions in labour camps.[3] A roll of honour at 317 Edgware Road recorded the names of sixty-two employees killed on active service, and thirteen victims of air raids. Unsurprisingly, *PIVOT*'s pages also noted a sudden upswing in marriages and its 'Wedding Bells' pages were filled for many months. Smiths still largely operated for MAP—almost every part of its organization was geared to war production, from the Home Counties to the West Country, Wales, and Scotland, but life was changing at every level as the firm began readjusting to peacetime operation. The creation of new jobs was important, but Stafford Cripps, to whom Smiths had become close, had moved from MAP to the Board of Trade, and though employment was crucial, he ranked it behind exports and achieving dollar earnings—and Smiths settled into a business strategy that was geared to achieving Cripps's goals.

Irrespective of the dominant contribution of the motor element of Smiths, Allan Gordon-Smith's immediate post-war priorities lay elsewhere. When Lionel Fraser and James O'Brien of Helbert, Wagg visited him at Cricklewood in February 1945, they listened to his post-war plans, recording: 'the biggest expansion anticipated will be in the production of all kinds of clocks and watches ... as many as eight factories will be engaged ... H.M.G. were determined to see an efficient clock industry established.'[4]

Reviving the 1942 plan for mass production of spring-wound alarm clocks, a factory was to be built either at Ystradgynlais or Elstree, but Cripps intervened and persuaded Smiths to site production at the MAP factory in Carfin, Lanarkshire, where aircraft instrument production would run down and in an important development area.[5] Smiths agreed, despite a lack of space, and were producing 1,000 alarms per day by year-end, with a waiting list of 300 applicants for jobs, pending deliveries of machinery.[6]

The production of watches would operate on two tiers. Robert Lenoir would assist in developing high-grade watch manufacture at Cheltenham, but volume production would be sited at Ystradgynlais, in partnership with Ingersoll, with whom Smiths formed the Anglo-Celtic Watch Company in May 1945, taking 50 per cent each. The Board of Trade commenced building a 'standard' pattern factory.[7] Vickers-Armstrong joined the consortium, taking a one-third share, soon after.[8] At inception, the factory worked on piece-part production of an Ingersoll-designed pocket watch, moving to the manufacture of inexpensive wristwatches in 1948.[9]

Helbert, Wagg had acted as financiers to Smiths for a decade. After 1945, when Lionel Fraser dominated the firm, arranging numerous capital raisings for firms such as Tube Investments, Leyland Motors, and Standard Motors, it was to him that Allan and Ralph Gordon-Smith naturally turned for financial advice and transaction execution.[10] For a while in late 1945 there was even a plan to recruit one of Fraser's colleagues, Gordon Munro MC, as Smiths' 'Financial Director'.[11] To fund Smiths' capital expenditure, early in 1946 Helbert, Wagg successfully raised £640,000 in a fully underwritten new share issue, over 90 per cent of which went to existing shareholders.[12] This put the firm in a position to press forward during the year with factory acquisition and expansion. Autop, a small die-casting company, was acquired to produce tin, Mazak, and aluminium castings for Cricklewood and Witney.[13] Bridge Works, adjoining the Cricklewood site, was added to the property portfolio, while Allan Gordon-Smith went on government-supported shopping trips to Switzerland, to buy machine tools, materials, and parts.[14] Reflecting its financial support, the machine tools installed at Ystradgynlais bore a metal 'Ministry of Supply' plate.[15]

This period was characterized by shortages of all sorts—the motor industry suffering, for example, from a quota system under which scarce steel was allocated according to success in meeting export targets.[16] Smiths, Ingersoll, and Vickers also planned volume watch production on Tyneside, but the necessary Swiss machinery could not be secured.[17] While strikes became more common at the motor manufacturers, the problem for suppliers such as Lucas and Smiths was availability of labour.[18] Barrett wrote to Stafford Cripps in early 1946, 'our prime factories . . . have between half and five-eighths of the complement of personnel they require and absenteeism is on a much higher scale than it should be'.[19]

With more manpower available in Wales, Smiths wanted a second factory (62,000 ft^2/5,800 m^2) built at Ystradgynlais, under the Distribution of Industry Act (1945), to which the Enfield clock business would be moved, and spent the rest of 1946 struggling through bureaucracy to secure approval. Construction commenced in early 1947, on land sold to the government by Smiths.[20] With Cricklewood bursting at the seams, the coil-winding operation was moved from London to Wales, while in Scotland conditions were immediately very cramped.[21] The shortages extended to workers' accommodation. Just as Smiths had needed to buy or build houses at Cheltenham and Carfin, now they needed to do the same in Wales, and twelve were under way by the autumn, with more planned.[22] At this stage, Smiths was happy to expand its housing portfolio, and acquired MAP's interest in the Meadoway Estate in Cheltenham. From financing and building houses, the natural extension was to finance individuals, and in May 1947, the board agreed to advance up to a total of £10,000 to assist key staff to buy houses.[23]

A harsh winter: 1947

Provided the position did not worsen in regard to the delivery of materials and labour supply, they could look forward to the future with reasonable confidence.

(*The Economist*[24])

The winter caught everyone unawares and brought problems. Severe snow in late January 1947 and a coal shortage combined to create a national fuel crisis. With bread in short supply, existing coal stocks frozen, and little sign of respite in the weather, Manny Shinwell, Minister of Fuel and Power, was forced to announce 'the most drastic restraint of industry ever known in this country'.[25] With a ban on the use of power for industrial purposes, factories across the country closed for extended periods. Smiths endured a forced three-week stoppage at its London factories, leading to significant losses, though a small benefit came from the reorganization of the workload to use heavier load machines at night, leading to a 30 per cent reduction in daytime power use.[26]

But expansionist planning continued. In view of the importance of Scotland in Smiths' new structure, it appointed to the main board one of Scotland's leading industrialists, Sir Frederick Stewart, already well-known as chairman of Kelvin, Bottomley & Baird. Scottish Industrial Estates, established in 1937 to create factories in 'distressed areas', was Smiths' landlord in Carfin and Stewart's role was to cut through bureaucracy holding up expansion.[27] Eventually a small extension was agreed in May 1947, tied to jewel manufacture—a strategic project 'subsidized heavily' by MoS, described as 'the one serious effort to produce high-grade watch jewels in the UK'.[28] Smiths managed the jewel project at Avon House Works in Warwick, and in June formed a dedicated subsidiary, Synthetic Jewels Ltd, under Wilf Kelly. It was scheduled to move to Exeter, then to Ystradgynlais, but finally moved to Carfin in late 1947, with six staff, leading in turn to the purchase of further houses.[29]

Smiths' internal documents show a heavy focus in 1946–7 on the clock and watch businesses. During 1947, SEC's new home, Sectric House, was completed at Waterloo Road, Synchro Time Systems changed its name to English Clock Systems, and another clockmaking business, Grimshaw Baxter & J. J. Elliott, was acquired.[30] October 1947 saw the opening for business of the National College of Horology at Northampton Polytechnic, another long-standing project of Allan Gordon-Smith's, influenced by his early experience in Biel and plans for British horology. It was not to have a long life, disappearing in 1960, but it commenced with significant support at an official level from the MoS, TUC, LCC, and NPL, and from firms such as Ferranti and English Electric. Gordon-Smith was the first chairman, and Smiths lay at the heart of college life—contributing towards the 'Allan Gordon-Smith scholarship'. The details of ninety-six alumni (out of a total of 127) are detailed in a 1960 history, and at that date forty-three had worked for a Smiths group company at some stage, several in significant roles.[31] This emphasizes the role of Smiths at the heart of reconstruction and the training of a skilled workforce.

Export or perish

> *Some of you may well ask what is wrong. The simple explanation is that we are living above our means on loans and subsidies and further, we are not paying our way by exporting to the value we are importing.*
>
> (Allan Gordon-Smith speech to Cricklewood
> workers, March 1947)

Clocks and watches were still a junior part of the group in financial terms, and the motor division continued to be the backbone, headed by Charles Nichols and Frank Hurn, delivering solid results, with new products showing promise—in particular the car heater was moving from being a luxury to becoming standard, and Radiomobile radios were doing the same. The watchword of the time was 'exports' and Smiths' *PIVOT* magazine constantly reflected this national obsession. Frank Hurn, commenting on UK vehicle production numbers for September 1947, noted that 'more than 64 per cent of all the cars made during the month were destined for overseas markets. Practically every vehicle...fits some or all of the equipment produced within this Division.'[32] The issue featured good publicity from a Rolls Royce export drive, involving seven cars that toured America in the autumn, featuring Smiths radios and a complete range of instruments—having been seen off on their trip by Stafford Cripps and 'new Cabinet boy Harold Wilson', featured by British Pathé in its October 1947 film 'Britain Gets Down To It'.[33] Other articles on aviation and industrial instruments all supported the government line on exports, articulated particularly by Hugh Dalton and Cripps, both friends to the firm—Dalton opening the Ystradgynlais works on 15 March, seeing through an initiative he had been involved in from the outset.[34] The other new venture, at Carfin, was up to speed, exporting a third of its production, and produced its millionth alarm clock in August 1947, prompting congratulations from Cripps.[35]

KLG arranged a novel export in late 1946. The government had allowed Rolls Royce jet technology to transfer to Russia (surprising in retrospect), and KLG echoed this with an extendable five-year deal to provide the Russian authorities with technical advice and training for six engineers in manufacturing aero and commercial plugs, for £30,000 up-front and £6,000 per year for the last three years.[36] KLG's other novelty were ceramic guides for the textile industry, signalling the birth of a new and non-motor-related ceramics business line.[37]

The industrial instruments business was also exporting widely, with AT hand tachometers shipped in large numbers, as well as thermometers and gauges from Harcourts. In October 1947, a share exchange finally brought together Henry Hughes and Kelvin, Bottomley & Baird in a new majority-owned company, Kelvin & Hughes, marrying complementary interests in aviation and marine instruments, all heavily exported. Perhaps most notable, certainly in the press, was the aviation division's successful launch on 21 September of the SEP1 all-electric automatic pilot, developed for the government and the brainchild of Smiths' highly talented engineer F. W. Meredith, who received a gold watch to commemorate the event (see Plate 35).[38] There is a remarkable back story to Meredith. Categorized as a 'left-wing agitator at the time of the General Strike in 1926' and as 'one of a group of Soviet sympathisers' at the RAE from 1932 to 1938, his MI5 case file had long been open.[39] Under interrogation by William Skardon in early 1949, Meredith admitted passing secrets to a Soviet handler between 1936 and 1939, including details of a Smiths bombsight. Allan Gordon-Smith was taken into MI5's confidence, and Meredith's career with Smiths continued, the view being taken that, following his confession, ongoing security risks were outweighed by the contribution to be had from someone described as 'little short of a genius'.[40]

A change at the helm

It is not easy to follow such a man, and his son Mr. Ralph Gordon-Smith has that task to face.

(*PIVOT*, August 1947)

In 1947, Allan Gordon-Smith clocked up thirty-three years as managing director of a group that now included more than twenty companies and more than 10,000 employees. In August, changes that had been agreed by the board more than a year earlier were implemented, and he stepped down as managing director in favour of Ralph, though remaining as chairman.[41] This moved Ralph onto an increased salary of £10,000 plus 2½ per cent of profits, with generous expenses. This should be seen in the context of Allan's arrangements, set to run to August 1952, totalling £20,000 in salary, plus 5 per cent of profits (in a combined minimum of £30,000) (2010: £915,000), and nearly £8,000 in expenses. Recalling Dennis Barrett's comment that, while Allan was alive there was no doubt who was running the firm, the compensation arrangements offer compelling evidence. It is also debatable whether Allan Gordon-Smith was happy to begin succession planning with Ralph's appointment. The two apparently never got on particularly well and it was clear to all that they were from quite different moulds. Ralph, the quieter, more studious type, was dominated by his wife Beryl whom he used as a shield—Allan apparently never forgave Beryl for arranging her marriage for the same day as the Ascot Gold Cup in 1932.[42] By contrast, Allan was a commanding presence, dominating conversation and probably many relationships—outspoken, lively, passionate, and highly competitive. Rex Smith, his nephew, was similar, and was also helping to run the clocks business, Allan's baby. As a result, Ralph's mother Bea felt the need to fight his cause and to advance his interests.[43] Just as we have seen that it was unlikely that Ralph made much of the running during the war, while Allan was notionally engaged at MAP, it seems likely from August 1947 onwards, though Ralph presented reports and plans at board meetings, that his father still pulled the strings.

Progress despite severe shortages: 1948

We are now the largest producers of motor car instruments in Europe, probably the largest single manufacturer of clocks and watches in the world, and makers of more aircraft instruments than any other concern.

(Chairman's speech, 1949)

The motor division continued to move powerfully ahead, with Bluecol, the anti-freeze developed with ICI, establishing itself as an industry standard, while car ventilation and Radiomobile sets led the main charge (see Plate 23). Richard Cave, a future managing director, had joined Radiomobile as commercial manager back in 1946, but a wider

Smiths audience will first have encountered him in a 1948 cartoon in *PIVOT*, titled 'meet the Radiomobile new boys'.[44] These included Peter Blair (drawn rather short), who would later succeed Rex Smith as head of publicity, but most noticeable was Cave, shown next to Blair at twice his height and cutting a very imposing figure— reminiscences of Cave invariably start with his height.

In addition to instruments sold to exporting manufacturers, a new development was Smiths' success in securing direct export orders for instruments themselves. But as with much of industry the problem of a lack of raw materials remained, leading to high prices and a tendency by firms to stockpile against the risk of shortages. This in turn led to higher figures for stock across manufacturing industry, and the Smiths board was conscious of the need to reduce the amount of working capital tied up.[45] Concern at the high prices of raw materials led to a £50,000 reserve in the year-end accounts against possible losses should material prices fall. Similarly, having finally purchased the Stoll building at Cricklewood from MoS, the firm quickly explored sale and leaseback options to release cash. Overall, the firm took a cautious approach, since though profits exceeded £1m for the first time, taxation was still running at 60 per cent.

At Cheltenham, the high-grade watch project was progressing rapidly but it was not just materials that were short—more labour was needed. At a planning meeting in mid-1947, it was reported of the factory that 'at the moment it has only 60 per cent of the required labour force'.[46] Machine tools were hard to secure, and Dennis Barrett was detailed both to help source these and to help arrange financing. As with the Ystradgynlais machinery, it was the MoS that was key, and Barrett succeeded in getting the ministry to finance equipment, on a rental basis.[47] With demand for housing, and further recruitment plans, the need for new building threw up a debate over the competing uses for local land, whether for agriculture while food was still rationed, or for new houses—a debate reflected in stormy planning meetings and angry letters to the local press over the course of 1947–8.[48] Smiths boosted its investment in the Bishop's Cleeve Housing Association, which in turn commenced work on a further seventy-six semi-detached houses in mid-1948, partly in anticipation of the move of all remaining aircraft engineering work to Cheltenham by year-end. No longer a shadow factory, Smiths' visibility at Cheltenham was increasing—sufficient to attract the BBC, and a highlight for several staff in August 1948 was the visit of Richard Dimbleby for his *Down Your Way* programme, interviewing Sylvia Moulder and Joan Wright on their delicate work of clock assembly and hairspring fitting.[49] At the same time, a heavy workload for the aircraft instrument side of the business is explained throughout the fifteen years after the war by the significant growth in passenger miles recorded—see Figure 6.2.

Conditions were much worse in Ystradgynlais (known to many as 'I strangled Alice'). The 'standard' factory had numerous problems, with its roof, windows, and solid-fuel heating making it 'far from ideal for the production of high precision instruments, such as watches, for which dust-free conditions are a prerequisite'.[50] A second factory had been built in early 1947, for the rehoused Enfield clock operation, but Smiths desperately needed an extension to the watch factory 'as a means of obtaining dust-free working conditions and additional assembly space'. Barrett spent

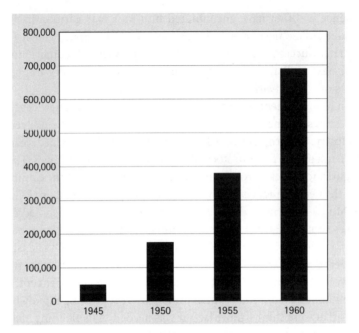

FIGURE 6.2 Scheduled service, revenue traffic passenger miles (1945–1960) (millions).

Source: ICAO (data for member countries only)

the rest of 1948 lobbying the Board of Trade, various ministries, and local Welsh offices. With a general reluctance to commit to any further public expenditure, Smiths was not helped by the fact that at one point its glazing requirements alone represented one-sixth of the glass nationally available, owing to a soda ash shortage.[51] Under heavily improvised conditions, Smiths achieved 10,000 units per week by late 1948, but the target was double this and growing, and the economics were not looking good. Anglo-Celtic had lost nearly £57,000 (2010: £1.7m) since inception, and lost a further £41,000 in 1948 as it failed to achieve volumes and efficiencies. The tough conditions at the plant will have contributed to the decision to send one of Smiths' key generals to run it—Harry Norman Walford, whom we last met running the Enfield operation.[52]

A tough environment, yet growth: 1949

Roll up sleeves, Loosen collar,
Speed production, Win the Dollar.

(Winning entry, KLG slogan competition)

The theme of shortages extended into 1949. Yet more space was called for at Cheltenham for aviation, plus the clocks and watches, while the motor division needed a whole new site for the expansion of its heater operation, experiencing strong demand from a market that, despite an austere climate, demanded car heating as standard.[53] The solution came in September with the purchase of significant land and factory space on a former airfield at Witney, previously a 'civilian repair unit' at which de Havillands had serviced Spitfires and Hurricanes.[54] Unsurprisingly, given experience elsewhere, thoughts soon turned to the purchase of houses at Witney, or to financing their construction. This marked the beginning of a major site for Smiths (see Plates 36 and 37).

In Scotland, the Carfin factory produced its third, and then fourth millionth alarm, squeezing the fifth in between Christmas 1949 and New Year, but cramped conditions necessitated action—a MoS official reported 'conditions are critical. Overcrowding is such that if there should be any fire the results could lead to heavy loss of life.'[55] This called for urgent action, and towards year-end, Sir Frederick Stewart opened negotiations with Scottish Industrial Estates to secure a new site for alarm production.[56]

While shortages of labour, space, and raw materials were constant themes, the firm nevertheless managed to continue growth, in sales, profits, and net assets, with a large percentage of its production exported, whether directly or indirectly. To promote those exports, Allan Gordon-Smith, Bea, Major Carington of KLG, and his wife, completed a 27,500 mile world tour in early 1949, taking in America, Canada, New Zealand, and Australia, meeting governments, clients, and employees. The government took drastic action with the devaluation of sterling by 30 per cent in September, in recognition that it was overvalued and largely to support exports, triggering a spate of competitive devaluations elsewhere. Remarkably, the move, though a shock to many in the sterling area, appears to have been of no consequence to Smiths at all—meriting a cursory mention in *PIVOT* six months later, but going entirely unnoticed in board minutes and in Gordon-Smith's year-end address to shareholders, when he chose instead to focus on the perils of nationalization, which he argued would 'stultify enterprise and initiative'.[57] Smiths was clearly untroubled by a move that would most likely be for the benefit of its main clients in the motor industry, coming at a time when Britain was the world's leading car exporter, representing close to half of the world's total.[58]

If Smiths' management did not like nationalization, it nevertheless wanted strong state assistance of various sorts, especially for the clocks and watches. A transaction in Scotland hints at a *quid pro quo*. ICFC's joint ventures with the Treasury through its DATAC committee to finance small companies in the late 1940s had not been successful.[59] One of these was Ming Ware of Dundee, a struggling watchcase-making firm that had been nursed for some time before Smiths took a controlling interest in 1950. The Treasury and Smiths each advanced £50,000 to recapitalize the firm and ICFC wrote off 60 per cent of its loan. It may have been a natural fit, but the suspicion lingers that Smiths were encouraged into what would prove a poor acquisition.[60]

Despite the difficult environment, aviation, the motor division, marine instruments, and clocks were all profitable. Watches on the other hand represented a drag as the businesses were slow to develop. Anglo-Celtic was still losing money, while Cheltenham's stubbornly high production costs continued to necessitate an internal subsidy in order to achieve a workable retail price.[61]

Factory enlargement

The Ministry of Supply strongly supported Smiths' application for the Gowkthrapple factory and are most anxious to see Smiths in operation as soon as possible.

(MoS memorandum, 1950[62])

Allan and Ralph Gordon-Smith made their first visit to Gowkthrapple, six miles south-east of the Carfin plant, in early January 1950 and saw the 153,000 ft² (14,200 m²) factory, only recently completed by MoS for the Brush Electric Co., which had altered its plans.[63] Immediate estimates were that at least £100,000 would be needed to equip it for the transfer of alarm clock production, with a plan to leave jewel production occupying a quarter of the old Carfin site. The plan saw peak employment of 1,200, of which 785 would be women, 305 men, and 110 'juveniles'.[64] Continued support from Scottish Industrial Estates saw the local authority absorb costs relating to Smiths' improvements.[65]

In the motor division, Hurn will have been busy supervising the large 140-acre Witney project, to which all heater production would be moved, together with flexible drives, under the management of Harry Smith.[66] As elsewhere, the move immediately created housing problems, leading to the creation of the Windrush Housing Association and the purchase of a remarkable further 250 acres of land.[67]

With major plans for two sites, Smiths wanted the latest thinking, and despatched a team to America under Bruce Hills, company secretary and group comptroller, which included key factory managers from around the network—Clarence Griffin of Waterloo Rd, Eric Desmond of Production Engineering, his assistant Stanley 'Brad' Bradfield, and Harry Smith of Smiths Jacking—with a brief to study factory layout, production methods, and costs.[68] Having digested their report and recommendations, consideration mid-year turned to the continued demand for more space in the motor division. Cricklewood was groaning at the seams and badly needed rationalizing and reorganizing. Hurn and Haviland both advocated securing a further 70,000 ft² (6,500 m²) of space, to accommodate the service and trade sale sections, freeing up more instrument-making space, mainly in the Stoll building at Cricklewood.[69] In November the board sanctioned a further £465,000 of further capital expenditure on plant for all the units, and for much-needed modernization at Cricklewood, but against a backdrop of the Korean War unfolding, and confidence evaporating, further new factories would have to wait.[70] However, by the end of 1950, the overall area of factory space in the group had already increased by a factor of eight, shown in Figure 6.3.

The continued strategic nature of the commitment to watch, hairspring, and jewel manufacture, now five years after the war had ended, is clear from the acknowledgement in both Smiths' papers and MoS minutes that Smiths and the Ministry were still subsidizing losses. At Cheltenham, 'after several years of difficulty', a man's watch was in full production and the next important development was a small ladies watch (the

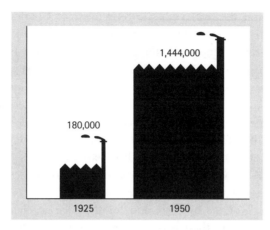

FIGURE 6.3 Factory area 1925/1950 (ft²).

Source: Smiths in 1950

size of an old sixpence), a first for the UK.[71] A large model was shown to great interest at the British Industries Fair, but it was clear that developing these watches was slow and expensive—15,000 hours of development time in the tool room alone.[72] Smiths provided an internal subsidy of 12s 6d per watch, but Barrett was also lobbying long-term for further help from MoS. Smiths bore the loss within the clocks division, which generated profits from the mass production and export of alarms, mechanical and electric domestic clocks, a business it continued slowly to build, with the purchase of Dennis & Robinson, case-makers in Brighton, and a recommitment to the training school at Cheltenham, for which a new building was commissioned.[73]

Long careers and benefits

> *May's been with us since 1936. As May has four brothers and a brother-in-law working at Cheltenham, a brother at Ystradgynlais and ten of out eleven members of her family have worked for Smiths there's no wonder if she feels that the place partly belongs to her.*
>
> (*PIVOT*, May 1950)

Many of the employees had been with the firm for several decades, and the presentation of gold watches for long service happened frequently. A regular feature of the bi-monthly *PIVOT* was a feature 'It's My Job' involving a series of six-page illustrated tours, taking in the main factories in turn. Employees were pictured at their worksta-tions, with an explanation of their job. A noticeable feature of the captions is the mention of length of service, frequently running to ten years, sometimes over twenty, in some cases over thirty. Smiths was presented as a happy and unified family of workers, working in different parts of the country and not necessarily knowing much about each other's work, but unified. In November 1949, *PIVOT* had described the sense of shock running around the firm with the retirement of Charles Nichols, the most senior sales figure in the motor division and someone who had worked very closely with Allan Gordon-Smith since 1901, for close to fifty years.[74] His departure meant Frank Hurn became general manager and therefore the most senior officer in the motor division—the 'father of the other divisions' as Gordon-Smith called it.[75] Among other significant figures, the shock death of Sir Frederick Stewart early in 1950 robbed Smiths of a main board director, to be replaced later in the year by James Reid-Young, then director of finance at Vickers-Armstrong.[76] Another significant death, in August 1950, just as he reached retirement, was that of Primus Otto Dorer, recruited by Allan Gordon-Smith back in 1903 and the designer behind scores of inventions and Smiths patents.[77]

There were 12,500 workers by 1950, and for the salaried element a pension had been in place since 1933, but there was pressure to provide wider benefits. In March, Nichols (now a non-executive director) gathered with the shop stewards to discuss the balance of the wartime Hard Luck Fund he had started in 1940. The conclusion was that a workers' convalescent home should be acquired, with the firm and the athletics club jointly funding running expenses.[78] A search resulted in the purchase mid-year of Solent Edge, a former guest house on Bluett Avenue in Seaview, Isle of Wight—a choice approved by Bill Lewis, the personnel manager, whose retirement neatly coincided, allowing him and his wife to move to the Isle of Wight as first caretakers in early 1951, with nine ex-Smiths 'guests'.[79] By late 1952, as many as 300 Smiths workers had visited, rising to 1,000 by the end of 1955.[80]

The horns are drawn in: 1951

> There is, in short, a very real danger that in the next twelve months the British people will experience a fall of the value of their money such as they have rarely if ever known before.
>
> (*The Economist*, March 1951[81])

1950 had seen Labour retain power with a significantly reduced majority, against a backdrop of impatience with continued austerity some five years after the war's end. Britain's involvement in the Korean War from mid-1950 was deeply unpopular, but firms like Smiths would initially have seen some benefits from increased military spending, though other wider economic effects soon started to bite. At the January 1951 board meeting, which Allan Gordon-Smith attended, there was naturally mention of the fact the firm had entered its centenary year, but it was decided to defer discussion to a later meeting. Instead, the meeting largely centred around Ralph Gordon-Smith's analysis of the firm's resources versus its commitments:

> It was agreed that in view of continued inflationary tendencies, re-armament and
> the general international situation, no further schemes . . . involving capital expend-
> iture or the acquisition of further businesses should be contemplated other than
> those that are absolutely essential.[82]

After months of careful planning and liaison by Helbert, Wagg with Smiths' institutional investors, early in 1951 the firm went through a major reorganization of its capital
structure, simplifying the share issues, capitalizing reserves, and also raising £900,000
in new money.[83] With increased gross profits of £1.1m and £420,000 net for 1950, the
chairman's speech in early December had been bullish, full of both good news on
strong past performance and full of promise for the developments ahead, so the tone of
the January board meeting reflected a quite different sentiment. As *The Economist*
pointed out, wholesale prices had risen 19 per cent from June 1950 to February 1951.
Smiths' situation was common across manufacturing industry—depreciation of historic prices failed to reflect rising replacement costs, while increased turnover, though
welcome, required further financing of more costly stock and work-in-progress. Cash-
flow was pressed, hence the importance of official assistance where possible—an
example being government support for two-thirds of the cost of a proposed new
Basingstoke factory for Kelvin & Hughes (see Plate 48).[84] It was a rocky year econom-
ically, with meat rationing at its worst ever, corporate taxes rising, and reverses for the
motor industry with purchase tax on cars rising significantly. Despite the long-standing
national emphasis on exports, which Smiths continued to follow, a balance of payments crisis further dented Labour's position. The political colour of Smiths' board was
probably uniformly Conservative, despite close relationships with key Labour figures
over many years—witness the firm's contribution of £5,000 in 1951 to the United
Industrialists' Association (2010: £120,000), a Tory fundraising organization. This
was a regular contribution over many years, with Dennis Barrett (an Association
board member) always presenting the contribution for approval.[85] On political
grounds, the Conservative win in the winter of 1951 election will have been welcome,
but the economic consequences less so.

National housing programmes under any government were still failing to meet
demand for homes, and *PIVOT* devoted a double-page spread in September 1951 to
explanations of Smiths' plans.[86] Beyond the original wartime constructions of fifty-
three houses and 124 bungalows at the Cheltenham site, Smiths had now supported a
further 150 houses at Bishop's Cleeve, with 140 more planned and under way, reflecting
less the watch business and much more the growth of aviation—led by national defence
spending. At Ystradgynlais, twenty-four houses had been built, and fourteen had been
purchased at Carfin, while at Witney permission had been granted for the first 100
houses on the Windrush Estate, to be ready mid-1952. By the time the houses would be
ready, Smiths' policy would alter again—rather than being content to fund a large
portfolio of houses, whether directly or through financing housing associations, 1952
would see a new desire emerge, to sell houses to their occupants wherever possible, to
free up cash.[87]

The Guvnor's gone

When the life of this great man comes to be written in full what a story there will be to tell.

(*PIVOT*, May 1951)

Looking back to 1950, one of the most memorable stories in Smiths' folklore involved a race. Allan Gordon-Smith had moved on from Walhurst Manor at Cowfold. Graham Smith speculates he never quite fitted into the local 'set'. For example, in a race at the Crawley and Horsham point-to-point, where by tradition members only would compete, he had been known to enlist John Hislop, his favoured jockey, who though amateur was clearly a leading National Hunt competitor—hardly endearing, but reflecting an intensively competitive streak. In 1946, Allan and Bea moved to Molecomb, a grand house on the Goodwood Estate, reached by a mile-long drive, where Gordon-Smith could extend his stables.[88] He was a good friend of his landlord, Freddie, 9th Duke of Richmond, and once settled there seems to have been better accepted into the local racing fraternity. Entertainment was lavish and Graham Smith recalls extraordinary parties—'champagne on the lawn, and Christmas was fantastic'. The social programme continued to include shooting, and an annual trip to Scotland where Gordon-Smith would take a large house, travelling up by train, while Wally the chauffeur would take two days with the luggage. Roger Hurn recalls his father's stories of the shooting where, owing to the lack of a neck cord on Gordon-Smith's eyeglass, the recoil of his shotgun would frequently mean the loss of a lens as it popped out and fell to the ground. His loader would keep a stock of spares in a waistcoat pocket, ready to hand over both gun and replacement monocle when needed.[89]

Gordon's sporting determination led him over years to mount challenges in the key meetings of the racing calendar—he was a steward at Goodwood and a member of the National Hunt committee from 1949. He had won the Ascot Gold Vase in the 1930s with Fearless Fox, but his campaign towards a Grand National win started in 1947 with Kami, ridden again by Hislop, finishing third. Losing Kami to a fall in January 1948, Gordon-Smith and Jack Olding purchased Cloncarrig, the horse that has gone down in posterity linked to Gordon-Smith.[90] This led to wins in the Molyneux Chase in 1949 and 1950, and the Becher Chase in 1950. In the 1949 Grand National, Cloncarrig fell, but was favoured to do well the next year. In the 1950 Grand National, starting at 25-1, Cloncarrig was ahead at the twenty-ninth fence, with Freebooter beginning to overhaul over the last half mile—'there were no whips out and both seemed to be going really well'—but then at the final fence, neck and neck, 'Cloncarrig just touched it and fell on landing'.[91] Gordon-Smith's chauffeur recalled 'the Guv'nor turned to me and all he said was "Well, that's how it goes, Wally"'.[92] Eddy Downey remembered 'the whole company cried when his horse fell at the Grand National. They talked about it for days afterwards. Messages were sent to him from ordinary people on the shop floor about how sad they were for him. It was a dreadful thing.'[93] It is revealing that Gordon Smith's relationship with his workforce, forged over years of promoting sports events, even taking part in early matches himself, bridged a divide that might otherwise have existed—factory floor workers 'on-the-clock' were proud of their chairman's race-horses and shared his victories and disappointments.

The board meeting of January 1951 was the last Allan Gordon-Smith attended. It was apparently already clear that he was gravely ill. Staying at St Ermin's Hotel in West-minster, as was his habit from before the war, he died on 12 February 1951. The flag on the 'whited sepulchre' of 317 Edgware Road was lowered to half-mast as staff around the country went into shock—Rex Smith simply told his son 'the Guvnor's gone'.[94] A memorial service at St Paul's, Knightsbridge, a week later, was remarkable for the breadth of mourners. Beyond family they included Members of Parliament, close colleagues from MAP days, eminent bankers, representatives of the motor industry, and from the horological world came the Astronomer Royal and liverymen of the Clockmakers Company, and many from the firm and its clients.

An intriguing mystery emerged in April with the publication of his will. It was clear with his father Samuel that some shrewd estate planning had been achieved. In Allan's case, the evidence tends more to suggest he had burned through the significant sums received over the years from the firm. The gross value of his estate at £60,260 was modest, in relative terms (2010: £1.5m), given the amounts he earned. The net amount proved was just £464, provoking some comment. The *Daily Telegraph* remarked 'his solicitors refused yesterday to make any statement on the liabilities' before continuing to catalogue rather pointedly and in some detail the sort of dividends and income Gordon-Smith might have enjoyed.[95] A life lived at full throttle left the tank empty at the end.

The loss of Allan Gordon-Smith altered the balance of power significantly. Although Ralph was appointed chairman at the next board meeting, his nephew Rex was later to recall there were questions as to whether an external chairman should have been brought in.[96] For months much administration was needed to readjust the boards of group companies reflecting Allan's death, including the board of EMI, where Ralph replaced his father. Bea was awarded a lifetime pension of £2,000 per annum, and Frank Hurn and Dennis Barrett (newly CBE) both joined the main holding company board, where James Reid-Young of Vickers received a knighthood in the Birthday Honours.[97] The first of many signals that, in losing Allan Gordon-Smith, the watch and clockmaking business was also losing its champion came with Professor Indermuehle's decision to leave the Cheltenham school in the autumn of 1951.[98] In an editorial for the *School Digest* at Easter he wrote 'the school has lost its best friend and staunchest supporter', just as the school was about to transfer to its own new building in May.[99]

'The rebirth of an industry?'

> *As a matter of national policy a clock and watchmaking industry would be developed and maintained in the country after the war.*
>
> (Dennis Barrett, 1952)

If the clocks and watches had lost their champion, nevertheless they had a new one. Under this title and with the policy comment quoted, Dennis Barrett contributed the lead article to the March 1952 *PIVOT*, which also marked the death of George VI.[100] He rehearsed the familiar history of pre-war German competition and the efforts of Smiths to recreate a national horological industry, as part of a patriotic effort to generate export earnings and to ensure more precision-engineering capacity as a strategic standby. Whether in *PIVOT*, or throughout board minutes over the next year and more, or lobbying government departments, or speaking as chair of the British Watch and Clockmakers, Barrett, 'who could talk the hind leg off a donkey', provided a 'powerful voice' in support of the industry.[101]

Extensive expansion was well under way, irrespective of Allan Gordon-Smith's death, and both Witney and Gowkthrapple (hereafter Wishaw) opened for business. Peter Graham remembers working on the scale planning model of the Wishaw factory in 1950, but the real thing was opened in September 1951 by George Strauss, Minister of Supply, revealing 150,000 ft² (14,000 m²) of the most up-to-date mass-production equipment, designed to handle 90,000 clocks per week, or 4.5m per annum—Strauss was handed Smiths' nine millionth alarm clock at the ceremony.[102] Eric Desmond, project engineer, claimed it to be 'the finest of its kind in the world', following Smiths' 'study of many of the world's outstanding flow production factories'.[103] One extraordinary feature solved the problem of adjusting to time the large volume of clocks. Desmond's answer was 'a specially constructed overhead conveyor carrying on average 50,000 clocks', stretching round the entire site. This was in itself 'a master clock making a circuit once in 24 hours to an accuracy of a fraction of a second', the timing perfected by English Clock Systems.[104] A finished clock was placed on the belt, and would return to the same spot exactly 24 hours later. If it showed a different time from the 'standard' time of the conveyor belt, a quick adjustment could be made—a simple yet remarkably elegant solution (see Plates 40 and 41).[105]

Much of the internal management discussion for the balance of the year revolved around the clock division, where we have seen there were internal cross-subsidies, with profits from volume production covering losses on the developing speciality lines. Barrett faced several difficulties, for example in sourcing steel, and the fact that alarm clocks were subject to Board of Trade 'price control orders', though he successfully negotiated to raise the limits in February 1952, allowing a 7–10 per cent price increase, reflecting the change of political climate under the new government.[106]

Several plans to move operations from one plant to another were discussed during the year, in an attempt to increase efficiency for both the motor division and the clocks and watches, finally resulting in a decision to close the original Enfield clock factory in London, to move watch-case manufacture from Dundee to Ystradgynlais, and then to close Ming Ware in Dundee altogether. Clock-case manufacture by J. E. V. Winterbourne (acquired in 1939) would cease at the Goodwood Works on the North Circular Road, presumably to be concentrated in Dennis & Robinson of Brighton, leaving space for Radiomobile to be rehoused.[107]

Fortunately for Barrett, more than a year's lobbying paid off in July 1952 and MoS, now headed by Duncan Sandys, finally agreed to subsidize the manufacture of high-grade watches, ending the need for an internal subsidy, but the division was in trouble.[108] Having budgeted to make a profit, Barrett knew months before the August year-end that he would break even at best. New restrictions on imports imposed in South Africa, New Zealand, and Australia (also major markets for the motor division) were damaging sales, and stock was building, absorbing cash. To make matters worse, Barrett could not easily reduce production, as he was locked into material supply contracts that his counterparts refused to alter.[109] Although invisible in the year-end accounts, a significant write-down on the stock of clocks and watches occurred.[110] Then in the autumn, margins came under the spotlight. Barrett was achieving less than 3 per cent on sales, while Ralph argued the firm had to target 25 per cent at least, and expenses at 19.5 per cent of sales needed cutting. Revealing little emotional tie to clocks and watches, the chairman instead showed distinct frustration with the state of the business.[111] It is telling that during the year a focus on income through reducing costs (versus increasing sales) was discussed as a strategy for profits.[112] Despite the gloom, some optimism must have been behind the purchase of control in Tyme Ltd, on the corner of Piccadilly and Old Bond Street—now Watches of Switzerland—presumably as an outlet for Smiths' watches, alongside competing Swiss brands.[113]

Despite the apparent strong management focus on clocks, there was plenty of activity elsewhere in the business. At Witney, production was well under way, with a workforce of 650 producing 7,000 heaters and up to 40,000 flexible drives each week.[114] Close ties to government in defence matters are revealed in deliberations on the future of the Enfield factories and whether these might be wanted for fuze manufacture.[115] At Cheltenham, a further unit, CH4, was under construction, but this was entirely government-funded and was to be devoted to guided weapons—a signal of the way the Cheltenham site was to move, heavily oriented towards aviation research and development, often led by military requirements.[116] CH4 would be significantly more heavily secured than other units, and its subsequent history is not easy to follow 'since it is necessarily shrouded in secrecy', but *PIVOT* later commented: 'the work under-taken by this Branch involves complicated mathematical investigations into controlling missiles in supersonic flight, and the design of special instruments which must work under these conditions'.[117] Not everything was defence related, of course, and the firm took particular pride in the launch of the new Comet jet in 1952, since it was largely populated with all the usual Smiths instruments, compass, sextant, gauges, and carried the automatic pilot.[118] The captain of the first scheduled passenger-jet service, from Heathrow to Johannesburg in May 1952, was Captain Alastair (Michael) Majendie, whose career path would lead him to a directorship of Smiths.[119]

The firm also had various sorts of battles on its hands. The long-standing licensing relationship with Bendix in the US, dating back to the 1930s, had soured in view of the American firm's refusal to pay royalties, now totalling £393,000 (2010: £24.4m), and Smiths finally decided to issue proceedings, beginning a long saga. Closer to home, there was a very different conflict to handle.

'Smiths workers demand work or pay'

In view of the fact that this firm is engaged on defence orders, among other things, has the Minister any information to show that this strike is in any way Communist inspired?

(*Hansard*[120])

The new Conservative government included Walter Monckton as Minister of Labour, vilified by some for having appeased the unions, but more generally assessed as an 'emollient and conciliatory' minister who kept industrial relations on an even keel.[121] Smiths, although relatively small fry, nevertheless crossed his sights.

Lawrie Nickolay was an instrument maker by training, who had joined Smiths in 1940, following in the footsteps of his older brother Phil, whose Communist politics he shared.[122] A move to Cheltenham led to two major developments: the first was Nickolay's appointment as a shop stewards' convener and then the formation of a 'combine' of shop stewards, which met monthly, bringing together representatives of the various Smiths factories. This was one of the first of such combines in the UK, allowing conveners at different factories to compare rates for piece work and to present a unified negotiation front to management. Other early examples were those at Fairey (1941), and at Vickers and English Electric (1943).[123] Nickolay was a highly active secretary for the pioneering Smiths' combine, and from then on he was to the fore in negotiations with management. The second development was a personal one, since Nickolay soon met Alys Hurley at Cheltenham, a skilled operator working on precision bench work. A Communist party member through a deep sense of natural justice, and 'not for any political conviction, because I hadn't any', she had progressed to being a shop steward, in the GMWU, the union to which most of the women belonged. Drawn together through shared ideals and union work, an affair blossomed, despite Alys already being married. This prompted a transfer away from Cheltenham in late 1944, to Smiths in London. Post-war, Nickolay became more active in the London Communist party—for example, being involved in the London squatters' movement—and as shop stewards' convener at MA2 in Waterloo Road.

This sets the scene for April 1952, when Smiths learned the Australian government was cancelling its order for £300,000 worth of clocks and watches, adding to the problem of troublesome stock levels. On 28 April, Smiths told the MA2 workers that 150 to 200 of them would be made redundant—bearing in mind this was a period when employment documentation was rudimentary, with minimal or no notice provisions. The immediate result was that 1,000 downed tools, and 500 marched to Cricklewood Broadway, led by Nickolay, to confer with shop stewards there.

Nickolay now hit the national press for the first time, emerging as the strike leader— 'Unless the management agrees to our request to protect the redundant people then workers at both factories may come out on strike.'[124] The demand put was that 'pending suitable alternative employment [the workers] remain as employees of

S. Smith & Sons', and that either Smiths or the Ministry of Labour should help find that employment. This was a 'basic principle' that the shop stewards wanted firmly established, irrespective of the availability of other local work.[125] Over the course of the next few days, about 1,000 remained on unofficial strike, while the likely redundancies rose to 350. The press and parliament were alive to the political backdrop—Nickolay's politics were well known. Several newspapers touched on the similarity between the action taken and that proposed at recent conferences, such as the Communist party congress at Easter and the Sheffield Action Committee's conference of engineering shop stewards—what the *Financial Times* classed as 'Communist and extreme Left Wing circles'.[126] The demands made were variously described as 'preposterous' and 'unprecedented' in the press, and questions were asked of the Minister of Labour in parliament, notably by Charles Fletcher-Cooke (Con).[127]

According to the *Financial Times*, Smiths 'emphasised yesterday that there was "no chance whatsoever" of meeting the men's demands', but over the course of the first week of May a compromise was worked out which can be argued to have established important new rights and to have set 'a high standard for the industry'. Nickolay's notes from June 1952 record:

> We returned to work after 9 days' strike on the basis of an agreement which sets a precedent for the industry: one month's notice of redundancy, the Ministry of Labour to work from the factory and time off to look for another job.

It was in this strike that another important figure in Smiths' industrial relations was first to rise to prominence—Emily (Emmy) Garvey, the women's convener since 1935: 'a blue-eyed blonde woman trade unionist is taking a leading part as "peace-maker" to avoid a possible spread of the strike which on Monday paralysed production'.[128]

While there was no further major strike action for nearly a decade, it is clear from the records of the Smiths Combine that it remained highly active, meeting regularly at the Cora Hotel in Euston, and maintaining constant pressure on management to increase wages, remove anomalies between factories, and to increase or standardize benefits. Nickolay left Smiths in 1956—most probably sacked, based on correspondence from the AEU, which describes his fall 'in battle with the employers'.[129] That he was seen as problematic, not just by Smiths, is revealed by a chance encounter in a Kilburn pub, early in the 1950s, when Eddy Downey was pushed aside roughly by his good friend Bill Jordan of Special Branch, not wanting to be recognized while on plain-clothes duty, following Nickolay—all part of the routine surveillance and wire-tapping that Stella Nickolay recalls being part of life, growing up in a Communist household.[130]

Smiths eventually decided it was time to secure 'the benefit of an expert adviser on Trade Unions, labour and similar matters and that a consultant should be engaged, either full or part-time', but apart from reports of high absenteeism at Ystradgynlais, its own industrial relations record reveals relatively few strikes over the years, though with such a strong reliance for business on the wider motor industry it could not help suffering when disputes happened elsewhere.[131] Austin's and Morris had merged in 1952 with a new holding company, British Motor Corporation. Charles Nichols's old friend, Lord Nuffield, had ceded control to Leonard Lord of Austin's, who took a firm stand against the National Union of Vehicle Builders at the beginning of 1953 when John McHugh, secretary of the joint shops stewards' committee, was made redundant. This led to the 'McHugh Strike' which lasted months, leading to significant damage at BMC, but also at Smiths, where Hurn had to report a downturn on the motor side as a result, despite promising development results emerging from new products on the car heating and space heating front.[132]

A difficult climb ahead: 1953

Everest conquered . . . a triumph for Smiths De Luxe watches.

(Advertisement)

Over in clocks and watches, Barrett continued to struggle. In early 1953, Ralph Gordon-Smith reviewed the clock and watch divisions, which had achieved annual sales of £3.3m, using capital of £2.4m. A 40 per cent reduction in capital employed was now targeted, and a 10 per cent return on equity (the group target remained 20 per cent).[133] Through running down stocks, Barrett had some success releasing capital, but the profit figures remained poor, ending up close to break-even.[134] Clocks per se made money, whether 30-hour alarms or designed for the mantelpiece. With 100,000 registered pigeon fanciers in the UK alone, Smiths believed it could even make money with specialist clocks used for races, producing the Skymaster.[135] But watches were different. Anglo-Celtic could break even with volume production, but 'the high grade watch made at Cheltenham was a different proposition'. Barrett 'could not see a profit on the sale of high grade watches for three or four years'.[136] Smiths even backed a jeweller in Cardiff, Mr Keir, who provided hire purchase terms to buyers of Smiths watches.[137] When this proved a success, Smiths rapidly moving to acquire the entire financing operation, but this meant it was financing the making of expensive watches at a loss, and financing retail clients to buy them.[138] Despite this dismal outcome, one bright spot was a significant government contract for the development of a watch to be used by all three services.[139]

In May 1953, the watches then achieved an extraordinary fillip with the successful climbing of Everest by Edmund Hillary and Tenzing Norgay. While Norgay wore a Rolex to the summit, Hillary was wearing a Smiths De Luxe, made in Cheltenham, for which Smiths had developed a special low-temperature lubricant.[140] In October, Ralph hosted a celebratory dinner at the Savoy for the sportsmen of the year, featuring Hillary, and the firm went on to develop a new 'Everest' model and to launch a strong advertising campaign—in 1954, a total of £100,000 was agreed for a 'prestige' advertising campaign which focused heavily on the watches.[141]

Expansion and consolidation: 1953–1955

The increase in turnover, employees and productive capacity arises mainly
from the large expansion of the motor accessory division.

(Chairman's speech, 1955)

Frank Hurn was kept busy in 1954–5 by major plans to expand the motor business yet
further. With existing space, such as Witney, he was faced with acute housing shortages, leading to further house-building schemes and arrangements to provide interest-
free loans to staff. On the products, significant resources were being committed to the
long-term development of a magnetic clutch, in a joint project with Eaton Corporation
of the United States, and at least 40,000 ft² (3,700 m²) of further space was needed.
Meanwhile, Smiths acquired more subsidiaries and redeveloped other sites: 51 per cent
of Uni-Tubes at Slough (conduit and tubing manufacture) was acquired in 1953; the old
Addressograph site on Oxgate Lane (near MA2) was acquired in early 1955, later
housing motor sales and service; extensions at the Witney site were completed over
1954–6 for expanded car heater production; finally the Wickmans factory on Edgware
Road was acquired early in 1955, for the motoring division's trade and sales departments, freeing up Cricklewood space. Since 1947, Labour's policy of directing investment into development areas had been relaxed, with the abolition in 1954 of
controversial building licences. In practice it was now easier to build in the Home
Counties and Smiths agreed a deal with John Laings for the building of a new 75,000 ft²
(7,000 m²) factory on Otterspool Way, Watford, completed in late 1955, which became
the new home for Petro-Flex tubing (see Plate 53).[142] All this expansion meant Ralph
Gordon-Smith could claim total floor space grew by a further 14 per cent over 1954–5,
probably to near 1.8 million square feet, and with it the workforce expanded to over
17,000.[143] A major development for many of these mainly hourly paid workers was the
introduction during 1955 of a non-contributory retirement and death benefit scheme,
established with an initial transfer of £178,000 (2010: £3.6m), half of which was met
from the year's profits and the balance from existing pension reserves.[144]

Away from motor and clocks and watches, an important consolidating move
occurred in late 1953. Smiths had until then owned 53 per cent of Kelvin & Hughes,
but in a share swap completed in the autumn, the remaining 47 per cent was acquired,
and early in 1954 George B. G. Potter, the managing director of Kelvin's, was added to
the main board.[145]

Consolidating its hold on other subsidiaries, Smiths acquired Vickers's holding in
the Anglo-Celtic Watch Company, early in 1954, and in mid-1955 acquired Amalgamated Wireless' stake in their joint Australian operation. Radiomobile was next, and
Smiths bought out EMI's half-share as of August 1956.[146]

Motoring in reverse: 1956

Owing to difficulties occasioned by the recession, mainly in the motor industry, we have reluctantly had to dispense with the services of a small number of employees.

(Chairman's speech, 1956)

Good news in early 1956 arrived with a ruling, in the long-running dispute with Bendix in the United States, in Smiths' favour, though it was appealed.[147] But Smiths gained confidence that they might either win again, or settle on good terms, and the sums involved were significant. This mattered as the news elsewhere was not so good—cash-flow was under pressure, against a backdrop of inflation in both wages and prices, a balance of payments deficit, and approval ratings for Prime Minister Anthony Eden, only a year into the job, plummeting. Purchase tax rises and a credit squeeze, with Bank Rate rising to 5½ per cent in February, saw the car industry immediately suffer sharply reduced sales, with inevitable knock-on effects for Smiths. In April, Hurn reported that he had managed to reduce stock by £100,000, but the target was £1m by mid-year, to free up cash.[148] To increase competiveness, he advocated reducing margins to just 5 per cent, putting some factories on a four-day week, and finally making some redundancies. By June, deliveries from Cricklewood were 35 per cent down on the average from only a few months' earlier, and 'it was obvious that a serious redundancy situation was present, particularly in connection with indirect workers'.[149] Steps were taken to retire workers who had reached retirement age, added to which a further 300 to 400 were made redundant. With the onset of the Suez Crisis, matters worsened and for the financial year ended August 1956, the motoring division's profits were halved, year on year, but overall net profits fell by only 15 per cent to £1.17m on the back of a strong performance from aviation, industrial, and marine, a result of stronger defence contracts—the positive flipside to the Suez Crisis.

Back into forward gear: 1957

I am very pleased to draw your attention to the overall recovery in profits . . . now almost restored to the level of three years ago.

(Chairman's speech, 1957)

With the arrival of Macmillan as prime minister, the first half of 1957 saw heightened confidence, with an overall improvement in the economy—in a year perhaps remembered best for his comment that 'most of our people have never had it so good'. The motoring public was cheered mid-year by the removal of fuel rationing, a hangover of the Suez Crisis, allowing parts of industry on four-day weeks to return to normal operation. Hurn reported bullishly on the motor trade in April.[150] Underlying sales of cars were recovering, though investments in motor accessories in Australia were yet to pay off. Investment and restructuring continued, keeping motor instruments at

Cricklewood, and consolidating 'hardware' at Witney—mainly the heater business (and Smiths Jacking Systems from 1958), flexible drives, but also the significant work on magnetic coupling for automatic gearboxes.[151] Hurn also reported initial discussions with a potential buyer of the same (probably Rootes) but this was long-range planning.[152] Overall, it was a busy year for the motor division, with *The Economist* featuring in detail the 'Recovery in Motors'.[153] The new Watford factory for Petro-Flex was completed, and both World Radio and R. M. Papelian Ltd were acquired from Richard Papelian to complement Radiomobile, giving Smiths access to American (Motorola) technology updates (see Plate 53).[154]

Any emphasis on factories outside London went hand-in-hand with a need for more houses, although Smiths continued wherever possible to sell properties to their tenants. At Witney, Smiths advanced the necessary 10 per cent needed by the housing association to build 100 more homes, the balance coming from the local council—an arrangement repeated in 1958 for a further sixty.[155] As an interesting social comment, when C. S. Steadman was made general manager at Witney and wanted a new house built, the board noted 'he had been asked to have one built commensurate with this station', and lent him £3,000 to help.[156]

Hurn, newly elected a vice-president of the SMMT, was met with two less comfortable issues mid-year.[157] Harry Smith of Smiths Jacking Systems had been with the firm for twenty years, but the lifting-jack business was no longer viable, and a settlement was agreed under which he left to work at a subcontractor.[158] More dramatically, the parent company, Smiths Motor Accessories, KLG, and British Jaeger were visited by the Monopolies Commission in connection with an enquiry into electrical equipment for vehicles which would run for several years, revealing the cartel arrangements Lucas and Smiths made in 1930 to divide business between them, terminated only recently in March 1956—Smiths having understood the 'indications of disapproval to the existence of such agreements' from the legislature.[159]

If the motor sector's prospects looked rosy, the same was not true of the clock and watch divisions. In 1943, Smiths workers had responded strongly to calls for aid to the Soviet Union and raised money for the Stalingrad Hospital Fund.[160] Pro-Soviet rhetoric still coloured comments in *PIVOT* immediately after the war, but enthusiasm naturally waned as the political map changed. Contact was however maintained, and among the regular visitors to Smiths' factories Robert Lenoir hosted a delegation led by Mr Britsko, the USSR Deputy Minister of Medium Machinery Construction, at Cheltenham in July 1955.[161] A return invitation to Russia was issued—an offer taken up by a hand-picked crack team in the autumn of 1956, including Barrett and Lenoir, all briefed to record in great detail their findings at Moscow's No. 1 and 2 watch factories.[162] Barrett returned more concerned than ever. With a total ban on imports, significant investment, and a commitment to technical training, Russia was producing 24m watches per annum, with plans for 50m. Barrett commented Russia had 'but to press the switch to divert supplies to Britain to cause us real problems'.[163]

In horological circles, Smiths and its friends continued to be influential—Harold Buckland was master of the Clockmakers Company in 1957, and Smiths still dominated the BWCMA—but close to home Barrett was faced with underloaded factories, and over-high stock levels, inflated by items for Smiths Industrial.[164] A £175,000 order from Poland for clocks and watches, financed by Warburg (a first mention of the firm's involvement with Smiths), would have been welcome, but the high-grade watches were still budgeted to lose £20,000, as well as consuming £100,000 (2010: £1.9m) in 'prestige' advertising.[165] Budgeting itself was a sore point— in autumn 1956 Barrett had forecast a respectable profit, but in January, March, and April 1957 had to announce successive downward revisions. A symbolic blow for clocks now fell. Since late 1942 the bi-monthly in-house news magazine had been called *PIVOT*. Clocks and watches had long been at the heart of Smiths but Graham Smith believes this name, and its close association with the division, did not sit well in an increasingly diversified group, and the September 1957 issue was the last. The more journalistic *Smiths News* was launched in October, in tabloid size and with larger pictures, rapidly reaching a circulation of 18,000, of which 3,000 were distributed outside the company.

The aviation business was riding relatively high, despite government cutbacks, in the slipstream of strong demand for autopilots and flight systems for civil aircraft— which is not to say the government business was not important. A budget discussion for 1957/8 made clear the division's figures could vary by £200,000 dependent on changes of government policy on armaments and development programmes. The relative importance of aviation is marked (in terms of returns)—the division was budgeted to make a 21 per cent margin on sales, exceeded only by Kelvin & Hughes, at 23 per cent, while motor and clocks and watches were both expected to produce just 7–8 per cent.[166] At the AGM in December 1957, reflecting the strong adoption of a modern model, Ralph Gordon-Smith emphasized the value of splitting a business into the different divisions, articulating a principle closely associated with several of his successors—a policy of 'Three D's': decentralization of operations, delegation of responsibility and authority, and diversification of products. He also announced a turnaround after two softer years, with net profits approaching £1.3m. Bringing issued capital closer into line with capital employed, nearly £3m of reserves were capitalized, approximating to the amount reinvested in the business over the previous three years.

Expeditionary force

> *I was very proud to have with me personally the Smiths Pocket Chronometer used by Captain Scott. This watch although over 46 years old gave precision timing and was carried by me throughout our long trek.*
>
> (Vivien Fuchs to Ralph Gordon-Smith[167]—see Plate 12)

The Commonwealth Trans-Antarctic Expedition had been years in planning, culminating in a ninety-nine-day overland crossing, during which Vivien Fuchs reached the South Pole on 19 January 1958. David Pratt, a D-Day veteran, was the engineer responsible for heavy modifications to the Sno-Cats and tractors. He recalls a team of several dozen from Smiths 'brilliantly rewired all my vehicles with silicone cables to deal with operating temperatures down to minus 65 F. They also installed the battery temperature thermometry I had decided on and . . . did a great job against the clock. Smiths gave their work in support of the Expedition for which we were most grateful. They also gave each member a gold wrist watch.'[168] In addition, Smiths donated clocks, sledge meters (just as it had for Scott's original expedition), instruments, and a variety of engine and cabin heaters from Witney, which endured their most severe test to date, and much more—in all equipment worth £15,000 (2010: £275,000).[169] All of this combined to provide excellent advertising material, coupled with the earlier association with Hillary's ascent of Everest with a Smiths watch and the efforts of a full-time competitions team—keeping Smiths' name associated with firsts and records (see Plate 50). Within months, a major advertising campaign would commence, emphasizing the breadth of the Smiths group, to ensure the brand was not associated solely with volume production items, but also with prestige and high-tech items—all under the strapline 'Smiths—a name with a world of meaning'.

The recovery in the motor industry through 1957 accelerated into an 'outright boom' in 1958 according to *The Economist*, and Smiths rode the wave, paying a special interim dividend 'not to incur additional liability for profits tax'.[170] It could claim other successes, for example with the commissioning in 1958 of the Comet IV airliner, which was to have a thirty-year life, populated with Smiths instruments, and its automatic pilot. Extensive developmental work was also being undertaken in collaboration with the government's Blind Landing Experimental Unit (BLEU), using Smiths' autopilot as the basis for joint development work. 'By October 1958, BLEU, in conjunction with Smiths, had completed more than 2,000 automatic landings using this system'.[171] Cheltenham was also selected to collaborate on the control system for the experimental Black Knight ballistic research vehicles, tested at Woomera from 1958 onwards, which yielded positive results.[172] Much of this developmental work will have been supported by new 25,000 ft^2 (2,300 m^2) research laboratories opened at Cheltenham mid-year, housing 150 staff and SEDA, an analogue computer 'used to work out aerodynamical problems'.[173] Defence contracts were crucial at Kelvin & Hughes at well, and its 'rapid photographic projector' was now used as part of the United States 'early warning system'.

It was good publicity to have De Luxe watches taken up Everest and to the South Pole, but these were all manual-wind models. In late 1958, Cheltenham finally announced an automatic version, to which Richard Goode and Major Andrew Fell contributed much, but the business still struggled and it would be April 1961 before production commenced.[174] The wider clock and watch business relied on more prosaic products, such as electric timers, which were apparently doing very well, but the result was still a profit of only £45,000, against a budget of £325,000.[175] Things did not improve as 1959 opened with Barrett once again explaining why he was so far below budget, dealing with a worldwide recession in the clock industry.[176] For the May 1959 board meeting he prepared a detailed report on his division, going back over five years' history, and providing forecasts. The business in time and control switches was presently one of the strongest elements, and overall the division was in reasonable shape, except for the high-grade watches, and on the horizon, tariff reductions were looking threatening. Ralph Gordon-Smith had his own prepared remarks on the report, which were tabled at the same time. These laid down firm guidelines:

- High-grade watches were to be segregated out and monitored separately.
- The immediate target was to achieve a 15 per cent return on the (approx.) £2m of capital employed, rising to 20 per cent by 1960.
- The factories were to be kept fully loaded at all times.
- No increase in productive capacity would be sanctioned.
- If demand from elsewhere in the group overloaded the factories, the least profitable clock lines would be dropped.

The most important issue was to keep the factories fully loaded. Barrett's defence of Allan Gordon-Smith's legacy was not proving easy. For Hurn, at least the broader motor industry was enjoying a return to strength with increased sales, but in July he had to report on the automatic gearbox that 'he and the chairman had been obliged to agree prices with Rootes which would not yield any material profit to Smiths but ought not to lose money after the smaller initial deliveries had built up'.[177] The press launch for the 'Easidrive' system fitted to a new model of Hillman Minx finally came in September—'by adopting the system of automatic transmission developed in conjunction with Smiths Motor Accessories, the Rootes Group has succeeded in marketing the first British volume-produced car . . . to be fitted with self-changing gears'.[178] The car attracted interest at the Motor Show in October, and overall press coverage was positive—even making 'car of the month' for the *Illustrated London News* motoring correspondent.[179]

While Hurn had waited for Rootes to confirm they were proceeding, and Barrett was struggling to defend his corner, another transaction occurred which at the time was not of great consequence, but which would grow in significance over time. In early 1958 Uni-Tubes (part of the motor accessory division) had acquired from Switzerland both machinery and patents from Kopex, which allowed the processing of strip material into convoluted tubing.[180] In a second transaction, closed near year-end, Uni-Tubes acquired another firm that would prove to be the foundation of a critically important future business line.

Serendipity in glass eyes

> *The war was the catalyst for the birth of the modern-day plastics industry . . .*
> *Dr Leader was therefore in the right place at the right time to experiment.*
>
> (History of Anaesthesia Society, *Proceedings*, 1988)

Solomon Leider, probably born in Poland, was a talented and driven man who progressed from an early start in Whitechapel to private practice in Harley Street, securing more than twenty patents between 1930 and 1950.[181] Changing his name along the way, Dr Sidney Arthur Leader (known as 'Pluto') qualified as both a dental and ophthalmic surgeon and established Portland Plastics in August 1940, working from his flat at 214 Great Portland Street.[182] Here he experimented with new materials for prosthetic eyes and teeth, replacing traditional ceramics and glass. He also pioneered 'plastic skin', a liquid plaster that would set to cover wounds.[183] In 1943, a visit to Major Thornton, an anaesthetist of the RAMC at Basingstoke, resulted in the idea to use PVC tubes in tracheal intubation—involving a tube inserted through the nose or mouth to maintain an airway.[184] Clinical trials by Thornton on Leader's tubing were reported on positively in the *British Medical Journal* in mid-1944, and military orders probably followed.[185] In late 1945, a fire in the cramped London accommodation led to a move to Dover, and what were expected to be temporary premises in Cherry Tree Avenue.[186] Here, 'government and export orders' were fulfilled but there was hope of future 'large potential commercial aspects' for development: 'The plastic skin and plastic surgical tubing are becoming increasingly popular in hospitals'.[187] Just as Smiths had developed factories with assistance, so Portland Plastics was helped by both local and central government, with a site for a new £50,000 (2010: £1.6m) factory compulsorily purchased, where construction commenced in early 1947. This was at Charlton Green, one of the most heavily war-damaged areas of Dover, but the project was mired in problems from the beginning, not least when the national fuel crisis stopped all production in the existing works.[188] Local opposition to the loss of buildings was significant, and the project was at the heart of a fight between local politicians, reported on by the partisan *Dover Express*.[189] Construction ceased in the autumn of 1947, probably owing to a shortage of funds, and Portland Plastics remained at Cherry Tree Avenue for a number more years. Expanding with a second works at Wear Bay Road, Folkestone, the firm moved gradually away from prosthetic eyes and teeth towards the development of new techniques for blowing (manufacturing) nylon film and the extrusion of nylon tubing. In 1953, the whole manufacturing operation was moved to Bassett House in Hythe, a large country house, and administration, which had been at 6 Victoria Street in London, was incorporated as well.[190] Leader and his family lived on the top floors, and his nephew 'vividly remember[s] that the manufactured goods were stored in the main hall which had a minstrel's gallery. It was here that there were tubs (possibly 4ft tall, 2–3ft in diameter) filled with plastic eyes of all shades. Obviously, some disappeared into my 11 year old pockets and were a great hit later that year when school resumed!'[191]

Advertising in *The Times* in 1955, Leader sought senior management help, or 'alternatively would consider amalgamation with London organisation, compatible interests, possessing requisite facilities'.[192] In the mould of Allan Gordon-Smith, Leader lived well, with fine houses, rented villas in Spain, and a Rolls Royce Silver Cloud for transport—though the clear impression is that he had a long-term problem with a shortage of capital and a lack of capacity to develop his business.[193] But his techniques in producing specialist nylon tubing were of great interest to Uni-Tubes, and by extension Smiths, for motor and aviation instrument applications. Leader sold his business to Smiths for £67,000 (2010: £1.2m) in December 1958, and though the initial interest came from elsewhere in the group, this serendipitous acquisition can be argued to be the foundation of the modern Smiths medical business.[194] Leader himself retired from active management, and remained a consultant for the remaining few years of his life.

People and places

> *Len and Ann Sharp have a total of 84 years' service between them—he joined the Company in 1915 and she followed in 1919. They celebrate their silver wedding this year.*
>
> (*Smiths News*, February 1959)

1959 saw a number of changes to the property portfolio. Kelvin House at Wembley Park was opened in May by David Eccles of the Board of Trade. Built at a cost of £250,000 (2010: £4.5m), this now housed the management, administration, and sales of the aviation and marine businesses, while Kelvin & Hughes secured consent to spend £75,000 on further building at their Barkingside site. Having leased the new Petro-Flex Watford factory, Laing's now wanted to sell it and approached Smiths as a natural buyer, a transaction agreed in August. At the same time, the factory adjoining the Chronos Works, occupied by Fanfolds, which Smiths had looked at before, became available again, and Smiths also agreed to purchase, creating Chronos II.[195] At the wholesale end of the business, Tucker Nunn & Grimshaw gave up their various City buildings and consolidated at Rhodesia House in Hatton Garden.

For the staff, notable appointments in 1959 included J. Anthony (Tony) Blair becoming company secretary of the parent company, on a pathway to greater things. Cambridge educated, he had served in the Royal Artillery and then trained as a lawyer, joining Smiths in 1952 to establish a legal department. Joseph Lockwood, well-known to Smiths as chairman of EMI, former partners in Radiomobile, was appointed to the main board in August.[196] There were notable losses as well, in Ben Haviland who finally retired after forty-five years' service, while his deputy for many years at Cheltenham, William E. Watson, now works manager, died aged just 56 in July. On the issue of loyalty and long service, it is worth noting that when Ralph Gordon-Smith had decided to award gold watches to those with twenty-five or more years' service there were over 400 recipients.[197] At the presentation dinner in January 1956, 250 of these were present—a large proportion had served more than thirty years. Remarkably, fourteen had served forty or more years.

Financial overview: 1946–1959

> *For each of the industries we serve, the nature of our production is so specialised that it is impossible for us to equate expansion in one against contraction in another.*
>
> (Chairman's review, 1959)

Despite Ralph Gordon-Smith's cautionary note, if the diversified portfolio of businesses in Smiths did not hedge each other perfectly, yet there were times when weak performance in one division could be compensated by strength elsewhere, so Smiths weathered two crises in the 1950s without serious damage. The figures for the first few years post-war are skewed by several factors, including the process of readjustment to peacetime manufacture. High corporate and purchase taxes continued to the early 1950s, and Smiths carried a reserve of £150,000 for excess profits tax all the way through to 1953, when a settlement was finally negotiated.[198] The firm adopted a broadly cautious approach for much of the post-war decade—for example, though it suffered rises in costs, of raw materials and through national wage agreements, it regularly held back on price increases to its own clients, nervous of losing market share. This compounded the effects of the 1951 crisis, influenced by the Korean War, when its profits fell markedly. Profits were reduced again against the backdrop of the Suez Crisis, but otherwise the period shows fairly consistent growth in overall profitability, despite the mix in fortunes of the different divisions at different times. Sales grew each year from £26m in 1955 to £40m in 1960. By the mid-1950s, the firm was earning £2–3m profit per annum, and above £3m per annum in the latter years—a return of more than 20 per cent on capital. With the exception of £900,000 in new equity raised in late 1950, growth was funded with internally generated funds, the profit and loss account being largely capitalized, in 1954 and 1958.

Towards the white heat

It has gone off rather well.

(Harold Macmillan, election day 1959)

Smiths emerged from the war as part of the military-industrial complex. Allan Gordon-Smith and his acolyte Dennis Barrett saw the continued development of the British watch and clock industry, which they had pioneered from the early 1930s, as a match of defence requirements and labour policy goals in which Smiths could continue to lead the industry—but it depended upon protectionism and subsidy. With the loss of champions such as Gordon-Smith and Cripps, and in the more liberalized trading environment under the Conservatives of the 1950s, international competition bit hard, added to which Smiths were attempting everything from luxury wristwatches to boiler clocks. It would continue to be a struggle.

The aviation industry offered great promise. The growth in civil air travel boded well for the supply of instrumentation while the Korean War and rearmament offered the prospect of longer term military development contracts and the resulting manufacturing work, though policy changes and cutbacks frustratingly emerged. Continued strong demand for Kelvin & Hughes hi-tech equipment (radar, echo-sounders, etc.), produced good returns, and on occasions helped to offset dips in performance elsewhere.

The difficulties of the period were felt most acutely in the motor accessory division, with shortages of materials (whether actual or through quotas), an increasingly militant shop-floor, a lack of labour in central locations, and inflation in raw material costs. Nevertheless the division reaped the benefits of strength in overseas sales—with the UK accounting for 52 per cent of world car exports by 1950, though this figure then declined by a half over the following decade.[199] For the business overall, it is clear that there was remarkable consistency in the long-term nature of people's careers, from the board downwards, but its most senior managers were now beginning to near the end of their careers. Succession began to become an issue.

Notes

1. Interview, 15 July 1998.
2. *HC Deb* (16 Oct. 1945), vol. 414, cc. 1045–50.
3. *PIVOT* (June 1945) 16 and (June 1946), 12–13, 18.
4. Meeting notes (7 Feb. 1945), Schroder Archive, SH 851.
5. Pressure also came from the BOT's committee on Control of Factory and Storage Premises and the Official Committee on the Balanced Distribution of Industry. TNA: BT177/910.
6. TNA: BT177/1122, 'Notes on a conference, for information of BOT' (4 Apr. 1946); Barrett to Cripps (19 Jan. 1946).
7. TNA: BT 96/225, 'Notes on a meeting with Ingersoll' (29 Jan. 1945); TNA: BT177/1122, 'Notes on a conference, for information of BOT' (4 Apr. 1946).
8. Date unknown, but predates *Minutes* (31 Oct. 1946).
9. Evans, *Time Again*, 30.
10. Richard Roberts, *Schroders: Merchants and Bankers* (Basingstoke: Macmillan, 1992), 397–409.
11. Barrington to Munro (9 Nov. 1945), Schroder Archive, SH851. Munro instead took a post as a Treasury representative in Canada.
12. *Minutes* (31 Dec. 1945, 14 Feb. 1946); Schroder Archive, SH851.
13. *PIVOT* (July 1955), 11. Autop also produced non-ferrous casting for aircraft companies. Mazak is an alloy of zinc, magnesium, aluminium, and copper.
14. *Minutes* (25 Apr., 11 July, 31 Oct. 1946).
15. Evans, *Time Again*, 18.
16. For this period, see e.g. R. A. Church, *The Rise and Decline of the British Motor Industry* (Cambridge: CUP, 1995), ch. 2 passim.
17. The Tyneside Watch Company. TNA: BT 177/1122, Barrett to Sadler Forster (19 Feb. 1948).
18. Harold Nockolds, *Lucas: The First 100 Years*, ii. *The Successors* (Newton Abbott: David & Charles, 1978), 89–90.
19. TNA: BT177/1122, Barrett to Cripps (19 Jan. 1946).
20. TNA: BT177/1122, passim; *Minutes* (11 July 1946). NB Smiths overestimated the Welsh labour supply.
21. *Minutes* (30 May 1946); Evans, *Time Again*, 21.
22. *Minutes* (26 Sept. 1946).

23. *Minutes* (21 May 1947).

24. 4 Jan. 1947, 45.

25. *The Times* (8 Feb. 1947), 5.

26. *Minutes* (19 Feb. 1947); Allan Gordon-Smith, speech to the workforce (12 Mar. 1947), *PIVOT* (Apr. 1947), 1.

27. D. I. Trotman-Dickenson, 'The Scottish Industrial Estates', *Scottish Journal of Political Economy*, 8 (Feb. 1961), p. 45–61.

28. TNA: BT 177/910, Wilson to Sadler-Forster (30 Dec. 1947).

29. TNA: BT 177/1122, Stoodley to Broadhead (28 Nov. 1945); Percival to Barrett (25 Feb. 1946); *Minutes* (25 June, 23 July, 27 Nov. 1947).

30. For £50,000. *PIVOT* (Apr. 1947), 27, and (Oct. 1947), p. 12–13; *Minutes* (16 Apr. 1947).

31. Thomas Henry Holmes, *A Brief History of the National College of Horology and Instrument Technology* (London: NCH, 1960).

32. *PIVOT* (Christmas 1947), 27.

33. *PIVOT* (Christmas 1947), p. 24–5.

34. Evans, *Time Again*, p. 15–16.

35. *PIVOT* (Oct. 1947), 26; *1948 Report and Accounts*, 19.

36. *Minutes* (31 Oct. 1946).

37. Cann, 'Chronological Record', ii. 174.

38. *The Times* (26 Sept. 1947), 2.

39. TNA: KV2/2200, 2201, 2202.

40. A former RAE colleague of Meredith's, Group Captain 'Tubby' Vielle, takes a less charitable view, arguing Meredith had successfully obstructed vital instrument development in the late 1930s. See E. E. Vielle, *Almost a Boffin* (Thatcham: Dolman Scott, 2013), 168, 170–2, 229, 314–17.

41. *Minutes* (18 July 1946).

42. 16 June 1932.

43. Graham Smith, interview (2013).

44. *PIVOT* (Feb. 1948), 19.

45. *Minutes* (24 Mar. 1948).

46. *Cheltenham Chronicle* (17 May 1947), 4.

47. *Minutes* (24 Mar., 23 Apr. 1948).

48. Based on a digital search of the *Gloucestershire Echo* and *Cheltenham Chronicle*.

49. *Gloucestershire Echo* (19 Aug. 1948), 1.

50. TNA: BT 177/1122, Barrett to Sadler Forster (19 Feb. 1948).

51. TNA: BT 177/1122, Fraser to Sadler Forster (4 Feb. 1948).

52. *Minutes* (24 Sept. 1948).

53. *Minutes* (25 Feb., 6 May 1949).

54. At a cost of £58k (2010: £1.6m).

55. *PIVOT* (Mar. 1950), 18; TNA: BT 177/910, Hooper to Hunt (20 Feb. 1950).

56. *Minutes* (17 Nov. 1949).

57. *PIVOT* (Mar. 1950), 3; *Financial Times* (28 Nov. 1949), 8.

58. Church, *Rise and Decline*, 47.

59. R. Coopey and Donald Clarke, *3i: Fifty Years Investing in Industry* (Oxford: OUP, 1995), 49, 69–70.

60. *Minutes* (21 Oct. 1949).

61. *Minutes* (6 May 1949).

62. TNA: BT 177/910.

63. TNA: BT 177/910, Hooper to Hunt (20 Feb. 1950).

64. *Minutes* (20 Jan. 1950); TNA: BT 177/910, 'production department report', undated.

65. *Minutes* (21 July 1950).

66. *PIVOT* (July 1950), 18.

67. *Minutes* (3 Mar., 22 Sept., 3 Nov. 1950, 26 Jan. 1951).

68. *Minutes* (20 Jan. 1950); *PIVOT* (July 1954), 6.

69. *Minutes* (21 July 1950).

70. *Minutes* (3 Nov. 1950).

71. *PIVOT* (Sept. 1950), 29.

72. *The Year 1950–51* (London: Smiths, 1951).

73. *Minutes* (3 Mar., 1 June 1950).

74. *PIVOT* (Nov. 1949), 4–5.

75. *Financial Times* (28 Nov. 1949), 8.

76. *Minutes* (30 Mar., 22 Sept. 1950).

77. *Minutes* (4 May 1950); *PIVOT* (Nov. 1950), 20.

78. *Minutes* (3 Mar. 1950).

79. *PIVOT* (July 1951), 14.

80. *PIVOT* (Nov. 1952), 27; *The Times* (15 Dec. 1955), 16.

81. 17 Mar. 1951, 578.

82. *Minutes* (26 Jan. 1951).

83. 'S. Smith & Sons—reorganisation of capital—negotiations file', Schroder Archive, SH 852.

84. *Minutes* (27 July 1951).

85. A first donation of £2,500 was made to the Home Counties Industrialists' Association in June 1948. Thereafter, it was usually £5,000 to the United Industrialists, a company which featured in Commons debates on the funding of political parties over more than thirty years. See e.g. *HC Deb* (18 June 1964), vol. 696, cc. 1577–1651.

86. *PIVOT* (Sept. 1951), 16–17.

87. *Minutes* (25 May, 26 Sept., 31 Oct. 1952).

88. 'Court Circular', *The Times* (18 July 1946), 6.

89. Sir Roger Hurn, interview (27 Feb. 2013).

90. *The Times* (19 Jan. 1948), 6; (29 Jan. 1948), 2.

91. *The Times* (27 Mar. 1950), 6.

92. Pam and Peter Wotton, *Sir Allan, Smiths and SEC* (self-published, n.d.), 22.

93. Downey interview (2013).

94. Graham Smith, interview (2013).

95. *Daily Telegraph* cuttings file on AGS (26 Apr. 1951).

96. Graham Smith, interview (2013).

97. *Minutes* (27 Apr. 1951); *The Times* (7 June 1951), 3.

98. *PIVOT* (Sept. 1951), 4.

99. Foreword, *School Digest* (Easter 1951), courtesy of Peter Graham.

100. *PIVOT* (Mar. 1952), 3–4.

101. Graham Smith, interview (2013).

102. Peter Graham, 'Reflections on a Life Influenced by Smiths', kindly communicated to the author (Mar. 2013); *The Year 1950–51*.

103. *PIVOT* (Nov. 1951), 10.

104. *PIVOT* (Mar. 1952), 5.

105. Peter Graham, personal communication; *PIVOT* (Nov. 1951), 10.
106. *Minutes* (29 Feb. 1952).
107. *Minutes* (25 July 1952). James Edgar Vincent Winterbourne was originally based in Clerkenwell, and secured several co-patents with Smiths; Cann, 'Chronological Record', ii. 148.
108. *Minutes* (25 July 1952).
109. *Minutes* (23 May 1952).
110. *Minutes* (25 July 1952).
111. *Minutes* (26 Sept. 1952).
112. *Minutes* (23 May 1952).
113. Cann, 'Chronological Record', ii. 184.
114. Cann, 'Chronological Record', ii. 183.
115. *Minutes* (25 July 1952).
116. *Minutes* (28 Mar. 1952).
117. *PIVOT* (July 1955).
118. *PIVOT* (July 1952), 5.
119. *Flight* (5 Feb. 1970).
120. *HC Deb* (6 May 1952), vol. 500, c. 161.
121. Andrew Roberts, *Eminent Churchillians* (London: Phoenix, 1994), 258–77; R. A. C. Parker, review of *Churchill and Consensus*, *Historical Journal*, 39/2 (June 1996), 567.
122. Material on Lawrie and Alys Nickolay is drawn from personal papers, kindly provided by Stella Nickolay. I am indebted to Graham Stevenson, convener of the Communist History Group, for arranging an introduction, and for his comments on Nickolay's significance and the concessions won by the strike.
123. Edmund Frow and Ruth Frow, *Engineering Struggles: Episodes in the Story of the Shop Stewards' Movement* (Manchester: Working Class Movement Library, 1982), 202–9.
124. *The Times* (29 Apr. 1952), 4.
125. *Financial Times* (2 May 1952), 5; *The Economist* (3 May 1952), 283.
126. *Financial Times* (1 May 1952), 5; *Daily Express* (6 May 1952), 4.
127. *HC Deb* (6 May 1952), vol. 500, c. 161.
128. *Willesden Citizen* (2 May 1952); *Smiths News* (July 1958), 1.
129. District Secretary to Nickolay (11 July 1956), Nickolay papers.
130. Downey, interview (2013); Stella Nickolay, personal communication (May 2013).
131. *The Economist* (19 Nov. 1955), 675; *Minutes* (24 Sept. 1954).
132. Martyn Nutland, *Brick by Brick* (Google eBook, 2012), 191–3; *Minutes* (24 Apr. 1953).
133. *Minutes* (16 Jan. 1953).
134. *Minutes* (27 Mar. 1953).
135. *Minutes* (26 Jan. 1951, 26 Feb. 1954); *PIVOT* (Mar. 1954), 5–6.
136. *Minutes* (27 Feb. 1953).
137. *Minutes* (27 Mar. 1953).
138. *Minutes* (29 May 1953). The operation was called Roath District Supply.
139. *Financial Times* (19 June 1953), 7.
140. Cann, 'Lenoir', 33.
141. *Illustrated London News* (31 Oct. 1953), 699.
142. *Minutes* (14 Dec. 1955). Petro-Flex left the Cassiobury Works it had occupied for some years.
143. *The Times* (15 Dec. 1955), 16.

144. *Minutes* (29 Apr. 1955); annual report (1955).
145. *Minutes* (30 Apr. 1954).
146. *Minutes* (15 Dec. 1953, 29 Apr., 3 June, 30 Sept. 1955, 29 Mar. 1957).
147. *Minutes* (24 Feb. 1956).
148. *Minutes* (23 Mar. 1956).
149. *Minutes* (29 June 1956).
150. *Minutes* (29 Apr. 1957).
151. *Smiths News* (Dec. 1958), 3.
152. *Minutes* (29 Mar. 1957).
153. *The Economist* (30 Nov. 1957), 793–5.
154. *Minutes* (28 June 1957). Consideration £130,000.
155. *Minutes* (27 Sept. 1957, 1 Jan. 1958).
156. *Minutes* (11 Dec. 1957).
157. *Commercial Motor* (24 May 1957), 56.
158. *Minutes* (28 June 1957).
159. *Minutes* (26 July 1957); Monopolies Commission, *Report on the Supply of Electrical Equipment for Mechanically Propelled Land Vehicles,* HC 21, 1963–4, 94.
160. *PIVOT* (July 1943), 23.
161. Cann, 'Lenoir', 37–8.
162. The team included Eric Desmond, Michael Bateman of Ingersoll, Major Andrew Fell, and 'Wilf' Kelly.
163. Cann, 'Lenoir', 38; *Financial Times* (21 July 1958), 71.
164. *Minutes* (26 Apr., 28 June 1957).
165. *Minutes* (27 Sept. 1957).
166. *Minutes* (27 Sept. 1957).
167. 18 Mar. 1958.
168. Dr David Pratt, personal communication, Apr. 2013.
169. Cann, 'Chronological Record', ii. 201; *The Times* (21 Jan. 1958), 5.
170. *The Economist* (15 Nov. 1958), 544.
171. Ellis, *Smiths at Cheltenham*, 96.
172. *The Times* (11 Dec. 1958), 18.
173. *Smiths News* (Dec. 1958), 5.
174. *Smiths News* (May 1961), 2.
175. *Minutes* (5 Nov. 1958).
176. *Minutes* (7 Jan. 1959).
177. *Minutes* (1 July 1959).
178. *Financial Times* (4 Sept. 1959), 6.
179. *Illustrated London News* (2 Jan. 1960), 34.
180. *Minutes* (5 Feb. 1958).
181. *London Gazette* (6 Feb. 1931), 828, suggests Leider's country of birth was Poland, but Austria is another possibility, see History of Anaesthesia Society, *Proceedings*, 4 (1988), 45; TNA: HO 144/13915 and HO 334/114/19128.
182. He also worked from 73 Portland Place.
183. Patent GB566,760 (1943).
184. J. B. Booth, 'Tracheotomy and Tracheal Intubation in Military History', *Journal of the Royal Society of Medicine*, 93 (July 2000), 383.

by a former generation of Smiths managers on small-scale engineering (e.g. through the National College of Horology) had proved anachronistic. Smiths' commitment from the early 1960s to the training of future management, though admirable, still started with the bench and vice.

The first half of the century had been dominated by Allan Gordon-Smith. His failure to ensure an adequate succession policy was keenly felt by the 1960s, with his son Ralph proving ineffectual, allowing two management factions to emerge. The mid-1960s brought significant change, first with an inevitable handover to a younger generation as the old guard moved towards retirement, and then with a decisive boardroom split that defined the way the firm would be run for the rest of the century. Dick Cave, remembered by many as 'the best boss I ever had', rose to the top in 1967 from the motor side, and firmly established the policy of decentralized management—an emphasis his younger corporate staff described, years later, as critical to Smiths' success—'it gives you marvellous ladders from the furthest outposts of empire into the great big centre, to allow the best talent to come through'.[2]

Cave cemented the foundations of the conglomerate Smiths would become, with motor accessories at the centre, still earning a significant proportion of the firm's income—though diversification remained important. Cave worked hard to promote and grow the aerospace business, particularly in the US, and it was from the aerospace side that Cave's replacement, Roy Sisson, rose. In addition to a more analytical approach taking firmer root, Cave also focused on shareholder value, tackling waste and overcapacity—'cutting out the fat' as a colleague described it—which would see not only the closure of units, but the disappearance of the playing fields and sports days of previous decades.

The 1960s also saw the slow but steady emergence of a medical business, centred around Portex. Its products were used in pioneering operations and it won international awards, growing in size and quality of facilities through the period. By the mid-1970s, it offered an extra pillar to the entire business with strong potential, helpfully just as the 'British disease' would express itself most visibly in the motor industry's most troubled phase.

Aviation, in a fog: 1960–1962

No, no. Don't let him in. Shut the door. Lock the door.

(Labour members, in chorus)

It was April 1960 and the opposition were shouting to exclude Black Rod from the Commons, excoriating the Minister of Defence who had just confirmed the Blue Streak missile programme was to be cancelled.[3] The February Defence White Paper had largely given the game away, but Smiths had seen signals even earlier—in late 1959 it reclaimed from the Ministry of Aviation the heavily secured building at Cheltenham

(CH4) where work on missile control systems took place, and purchased the Ministry's equipment.[4] The focus had switched from conventional weapons to a nuclear deterrent with the 1957 Defence White Paper, de-emphasising manned aircraft in favour of missiles, but now even missiles were being cut. In theory, Smiths could win business under either emphasis, and the firm was still contributing to the long-running TSR-2 project, but there was an overall nervousness. A board paper in February 1960 covering aviation prospects 'in the light of the Government's policy in relation to the Industry' was pessimistic.[5]

Uncertain signals from government were not the only headache. The board also had concerns about the running of SAMI (Smiths Aviation, Marine, Industrial). In late 1960, SAMI was broken up into three new divisions (aviation, industrial, and Kelvin & Hughes—now 100 per cent owned) each with its own board.[6] Leonard Morgan still ran aviation, as he had done since 1937, but succession planning saw his deputy, Michael Majendie, given more responsibility.[7]

The aviation division, though troubled by high R&D costs and work-in-progress, plus staffing difficulties, was making some headway, particularly with a first order from Boeing for instruments for the 727 airliner. Smiths' autopilots were now used by more than forty-five different flight operators, but the biggest news was the rapid development of blind-landing equipment—December 1962 saw fog close London Airport for three days, but Smiths 'had been waiting for weeks for just such a "pea-souper"' and its Varsity plane 'made a perfect landing', making the front pages.[8] There was competition—Smiths' system was adopted for the BEA Trident project but Elliott Automation was fast developing a competing system for the BAC VC-10 airliner—all of this because air travel was beset by frequent weather-related delays and attendant costs, and solutions were keenly sought. It would take years of testing to achieve acceptance for true blind landing for civil airliners, but as the threshold of acceptable safety for the military was lower, by late 1962 more than 10,000 blind landings had been achieved, and the system was rolled out for the V-Bomber force, plus the Argosy and Belfast freighters.[9] Smiths therefore had significant (though less visible) military demand for its product already.

A more searching approach on the board

Some extravagances were bound to have arisen . . . during the 1956/60 expansion of trading. The Chairman asked Mr Proctor to consider means of instituting economies.

(*Minutes,* February 1961)

In 1961, a trend towards a more analytical approach in management was reflected in the appointment of the group accountant to the main board. Colin St Clair Proctor had joined Smiths in 1947, stepping into the shoes of Bruce Hills, the former comptroller, in late 1952.[10] From then on Proctor attended board meetings as group accountant, and from around 1960 onwards took more of a role in board discussions. Major Carington, who had joined KLG in 1918 and run it since 1927, was now in his mid-seventies. When he resigned his directorship in 1961, Proctor took his place, changing the board's composition.[11] Charles Nichols was in his late seventies. Frank Hurn had also been born in the previous century, whereas Proctor was just 47, a decade younger than Ralph Gordon-Smith, Dennis Barrett, and Sir Joseph Lockwood. All this was recorded by the even younger J. Anthony (Tony) Blair, still in his thirties. After a successful military career and then distinction in the Law Society's honours examinations, he had joined Smiths in 1952, helping to create a legal department.[12] The sense of the passing of an age will have been emphasized by the deaths of both Ben Haviland and Harold Buckland, veterans of the early days—both reported in the meeting at which Proctor was elected a director.[13]

Proctor focused the board's attention more on stock levels, budgeting, and project costs. The minutes over decades had recorded funding requests from division heads, with little apparent challenge in the approval process. In August 1961, the board ceded authority to Proctor to agree or veto capital expenditure—the plan for spending £1.6m that year was to be reviewed, with a view to cutting at least £100,000. He ended up cutting it by nearly £300,000, and the following year took over central coordination of annual expenditure approval.[14] On budgeting, the minutes note Proctor's scepticism with comments about figures being 'pitched high', or of 'forecasting errors'—increased stock levels were 'disappointing'.[15] His colleagues knew that too much capital was being tied up, but from now on Proctor issued more regular reminders. Aviation was a case in point. One problem had been acute staffing shortages at Cheltenham, but more significant in the long term was the classic problem of high-cost, slow-burn research and development-led projects.[16] This was highlighted by non-executive director Joe Lockwood, from EMI:

> In relation to the mounting level of work-in-progress at Cheltenham, and on Sir Joseph Lockwood's suggestion, it was agreed to examine the possibility of requiring advance payments on Civil Aviation contracts where the goods supplied involved a long production cycle.[17]

Staffing was also now reviewed more regularly. Overall numbers (now running at 23,000+) were kept under watch, as well as measures of profitability and sales per capita. Here Smiths scored unfavourably against its peers in engineering and industry (e.g. AEI, Albert E. Reed, BMC, BSA, EMI, and Monsanto), leading to a desire to cut numbers and increase productivity, though overall the commitment to finding and retaining the right staff remained—witness the fact that in the three housing associations Smiths had sponsored with local authority support, at Bishop's Cleeve, Witney, and Basingstoke, there were now 1,078 dwellings, housing 3,000 people, with 362 garages and twenty-two shops.

Industrial relations were problematic, with frequent unofficial stoppages, so in February 1962 Proctor advocated appointing a personnel director whose responsibility 'should include not only wage structures, term of employment, claims and negotiating machinery, but also welfare, education and training, management recruitment and succession'.[18] The management consultants Urwick Orr produced a report on industrial relations for the board in February 1963.[19] Proctor also recruited Booz Allen & Hamilton to advise on programming and production at Cheltenham, and the high levels of work-in-progress and stock—by May 1963, stock in the aviation division amounted to an entire year's production, which was inefficient and unsustainable.[20] Stock control was one of the principal arguments Proctor advanced in March 1962 for the purchase of a computer. Unsurprisingly for such a project, the budget was to overrun both in time and money, but an EMIDEC 1101 was eventually installed in a purpose-built computer centre at 317 Edgware Road.[21]

Bracken Hill House

One of the great features was that we were encouraged to own old cars and rebuild them, so we did. BHH car park was a sea of ancient, open-top, Morris 8s, Austin 7s and for the lucky ones, ancient MGs.

(Marcus Beresford, 2013)

A feature of Smiths, well-remembered more than thirty years after its disappearance, is Bracken Hill House (BHH). Just as there had been a school in Cheltenham, established by Allan Gordon-Smith to ensure first-class training, so Frank Hurn evolved the idea of a school in London that would mould future managers for the motor accessories division.[22] BHH was a large house at Northwood Hills in Middlesex, run from 1959 by Tim Beevers, a former housemaster from Harrow with a distinguished war record who, together with his wife Christina, was 'ideal to supervise eighteen-year-olds'.[23]

The annual intake—typically fourteen school-leavers with A-Levels, and four existing craft apprentices—spent eleven months on a residential course. Each week, two days were spent at Hendon Technical College, studying to ONC level in various engineering disciplines. Three days at BHH were spent in lectures from Smiths specialists, and in tuition in workshop practice from Pete ('2/10ths Pete') Nethersole and technical drawing (the language of engineers) from Ken Kneed. Beevers covered language and literature. Towards the end of the year, a mini outward-bound expedition took the students to Snowdon. Some students would go on to university before starting work, while others might spend three years rotating around Smiths before selecting a final job. Many managers across the motor accessories division of the 1970s, including Marcus Beresford, Mike Lowne, Michael Henderson, David Miller, Nigel Forsyth, and Nick Morgan graduated from BHH. What marked it apart from either apprentice or graduate schemes was the thorough mix of both academic work and the intense nitty-gritty of practical work, though a few critics argued it failed to produce 'businessmen'. No other manufacturer seems to have offered similar training, leading to a degree of poaching of BHH graduands by firms such as Rolls Royce.

Industrial relations: 1960–1961

Just how far it will benefit shareholders is a matter of some conjecture at this stage.

(Chairman's statement, 1960)

In 1960, to improve industrial relations, 'staff' status was granted to more than 3,000 who had previously been 'on the clock'—for all employees with a minimum service requirement, both men and women and unskilled and skilled. Ralph Gordon-Smith claimed the breadth of the measure to be 'unique in the engineering industry' in 'breaking down the distinction between the white collar and the overalls'. The working week was shortened from forty-four hours to forty-two, but though this was presented as a concession, it resulted from national negotiations between the EEF and union officials, against a backdrop of rising numbers of unofficial strikes across industry, and Smiths was merely carried on the tide.[24] It had its own fair share of strikes in the first half of the calendar year, and for the first time the board received detailed reports from Proctor on the cost of industrial action.[25] Other improvements for staff involved enhancements to the pension scheme, introducing a minimum fraction of final salary, together with enhanced benefits for executives. All workers were enrolled in the sports and social clubs, without a subscription, and more housing was built at Witney.

1960 had also seen the continuation of strong motor-car sales, but from 1961 onwards for several years the analysis of comparative figures and performance in board meetings tends to look back wistfully to the late 1950s as a golden age, hard to repeat. From near silence on industrial relations in board minutes, unofficial strikes and stoppages start recurring. In May 1961 there was a dispute at Witney. June then saw an unofficial strike by 113 workers at Watford, related to a bonus claim, but a far more serious dispute at Cricklewood. The beginning of the month saw the annual congress of the GMWU, at which Emmy Garvey, the women's convener for MA1, spoke. Her address focused on Smiths' drive towards greater efficiency—she was worried about 'automation "galloping in"'—a workshop that formerly employed forty-nine was now automated and achieved twice the output with four workers. Redeployed staff had seen their wages fall from £13 per week to near £8—was this fair?[26]

Garvey, the most vocal and visible shop steward at Smiths, had joined in 1932, on clock assembly, but latterly worked as forewoman on the cleaning staff. While avowedly not a Communist, she was naturally a key MA1 representative on the strongly left-leaning Smiths' Combine.[27] In 1958, she was selected to represent London at the GMWU conference, following this up a year later with a TV appearance, discussing redundancy at Smiths and the provision of alternative work.[28] She divided opinion strongly, recalled in very negative terms by some, but also remembered for being a fiercely protective mother hen to large numbers of Irish girls from Kilburn who worked at MA1. Bruce Alexander of MA1 described her as a fierce negotiator whose 'heart was nevertheless in the company, however loud she shouted'.[29]

A decade on from the last major Smiths' strike to hit the national press, Garvey's return from the 1961 GMWU congress coincided with the escalation of demands for significantly increased wages at Cricklewood. Deadlock in discussions led to an unofficial walk-out of 2,000 from 12 June which ended up lasting two weeks and a day—with Garvey as de facto strike leader. There were considerable ramifications as Smiths had an effective stranglehold on the supply of speedometers and heaters to most manufacturers. Within a week, shifts were being cancelled and men sent home at Standard Triumph, Jaguar, Pressed Steel, and elsewhere. By 21 June, 6,000 were laid off at BMC. There was a degree of industry stockpiling of largely complete cars, to which Smiths' parts could be retro-fitted, but storage capacity disappeared fast.[30]

The strike was notable not only for the toughness of negotiations with management (which pointed out an outstanding national wage claim, its granting of staff status to 3,000, and recently improved benefits) but also the slanging match between strikers and union bosses, who jointly called for a return to work. Jim Matthews of the CSEU cabled 'Dear Emily, please get girls back to work and leave rest to us'.[31] Bill Carron, the moderate AEU leader, received the simple anonymous cable 'Shut up and do something. Your AEU officials are not bothering', from factions anxious to return.[32] Carron did not help matters by announcing to the national press he believed 'subversive elements' (i.e. Communists) were responsible for the trouble, leading to Garvey's public announcement that Carron had 'no idea what is going on on the factory floor. He couldn't assemble a speedometer if he tried.'[33]

A compromise was eventually reached in which Smiths agreed to consider claims constructively, but the knock-on effects across the industry were severe, involving at least 10,000 workers and more than a week's lost work. Proctor's analysis showed the implementation of the national wage award earlier in the year had added £450,000 to Smiths' costs, and the May and June strikes a further £65,000.[34]

Monopolies and market forces: 1961–1964

Having regard to the figures given . . . it is of vital importance to a component maker to obtain and retain the custom of any of the Big Five and, particularly, of B.M.C. and Ford.

(Monopolies Commission, 1963)

1961 saw the millionth Morris Minor roll off the production line, every one since 1948 equipped with Smiths instruments, as was a rather different sort of vehicle, the E-Type Jaguar, the first of which emerged that same year. Soon after, figures from the Monopolies Commission report on electrical devices in the motor industry showed Smiths dominated in heaters (76 per cent market share) and instruments (66 per cent).[35] It also had around 8 per cent of the sparking plug market, but Hurn had been discussing with Lodge Plugs the possibility of acquiring the firm, with a further 12 per cent market share. Morgan Crucible created a shock in November by announcing its own bid, resulting in urgent meetings with the advisers at Helbert, Wagg, but Smiths' bid at a slightly higher level was accepted early in 1962, leading to the creation of a separate spark plugs and ceramics division.

Smiths had spent years developing (and now dominated) the market for car and commercial vehicle heaters. Symptomatic of the possibilities for expertise and technology transferring into other arenas, this led to an interest in space-heating for the home and then larger buildings. An initial move had been the acquisition of Camron Engineering of Chichester, makers of boiler parts, in early 1959.[36] By January 1960, an oil-fired domestic boiler had been developed at Witney, and a purpose-built factory was later constructed at Portsmouth. It was typical of Smiths' approach over many years that domestic boiler manufacture could be sited within the motor accessories division.

At the top, Hurn's service agreement was extended to 1963, but succession arrangements were well under way and by late 1962 the board confirmed it 'would be in order, in referring, at forthcoming Motor Industry functions, to Mr Cave as Mr Hurn's designated successor as head of the Motor Accessory Division'.[37] The division enjoyed good results in 1962–4, on the back of markedly reduced purchase tax on cars in 1962, better industrial relations for the whole industry, and limited impact from imports, though one significant blow was Ford's change of policy in February 1964, deciding to manufacture its vehicle instruments in-house, rather than subcontracting—a first major challenge to Smiths' dominant market position.[38]

Medical breakthroughs: 1960–1964

> *Brown, I now appreciate the full enormity of what you are proposing.*
> (Halliday, Smiths' chief scientist, on medical
> ultrasound, 1956[39])

In the early 1960s, both the marine and motors divisions contained fledgling medical businesses. Since the mid-1950s, Kelvin & Hughes had used ultrasound equipment, originally developed for flaw detection in metals, for medical scanning purposes. The key developmental engineer was a young Tom Brown, who spent years scrounging equipment, experimenting, and supporting Professor Ian Donald of Glasgow University, developing the Diasonograph, under the aegis of Bill Slater, deputy MD at Kelvin & Hughes, who provided 'such active encouragement and financial support as he could manage, sometimes almost in defiance of the rest of the Board'.[40] This had led to a ground-breaking article in *The Lancet* in 1958, launching the field of medical ultrasound.[41] Reportedly, Potter, then MD, had been 'somewhat unsympathetic to the medical ultrasound project', but with his departure, matters improved.[42] In 1962 the same technology was first used for scanning brain injuries.[43]

When David Deszo Rothman, co-owner of Uni-Tubes, died in late 1962, Smiths acquired the balance of the firm, and thereby complete control of Smiths' other medical business, Portland Plastics, for which a new factory was approved at Reachfields in Hythe.[44] This replaced Bassett House, destroyed by fire in May 1960 which led to uncertainty over the firm's future while production was farmed out among different Smiths units. Alan Hornsby recalls the insurance claim—'had we not wanted the business, we could have walked away with a profit. The decision to re-invest in Hythe was an inspired one by the SMA Board and the rest is history.'[45] From early on the firm's products were involved in landmark events—for example, its new tracheotomy tube played an important role in the first UK operation to install an artificial heart valve in 1964.[46]

Clocks to kitchen timers

His company was very involved these days in all sorts of instruments for cooking and heating. There was no end to it.

(Robert Lenoir, 1960)

These were Lenoir's comments at the end of a lecture on high-grade watchmaking, in March 1960, but as he admitted, Smiths was now working at the other end of the market, on domestic appliances, and for the clock and watch division at the beginning of the decade, this, for a while, was where the money lay.[47] As part of the development of the ideal home, automatic 'labour-saving' controls were the vogue. MA2, Witney, Ystradgynlais, Brighton, and Wishaw all contributed products to a new appliance control branch, including oven timers (gas and electric); the Defromatic which automatically defrosted a fridge daily; even the Hoovermatic washing machine.[48]

With a view to countering competition, Dennis Barrett was authorized to secure Swiss investment in Smiths' watch businesses in 1961, but nothing emerged.[49] At the high end, Cheltenham produced the first British automatic 25-jewel watch in 1961, while in volume production Barrett was presented with the thirty millionth alarm to come off the line at Wishaw in January 1963.[50] At Ystradgynlais, Ron Williams had joined Anglo-Celtic as chief accountant in 1959 (after training at Deloitte, Plender, Griffiths in Cardiff), attracted by an increased salary at one of the largest manufacturers in the region. He recalls a 'buzz' that came from an exciting and technically highly competent operation, producing high-quality products—a buzz reflected across the entire group. Nevertheless, at the 'Tick Tock', as the Ystradgynlais works was known locally, he recalls 'there was a big awareness that life was going to be a lot more difficult in the future'.[51] The consumer magazine *Which* reported very favourably on Smiths' watches in 1962, but despite such praise the dreams for the division which Allan Gordon-Smith, Barrett, and Lenoir had in 1945 lay in tatters.[52]

New blood on the board: 1963–1964

> *It made ten landings successively . . . with the pilot, Mr J.H. Phillips, sitting*
> *in the cockpit with his arms folded.*
>
> (*The Times*[53])

The importance of the US for the aviation business had commenced with the Boeing and Douglas contracts. Smiths now ventured further by collaborating with the Minneapolis Honeywell Regulator Co. to quote for autoland equipment to the specification of the US Federal Aviation Agency.[54] Back at home, the aviation business was rocked in the autumn of 1963 by the sudden death of Leonard Morgan, its managing director, leading to Michael Majendie's immediate appointment in his place. More significantly, October saw the election to the main board of Majendie, Dick Cave, and Tony Blair, the company secretary—a team with thirty-seven years' aggregate service between them, yet an average age of just 41. Motors were therefore now strongly represented by both Hurn and Cave, while aviation had a direct champion in Majendie.[55]

This was a tricky time for Majendie. Press reports of the first blind autolandings by the Trident in March 1964 were strongly positive and Smiths was acknowledged as the developer, but the aviation division was also carrying significantly expanded receivables from Hawker Siddeley, which it felt unable to press owing to faults in supplies to Sperry Gyroscope, one of Hawker's subcontractors. There were serious shortfalls in deliveries to other customers, and in May 1964 Majendie had to cut his forecast income figures back to near break-even.[56]

Cancellation of TSR-2: 1965

> *We all admire the technical skill that has been put into this aircraft.*
> *(Opposition shouts of 'Eyewash').*
>
> (Callaghan announces the cancellation of the TSR-2, *The Times*[57])

Without apparent irony, *Smiths News* announced in early 1965 that the Cheltenham factory was establishing a 'museum of the air'—an attempt to preserve examples of Smiths' aviation products from the last few decades.[58] Despite any inference that the division's products were being consigned to the past, there were grounds for concern. As with the cancellation of Blue Streak in 1960, the contractors and other insiders in military aircraft projects (now under threat since Labour's victory in the October 1964 election) were well aware which way the wind was blowing—Labour had opposed the TSR-2 project for years.[59] By January 1965, Majendie was warning the board of 'the current political uncertainty with regard the future of the British Government's three main military aircraft projects (TSR2, P1154 and HS 681) and the effect which a cancellation would have on the Aviation Division'.[60] Following crisis talks at Chequers, February saw the cancellation of the HS 681 and P1154, with large resulting job losses.

When the axe fell on the TSR-2 in April, the industry suffered further. Lucas, for example, had developed new equipment for the plane which had put it 'into a whole new field of business, much of which withered on the vine'.[61] Among smaller companies, H. M. Hobson of Wolverhampton, flying-control systems manufacturers, were crippled by the cancellation, leading eventually to their acquisition by Lucas. There were many more casualties, though Smiths' competitor Elliott Automation was largely untroubled, given its volume of development work. The Smiths' board met the day after the announcement:

> Mr Majendie . . . doubted if the 'Plowden Committee' could be expected to operate effectively whilst its appointers were taking fundamental decisions in quick succession. So far as [Smiths] was concerned it was difficult to adjust plans in such a fluid situation but an early manifestation of the Board's intentions would be desirable in the interests of morale.[62]

Tactically, it was better to wait to communicate with the staff, since though the military projects were called off, the year nevertheless saw the triumph of Smiths' 'Autoflare' system when on Thursday 10 June 1965 the eighty-eight passengers on a Trident jet from Orly to Heathrow were told on arrival that 'you are the first people ever to be landed by an automatic pilot' (see Plate 51).[63] This was reported around the world and attracted considerable positive coverage. Majendie travelled around the aviation factories, addressing 3,000 staff at Cheltenham on 22 July, where he emphasized that the firm was 'unsullied by the defence cut-backs'.[64] He acknowledged that it was civil aviation on which the firm should focus. 'That is our market', he said, 'And conservative estimates show that world travel will certainly treble and may even quadruple between now and 1980.' The UK experience, measured by passenger traffic, did indeed show a trebling, but Majendie's forecast was conservative, given the global growth of aviation (see Figure 7.1).[65] Smiths was well-placed in one sense. Unlike its customers (firms such as Hawker Siddeley, with so many eggs in the military contract basket that immediate job losses followed the project cancellations), Smiths, like Elliott Automation, had a more diversified mix of business, and could continue to provide instruments and flight systems to a growing international range of aircraft builders, allowing Majendie to claim 'We are, therefore, much better off than some other parts of the industry.'

There was, however, a lot of ground to recover. Smiths did not split figures by division, but Ralph Gordon-Smith had disclosed a year earlier that for a decade the aviation division had accounted for about a quarter of the group's assets, and nearly as much in turnover. From 1957 to 1960 it accounted for a full third of profits, but thereafter this fell to less than 10 per cent.[66] It was also the case that, despite a willingness (out of necessity) to emphasize exports, Smiths still felt the need to argue for more state support for aviation. When Ray Gunter, Minister of Labour, visited Cheltenham in autumn 1965 to open Smiths' new building, Majendie's speech pulled no punches: 'The public denigration of our own national efforts and products . . . has become something of a national pastime. We need to recreate a belief in our own destiny, and in our own capability—so as to present a better shop window to the world.'[67]

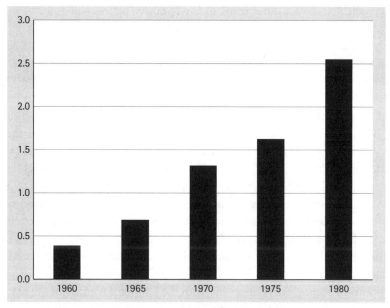

FIGURE 7.1 (US only) revenue passenger miles 1960–1980 (billions).

Source: US Department of Transport

In-house, there was recognition the US was the most important target market, and a first small acquisition was made in late 1965, with Gap Instrument Corporation in New York, a specialist avionics manufacturer. A more important acquisition was under way in the UK. In late 1964, Frank Clarke of Clarke & Smith approached Frank Hurn about selling their subsidiary Specto Avionics, a specialist developer of the heads-up display (HUD)—a logical corollary of faster, low-level flying requirements and related to projects such as Hawker Siddeley's cancelled P1154.[68] The subsonic VTOL P1127 (later the Harrier) was continuing in development and Specto retained the brief, but its small size was a problem for the Ministry of Aviation, leading to the idea of Smiths' acquisition. The transaction rumbled on through 1965 and was finally closed in January 1966.

Difficult times: mid-1960s

Signs of reduction in consumer spending were reported by Mr Barrett from the jewellery trade and confirmed by Mr Cave (cars) and Sir Joseph Lockwood (gramophone records).

(Minutes, May 1965)

Proctor's emphasis on staffing levels fed through to some rationalization, with numbers employed in 1965 per million of turnover falling from 530 to 470 over twelve months, but similar calculations for other firms showed Smiths' figures still high.[69] Proctor also turned the spotlight on the relative performance of the different divisions.

Having arrived in office with a larger than expected balance of payments deficit, the Labour government had introduced a raft of defensive measures to protect sterling and to contain credit expansion. Alongside the defence project cuts, the 'prestige' Concorde project was also to be reviewed, an import surcharge was introduced, and tax reform promised. With bank rate increased to 7 per cent, the board's 'attention focused on the increase of £10.5m in stocks and debtors over the period [5 years] and the cost of servicing working capital in the present era of high interest rates. It was agreed that more critical examination must be applied . . . to units whose return on assets employed was not comfortably higher than the cost of money and whose prospects of higher returns in the future were not clearly favourable.'[70] In August, Proctor tabled a schedule showing five activities (clocks and watches, aviation, Kelvin electronics, industrial ceramics, and automotive sparking plugs) which consumed over 50 per cent of the value of assets employed in the group but which contributed less than 20 per cent of the profits.[71]

In clocks and watches, the relationship with the Labour government of 1945 was now a fading memory. Barrett had kept faith, but he was nearing the end of his career. His executive appointments were renewed in 1965, but it was clearly understood he was to start delegating as soon as possible.[72]

The treadmill of inflation was beginning to feature in board discussions, and for the first time a decision was taken to revalue the firm's properties, at the end of 1965. At £9.2m this showed an excess of £3.9m over balance-sheet values, and the board decided to recognize £3m in an upward revaluation, and a further £400,000 came from a simple revaluation of stock.[73] The fixed assets mainly comprised factories and plant, the floor area having more than doubled in fifteen years (see Figure 7.2). From now on, however, this would begin to lose relevance, and ceased being published.

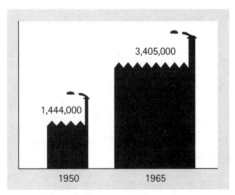

FIGURE 7.2 Factory area 1950/1965 (ft²).

Source: Annual reports

Two strategic decisions in 1964–5 reflected a tension in the direction for the firm. Ralph Gordon-Smith had made much in 1957 of his policy of 'Three D's': decentralization of operations, delegation of responsibility and authority, and diversification of products. In July 1964, Proctor proposed centralizing the head office functions of the entire group in a single building, probably influenced by consultants such as Urwick Orr and Booz Allen Hamilton, who had advised on stock control and production planning.[74] For Proctor, who championed efficiencies and cost-cutting, it will have been logical to propose common offices for several functions. Even he found himself on the defensive, having to admit Smiths had 876 staff in forty-four separate accounting units.[75] Computerization was already under way, but further simplification from the top-most management function down was desirable, certainly in Proctor's mind—a view he shared with Majendie and Blair. By August 1964, the purchase of eight acres at Sudbury Hill was agreed with J. Lyons, for £465,000, and planning commenced for a new headquarters.

Gordon-Smith's statement at the end of 1965 contains the telling sentence 'Whilst "diversification" may not be a dirty word neither is it a process which any company can carry on indefinitely without weakening itself.' He talked of eliminating or reducing activities that could not produce satisfactory returns, and commented that 'as we enter a new field we will probably have left one or two more old ones'. 70 per cent of the group's activities were carried out under the Smiths brand. Having invested heavily in the brand, and to emphasize that the firm was strong in a range of different industries, the decision was taken to drop the convoluted twenty-year-old name of S. Smith & Son (England) in favour of the more direct 'Smiths Industries', with effect from 1 January 1966.[76]

Smiths Industries, under close review: 1966

Operating managers could be made more forcibly aware of the effects of high working capital if an economic rate of interest on net working capital were to be charged in their management accounts.

(Proctor, *Minutes*, 1966)

At the first board meeting of 1966, Proctor set out a schedule of eight presentations to be made over the next year, each focusing on a business producing less than 7.5 per cent on assets employed.[77] Last in the series, and reserved for early 1967, were aviation and the clock and watch divisions. First up was KECO, the Kelvin Electronics company, established just a year earlier, at Kelvin's Hillington site in Glasgow, housing the more specialized and technically advanced products, including the industrial and medical ultrasound business. Despite appreciation of management's efforts, sufficient profitability seemed unlikely, and while the axe did not fall instantly, it was operating on borrowed time.[78]

Proctor's schedule of presentations saw ceramics, automotive spark plugs, and the Australian subsidiary examined in close detail over the coming months. The latter two, despite poor returns, were felt to be on a strong path to better performance. Ceramics were more problematic, as there were different business lines within the division, but the review of spark plug operations proved reasonably encouraging.[79] Management was put on notice of a two-year trial, to be followed up with further review.[80]

All of this review work was taking place against a backdrop of a deepening sterling crisis, with Wilson resolutely refusing to countenance devaluation. Over the previous year measures had gradually been introduced to curb demand—higher taxes, credit restrictions (including the tightening of HP terms, damaging the motor industry), import surcharges, and increased Bank Rate. A government showdown over wages with the striking seamen's union was just one of many negative factors and Wilson finally acted with the 'July measures', which ranged widely—the *Financial Times* commented 'Mr Wilson threw everything in within reach'—including a temporary freeze on wages, salaries, prices, and dividends.[81] Company reports did not break down the income statement to allow analysis of costs and sales margins, but Smiths' accounts that same July reveal some of the inflationary effects the firm had suffered in the past year. Despite sales advancing 3 per cent to £55m, inflationary cost increases amounted to more than £1.5m, not recovered in increased sales prices, and profits slumped from a high of £4m in 1965 to £2.9m—reminiscent of mid-1950s levels.

In-house, there were many concerns. One was funding—there was an over-reliance on overdrafts—and on the sales side, Smiths' customers were extending their use of deferred credit terms. Proctor argued profitability per employee needed to be higher, comparing Smiths with a range of twenty-four other industrials in April 1966. One of these would undoubtedly have been Lucas, which employed roughly three times the workforce, but achieved 50 per cent more profit per head. Stock levels were constantly too high—hence Proctor's observation that operating managers should be charged an economic rate of interest in the management accounts for the working capital they were using.[82] Over time, Smiths had consistently moved towards in-house manufacture, from raw materials to finished product. Its catalogues across the different divisions kept expanding, but now 'it was doubted whether the still rising [and therefore costly] trend of stock levels would be reversed so long as the variety of products subsisted and so many components of each product continued to be made in house'.[83]

Competition in clocks and watches: 1964–1968

Alarm from the clock industry.

(*Financial Times* headline[84])

Barrett's clock and watch division exemplified the problem of too large a product range. Increased foreign competition was also hurting. The Swiss exported a record forty-seven million watches during 1964, while the Russians sent more than £250,000 worth to the UK in the second half of the year. It was also the year Robert Lenoir retired. He had worked for Smiths since 1927, and delivered everything Allan Gordon-Smith had asked. But the world had moved on, and Barrett was left with a division which could not make adequate returns, forcing him on the defensive in board meetings. Graham Smith recalls Tony Blair commenting 'the Company would do better to wash their hands of clocks and watches and invest the proceeds in bricks and mortar', a sentiment he might have expressed any time in the mid-1960s, judging from the minutes.[85] In 1964, Barrett lost another ally, his long-term colleague Rex Smith, with whom he had built up the clock and watch business since the 1930s. Under the pressure of an unremitting long-term illness and the strain of looking after an invalid son, Rex retired. This left his son Graham the only other Smith in the business, besides his uncle Ralph, who had no children.

Sales were not being hampered purely by domestic considerations. John Boyd of the AEU executive had found on a 1966 trip to Hungary that alarm clocks were being exported at the 'quite fantastically low figure of one third of their actual prime cost'.[86] This was crippling for the Wishaw factory, which reduced its output, thus losing economies of scale. A long-term problem was one of factory capacity in the clocks division not being fully loaded, so the flagship alarm clock factory now accepted a contract to produce telephone automatic dials for the GPO, still rolling out its subscriber trunk-dialling programme.

It was no longer sensible to produce platform escapements at the Chronos Works, and in 1966 these were abandoned at the end of a thirty-five-year run.[87] Anglo-Celtic and Enfield were faring little better in Wales. To promote trade with Russia, the government nearly doubled the permitted value of imported Russian watches to £400,000 for 1966. In early 1968 it was increased further to £500,000 and this hurt Smiths and Ingersoll's directly.[88] The Economist commented on the damage the 1968 Anglo/Soviet trade arrangements agreed by Antony Crosland would have on the domestic British markets for cars and watches (a unique combination in Smiths).[89] A rare positive was the continuing business from the MoD for the supply of service watches—for example, an order for 10,000 in 1968.[90]

A bumpy ride for motors: 1965–1966

The Company is facing the most critical conditions experienced since the second world war.

> (Ralph Gordon-Smith to senior managers, November 1966)

From 1965 onwards, the motor industry behaved unevenly in terms of sales and therefore demand, making forecasting difficult and revealing budgeting exercises had been of little value. By August 1966, the board was discounting heavily its previous forecasts, while Proctor explained difficulties in short-term funding that might lead to long-term borrowing being necessary, even at present high rates. Against this gloomy backdrop, Cave wondered 'on a point of psychology' whether 'the board were in favour of a review of the desirability, in current conditions, of the Sudbury Hill project'.[91] Despite his reservations, the board pressed ahead, though noting the need for economies. The results for the year ended July 1966 were sufficiently poor (28 per cent down on 1965) that the dividend was reduced for the first time in twenty-five years. Ralph Gordon-Smith's internal memo to his senior staff in early November pulled no punches—likening the crisis to wartime conditions, he warned 'the Directors for their part will accelerate their review of those parts of the Company's business which have consistently failed to give an adequate return'.[92] Days later the board decided to bring forward the review of the clocks and watches division, but patience with Kelvin Electronics ran out completely, and Majendie was instructed to close it immediately, which he accomplished over the following months, with a loss of over 500 jobs. Despite having pioneered the fledgling medical ultrasound business, it disappeared to Nuclear Enterprises in Glasgow.

The winter of 1966 had seen news from the motor industry turn significantly negative, in the wake of the 'July measures' and the resulting credit squeeze. Over the following six months, up to 40,000 car workers were laid off at sixteen different plants, on the back of industrial action in protest at the redundancy of 11,000 at BMC.[93] At Joseph Lucas, a three-day week applied across eleven plants by mid-November, affecting 6,000 workers. Smiths avoided lay-offs, but the motor accessories division entered 1967 under the cloud of a depressed broader market. Aviation and marine nevertheless had respectable order books stretching out two to three years, and the contrast between the prospects for the two main elements of the business will in part have underpinned an audacious move by several members of the board.

The parting of the ways: 1967

> In the yard one day [Tony Blair] came up to me and said 'I gather you're a Cave-man'.
>
> (John Thompson, interview, 1998)

It will have been clear to the board that Ralph had been considering stepping down as MD for some time. It was also clear, not only to the board but to many of the senior management, that there were two broad camps into which the board was divided. One camp comprised Majendie, Proctor, and Tony Blair, who can be viewed as the centralizers—the architects and sponsors of the Sudbury Hill head office project. The other camp, headed by Dick Cave, supported particularly by Frank Hurn and Joe Lockwood, was opposed to the new HQ office project and strongly favoured the decentralization of management. Dennis Barrett engaged in a degree of shuttle diplomacy, trying to keep the peace. Sir James Reid was placed in a difficult position—he was Tony Blair's father-in-law—so he absented himself from the picture by resigning in January, ahead of action by Majendie, Blair, and Proctor, who wrote to Ralph Gordon-Smith in early February with a proposal related to issues of overall strategy, planning, and succession, embodying the suggestion that Majendie should succeed Ralph as MD.[94]

At the board meeting on 8 February 1967, Ralph tabled a resolution giving effect to his proposed changes, such that he would remain chairman and chief executive, reserving to himself certain rights to approve the appointment of another managing director. Majendie, Blair, and Proctor voted against, formalizing the split.

It is clear that Ralph had already agreed Cave should succeed him, and though Linklaters were present at the next meeting (a week later) to ensure due process, the resolution was once more passed. A four-hour discussion ensued, with the appointment of non-executive directors a major topic. It is also clear the proposal for Majendie to succeed Ralph was tabled again, but 'a compromise proposal' was agreed, probably referring to the appointment of John Tyzack of Tyzack & Partners, who then spent March and April 1967 formulating advice and proposals on 'the problems causing dissension'.[95]

When the board met on 10 May 1967, it was clear the Cave-men had won, and Majendie now had to make a tactical withdrawal. Over the coming weeks a leaving settlement was negotiated with both him and Blair. Majendie, a respected industry figure, was soon able to secure another post and left in September to become deputy chairman at Molins.[96] Blair was a different case, since he had no industry credentials. At this stage, Cave spoke almost daily on the telephone with Geoffrey Seligman of Warburg's, the company's main financial advisers, and persuaded him to offer Blair a job, though this did not prove to be a long-lasting appointment.[97]

Proctor, however, was a different matter. Having backed the wrong horse, he too might have been expected to leave, but whether it was due to his long service, or proximity to retirement, Cave retained him. It may in fact have suited Cave to restructure the board, removing Proctor as finance director but putting him in charge of a new operating division that drew together the industrial instruments businesses, and the clock and watch division, from which Barrett was retiring.[98] He probably felt these problematic businesses would benefit from Proctor's forensic approach, and should further closures be needed, it was politically astute to have him be the instrument. Robson, the group accountant, was quickly made a special director in charge of finance, reporting to Cave, and this also paved the way for the appointment of a new chief accountant, Alan Hornsby, who had joined back in 1955, gravitating up through positions in the industrial instruments and motor accessories divisions to be Robson's assistant, supported by Cave with whom he enjoyed a good relationship.[99] This was a significant move, as Hornsby began a long-term drive to force up the quality of accountancy across the whole firm, first at head office, and then throughout the group. A close colleague commented: 'When I arrived in 1960, the lawyers were in the ascendancy, and the accountants were "also-rans". That changed. Alan was a strong man and got what he wanted. His aim was to improve accounting standards, and any accountancy appointments were subject to his approval.'[100]

The motor accessory presence on the board was consolidated further with the appointment of Stanley Burlington, who now headed up the division. One of John Tyzack's recommendations was implemented with the appointment of two new non-executive directors; David Breeden, chairman of fellow motor accessory manufacturer Wilmot Breeden, and George, 2nd Earl Jellicoe, a director of SG Warburg Finance and Development, cementing further connections both with the City and Parliament.

Another survivor of the battle, much to his surprise, was Gerry Mortimer, who had worked for Proctor for some time, as investment manager for the company's pension fund. Trained as an economist and financial analyst, he had joined in 1961. Given that 'I was associated with the Blair/Proctor school . . . I thought [Cave] was going to give me the boot actually, and he offered me a job to go and investigate for him how we might go about things, particularly planning the company, and strategic planning—which we didn't think was a good description—so we called it forward planning.'[101] Initially Cave wanted economics and corporate planning departments, sending Mortimer to visit companies such as Dunlop and Eaton Corporation to assess their operations, but he returned to tell Cave 'you don't want either really . . . have a logical proposal but let people do it themselves—they run the business, we don't . . . and to Dick Cave that was music'.

A rising tide of inflation: 1966–1967

> *We built a bloody great new headquarters at Greenford and then never occupied it. IBM bought it, I think.*
>
> (John Thompson, 1998)

The project closely associated in everyone's mind with the centralizers was the Sudbury Hill office block, now nearing completion. One of Cave's first actions was to have the model of the new building removed from the Edgware Road foyer. With the power struggle clearly won, it was time to move on and Ralph issued a memorandum to senior staff, though the wording is perhaps Cave's:

> If a policy is established against the background of factors and philosophies which cease to be valid then the solution must be to change that policy, and the Board must have the courage and the flexibility to make that change. Sudbury Hill . . . would have housed . . . the bulk of the senior management . . . In those circumstances, and whatever the form or intention of an organisational structure, the consequences would have been a move towards centralisation. The emphasis of the new organisational structure will be a downward transmission of responsibility and initiative to individual managers, and this is, of course, a process of decentralisation.[102]

The economic backdrop had changed markedly since the headquarters project had started. The 'July measures' of 1966 had exacted a significant toll on the economy, but are generally interpreted to have failed to achieve the desired effect, since though demand was controlled (with unemployment doubling over twelve months) the trade deficit nevertheless widened, made worse by a Liverpool dockers' strike from September 1967, which saw export goods stockpiled in port. With sterling under pressure, and resisting to the last (with two increases in Bank Rate ignored by the markets) Harold Wilson finally agreed a 14.3 per cent devaluation of sterling on 18 November, arguably setting off an inflationary spiral that would last years—Smiths, for example, went through an immediate round of price increases wherever it could across its whole range.[103] The benefits apparently fed through to higher exports for Smiths in hi-tech products in the first half of 1968, but interestingly in his next chairman's report Ralph relegated such benefits to third place behind the gains made from controlling expenditure and the improvement in domestic sales of motor and consumer goods.[104]

An unlooked for inflationary benefit saw Sudbury Hill in the money, and in a neat transaction the firm sold it to the Smiths pension fund for £3.1m (2010: £42m), which in turn granted IBM a long lease.

Onwards and upwards in aviation: 1968–1969

> The significant pointer to the future is . . . that all sectors of the Company
> are now pulling in the right direction.
>
> (Chairman's statement, 1968)

With Majendie gone, Cave devoted considerable efforts to the aviation business, travelling extensively in late 1967/early 1968, in a drive to penetrate the US market, emphasized with a decision to create a plant at St Petersburg-Clearwater airport in Tampa, Florida, that would open in 1969, consolidating operations previously in Toronto and New York.[105] Possibilities for long-term supply contracts with Boeing and collaboration with Rockwell looked promising.[106] Good press coverage followed the 1968 decision to allow Trident autolandings with decreased visibility and the division began performing ahead of budget. There were frustrations as well, as the joint bid with Honeywell for flight control systems on the Lockheed L1011 Tristar failed, as did another joint collaboration on the Douglas DC-10.[107] Nevertheless, Smiths committed heavily to collaboration with Honeywell, particularly in radio altimeters, and to Bendix, on flight control systems, winning business for the A300 Airbus as a subcontractor. There was less good news at Gap Instrument Corp in the US, a 1965 purchase that had not worked out, and an exit was sought from mid-1969 onwards.[108]

Cave will have spent time assessing the senior management structure Majendie had left behind. By mid-1969 he was happy to see Roy Sisson, the aviation managing director, join the main board. Sisson had been apprenticed to Hawkers in 1930, served as a wartime engineer officer with Imperial Airways, then BOAC, becoming involved in introducing the Comet, finally joining Smiths in 1965 as technical services manager. Below him as technical director, following a slight juggle in mid-1968, was Bill Mallinson, a gifted engineer with significant experience in guided weapons, recruited from Ferranti to replace Ken Fearnside, who left to go to Plessey.[109]

Time begins running out: 1968–1971

> *The process of getting out of the clock and watch industry was also traumatic, but it was necessary because the business declined so dramatically.*
>
> (Ron Williams, interview, 2013)

From mid-1968, withdrawal from the horological industry commenced with the closure of Synthetic Jewels at Carfin, and then the winding down of the Enfield clock operation in Wales, allowing part of Kelvin & Hughes to be moved there, followed by vehicle instruments from early 1969.[110] This formed part of a wider plan for Proctor's operational division, which became Group C (clocks and watches, appliance control, industrial instruments), increasingly seen as the problematic remnants of older businesses which might not have a future. Smiths had premises, machinery, a trained workforce—was there a better use for these resources? In June 1968, this thinking underpinned the emergence of an idea to purchase from Ingersoll its 50 per cent of the Anglo-Celtic Watch Company, thereby gaining control of the Ystradgynlais site for more profitable activities.[111]

Mechanical wind-up clocks were giving way to battery-driven versions—using the new 'Sectronic' movement—which could be volume-produced in Cheltenham. The technology was still relatively traditional, but Smiths was already exploring the possibilities of quartz as an oscillator, not only in clocks but in watches. By early 1969, Proctor was outlining the dilemma of 'whether to advance the quartz crystal development at the expense of the Sectronic watch project'.[112] Overall, Group C's performance was lacklustre in 1968–9. Price increases were achieved 'without any great adverse reaction', but several parts of the division showed sales well below budget.[113] Appliance control suffered from labour shortages, and both its output and market demand were well below forecast—leading to losses overall and a decision mid-year to cease manufacturing cooker controls.[114] Over the course of the following year, Brighton was wound down and the factory finally closed in the spring of 1970.[115]

In the absence of a champion like Barrett, and given Proctor's lack of line experience, the business drifted, although by mid-1969 it was clear that emphasis would be placed on developing a quartz clock over the next year.[116] It was finally decided in early 1969 to bid £135,000 for the balance of Anglo-Celtic, a transaction agreed soon after, and for all the romance of its wartime origins, British Precision Springs in Cheltenham was now an anachronism, and its thirty-year life as a separate company came to an end.[117]

Into 1970 and clocks and watches were performing abysmally. Proctor announced cuts 'in expenses and forward technical developments'.[118] Recognizing the strength of the brand, but the lack of economics in home manufacture of movements, he also announced a strategy of moving entirely to Swiss-made movements by the end of 1971—an ironic return to the practice of Samuel Smith a century earlier. In September 1970, Cave announced that high-grade watch production would cease at Cheltenham, and the closure programme was complete by March 1971, with aviation taking the redundant space. A small team under Dr Shelley of the Special Horological Products Unit continued to work hard on the development of quartz clocks and watches. It was to develop a cutting-edge quartz watch—the Quasar—launched at the Basle Fair in 1973, but abandoned soon after, probably in acknowledgement that Seiko had developed a much superior watch in the calibre 38 series, while Omega had already successfully launched the Megaquartz.

The move into distribution: 1969–1972

> We decided to stick to our muttons. We thought we knew something about the motor industry . . . the distribution business was in chaos, so we decided to stick our toe in the water.
>
> (Gerry Mortimer, 1998)

Cave's vision for the firm was not all grand strategy, and there were more than economic reasons behind his decision to scrap wine in the directors' dining room. The cosy atmosphere of 317 Edgware Road needed shaking up. In July 1969 he noted 'a common ill was the inability to contain cost inflation by price increases or cost reductions with a consequential increase in the break-even point'.[119] There was also 'undue optimism' which 'inhibited reductions to a lower base line of expenditure' and more pressure was needed on stock reduction. As he outlined to the board in his paper on 'growth strategies' in October 1969, it had to be 'recognized that internal growth from the traditional activities of Smiths Industries was less assured than previously'.[120] Cave's vision saw the pace of acquisitions increasing significantly. In the motor division, whether in spark plugs or in other accessories, it had been clear for a long time it was hard to make money as an original equipment manufacturer (OEM)—more value was created in the after-market or the supply of retro-fitted accessories. Spark plugs were a good case in point. These were sometimes a loss-leader when sold to car companies on an OEM basis, but were sold at significant margins to the service trade. Since servicing was relatively predictable and also relatively inelastic in relation to annual car sales, it provided a solid after-market for volume sales. It was this fundamental logic that underpinned Smiths' bid for Halfords, the high street motor accessory retailer, in late 1969—part of a strategy suggested to Cave by Mortimer, with input from Professor Tony Merritt of the London Business School. The M&A team at Warburg's cranked into action and Cave went to see the chairman of Halfords, but an unexpected and much higher bid from Burmah Oil scuppered the deal. Smiths wanted to see a 15 per cent return on investment and Halford's most recent figures offered no such prospect. Further, as a matter of policy over the long term, Smiths would not consider a hostile or competitive bid—it was their style to reach agreement with the owners and managers of any takeover target. A LEX column in the *FT* headed 'Burmah's Overkill Bid', opened with Mortimer's assessment—'There are bids, dear bids and oil company bids'.[121]

With difficulties in consistent production in the motor division and the spectre of both collapsing profits at BLMC in 1970 and its decision to adopt dual-sourcing for the first time, the strategy of focusing less on the tricky OEM business and more on the after-market made sense. Two large transactions that year were the purchase of Yorkshire Factors, a wholesale factoring business, and Smiths' first venture onto the high street with Longlife, a chain of retail motor accessory outlets, all designed to capture significantly larger margins, though bringing further overheads and administrative burdens as well. Yorkshire Factors was acquired as a motor business but it 'turned out to be a general factor of everything including wirelesses and televisions, and goodness knows what'.[122]

With the arrival of the Conservatives in power from June 1970, Earl Jellicoe resigned his directorship, becoming Lord Privy Seal, but the board was strengthened in two ways—first with a further non-executive, Barrie Heath.[123] A distinguished wartime Spitfire pilot, Heath entered the motor industry in 1960 as MD of Triplex Safety Glass in the Pilkington Group, becoming chairman in 1965.[124] Described by Roger Hurn as an 'absolute archetypal natural leader', with relevant motor experience, he was a vocal and valuable addition.[125] Early in the year, Robson, special director of finance, had been elevated to the board. This was a challenging period as inflation began to accelerate and interest rates moved up smartly—real rates turning negative. Robson was heavily occupied in consolidating the firm's short-term finances and then working mid-1970 on a twenty-five-year debenture issue, designed to reduce volatile short-term borrowings against a backdrop of uncertainty where rates might go and how easy liquidity might be.

Crippled by rising development costs for its RB211 jet engine, Rolls Royce was forced into bankruptcy in February 1971. Smiths' monthly deliveries were valued at £160,000, and total outstandings exceeded £0.5m, but it was only Rolls Royce shareholders that ultimately took a haircut, offering a salutary lesson for industry of the need to control costs and stock. Cave's plan for growth in motor accessories via acquisition became more active throughout 1971, with the purchase of several small motor factors (see Appendix IV) and the largest deal to date by Smiths, purchasing Godfrey Holmes, first considered for £3m mid-year, and finally acquired for £5.75m at year-end. Based in Lincoln, with thirty-eight nationwide branches, Godfrey Holmes was 'one of the largest specialist distributors of vehicle component parts in the UK', and formed part of a decision 'to specialize in what we called vehicle stoppers (brakes), clutches and bearings'.[126]

Acquisitions continued in 1972, with more motor factors acquired around the country leading to the creation of a holding company, Affiliated Factors, based in High Wycombe, in the autumn, run by F. E. G. ('Ricky') Morris. Amalgamating ten companies, further acquisitions were then folded in over time, taking advantage of centralized administration. On the manufacturing side, rationalization meant letting go the spark plug operation in Treforest—originally a shadow factory—which was sold to Ford (effective mid-1973), while modernizing production at Rugby.[127] The inflationary backdrop meant that wage negotiations remain a constant theme in board discussions, as well as the price war in the motor industry OEM market, where increasing use of dual-sourcing, particularly by British Leyland, was having a marked effect. It was clear as the first half of the 1970s unfolded that revenues and profits from aviation and the various distributive trades were fast outstripping the returns from supplying the motor industry.

Industrial relations: 1970–1975

The relationships were valuable. You could say to Scanlon, 'I'm in trouble, there's no way I can give any more', and he'd say, 'OK, I can accept that's your last offer.' And then he'd sell it for us.

(Gil Jones, 2013)

In addition to growth through acquisition, Cave planned to shake up Smiths in other ways, and as part of these head-hunted Gil Jones from Dunlop in 1970, first looking after industrial relations and then as personnel director—'at the start of the big change' as he recalls.[128] An early task was to close the Godalming aviation factory, only opened in 1965, so production could move to Basingstoke. All part of a process of moving towards an emphasis on shareholder value, Cave had an eye to 'cutting out the fat'.

Jones replaced Bob Aldrich, who had run personnel since 1950, dealing with the Smiths Combine and the post-war militancy of the unionized workforce. Despite management trying to ignore the combine from 1951, and sacking its most charismatic Communist leader, Lawrie Nickolay, in 1956, the conveners had succeeded in maintaining a negotiating front that united the factories. One of Jones's missions was to break this down and return to a system of unilateral negotiation with each factory. Viewed with suspicion as an agent of central management with no good intentions by the workforce at MA1, Cheltenham, and Witney, he had an uphill task. BLMC, with the largest car plant in the world at Longbridge, famously had its own combine, headed by Dick Etheridge, with Derek Robinson (later 'Red Robbo') as deputy, but as Jones recalls 'we had our own reds—particularly at Witney, where one man continually led the workers out on unofficial actions. His trick was to bring a different department out each week', thereby disrupting overall output.[129] BLMC was beginning to flex its muscles to increase competition among its suppliers, and Smiths failed to win a supply contract for a vehicle heater for the first time in a decade.[130] BLMC's rationale for not awarding Smiths the contract was reportedly its concern at Smiths' labour troubles, which were particularly focused at Witney, the heater factory, and the question whether Smiths could maintain a supply schedule. On one occasion, the highly colourful Reg Birch, then a senior officer of the AUEW, was of surprising help, getting up on the back of a lorry to address workers at Witney, successfully getting them back into work by leaning on the convener.[131] Being able to count on a good working relationship with senior union officials in the 1970s was valuable, and to promote this Jones recalls an annual dinner at St Ermin's Hotel in Westminster—'it included Jack Jones, Hugh Scanlon, Clive Jenkins, Bill Jordan, Sir John Boyd, the lot'.[132] These events are remembered by many—Roger Hurn recalls Gil Jones's remarkable gift for telling priceless jokes in a dry Welsh accent that had the room rolling in laughter. Others remember some of the guests making good use of Smiths' hospitality and bottles disappearing up to hotel rooms late on—though in deference to the teetotal Boyd of the AUEW, lifelong member of the Salvation Army, the assembled party would stand to sing 'The Old Rugged Cross' at the end of the evening.[133] Marcus Beresford believes such evenings, with so many key union leaders together in such informal circumstances, may well have been unique.[134] The relationships strengthened on such occasions would be vital in the early 1980s.

The 1970s saw industrial relations crises at a national level, but Jones recalls Smiths being affected to a lesser degree, in his view partly down to an environment—even perhaps a loyalty—at factory level that was the legacy of the Smith family. Witness the hampers sent out to long-serving retirees each year and the remarkable sports facilities that supported football, cricket, archery, darts, bowling, tennis, and more besides. These were all over the country, maintained by staff, including green-keepers. Witney's cricket ground was used for minor county matches—'but when you asked how many Smiths employees played there, it was the captain of the seconds. No other Smiths employees. It was the same with lots of these facilities.'[135] Leisure patterns were changing—television being just one obvious factor—and sport at Smiths dwindled. The grounds were gradually sold and sports clubs made to become self-supporting, though Jones admits soft-pedalling on the yacht club on the Welsh Harp—'Cave was commodore, you see'.

Aviation management: 1971–1973

> *To become an emasculated appendage of the French aerospace industry does not feature in our forward planning.*
>
> (Roy Sisson, 1973)

With comments largely directed at Michael Heseltine, Sisson 'hit about him in a style that brought fervent applause' at the Society of British Aerospace Companies' dinner in 1973.[136] In 1971, Smiths had joined a group led by Société Française d'Equipements pour la Navigation Aérienne (SFENA) of France, working on the A300 Airbus automatic pilot—the same year that Sisson was elevated to be deputy managing director of the group, raising the standing of the aviation division further.[137] In an era of collaborative European aviation projects, Sisson's speech reflects a common desire to protect the British aerospace industry. In the year Britain joined the EEC, Smiths even went on the offensive with a plan to acquire 40 per cent of SFENA, to take it into the heart of the French aerospace industry, but it was insufficiently aggressive and lost out to a French consortium headed by Crouzet. More positive news emerged on military equipment, however, with the HUD product taken up by Sweden for its JA37 Viggen aircraft, while a first supply deal with the US Marine Corp for Harrier displays was agreed, announced by Bill Mallinson.[138]

Mallinson had followed Sisson's path, moving from technical director in aviation to managing director, and then to running both aviation and Kelvin & Hughes, though the latter produced lacklustre performances, leading to informal discussions with Plessey, and later on RACAL, on its possible disposal, though without any success.[139] Colin Proctor, retained by Cave after the 1967 board room struggle to handle some of the 'legacy' assets, finally retired after twenty-five years' service in July 1972. This left space for Mallinson to fill and he joined the main board, bringing a strong engineering and technical focus.

New technology: 1970s

'This is something completely new in instrumentation—not a gimmick',
said Walter Bischoff.

(*Financial Times*[140])

Smiths was a pioneer on many occasions, although sometimes it was not the company to develop fully some of the technically brilliant ideas that emerged. The idea of a heads-up-display (HUD) for motor vehicles is only beginning to gain acceptance in the twenty-first century, yet Bischoff and his development team at Smiths were trialling HUDs on police cars in 1973—technology developed from 1970 with the Transport and Road Research Laboratory, an idea too far ahead of its time.[141] It was another fifteen years before Nissan and GM tentatively tried again.

In the mid-1960s, another Bracken Hill House graduate, David Miller, at the newly formed Access Control Unit, helped to develop the cash dispenser, or ATM. Collaboration with Chubb came through a close relationship between its chairman, Lord Hayter, and Peter Blair, Smith's PR director. In late 1966, a deal was agreed with Westminster Bank (later NatWest) to fund development, but time was of the essence as the bank planned to introduce ATMs ahead of Saturday closing. The first models (the MD2—'money dispenser 2') emerged in mid-1967, and though Westminster's thunder was stolen slightly by Barclays' contemporary cheque-cashing machine, the Smiths/

Chubb card-operated cash dispenser using a four-digit PIN was the first ATM in the world. The card was retained and returned to the customer in the post, while the later MD4 used a returnable card, using credit card technology. Alan Smith remembered, 'We had one of the earliest cash dispensers at our Cricklewood HQ. We made the clever bits, Chubb made the safe... our system worked. It had a card with perforations in it. Put that in and you got £10.'[142] But Smiths was nervous at the amount of technology required and the scale of potential competition—Miller recalls Cave telling him he had 'an insurmountable mountain to climb'.[143] Following a distribution agreement signed with Diebold of the US in early 1971, Smiths' interests, and Chubb's, were transferred to Diebold entirely in 1973. It remains a world leader in ATM technology and manufacture.[144]

Grappling with change in motors: 1973–1975

They were the fifth largest car hire company in the country.

(Gerry Mortimer, 1998)

A further move into distribution occurred mid-1973 with an agreed bid of £6.2m (2010: £58m) for Claude Rye, a family-owned and controlled ball-bearing importer and distributor. This was an example of a strategy that would be repeated, of acquiring a company for a single business line, and disposing of unwanted parts. Smiths wanted the ball-bearings business, but Claude Rye also operated in vehicle sales, hire purchase finance, and contract car hire, none of which was wanted, leading to the rapid disposal of the sales business, though the contract car hire took much longer. Another transaction a few months later was the £1.8m purchase of Tudor Accessories, based in Glamorgan, which, with 90 per cent of the UK market for car windscreen washer equipment, enjoyed the sort of market power Smiths targeted.[145]

With the Claude Rye transaction closed, Ralph Gordon-Smith signalled his intention to step down as chairman, and from August 1973 he accepted the honorary title of President, with Cave replacing him as chairman, and Sisson stepping up to become managing director.[146] At around the same time, Earl Jellicoe (who had been active in the sales effort for Concorde) resigned his government post, leaving him free to rejoin the Smiths board in October, along with John Thompson, who was responsible for all the vehicle equipment businesses.[147] Thompson, an engineer to the core, had joined in 1949 and spent many years in Coventry running the technical sales department, covering the motor manufacturers, under the sponsorship of Frank Hurn—a hugely successful operation that gathered information and acted as an interface between Cricklewood and the assemblers. Cave had brought him back to London in 1963 with a view to becoming chief engineer, and then surprised him by making him a director—'I didn't really expect it. The board in '73 was a very prestigious thing, actually. Lots of knobs, you know, as far as I was concerned. All pretty big cheeses. Pretty daunting.'[148]

October 1973 saw the start of the OAPEC oil embargo that followed on the Yom Kippur War, with knock-on effects across industry and the economy. The quadrupling in the price of oil led to a fall in demand for new vehicles, and the value of UK car sales for 1974 fell 24 per cent year-on-year to £1.3bn (see Figure 8.1 for the wider decline in production).[149] Production itself was severely affected by rising energy costs, the problem compounded yet further by the introduction of the three-day working week from January 1974. In a showdown with the unions, particularly the striking miners, Heath decided to call a snap election in February, largely on the question of who should govern Britain. From discussing production priorities in January, the board moved to considering reductions in staff and the possible outright closure of the Watford factory. Having sold the Treforest spark plug operation, Thompson had ambitious plans for the industrial ceramics business, but with Wilson back in power (although in a hung parliament) the climate was not judged right and plans were put on hold.[150] Other far-reaching changes were afoot in vehicle instruments, with the beginning of a focus on electronic as opposed to electro-mechanical instrumentation, and in mid-1974 Thompson was outlining major capex plans on electronic speedometers, as well as expenses in reorganizing the Ystradgynlais site for the vehicle instrumentation division. In October, Wilson returned to the country, narrowly gaining an overall majority after having settled the miners' strike. Meantime, the motor industry was dominated by negative news, not only from BLMC, but from Chrysler, Vauxhall, and even Ford. Rampant inflation and appalling industrial relations saw costs for all manufacturers increase, and these were only partly recovered in price increases. BLMC haemorrhaged cash, slipped into the red, and passed its final dividend in December. With the equity raised from the City just two years earlier now fallen by more than 80 per cent in value, the situation was grave. Tided over with a £50m government short-term guarantee, Sir Don Ryder of the National Enterprise Board headed a committee formed to conduct an enquiry and make recommendations—producing the ill-fated and wildly optimistic 'Ryder Report' which, in a nutshell, urged colossal capital expenditure and organizational change—none of which achieved its desired goal.[151]

Overall, 1975 was a disastrous year for the UK motor manufacturing industry, with production, domestic sales, and exports all down on the previous year. Most notable was the bankruptcy and nationalization of BLMC. On sales to the motor manufacturers of £23m, Smiths earned less than 3 per cent net profit, by contrast with the 12 per cent earned on £26m of sales to the aerospace industry, a margin closely comparable to that made on the distribution businesses, validating the strategy of the past few years to build this segment of the company. Exports (both direct and indirect) accounted for nearly half of sales. One bright spot in the motor division involved exports of plant and know-how. Back in 1968, Cave had travelled to Moscow with Sir George Harriman of BMH and others to promote UK involvement in the Russian motor industry.[152] As a result, Stephen Gortvay, a Hungarian émigré remembered for his great presence, and a senior marketing officer in the spark plug operation, had negotiated the first of three deals in 1969 to export specialist spark plug machinery, materials, and know-how to Russia.[153] The third deal, in spring 1975, was worth £3m alone.[154] These transactions led to later success in similar operations to export both licences and manufacturing plant to Poland, Yugoslavia, Israel, and Egypt, but the senior engineer responsible, Trevor Leader, remembers the Russian deals as the most ground-breaking, involving heavy security surveillance and significant difficulties in completing each step of the negotiations in what were still the depths of the Cold War—they opened people's eyes to the possibilities of working in 'closed' Communist countries.[155]

The rise of medical: 1970–1975

> It is probably true to say that no person made a greater contribution to the growth and shape of SI, as we know it today, than Frank Hurn.
>
> (*SI News*, April 1973)

The 1970s saw a baton pass from one Hurn generation to another. In December 1972, Frank Hurn finally retired from the board, after twenty-one years, ending a fifty-three-year association with the firm, but sadly he was to die just weeks later. The board always marked the loss of a former colleague—for Frank Hurn, however, the minutes record that for the first time the directors stood in silence, to mark his memory.[156] His legacy extended far outside motor accessories, for while he might have been exasperated at the terms agreed by Proctor and Blair for the acquisition of Uni-Tubes, and was furious to discover its subsequent purchase of Portland Plastics as a fait accompli (which he attempted to have put aside), these were businesses that had flourished on his watch.

Portland's telex code 'Portex' was a natural choice for a change of company name from 1967, and by the early 1970s, the firm was already significant, 1972 seeing a large expansion in premises at Hythe. An agency in Canada had been acquired in 1960 through the purchase of Cribb Associates and then, to support further North American exports, an assembly operation was established in Wilmington, Massachusetts, in 1973, and the same year, in an early move to lower production costs, Smiths moved some assembly to Madeira, recruiting former lace workers. But the Portuguese revolution rapidly curtailed matters, with rapidly escalating labour rates, and Smiths hired a plane to evacuate its plant, leading to a costly dispute with the Blandy family (of Madeira fame, and Smiths' local sub-contractor). Employee numbers went through the 1,000 barrier in 1974, while the firm boasted a string of international industry awards.[157]

In the spring of 1974, Frank Hurn's son Roger was appointed managing director of Group O, chiefly comprising Smiths' international businesses, with Portex added to the portfolio.[158] Roger Hurn had enjoyed a meteoric rise, joining in 1958 after two years at Rolls Royce, persuaded on board by Dick Cave, who in turn had been introduced to Smiths by Frank Hurn. After short periods spent at Jaeger in France, then in North America, and having completed his national service, he spent time in technical selling to the European motor industry, being promoted as a divisional director and export manager for the motor accessories division in 1969, at the age of 30.[159] Within months, Cave had created Group O (handling overseas subsidiaries) with himself in charge. Hurn was moved to assist him, becoming special director, international operations soon after.[160]

Back to 1974, and with Hurn now responsible for Portex, plans were announced for a £650,000 investment in a manufacturing facility across the Channel in France, at Berck-sur-Mer, which would be completed in mid-1978.[161] Within months, Hurn was back before the board to outline plans for a further £415,000 investment in the existing assembly facilities in Boston, Massachusetts, for completion in 1977.[162] Ron Williams, who had been recruited to London from Anglo-Celtic by Alan Hornsby, was appointed a divisional director in October 1974, with special responsibilities for the medical division (and Claude Rye), and a close working relationship with Roger Hurn commenced that would last more than two decades. In May 1975, in a rearrangement, a new Group M was created, including Portex, spark plugs and ceramics, and the industrial instruments and pressure devices, run by Hurn, with Williams as financial controller.[163]

Financial overview: 1960–1975

It is again apparent this year that profits are not sufficient at present rates of inflation to generate adequate funds for long term investment programmes.

(Chairman's statement, 1975)

From so many never having had it so good in the late 1950s, the 1960s saw a radical change in the backdrop, though the stop-go cycle continued. The significant government emphasis on exports as a measure to rein in the balance of payments continued, but inflation was a significant threat, leading to a series of attempted controls through pricing and incomes policies, and credit restrictions. In the case of Smiths, the period opened strongly. Though the current account turned negative in 1960, UK car output rose from 36,000 per week to 44,000. Despite aviation underperforming, this unexpected upturn fed increased profits, taking return on capital to a record 23 per cent. Between then and 1965, the situation was mixed. Strikes and national agreements on wages had negative impacts. Selwyn Lloyd's 'mini-budget' of July 1962 did not help, with credit restrictions softening demand—it was also a year when inflation spiked, and Smiths' returns fell below 10 per cent. Confidence was sufficient to allow major capital expenditure, but nervousness over funding led to a £4m issue of 6 per cent debenture stock via Warburg's in early 1963 (despite the thirty-year relationship with Helbert, Wagg). Two reductions of purchase tax on cars in 1962 from 55 to 25 per cent and stronger military aviation demand meant Smiths' figures bounced back, but 1964 saw aviation orders fall away as Labour took power. Tightened credit restrictions particularly hit the motor industry, and the cancellation of TSR-2 emphasized the need to develop civil aviation. Overall, returns remained healthy at around 15 per cent for four of the five years to 1965.

However 1966 and 1967 saw a marked downturn, with profits and returns halving. While inflation had eased, Smiths nevertheless found rising costs could not be adequately recovered in price increases. The 1966 'July measures' hit hard—interest rates rose and tighter hire purchase terms depressed demand for cars. Smiths revalued its properties upwards for the first time. With sterling under pressure, and rates rising yet further, devaluation eventually came, and this was partly responsible for improved results in 1968, though Smiths downplayed benefits to exports. With boardroom conflicts resolved, management succeeded not only in driving the business forward but also controlling costs and expenditure. Better stock control and sale of properties in 1968 all fed into a record year, with returns up from 7–9 per cent to over 12 per cent. Despite reinforced lending limits from mid-1968, record turnover and profits were achieved again in 1969 but there were notable negatives—in appliance controls, at Kelvin & Hughes, and in Australia, plus costs of contraction and relocation. The Conservatives regained power in 1970 with inflation over 5 per cent and rising, influencing record turnover, but profits declined markedly, blamed squarely on the chaotic state of the motor industry, and Smiths' response included a 7 per cent reduction in the workforce. Inflation neared 10 per cent in 1971, leading to uncertainties and a decision to lock in more long-term funding with further debenture stock. By now, sales of non-Smiths products through newly acquired distribution channels were significant, at more than 15 per cent of sales in 1972—the returns from new activities exceeded those on traditional businesses.

There was some respite in 1973, with a wage freeze in operation, and Smiths earned significant amounts from the motor industry both on the OEM side and in distribution, overall returns exceeding 20 per cent for the first time since 1960, though crucially not allowing for inflation effects. With inflation reaching the mid-teens and rising, Dick Cave's address to the workforce in the first issue of *SI News* in 1974 was headed 'The Crisis', emphasizing the seriousness of the economic situation. The three-day week and marked labour and material shortages were crippling the car industry and Smiths' OEM business with it. Workforce numbers always fluctuated, tending naturally to match production demands, but 1975 saw the most significant reduction, at 2,100 or 9 per cent, requiring £620,000 in redundancy payments. Despite this, a notable change was the significant increase in numbers of 'staff' versus those 'on the clock', reaching 56 per cent in 1974 and then 77 per cent in 1975. Inflation soared to over 26 per cent mid-year, and though weak sterling helped exports, such high inflation was a severe drag, offsetting the gains. It also fed a growing debate on the validity of historical cost accounting, either for evaluating companies, or for management to make informed decisions. A report in 1973 by the National Economic Development Office which examined the accounts of 126 quoted UK firms between 1965 and 1971 highlighted the marked results from reinterpreting figures on an inflation-adjusted basis, unsurprisingly uncovering weaker results. Notably the firms had reinvested only a small portion of their real earnings—profits that appeared to have been ploughed back were illusory.[164] Following the lead of firms such as GKN and Tube Investments which in 1974 had revealed surprisingly lower inflation-adjusted figures in their annual reports, the 1975 Smiths accounts saw the first appearance of (alternative) 'current purchasing power' figures, illustrating the damage of inflation.[165] Significant effort was required in such an environment to manage credit terms on both sides of the business and to ensure sufficient liquidity not only as working capital but for investment—a need partly met with a rights issue that raised £8.7m mid-year.

Conclusions

> *For one brief period the British motor industry was successful. It was brief!*
>
> (John Thompson, 1998)

The period 1960–75 opened with Ralph Gordon-Smith increasingly marginalized and the senior members of his board moving towards retirement age, without any clear succession plan. The result in the mid-1960s was the division of the board into two factions, and a showdown in early 1967 that saw Dick Cave emerge victorious, backed by Frank Hurn. It was therefore Cave's vision for a highly decentralized corporate structure that was firmly adopted, shaping the management of the firm for the rest of the century. It also heralded a distinct transition from the slightly cosy 'family firm' to a significantly more dynamic and professional firm.

Motor accessories remained at the heart of the business, though the importance (and potential) of aviation was clearly understood—the division survived the vagaries of uncertain government procurement policy and laid the foundations of important future civil business with majors such as Boeing. The clocks and watches division, despite vigorous championship from Dennis Barrett, could not withstand the fierce competition emerging, particularly from Switzerland, Russia, and Japan, and its fortunes declined.

With car ownership still growing, albeit at a slower rate, the car industry involved mass production and high-value goods, forming a natural target for fiscal measures to regulate spending. The high point of UK car production fell in 1972, but the journey to the peak had not been smooth—between 1957 and 1968 there were eleven changes to hire purchase terms, and seven changes to the purchase tax rate.[166] The performance of Smiths' accessory business was inextricably linked to the changing fortunes of an industry that was declining in productivity and profitability. On a broader front, and in common with almost all industry, Smiths suffered from two memorable characteristics of the late 1960s/1970s: (i) the rising militancy of the engineering unions (though to a lesser degree than its car manufacturing customers), and (ii) the rapid acceleration of inflation.

A long-term reputation for innovation and R&D is evidenced in a role in hi-tech areas such early medical ultrasound technology, heads-up displays, and ATM technology, although intriguingly sometimes Smiths' role could be limited to that of incubator, with the technology moving on to be developed by others.

Having cut his teeth on the motor side, particularly in motor accessories, and then having run the export business, Roger Hurn was a rising star, emerging in 1975 with a new division that included Portex, by now growing from strength to strength and establishing medical as a business line in its own right. Around Hurn, a remarkably talented team that would drive Smiths forwards over the next two decades was falling into place.

Notes

1. *Mar. 1960*, 4.
2. John Thompson, interview (15 July 1998).
3. *The Times* (14 Apr. 1960), 10; *HC Deb* (13 Apr. 1960), vol. 621, cc. 1265–75.
4. *Minutes* (9 Dec. 1959).
5. *Minutes* (6 Jan. 1960).
6. *Minutes* (13 Oct. 1960, 11 Jan. and 7 May 1961).
7. *Minutes* (6 July 1960).
8. *Daily Express* (5 Dec. 1962), 1.
9. *Financial Times* (8 Dec. 1962), 8.
10. *Minutes* (31 Oct. 1952).
11. *Minutes* (8 Feb. 1961).
12. *Smiths News* (Sept. 1959), 3.
13. *Minutes* (15 Mar. 1961).
14. *Minutes* (4 Oct. 1961, 11 Apr. 1962).
15. *Minutes* (15 Mar., 2 Aug. 1961).
16. *Minutes* (11 Jan. 1961).
17. *Minutes* (19 Apr. 1961).
18. *Minutes* (14 Feb. 1962).
19. *Minutes* (14 Feb. 1962); Cann, 'Chronological *Record*', ii. 226.
20. *Minutes* (13 Feb., 22 May 1963).
21. *Minutes* (21 Mar., 7 Nov. 1962, 5 Aug. 1964).
22. *Smiths News* (June 1959), 9.
23. Marcus Beresford, personal communication (July 2013).
24. For the background, see Eric Wigham, *The Power to Manage: A History of the Engineering Employers' Federation* (London: Macmillan, 1973), 189–211.
25. *Minutes* (4 May 1960).
26. *Guardian* (9 June 1961), 7.
27. *Smiths Combine minutes*, Nickolay papers.
28. *Smiths News* (July 1958), 1.
29. Personal communication (11 June 2013).
30. *Guardian* (21 June 1961), 3; *The Times* (24 June 1961), 8.
31. *Guardian* (24 June 1961), 1.
32. *Guardian* (22 June 1961), 22.
33. *Guardian* (21 June 1961), 3; *The Times* (24 June 1961), 5.
34. *Minutes* (11 Jan., 12 July, 2 Aug. 1961).
35. Monopolies Commission, *Report on the Supply of Electrical Equipment for Mechanically Propelled Land Vehicles*, HC 21, 1963–4, 4.

36. Cann, 'Chronological *Record*', ii. 205.

37. *Minutes* (3 Oct. 1962).

38. *Minutes* (12 Feb. 1964).

39. Tom Brown, personal communication (3 June 2013).

40. E. M. Tansey and D. A. Christie (eds), *Looking at the Unborn: Historical Aspects of Obstetric Ultrasound*, Wellcome Witnesses to Twentieth Century Medicine, 5 (London: Wellcome, Jan. 2000), 18.

41. *The Lancet*, 271/7032 (7 June 1958), 1188–95.

42. Tansey and Christie, *Looking at the Unborn*, 18.

43. Cann, 'Chronological *Record*', ii. 223.

44. *Minutes* (3 Oct. 1962, 16 Jan., 22 May 1963).

45. Alan Hornsby, personal communication (June 2013).

46. *SI News* (June 1964), 5.

47. R. Lenoir, 'Progress of High-Grade Watch Production', *Society of Engineers' Journal*, 51 (1960), 59–77.

48. *Smiths News* (Dec. 1959), 2, and (May 1961), 1.

49. *Minutes* (19 Apr. 1961).

50. *Smiths News* (Feb. 1962), 2.

51. Ron Williams, interview (26 Feb. 2013).

52. *Smiths News* (June 1962), 1.

53. 5 March 1964, 17.

54. *Minutes* (17 Apr. 1963).

55. Hurn retired as an executive from 31 July.

56. *Minutes* (20 May 1964).

57. 7 Apr. 1965, 15.

58. *Smiths News* (Apr. 1965), 6.

59. See e.g. George Brown's comments, *HC Deb* (13 Nov. 1963), vol. 684, cc. 175–305.

60. *Minutes* (13 Jan. 1965).

61. Harold Nockolds, *Lucas: The First 100 Years*, ii. *The Successors* (Newton Abbott: David & Charles, 1978), 287.

62. *Minutes* (7 Apr. 1965).

63. *The Times* (11 June 1965), 8; *ILN* (19 June 1965), 5.

64. Cann, 'Chronological *Record*', ii. 242; *Smiths News* (Aug. 1965), 1.

65. 'Air Transport Statistics', *Commons Library Standard Note*, SN03760 (July 2011), 15.

66. Chairman's report (1964).

67. *Smiths News* (Oct. 1965), 10.

68. *Minutes* (5 Aug., 16 Oct. 1964).

69. *Minutes* (19 May 1965).

70. *Minutes* (7 July 1965).

71. *Minutes* (4 Aug. 1965).

72. *Minutes* (9 June 1965).

73. *Minutes* (4 Aug., 3 Nov. 1965).

74. *Minutes* (8 July 1964).

75. *Minutes* (20 Mar. 1963).

76. *Minutes* (9 June 1965).

77. *Minutes* (12 Jan. 1966).

78. *Minutes* (9 Feb. 1966).

79. *Minutes* (8 June 2013).

80. *Minutes* (9 Mar. 1966).

81. *Financial Times* (21 July 1966), 14.

82. *Minutes* (18 May 1966).

83. *Minutes* (6 July 1966).

84. 30 Nov. 1967, 8.

85. Graham Smith, interview (2013).

86. *Smiths News* (Mar. 1966), 6; *Financial Times* (30 Nov. 1967), 8.

87. Cann, 'Chronological Record', ii. 247.

88. *Minutes* (16 Feb. 1967).

89. *The Economist* (15 June 1968), 64.

90. *SI News* (Jan. 1968), 12.

91. *Minutes* (3 Aug. 1966).

92. RGS, MD's memorandum no. 190 (3 Nov. 1966).

93. *The Times* (11 Nov. 1966), 12.

94. *Minutes* (16 Feb. 1967).

95. *Minutes* (3 Mar. 1967).

96. *Minutes* (2 Aug. 1967).

97. Information kindly supplied by John Goodwin and Sir David Scholey. Personal communication (May 2013).

98. RGS, MD's memorandum no. 197 (5 July 1967).

99. Cave, MD's memorandum no. C18 (8 Apr. 1968); Alan Hornsby, interview (24 July 2013).

100. Martyn Wenzerul, interview (21 Aug. 2013).

101. Mortimer, interview (1998); Cave, MD's memorandum no. C23 (17 June 1968).

102. RGS, MD's memorandum no. 200 (12 July 1967).

103. *Minutes* (10 Jan. 1968).

104. *Chairman's Report* (1968).

105. *Minutes* (4 and 25 Oct. 1967, 25 Sept. 1968).

106. *Minutes* (14 Feb. 1968).

107. *Minutes* (10 Apr., 7 Aug., 23 Oct. 1968).

108. *Minutes* (14 May 1969).

109. *SI News* (June 1968), 1.

110. *SI Digest* (Apr. 1968), 1; *Minutes* (15 May 1968).

111. *Minutes* (12 June 1968).

112. *Minutes* (8 Jan. 1969).

113. *Minutes* (25 Sept. 1968.

114. *Minutes* (10 July 1969).

115. *Minutes* (12 May 1970).

116. *Minutes* (9 Apr. 1969).

117. *Minutes* (8 Jan., 12 Feb. 1969). Hairspring production continued at The Grange till the late 1970s, when a management buy-out of British Precision Springs took place.

118. *Minutes* (12 Feb. 1970).

119. *Minutes* (10 July 1969).

120. *Minutes* (7 Oct. 1969).

121. *Financial Times* (3 Dec. 1969), 31.

122. Mortimer and Williams, interviews (1998).

123. *Minutes* (6 Oct. 1970).

124. *Flight International* (11 Feb. 1965), 223.
125. Roger Hurn, interview (1998).
126. *SI News* (Feb. 1972), 1; Mortimer, interview (1998).
127. *Minutes* (13 July 1972).
128. *SI News* (Dec. 1970), 1; Gil Jones, interview (14 June 2013).
129. Jones, interview (2013). It was probably Ray Brown.
130. The AD028 heater. *Minutes* (10 July 1969).
131. Jones, interview (2013).
132. Jones, interview (2013).
133. Hornsby, interview (2013).
134. Marcus Beresford, personal communication (13 July 2013).
135. Jones, interview (2013).
136. *Financial Times* (28 June 1973), 27.
137. *SI News* (Feb. 1971), 5; *Minutes* (14 Oct. 1971).
138. *Minutes* (8 Mar. 1973); Wenzerul, interview (21 Aug. 2013).
139. *Minutes* (11 June, 10 Sept. 1970).
140. *Financial Times* (14 Aug. 1970), 21.
141. *SI News* (Nov. 1973), supplement. The technology was transferred to the NRDC in late 1974—*Minutes* (10 Oct. 1974).
142. Alan Smith, interview (1998).
143. David Miller, personal communication (Aug. 2013).
144. *Minutes* (14 Jan. 1971, 13 Apr. 1972, 10 May 1973).
145. *Minutes* (24 Sept. 1973); *SI News* (Feb. 1974), 1.
146. *Minutes* (12 July 1973).
147. *Minutes* (11 Oct. 1973).
148. John Thompson, interview (15 July 1998).
149. R. A. Church, *The Rise and Decline of the British Motor Industry* (Cambridge: CUP, 1995), 109.
150. *Minutes* (14 Mar. 1974).
151. Church, *Rise and Decline*, 104–6.
152. *SI News* (Apr. 1968), 1.
153. Born Istvan Grunwald in Israel in 1906. He had built a spark plug factory in Hungary by the 1930s, only to lose it in the 1956 uprising. He was naturalized in the UK in 1963.
154. *SI News* (Apr. 1975), 1.
155. Trevor Leader, personal communication (8 Aug. 2013).
156. *Minutes* (11 Jan. 1973).
157. *Portex Communiqué* (1977).
158. *SI Digest* (Apr. 1974).
159. *Minutes* (12 Mar. 1969).
160. *Minutes* (14 May, 7 Oct. 1969).
161. *Minutes* (14 Mar. 1974); *SI News* (May 1974), 1.
162. *Minutes* (10 Apr. 1975).
163. *SI News* (May 1975), 1.
164. P. W. Parker and P. M. D. Gibbs, 'Accounting for Inflation: Recent Proposals and their Effects', *Journal of the Institute of Actuaries* (Dec. 1974), 353–4.
165. *Financial Times* (15 May 1974), 10.
166. Graham Turner, *Business in Britain* (London: Eyre & Spottiswoode, 1969), 379.

CHAPTER 8

....

1976–1990

Shocking the Markets

....

DoI officials now recognise that BL's chances are less than even. We regard them as nearly zero.

(John Hoskyns to Margaret Thatcher, 1979[1])

THE second half of the 1970s saw the Labour government continuing to grapple with the serious problems of both high inflation and unemployment. Experiments with managed pricing and incomes policies were failing and the mid-1970s saw the abandonment of demand management. Catastrophic industrial relations remained a constant trope for the period—usually summed up decades later by reference to BL's 'Red Robbo', the car manufacturer's most militant shop steward, whose name typically evokes the decline of UK industry, particularly automotive. The arrival of the Thatcher government in 1979 signalled a determined move to allow markets to function freely and to use their operation to encourage competition—indeed to determine survivorship—placing BL squarely in the spotlight.

UK manufacturing in general declined in both output and productivity through to 1979, and the motor industry, still the most important sector for Smiths, offers strong evidence—production declined by 40 per cent in the 1970s alone (see Figure 8.1).[2] From the mid-1970s, car imports exceeded exports, and a combination of both disastrous management strategy (e.g. the 'Ryder Report' and its outcome) and productivity losses forged a near terminal decline. The UK's cocktail of high inflation, poor industrial relations, and relative declines in productivity and competitiveness left Smiths' two best-known businesses in dire straits by the mid-1970s. Over at Lucas and GKN, two other firms with a major stake in the declining UK motor industry, their strategies nevertheless contemplated continued involvement in the automotive sector. Smiths' response, however, stunned the markets. When Roger Hurn became CEO in 1981, he and his team had grown up together over decades in the motor business, yet they decided to abandon the firm's roots, in both motors and clocks/watches. It took till the mid-1980s to manage the reorganizations and disposals, but the firm that emerged, with the triumvirate of aviation, medical, and industrial, provided a structure that would last another twenty years, producing healthy returns and capable of weathering the economic cycle.

FIGURE 8.1 UK car production (1966–1980) (millions).

Source: SMMT

Over the long term, the 1987 purchase of Lear Siegler businesses proved to be the most far-sighted acquisition of the period—but easily the most significant decision, indeed of the post-war period, was the disposal of the motor accessory business in 1983. John Thompson later turned down Harvard Business School's request to turn it into a case study, but the request was predictable—examples of firms abandoning the business lines with which their brands are most closely associated, and have been for many decades, are hard to find. The story, as well as illuminating another facet of the decline of the UK motor industry, provides a compelling example of Smiths' ability to adapt over the long term to changing circumstances.

Management change: 1976

One of the most drawn-out succession sagas in the history of British business appears to have come to an end.

(*Financial Times*[3])

Five and a half years after Sir Jules Thorn had announced he would retire 'within a year' from Thorn Electrical Industries (and a few days after Harold Wilson's resignation), he finally announced in 1976 he was stepping down as chairman of the firm he had founded forty years earlier. His chosen successor was Dick Cave, whose achievements at Smiths over nine years had, according to *The Times*, 'made him one of the City's hottest management properties'.[4] Cave's colleagues at Smiths were shocked he could be 'tempted away to go and run Thorn at the height of his powers', but Jules Thorn knew he needed someone 'to lift the company [Thorn] from its older electro-mechanical activities into the electronic age'—echoing a broader meta-narrative of the challenge facing Smiths and large numbers of engineering companies worldwide, whose products had previously relied on lathes and coil-winding machines, but which would in future depend heavily on the flow-solder machine.[5] While Cave (now Sir Richard Cave) went on to execute bold manoeuvres such as the acquisition of EMI in 1979, 'his time at Thorn was less happy than at Smiths', and his seven-year term was dogged by several poor performances.[6] Hurn recalls that, 'for all he ran a much bigger company he never felt very much at home there', reflecting the way Smiths' culture became deeply ingrained.[7]

Cave's departure propelled two senior aviation figures to the top, with Roy Sisson becoming chairman, and Bill Mallinson, the archetypal hi-tech engineer, becoming managing director. The final move on the board saw Roger Hurn appointed director. Sisson's arrival signalled a change in culture for the corporate staff. Cave, a lifelong motor man, had worked hard to master the aviation brief, and is remembered as 'a demanding taskmaster', though 'there was a huge respect, tempered with a degree of fear'.[8] Sisson's style was significantly more relaxed and hands-off—he knew his own sector but did not enquire too deeply elsewhere, allowing people to operate without intervention. He also inspired significant loyalty, and is fondly remembered for a tremendous (and bawdy) sense of humour—'the schoolboy who had found a bag of sweets'—though he was also shrewd and a hard man, if crossed.[9] Mallinson's appointment as managing director lasted through till August 1978, when he was elevated to vice-chairman, with Roger Hurn, who had only joined the board two years earlier, leapfrogging his fellow directors to the position of managing director, though technically Sisson remained CEO.[10] It was clear Mallinson, despite a brilliant intellect and a distinguished track record in guided weapons at Ferranti, was no manager—as Joan Berry, his secretary, commented, 'he never really fitted in, not having come up through Smiths'.[11] John Thompson became deputy managing-director, and Alan Hornsby ('the cleverest of all of us', according to Thompson) joined the board as finance director, stepping into the shoes of his former boss, 'Robby' Robson, who had died unexpectedly in January. Here he was in a position to continue the drive towards financial discipline and higher standards in accounting.

A decade had elapsed since Cave had won the boardroom battle. Under his command, some rationalization had occurred, for example in clocks and watches. Aviation had been strongly supported, and the motor business had been diversified with the move into the motor factors. But by the late 1970s it was obvious more rationalization was needed. Various trading environments were proving too hard for any chance of sustainable growth or profitability. Physically it was time for change as well, and a new site was acquired at Child's Hill, Finchley, in 1978, where work started the following year on a new (and small) corporate headquarters building (see Plate 57). Cricklewood was beginning to fade.

Aviation: steady but unspectacular, 1976–1980

> On September 1, 1980, Marshal of the Royal Air Force, Sir Denis Spots-wood, GCB, CBE, DSO, DFC, FRAeS, joins the Company as chairman of SI's international aerospace companies.
>
> (SI News, 1980)

In the period 1975–8, profits from aerospace declined, reflecting a deeply competitive environment, and problematic defence contracts. The MRCA (Tornado) programme offers an obvious example. In 1975, the UK announced a desire to slow the production rate, with an eye to containing its defence budget.[12] With costs soaring, 1976 saw delays through problems with engine components being developed by Rolls Royce.[13] A continued combination of concern over costs and delays from refining new technology fed through to a drain on defence avionics suppliers such as Smiths.

On the civil front, the mid-to-late-1970s saw agonizing over how the airlines' requirements would be met for the several thousand aircraft estimated to be needed over the following decade, in part to replace existing and ageing stock, and in part to support anticipated demand, particularly in the short-to-medium-haul sector. Boeing, which accounted for more than half the world's commercial fleet now faced the threat of competition from Airbus. All constructors faced significant development costs, and many of their airline clients were financially weak.

Smiths' preparation for an up-turn, as airlines eventually had to commit to purchases, rested on continued technical development and the maintenance of a presence in both the UK and US markets. The up-turn began in 1978, with Boeing's selection of Smiths to provide autothrottles for the 727 and 737 aircraft and engine indicators for the 747—a contract worth £1m per annum—and then stall-warning equipment from 1979. Having lost several other Boeing contracts to the same competitor—Harowe Systems of West-Chester, Pennsylvania, part-owned and run by Geoff Hedrick—Smiths took the sensible course of buying the company, in early 1978, adding new primary flight instruments and on-board computers to the product range.[14] On technical development, the broad switch from electro-mechanical to pure electronic was taking place in all of Smiths' peers in industry, including Dowty, best-known for its landing gear. Dowty also had ambitions in fuel systems and the two firms pooled their resources in 1977, forming Dowty & Smiths Industries Controls, focusing on aircraft engine control—leading to closer long-term contact between the parent firms, fostered also by a long-term relationship between Sisson and Bob Hunt, Dowty's chairman.

In 1979, Smiths rearranged its activities and formed a new company—Smiths Industries Aerospace and Defence Systems (SIADS)—in place of the old aerospace divisions, recognizing the sense in grouping non-aerospace defence work within the same area. In September 1980, Smiths hired Sir Denis Spotswood, who had been vice-chairman at Rolls Royce, and a recent president of the Society of British Aerospace Companies (SBAC), following in Sisson's earlier footsteps. Spotswood, who also took up a directorship at Dowty, became chairman of the aerospace division, with a role 'to evolve a strategy to maximize the efficient use of our Aerospace resources'.[15] Geoff Hedrick recalls his effectiveness: 'what he did was to take the hard decisions about how to make the aerospace companies work together'. There were a number of difficulties between units. For example, salary differentials between the US and UK were high. Then there was friction between the sales operation in Clearwater, Florida, and a new unit established by Doug Gemmell in Seattle, deliberately close to Boeing. Gemmell, head of the Cheltenham unit in the 1970s, was a forceful character—some might argue a maverick—determined to win more business from Boeing, and his decision produced a natural conflict, resolved by Spotswood's appointment of Hedrick as overall CEO of all

North American operations with a brief to get the units working together, achieved with some reorganization and rationalization.

However, the backdrop was not all positive. Confidence that airlines would commit to replace their ageing fleets gave way to disappointment as the worldwide economic slump of the early 1980s unfolded. On the military side, a feature of the slump was a move by governments to defer spending, observable through to at least 1983. To a degree, however, Smiths bucked this broader trend through its involvement in two programmes. Deliveries of the Panavia Tornado commenced in 1979 and, throughout the first half of the 1980s, when several hundred aircraft were built, Smiths contributed the HUD, engine instrumentation, and control (in collaboration with Dowty), producing good revenues and profits. Similarly, the AV8B (Harrier II) programme used Smiths' HUD and head-down displays, and controls for the Rolls Royce Pegasus engine. The rapid response of the Cheltenham electronics team, supporting the Sea Harrier HUD during the Falklands War in 1982, and winning a third Queen's Award that same spring, all contributed to a boost for morale, but this was more than offset by the announcement of 400 redundancies at the factory, reflecting the constant news of deferrals and cancellations of aerospace orders in both civil and military spheres.

In October 1981, perhaps mindful that Mallinson, another senior aerospace man, had been largely marginalized as vice-chairman since 1978, and the division lacked dynamic and decisive line management, Roy Sisson recruited (in true Sisson fashion, over a number of whiskies) his good friend Hugh Pope, the director of Dunlop's aviation business (and current president of the SBAC), to become operating managing director of the division.[16] Pope had been well-known to Sisson, Hurn, and other Smiths colleagues for years and was recruited to provide more energetic and 'hands-on management . . . he knew every element of the business, every political nuance, every player'.[17] Having settled into the role, Pope joined the board in May 1983, on the same day as George Kennedy in medical.

Pope joined a business heavily involved in long-term defence development and contract work—particularly for projects such as BAe's Agile Combat Aircraft (which morphed into the Eurofighter via the Experimental Aircraft Project) and the Anglo-Italian EH101 helicopter, replacing the Sea King. Both turnover and profit remained unspectacular through until 1984, but the following year saw an upturn in civil aviation, and 1985–6 witnessed healthy deliveries of instruments and engine control systems to Boeing for the 737-300, and the fuel management system for the Airbus A320. This followed on earlier contracts for the A300 flight guidance system—all theoretically good diversification (to work with Airbus as well as Boeing) but in reality difficult business, offering technical challenges that were not always welcome. The same period saw another significant contract from McDonnell Douglas, covering solid-state displays for the MD88—part of the strong trend away from using mechanical dials for aircraft instrumentation.

Medical shows strong growth: mid-1970s to 1979

We focused on exports. Sales to a UK hospital involved boxes. Exports sales were in bulk.

(George Kennedy, 2013)

George Kennedy moved south from Scotland in his mid-twenties to play for Hull Kingston Rovers, but he forsook professional rugby for a commercial career, moving in 1967 to Brunswick Corporation in its developing medical division. Having run Brunswick's newly established Tokyo unit for a year, networking through the medical conference world brought an introduction to Portex and a job back in the UK as marketing director, from January 1973. Here he rapidly established himself and a year later was placed in charge of the Hythe factory.

Kennedy now worked hard to develop exports—already accounting for more than half of sales. Closest to home, France was an important target. Plans for expansion across the Channel had been in place since 1974, recognizing the strong protectionism that required local manufacture (or assembly) to gain market share. A new factory at Berck-sur-Mer was finally completed in 1978, so temporary premises were used for assembly in the meantime, including (remarkably) the Mairie, lent by the supportive mayor, leaving residents to conduct their weddings and funerals elsewhere.[18]

Japan was another key destination, to which Portex had exported since 1971 through a small firm, Japan Medico, run by Hiroshi Mikami. To add some needed substance, Smiths arranged for the more established Kuraray, a synthetic fibre company from Osaka, to acquire control of Japan Medico, but long discussions finally resulted in a 50:50 Portex/Kuraray joint venture from 1976. Smiths faced limited competition in Japan, where the manufacturing focus was significantly skewed towards hi-tech and high capital value areas, such as X-ray and other scanning equipment. In single-use items, Japan became a critically important market thereafter for Smiths, and when the underlying business mushroomed rapidly in growth, the firm found itself with a long-term challenge to regain full control of its successful distribution outlet.[19]

International growth produced Queen's Awards in 1970 and 1974, but exports were not limited to products alone. Just as Smiths exported equipment and know-how in spark-plugs, so Portex developed the export of its technology and expertise. There were two features to the business: (i) the licensee could develop its local market, but not export any final products, and (ii) there was the prospect of follow-up business—'the gamble was to sell today's technology at a time when we had a new pipeline of stuff coming through'. Effectively crystallizing a degree of potential sales into the alternative of an up-front payment for a licensing deal bolstered Portex's growth at home.[20] The first deal came about with lengthy assistance from the CBI and DHSS, and resulted in a £1.25m deal in 1977 to supply airway management plant and machinery, plus know-how, to Licensintorg in Leningrad.[21] This part-financed the small acquisition that year of Surgical Equipment Supplies, in Acton, manufacturer of autoclaves and sterilizers, and a range of disposables, transferred into Portex.

In 1979, a second transaction involved a £2m sale to support a medical factory in Skopje in the former Yugoslavia.[22] Kennedy sees these licensing deals as vital—'To me, these were the two catalysts that brought money in . . . they were hugely profitable deals, and brought medical to the attention of the rest of Smiths'.[23]

Exports now accounted for more than 70 per cent of sales, and were a priority because they involved bulk quantities, but in the domestic market the single largest customer was, predictably, the NHS, giving rise to headaches for Ron Williams as financial controller, who despaired of profits focused at the end of the year. But this was a function of classic NHS budgeting. Kennedy explained: 'they guarded the budget till the last month of the year, till someone said "Whoops, we've got all this money. If we don't spend it, we'll lose it." We geared ourselves to that. We didn't build stock till the last quarter, when we knew we could sell it. A hospital would ring up and say "We've got x pounds, can you help?"'[24]

Another important factor was the realization Portex had proprietary products for which it could charge a premium price. Kennedy recalls, 'one of the first things I did when I came in was to put all the prices up. They had been too frightened to change them in years, and yet this was an inflationary time.' Indeed the medical business was an area where Smiths dealt well with inflation: 'you could get away with what appeared to be a 10 per cent price increase over everybody else, but if you got in early you started making money on it. The tail-end Charlies weren't making any'.[25]

In 1979, the firm added two further Queen's Awards (for both exports and technological achievement), and Smiths enlarged its business in the US, acquiring Concord Laboratories in Keene, New Hampshire. With sales of $10m per annum in a wide range of disposable products (including blood-gas analysis kits), this offered a neat complement to Portex's main lines. These had been rationalized early on by Kennedy, who abandoned projects in capital machines (such as glucose monitoring equipment), arguing 'these were losing money. First-in is not always a profitable strategy.' Instead, he focused on specialist disposable products familiar to consultants which would be asked for by name, rather than volume items associated with nursing, available via discounted bulk-purchase. The Concord acquisition saw Kennedy working with Gerry Mortimer for the first time, but an added step was the appointment of Mortimer as chairman. This approach to absorption into the Smiths ethos was described later by Hurn as 'nice, soft, cuddly entry . . . Gerry's in charge for a while and you report to him, chaps, because you met him during the acquisition process and due diligence, and you've got to know him and can even stand his jokes if you don't hear them too often.'[26] Such a kid-glove approach was rarely adopted by Hurn, but was occasionally crucial to maintaining the goodwill and close involvement of the entrepreneur selling their business to Smiths. Where this wasn't necessary, the standard approach was 'to hit them from day one with what they're going to be up against, and they should learn what we expect from them, which is the proper reporting line into the management at director level'.[27]

Project Lucy: 1982–1983

> *We were attempting to serve a bankrupt industry. If you are a supplier to an industry that isn't making any money, you are under siege because they want their supplies for nothing.*

> (John Thompson, 1998)

A number of serious threats to Smiths' automotive business emerged from the mid-1970s onwards, rooted in the broader industry. Failings in industrial relations, in the design and build of the product range, and in the quality of management and planning, all meant the UK car industry was in serious relative decline. It was not standing still—there were considerable technical advances being made—but foreign industries, notably the German and Japanese, were advancing faster and achieving higher productivity and build quality. The overwhelming backdrop for the UK was the rise of import penetration and the collapse of UK vehicle production by roughly 50 per cent from the early 1970s to early 1980s.[28] For Smiths 'this had the dual effect of crippling us and strengthening our competitors who saw their volume base increasingly rapidly'.[29] By the late 1970s, the Vehicle Instrumentation Division (VID), including Radiomobile, the after-market business, and industrial instruments were all facing serious decline. An increase in imported vehicles (minus any Smiths content) impacted the previously profitable after-market, and car radios were now fitted as standard, not retro-fitted, removing their historic profitability.

There was also industry-wide pressure to adopt emerging electronic technologies. For firms such as Lucas this meant the development of engine management systems and solid-state electronics for combined monitoring and control. In France it half-owned Ducellier together with Valeo (formerly Ferodo). Jeffrey Wilkinson, joint-MD, had been working for some time on Project LDP (Lucas, Ducellier, Paris Rhone), combining electronic ignition, fuel management, rotating machines (small motors, alternators, and starters), lighting, and instrumentation in a single enterprise, to compete with Bosch, with backing from both the UK and French governments. In Smiths' case, it had decades of experience in the design and manufacture of electro-mechanical instrumentation and it had also been one of the first firms worldwide to incorporate an integrated circuit in a production instrument—an electronic tachometer, using a Texas Instruments chip.[30] This advance, and the relationship with Texas, led to digital speedometers and solid-state displays using vacuum fluorescence, all providing a technological edge that supported export business (to Volvo, Renault, Fiat, and VW), matching the car makers' demands for 'hi-tech' products.

This edge was maintained with another hi-tech advance, involving voice synthesis warning and information systems—the 'talking dashboard'. Marcus Beresford (John Thompson's protégé who was now running VID) spent a lot of time in Japan, courting Nippon Seiki, to see if there were was room for cross-licensing or even equity proposals: 'we were therefore privy to some of the developments that were moving rapidly in Japan, principally in trip computers and voice synthesis'.[31] He persuaded Andy Barr of BL (who ran the Cowley assembly plant) and other senior BL colleagues to accompany Smiths to Japan, partly to see what was being done for Honda; 'they were very excited and impressed and decided this was exactly what they needed to do to raise BL's image'. Smiths therefore funded the development of the talking dashboard for BL's LC10 project, launched as the Maestro in 1983. This featured a thirty-two-word vocabulary, recorded for the English-language version by the television actress Nicolette McKenzie, though with only 64k of chip memory, the speech compression devised at Witney suggested a Japanese accent to some—strong folk memories remain of 'farsen sea bell prease'. There were teething problems and the dashboard, an expensive option, did not survive—John Thompson recalls 'one of the jokes was we had a claim from this girl for repeats!'[32]

Smiths were caught on the horns of a dilemma. Board minutes make repeated reference to the poor state of the motor industry and the need to cut costs, including headcount. Experiments with high-speed automation on the traditional instrument production lines were beginning, but Cricklewood was described as 'almost Victorian' by one former civil servant.[33] A remarkable (indeed harrowing) insight into the relentless work at Cricklewood appears in Miriam Glucksmann's *Women on the Line*—an eye-witness account drawn from her work there in 1977–8.[34] Her ethnographic survey vividly charts the mind-numbing process of work on an unforgiving high-speed production line, the relationships and tensions this forged between a diverse group of women drawn from multicultural late 1970s north London, building up to a description of a go-slow, strike, and sit-in lasting several weeks which resulted in 2,000 workers at BL Cowley being laid off.[35]

Cost-cutting at Smiths had driven down quality, leading to high warranty costs—overall, original equipment supply of the traditional instruments lost money, irrespective of the high margins earned on replacement and after-market sales. But the emerging electronic technology did not offer an easy salvation. Thompson remembers Beresford issuing serious warnings that the costs of developing solid-state vehicle instrumentation could prove crippling—it would involve vast cost, added to which the firm's main client, BL, had a highly uncertain future.[36] Thus if nothing changed, Smiths would lose money—and if it poured money into new technology, it still might lose money. Against this backdrop, and probably from the nationalization of BL onwards, Smiths started looking for the exit.

While thoughts of restructuring were being formulated, and the new headquarters at 765 Finchley Road were being built, a shift in top management was also under way. Both Sisson and Hurn were honoured in 1980—Sisson receiving a knighthood for his contribution to exports and in recognition of his contribution to the aerospace industry, while Hurn was voted the *Guardian*'s 'Young Businessman of the Year'—though the journalists could have no idea of the radical plans in Hurn's mind, profiling him as 'the boss who makes Smiths Industries tick'.[37] In mid-1981, as the firm moved into its new headquarters at Child's Hill, Sisson announced his decision to cede the role of CEO to Hurn, though he would stay on as chairman, and remained understandably interested in aerospace.[38] This formalized the role that, de facto, Hurn was already fulfilling, much of which involved facing up to the difficulties of dealing with problem businesses.

A critical goal was to find a route involving minimal damage to the balance sheet. A first step was to explore some form of collaboration with VDO of Germany, Jaeger in France, and Borletti in Italy, but fierce national protectionism made this impractical. Based on a history of close cooperation with Jaeger, including joint development and exploitation of the GITAC tachograph in the early 1970s, there were hopes of some arrangement, but Jaeger was in any event now part of the VDO group and discussions came to nothing.

Now the idea of an outright sale of Smiths instrumentation to VDO emerged, or possibly a junior role in a joint venture, and Hurn, Thompson, Mortimer, and Beresford travelled regularly to Frankfurt towards year-end, meeting Liselott Linsenhoff, VDO's owner. Memories survive of Linsenhoff, a former Olympic dressage gold-medallist, and feeding her horse Piaff under the watchful gaze of the heavily armed security guards at her house.[39] Beresford recalls the drawing-room, complete with plate-glass windows through to the dressage ring, and three bar areas, each with a refrigerator filled floor to ceiling with Dom Perignon 'which we did our best to make a dent in—quite a lifestyle'.[40] Such discussions were naturally top secret, but enough noise filtered down through Smiths, and the enterprising Ray Davidson of motor accessories sales and service organized German evening classes for his staff.[41] While Linsenhoff became hot to trot on a deal, her CEO and finance director were against it, probably concluding with the German and French markets already sewn up 'we would bring little to the party'—all of which was moot, since the Bundeskartellamt (German merger clearance office) vetoed any transaction.[42] Alan Hornsby also enjoyed the Linsenhoff visits, but recalls 'we were grasping at straws'. He believed withdrawal from the industry was unavoidable.[43]

In late 1981, Philips announced the closure of its car radio factory in Belgium, choosing to relocate to the Far East—part of a general trend in consumer electronics. Smiths likewise took the decision to cease radio manufacture at Radiomobile a few months later.[44] A different overall strategy began to emerge. Smiths and BL had a long-term supply agreement in place, embodying price increase mechanisms, which Smiths invoked to impose a 12.8 per cent increase in early 1982.[45] BL resisted on the basis it could source components more cheaply in France, at what Hurn termed 'distress prices' owing to under-capacity. Harold Musgrove of BL now professed himself 'fed up to the back teeth' with Smiths and commenced negotiations with French suppliers. Smiths realized it had reached a 'cliff edge' and there was no way forward, travelling on the same track.[46] Complete exit of the industry through a sale was now presented to the board as a choice, probably in June 1982.[47] Hurn recalled the reaction of Barrie Heath, former chairman of GKN:

> When we came to the board with the proposal that we exit the motor industry there were shocked faces around the table, except for Barrie Heath's. He said, 'If you can do it, it's absolutely the right thing to do.' He was extremely influential.[48]

There was now a clear mandate to press ahead with plans for disposal and John Thompson and Alan Hornsby moved into gear to execute.

Official support

Present problems [for Lucas] stem from the fact that its 'cash cows', its established UK businesses, are very sickly animals.

(DoI briefing notes, 1982[49])

There was much in the car industry to occupy minds in Whitehall in the early 1980s. In April 1982, Margaret Thatcher told the Commons 'at the moment the Government have provided £970 million of taxpayers' money to British Leyland'.[50] The firm had lost £497m the previous year, and had a monumental struggle ahead of it to achieve profitability. BL's industrial relations were at a low ebb—witness the 'tea-break' strike of November 1981, with thousands laid off, causing knock-on effects at firms such as Smiths, which shed 200 jobs at the Witney heater plant as a result.[51] Months earlier it had already trimmed the workforce from 1,500 to 1,150.

After two years of investigation, the Monopolies Commission issued its report into car parts in May 1982. It revealed the scale of the UK market—involving 'about 300 main manufacturers of components' with a large number of smaller firms, 'estimated to employ between 250,000 and 300,000 workers and create employment for perhaps as many again in the production of their materials'.[52] Sales were estimated at £2 billion in retail terms in the UK for 1981, and in excess of £2.2 billion in exports. The sector was therefore significant, reflected in the existence of the Component Industry Liaison Group (CILG) at the Department of Industry (DoI).

Besides BL, the government was also mid-negotiation with Nissan on its proposed investment in a new UK car-plant. By mid-1982, lobbying via the CILG over the minimum amount of locally sourced content was among several reasons Nissan continued to waver over its plans, as well as uncertainty over broader economic recovery and potential labour relations difficulties.[53]

The nexus for consideration of all these matters was the office of Robin Mountfield, Under Secretary at the DoI, running the Vehicles Division. Mountfield is remembered for persuading Keith Joseph to allow British Leyland more time to deliver on its corporate plan (for which Margaret Thatcher never forgave him), but also for steering the (ultimately successful) discussions with Nissan. Beyond the headline-grabbing problems of BL, Mountfield and his colleagues were also well aware that firms like Lucas needed to adapt to the fast-changing technological requirements of evolving car design, and that a balance was required between (i) supporting Leyland with components, (ii) developing an export business, and (iii) supplying newcomers such as Nissan. Mountfield's assistant, Michael Cochlin summarized: 'This was our last throw of the dice. We could see the component industry falling into foreign hands if we didn't act.'[54] In May 1982, the Vehicles Division submitted a paper to the British

Technology Group (BTG), arguing there was a case for assisting a company combining automotive electronic systems and instrumentation. It would offer competition for Bosch, Renix, Marelli, VDO, Jaeger, and Borletti.

At Lucas, Jeffrey Wilkinson zealously pursued his Project LDP vision for an Anglo-French vehicle electronics champion with Mountfield at the DoI.[55] Against this backdrop, Marcus Beresford at Smiths and Keith Wills at Lucas had been considering collaboration by early 1982. Memories have faded, but DoI papers suggest, by the summer, discussions between John Thompson of Smiths, Anthony Fraser of the SMMT, and Mountfield had already focused on how Smiths and Lucas might cooperate with a degree of government help. This led to a lunch in August, to which Wilkinson was invited. Despite Mountfield's notes that it was 'an unproductive meeting with Mr Wilkinson and Mr Thomson arguing' (an intellectual argument between friends over their firms' respective failings), a joint venture project was soon under way, codenamed 'Lucy' (i.e. LUcas-SI), and from the outset the two firms assumed there would be sizeable official assistance.[56] This would come from the Product and Process Development Scheme, designed to fund R&D for approved projects. Cochlin recalls Lucas and Smiths being encouraged to identify eligible projects—'they would have to satisfy the criteria under the rules, but we wouldn't be overly fussy'.[57]

Lucy would involve significant rationalization on Smiths' part—operations at MA1 and Oxgate Lane in Cricklewood would close. With the Humber Road and the old headquarters building at 317 Edgware Road closed by September 1982, the last links to Cricklewood would now disappear. People and equipment would move to Great King Street (Lucas's Birmingham site), and the Ystradgynlais and Hengoed factories in Wales would transfer ownership, as well as part of the Witney site, housing instrument engineering. In London, 900 jobs would go at Smiths, and 200 at Lucas in Birmingham, but 500 new jobs would be created, a reasonable proportion in the development areas in Wales.

By early November, a joint feasibility study convinced both firms the plan would work, though subject to some crucial caveats. Lucas would take 75 per cent of the equity, Smiths 20 per cent, and the BTG 5 per cent (though the latter proposal was soon dropped). The financial model presented by Wills and Beresford included elements shown in Table 8.1.

A vital element of the five-year projections for sales was the assumption that 52 per cent would come from BL at the outset, falling only to 41 per cent after five years, while exports would rise from an initial 13 per cent to 33 per cent over the same period. There was therefore a strong reliance on continued business from BL, which Wills and Beresford presented as a risk necessitating 'substantial assistance from the DoI and BTG'.[58] A file note records Wilkinson's comment that the 'BL/Smiths relationships are at zero—only talk with lawyers present', so rather more than financial assistance was actually needed.[59] At a meeting with Mountfield on 12 November, Smiths and Lucas asked for £30m in government help towards the £102m total.[60]

From November, the pace accelerated. Visits by the DoI to Lucas in Birmingham were arranged, copious amounts of information and projections were delivered, and between

Table 8.1 Financial model presented by Wills and Beresford

Costs to Lucas and Smiths	£ million
tangible assets transferred to JV, excluding industrial property	36
rationalization costs	5
In Lucy: five-year total (constant 82/83 values)	
set-up and reconstruction costs	4
working capital	22
capital expenditure	30
R&D	46
Total	102

the two firms there was a debate over the valuation of assets and stock that would be transferred to Lucy. Roger Hurn and Jeffrey Wilkinson lunched with Gordon Manzie, Deputy Secretary at the DoI, on 2 December, to discuss progress. 'Wilkinson did most of the talking', reflective perhaps of the different goals for the two partners.[61] For Smiths, Lucy meant an exit, with no consolidation in its accounts of the new venture—a recognition of the fact Smiths could take its motor business no further. Lucas on the other hand (or Wilkinson's part of it) remained heavily committed to the industry, and desperately needed to modernize, to put together an electronic package that combined instrumentation and fuel management. Wilkinson needed the deal and needed government support, just as he also needed French government funding for Project LDP.

Manzie's briefing notes reveal Lucas and Smiths now claimed the department was back-pedalling on 'special' assistance and was offering just 'standard percentage support under conventional schemes'.[62] The firms now wanted £35m and the department's internal calculations had suggested £15–20m might be possible, but 'we are limited in what we can offer if Brussels involvement is to be avoided'. Manzie reiterated strong support, stressing the completion of due diligence, while Wilkinson and Hurn stressed the need for speed—the possible spread of rumours meant the Stock Exchange would soon need notification of talks taking place.

Two weeks later, Wilkinson called Cochlin.[63] Giving ground, Wilkinson was now asking for just £25m, but needed a three-year contract from BL, and at current prices—not the reduced prices being demanded. The DoI spent December analysing how it might justify the funding, with site visits and analysis of projects put forward by Lucas and Smiths—an amusing manuscript addition on the voice synthesis papers noting 'the public may like talking to a car—I don't'.[64] On 8 January 1983, Smiths and Lucas made a joint announcement to the Stock Exchange to the effect that possible collaboration was under discussion.[65] In the meantime, DoI due diligence continued, including commissioning the EIU to test various project assumptions, asking Spencer Stewart to profile Keith Wills and Marcus Beresford, and requesting both firms to state their alternative strategy, should Lucy not proceed.[66] While perhaps predictable, the answers were unequivocal. In Lucas's case, while it would pursue a 'go-it-alone' strategy, it was emphasized 'we shall

40. Wishaw alarm clock factory (*c.*1951).

41. Wishaw production line (early 1950s).

42. Dennis Barrett (1901–1989).

43. Frank Hurn (1895–1973).

44. Ralph Gordon-Smith (1905–1993).

45. De Havilland Dove, 'the flying showroom' (late 1940s).

46. *PIVOT* cover (November 1954).

47. Typical Smiths sports day, tug-of-war (1950s).

48. Basingstoke factory complex (late 1950s).

49. SMA Oxgate Lane (late 1950s).

50. Ken Reaks, Smiths' instrument expert, in the cockpit of Bluebird CN7 (c.1960).

51. Trident G-ARPB making the world's first fully automatic landing (10 June 1965).

52. Sir Richard (Dick) Cave (1912–1988).

53. Smiths Watford (late 1950s).

54. Roadcraft Press, home to all Smiths' printing (*c.*1965).

55. Sir Roy Sisson (1914–1993).

56. Sir Roger Hurn (b.1938).

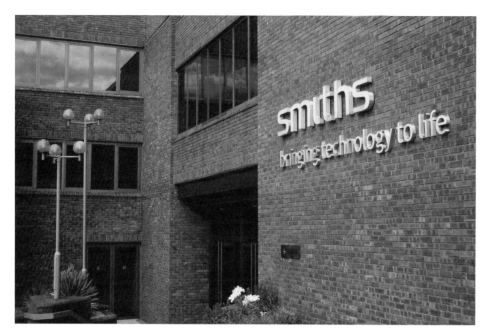

57. Head office (1981–2009), 765 Finchley Road.

58. Keith Butler-Wheelhouse (b.1946).

59. Smiths Detection's Sabre 5000, for detecting trace amounts of explosives.

60. Smiths Interconnect's DaVinci test socket, for ultra-high reliability semi-conductor testing.

61. John Crane's heavy duty coupling test rig—for testing high-performance new products.

progressively run down manufacture' at Great King Street, which employed around 2,100. This would produce high costs and the diversion of resources away from other UK-focused businesses and a need to source components from overseas.[67] John Thompson of Smiths was equally blunt—'the realistic alternative is, therefore, closure of the whole or closure of the major part . . . while the effects on employment are severe, our calculations indicate that closure could be achieved at little, if any, cash cost to SI'. Smiths had already indicated closure would involve 1,500 job losses, of which 1,000 would be in Wales.[68] To increase the pressure, he added, 'This increases the dilemma for SI when considering the further expenditure needed to launch the Lucas/SI joint company.'[69]

February passed with internal wrangling at the DoI. The Minister for Information Technology, Kenneth Baker, reluctantly agreed to support the transaction, but 'commented that the Department should not devise any more schemes like this, even if the companies are as important as the 2 in this case'.[70] Lucas was pressing for up-front assistance in a form that would not disturb its debt covenants, and absolutely ruled out raising equity, given its shares were trading vastly below net asset value.[71] There was now a period of horse-trading. A flurry of ministerial correspondence questioned if Lucas and Smiths were bearing their fair share of risk, and Mountfield and colleagues succeeding in negotiating Wilkinson down to just £12.5m by way of a ten-year loan on soft terms, with an increase in selective finance to £12.5m, subject entirely to individual project approval.[72] With terms finally settled, Smiths and Lucas announced to the Stock Exchange on 28 March the firms' agreement to merge Smiths' automotive instrument business and Lucas's electronics and systems businesses into Lucas Electrical Electronics & Systems (LEES), with Lucas taking 80.1 per cent of the equity, and Smiths the balance. The transaction involved five Smiths factories employing 2,715 and seven Lucas plants employing 5,000. Smiths valued its shareholding at £12m, the value of assets contributed—while sales contributed were expected to run at around £45m, out of a total projected £120m for the new venture.[73]

Post-mortem

> They had full due diligence. We told them exactly what it was like. They knew exactly what the business forecasts were. There was never anything held back from them. And they decided to buy it.
>
> (Roger Hurn, 1998)

Intense activity followed, with some Smiths staff making immediate preparations to move to new locations, although 900 were made redundant. Thompson recalled: 'our side of it was to close Cricklewood. Now that was a hell of a thing. Cricklewood was like Mecca to anyone that had worked at Smiths.'[74] Gil Jones and Thompson did much of the negotiating with the unions, explaining the inevitability of the move—some transfers, but many redundancies. Here relationships built up over years stood them in good stead. Towards the end of a long Friday of negotiations with union representatives, Thompson remembers the breakthrough—'"OK, we're convinced. How much?" I remember the words vividly'. A five-minute recess led to a concrete figure being accepted. 'We were as generous as we could be—we were talking about several hundred of my old friends. It was tough.'[75]

The transaction was formally closed early in May. Marcus Beresford moved from Cricklewood to Birmingham as general manager of LEES, though already planning a new head office in Paris, reflecting the central role the Ducellier element played in the vision for the planned firm. Smiths' transferees experienced a culture shock. Compared with the decentralized and largely non-political Smiths atmosphere, Beresford recalls Lucas 'was a nightmare environment':

> Lucas centralized most key functions, its accounting and financial control was very poor compared with what we had been used to, and the centralized functions were cumbersome and inefficient. There were two joint managing directors, Jeffrey Wilkinson and Tony Gill, deliberately put in conflict to see who should take over from Godfrey Messervy . . . The centralized functions of manufacturing and supply had greatly underestimated the complexity of Smiths components and both supply performance and quality suffered.[76]

Lucy's life was short. The power struggle at the top of Lucas ended with Wilkinson's departure in January 1984.[77] From Gill's point of view, Lucy 'ran counter to our agreed strategy, to progressively get out of the low technology electrical products business . . . the project was loss-making and needed to be "sorted out" when I took over'.[78] On the French side, increased inflation and budget deficits under the first Mitterrand presidency from 1981 led to 'le tournant de la rigueur'—the move to austerity—in 1983. As Keith Wills's contact at Valeo told him, 'les caisses sont vides'.[79] Gill pulled the plug, and Lucas's half of Ducellier was sold to Valeo for a nominal sum—crystallizing nearly seven years of loss-making support.[80] Beresford concludes: 'from this moment Lucy was dead. Lucas Electrical had even less export content than Smiths, and no realistic chance of winning any against Bosch and now Valeo/Ducellier.' He left for Plessey in early 1985, and Smiths wrote off its investment in LEES with a charge of £4.8m, transferring its shares to Lucas the following year.[81] The DoI will have been disappointed to have failed with the last roll of the dice—though Cochlin recalls the much larger issues of BL and inward Japanese investment 'probably meant we took our eye off the ball'.[82]

Coupled with factory reorganization and redundancy costs, the exit from the vehicle instruments business probably cost Smiths less than £10m in balance-sheet terms, spread over three years. However, as Alan Hornsby (finance director at the time) argues, there were two approaches in play: 'Lucas focused on profits, whereas I was focusing on cash'.[83] The sales of the Cricklewood and Oxgate Lane sites released significant cash. After the initial closure, two further transactions involved sales to Lucas of stock, notionally at discounted levels, but once more releasing cash. Corporation tax allowances for the factory reorganization costs also had a cash effect. 'I would not be surprised if, all things taken into consideration, we came out of the Lucas deal ahead on cash. And that's the way you *have* to look at it.'

With the benefit of hindsight, different views survive among the Smiths actors. Thompson felt 'there was no doubt about it. Lucas made a complete balls of it', arguing the failure to deal with expensive overheads, poor management, and inefficiency in the original Birmingham operation was fatal, a view wholly endorsed by Hornsby.[84] Hornsby also argues Smiths' choice to own 19.9 per cent of Lucy (i.e. it would not be consolidated) was a clear signal of a lack of optimism for its chances. Hurn is inclined to be more charitable: 'looked at from their point of view, they thought it a wonderful opportunity for once in fifty years to break out of their product range...a wonderful chance which, if they didn't take, somebody else would, and might even attack them in other areas'.[85] The disappearance of French support was a factor, but the story emphasizes the role of champions for an idea. At Lucas, Lucy and Project LDP were Wilkinson's babies—without him, they lasted months. At Smiths, vehicle instruments were of course only part of the business in motors, but the Lucy transaction was the critical catalyst for further action—'all the other five deals hinged on the Lucas deal'.[86]

While whole business lines would be closed or reorganized, parts of the long-term Smiths cultural heritage disappeared as well. Bracken Hill House closed in late 1982, after twenty-three years. Many alumni achieved senior positions, but with the emergence of the plate-glass universities it was losing relevance as Smiths' graduate recruitment modernized. Similarly, the Isle of Wight rest home, largely geared to the convalescence of production-line workers, was an anachronism. Gil Jones commented, 'by now the welfare people were hunting around for people to go there. Almost on holiday.'[87] After 6,500 visitors and thirty-two years' operation, it closed in 1983.[88]

Clocks—time runs out: 1978–1983

We worked hard to reach our bonus target early so we could have time to run a hairdressers for the dancing on a Friday night. Good times.

(Margaret Jack, Wishaw employee, 1965–76)[89]

From 1973 to 1978, the workforce at the Wishaw factory—once an extraordinary seat of hi-tech modern volume-production of alarm clocks—had fallen from 1,400 to close to 500. Despite attempts to diversify production, there was continued over-capacity. Russian and Asian imports had killed local manufacture and the firm was reduced to assembly and rebadging of imported movements. In 1978 a further 200 jobs were lost, bringing numbers down to close to 300. Mid-year, after a forty-year run, 115 jobs went with the closure of the Hewlett Road factory in Cheltenham, as it became impossible for Smiths' quartz clocks to compete with foreign products, mainly from the UTS division of Kundo from Germany, which had taken an early strategic view of the future for quartz and invested heavily. Later that year, much of the clock-related operations left in Smiths, including Tucker, Nunn & Grimshaw, were consolidated and from

January 1979 everything was focused at Wishaw. English Clock Systems were still manufacturing and selling industrial time-recorders, and Graham Smith (Allan Gordon-Smith's great-nephew) was made general manager in 1979.

In Wales, the Vehicle Instrumentation Division had occupied part of the site for years, and we have already seen that by 1980 significant attention was being paid to exiting that business. Though the motor business was significantly larger and perhaps most closely identified with Smiths, the association with clocks and watches was also historic and deeply entrenched in the minds of both the public and City analysts. There was therefore understandable surprise all round at the decision in January 1980 to stop manufacture of all pocket- and stop-watches at Ystradgynlais, and cease manufacture at Wishaw.

Cecil Boult, who ran Anglo-Celtic in Wales, phoned Dennis Barrett, now long-retired, to tell him the news, prompting a letter from Barrett to Graham Smith: 'what a tragedy this is as Smiths were once recognized as the leading clock people in the UK'.[90] The irrepressible and driven Barrett, never one to go down without a fight, still brimmed with ideas for ways to capitalize on the Smiths name—'millions have been spent in advertising this name and there are millions of clocks in use bearing it'. Barrett was well aware technology had moved on. He urged the building of a business using the cheapest quartz technology available, targeting the market for simple wall clocks he believed was being ignored. Intriguingly, Barrett laid the blame for the failure of Smiths' effort to break into the quartz watch market squarely at the door of Dr Shelley of the specialist unit at Cheltenham, which he had set up—'its only terms of reference were to develop a satisfactory quartz movement [but it was] disbanded by Dick Cave because it had substantially failed in its task, so in total getting on for £200,000 went down the drain'. Not everyone would agree. John Thompson recalls the Quasar watch that launched briefly at the Basle Fair before Cave pulled the plug: 'that's a case of a champion, again—"We've got to do this"—What he [Barrett] didn't know was that the Swiss, the Russians, and the Japanese were setting up to make trillions of the things. So perhaps his research wasn't good. It was ambition above skill.'[91]

Graham Smith was in no position to take Barrett's ideas forward—he was instead instructed to supervise the sale of English Clock Systems' time-recorder business to Blick in the closing months of 1980.[92] In fact Barrett's idea chimed with plans already in place at Wishaw. With the loss of 250 jobs, the operation was scaled back to deal with service requirements and the casing up of imported movements.[93]

The Dennis & Robinson subsidiary had switched from making clock-cases to kitchen furniture years earlier, but this small link to the horological past disappeared in 1982 with a convenient management buy-out. For the few remaining workers at Wishaw, the writing was on the wall, and in September 1983 the factory was told all manufacture would be phased out, as soon as remaining orders were fulfilled.[94] With the closure of the clock company, Graham Smith remained for a while, working on various special projects and finally at the environmental controls company from which he retired in December 1984, leaving the ageing Ralph Gordon-Smith, still president, the only remaining Smith.

Further disposals: 1983–1988

And of course Cricklewood is developed . . . there's nothing there whatsoever,
now, next to the railway bridge, to tell you Smiths was ever there.

(John Thompson, 1998)

Smiths' factory at Witney accounted for the bulk of BL's vehicle heater equipment, but it had one competitor in Delaney-Gallay in Wales (part of the Hanson Trust group), producing Delanair air-conditioning and car heater products. With the BL relationship at an all-time low in early 1983, Hurn recalls the client was 'playing fast and loose with the suppliers and they effectively fired us'. BL wanted Delaney-Gallay to replace Smiths, but it 'was not very sensible on their part [as they] had to buy our business. Had to, because otherwise there would have been no continuity . . . we could have stopped the production line.'[95] Thompson was once again at the heart of getting the deal done (codenamed 'Operation Truss'), in mid-1983—'tough lot, Hanson, actually'—but 'there simply wasn't enough business for two . . . so we either had to acquire them or they had to acquire us, and since we were getting out of the motor industry, they acquired us. A straightforward, cut and thrust deal.'[96]

These two transactions, with Lucy by far the most significant, unlocked a series of further sales and rationalizations. At Cricklewood—the heart of Smiths since 1915—a huge auction sale was conducted in April 1984 of all the machinery, even the desks and chairs, and the site was cleared.[97] Thompson recalled: 'I had an office on the top floor of the engineering block and I remember seeing some of my stuff being thrown out of the top floor window which rather broke my heart.' More amusing was the tale of one man who bought the remarkable tiled floor of the canteen, 'but when he came back two or three days later . . . they wouldn't come off the floor!'

While Cricklewood was being dismantled in the spring of 1984, discussions were under way with GKN about Smiths' remaining UK businesses in auto parts and accessories—Godfrey Holmes and Affiliated Factors. The move into distribution had been Cave's inspiration, to diversify within the motor business away from original equipment. For a time it had made a contribution, but as Hurn later summarized 'it was definitely a mistake to get into those businesses for a manufacturer. The fundamental control mechanisms and the management thinking of a manufacturer are absolutely not aligned with wholesaling and retailing.'[98] In response to the difficulties of managing the distributive trades 'we tried to hire in specialists [but] we just weren't comfortable with the way they thought about the things that made us spark: stock ratios, cash collection, all these things'—an important insight into the ingrained strength of Smiths' culture and its occasional impermeability. A deal was struck with GKN, still investing in, and diversifying, its own automotive division, to sell both businesses, nearly doubling GKN's (relatively small) share of the UK motor components distribution market.[99] Ironically, GKN was to have similar experiences. The head of its Driveline business, Trevor Bonner, eventually came to the same conclusions as

Hurn—'Some people tried to make a case for a connection between distribution and OE, but there wasn't one.'[100]

Another motor accessories outlet, Longlife Accessories, with a chain of eighty retail shops, had already gone. After significant losses, Hurn negotiated its sale in early 1982 to R. C. Hartley (Holdings), with a chain of more than 400 stores under the Motorist Discount Centre brand, but the market was tough and the whole enterprise was in receivership by late 1984.[101]

There were car heater and air-conditioning businesses outside the UK as well. One had operated in Australia for many years, but in mid-1978 had been transferred into a new joint-venture with Japan's Diesel-Kiki to form SIDK Pty. With Smiths' UK divestiture programme and the increasing Japanese dominance of the Australian car market, it made sense to sell out Smiths' 60 per cent stake in SIDK which Diesel-Kiki purchased in March 1985. In South Africa, a small heater and air-conditioning assembly operation had been established by Roger Hurn, while export manager, particularly to service BL requirements. An unspectacular performer, it had most recently provided an object lesson in the way management of foreign subsidiaries in locations such as Australia and South Africa could 'agree what the strategy and tactics were going to be, and the budgets and the forecasts, and how we were going to get there, and what we were going to invest in and what we weren't. And as soon as they got back home they'd start doing something differently.'[102]

Bearing in mind it was a heater and air-conditioning business, Hurn admits it was a surprise to find 'that we'd funded an oil-drilling rig—an offshore oil-drilling rig. We said "What the hell is this? We didn't agree . . .", and they said "Oh, it's a wonderful opportunity!"' A change of local management had been the response to this particular indiscretion, but 'after we'd sold the heater business to Hanson, it made no sense to stay in the motor industry in South Africa at all', so a sale was authorized. There were other concerns. South Africa had unified its dual currencies in 1983, dropping the financial rand, thereby providing foreign investors with an easier mechanism to repatriate funds. Widely seen as a mistake, and with foreign debt escalating and other pressures mounting, Ron Williams at Smiths was nervous a restrictive dual-currency policy might be reimposed. In early 1985, Smiths instructed NedBank to sell its subsidiary, even supplying the names of candidate buyers, but to no avail. Williams visited but NedBank reaffirmed 'there was no chance of selling it'.[103]

Back in his hotel, Williams recalls seeing 'a fellow a bit like Harvey Jones talking on television, telling everybody how to run industry . . . and I thought, "Well, he's the man, he'd be the fellow to buy"'. This was Albert Wessels, the founder of Toyota South Africa, whom Williams met in Johannesburg. 'He said he could spare me a quarter of an hour and in the end he talked to me for about two hours . . . I'd listened to everything he said and I'd told him about the problems of the business . . . and I'd really come to the conclusion that he could run it better than we could.' In his element, Williams ended up constructing an acceptable deal to sell to Metair Investments (Wessel's company), but he was still nervous about the local situation. He then devoted a lot of effort to persuading NedBank and the incoming managing director that it would be fine to gear up the local subsidiary and remit the loan proceeds to Smiths in London—the loan being equal to the entire purchase price agreed with Wessels. Smiths announced the sale at the beginning of August, stating this completed 'its planned withdrawal from the automotive sector worldwide', prompting a 6 per cent rise in the stock price.[104] With the closure of South Africa's foreign exchange market later in the month, Williams received several calls of commiseration, bemoaning the fact that Smiths had acted just a little too late to get its money out—except of course the sale proceeds had already arrived.

There was a still a rump portfolio of various distribution companies, assembled in the mid-1970s as part of Cave's diversification plan. In 1984, EMWE in Holland and Enterprise in Sweden were sold to their own management, whereas Simonsen & Nielsen in Denmark was sold to another local distributor, Erik Veng A/S. In the UK, the ball-bearings businesses of Claude Rye and M & E Bearings, acquired in the early 1970s, had been rationalized by 1981 into a single business, Mecro Ltd. This was disposed of in a management buy-out in late 1986.[105]

Smiths had been in South Africa for little more than a decade. It was a different story in Australia where Smiths went back some forty years. By the mid-1980s, the range of businesses included architectural hardware products, door-closers, locks, and other door furniture. Hurn recalls a portfolio 'of quite successful companies but with absolutely no rationale behind our owning them at all . . . really an oddball set of companies'.[106] At the end of 1987, the decision was taken to conduct 'a controlled auction of certain of the company's Australian subsidiaries'.[107] The job fell to Gerry Mortimer, assisted by David Flowerday (who did all the work), and involved 'six separate deals in Australia. We went out twice and completed the heads of agreement within ten days second-time round. We conducted a very, very rapid auction and actually forced them (which was a wonderful system because they knew we were going to get on the plane to go home on Friday) to do a deal. We got far better prices than we deserved.'[108] But just as with the disposal of the motors business, there was a lot of emotional baggage, as Hurn remembers—there were 'a lot of upset people, you know, "How can you possibly abandon us?" . . . You just live with that sort of thing. You treat them properly and you do it.'[109]

Supporting the executive throughout the process of rationalization, the non-executive directors played an important role. Barrie Heath had backed the exit from the motor industry, alongside Derek Birkin of RTZ—'a plain-speaking Yorkshireman, he had a forceful personality which acted as a foil to the more urbane style of Earl Jellicoe'.[110] Birkin left in 1984 to chair RTZ and his slot on the board was filled by Sir Alex Jarratt, in his last year as chairman of Reed International. In 1985, Mallinson retired, as did Sisson, relinquishing the chairmanship and leaving at the same time as his good friend Sir John Lidbury from Hawker Siddeley—'his shrewd financial brain served Smiths well'.[111] The Hawker's link was preserved with the appointment the same year of another of its directors, Sir James Hamilton. Sir Alex Jarratt stepped into Sisson's shoes as chairman in August 1985. Two non-executive veterans, Earl Jellicoe and Barrie Heath, retired the following year, giving way to Sir Peter Thompson, best known for the hugely successful privatization of National Freight Corporation, and Neil Shaw, chairman of Tate & Lyle. The last link to the motor industry, David Breeden, retired in 1987, to be replaced by Sir Austin ('Tin') Pearce, the outgoing chairman of British Aerospace—a natural fit for the newly evolved and largely aerospace-led Smiths.

Regrets, I've had a few

> It wasn't that they went and did their own thing. It's just that they didn't seem to mind when it wasn't going according to plan. And we did mind rather a lot.

> (Roger Hurn, 1998)

Despite a seemingly constant array of acquisitions, it was nevertheless the case that large numbers of potential purchases never took place, failing to make it through Smiths' rigorous due diligence process. 'We look at acquisition targets all the time—always have perhaps four or five targets under review. Some we start and never finish for a variety of reasons, others we never agree a price.'[112] But despite careful analysis, occasional mistakes were made. Interviewed in 1998 at the time of his retirement, Roger Hurn was asked what deals, with hindsight, should not have been done. Two came to mind that related to the early 1980s when the process of reshaping Smiths was still under way. One was the acquisition of Integrated Air Systems in Valencia, California, in 1981, a manufacturer of clean rooms and associated technology, mainly used in the semiconductor and medical industries, which on the surface of it fitted the hi-tech engineering world in which Smiths operated. Hurn's view was 'it taught us another lesson . . . there is something very different about doing business in the east coast of America and the mid-west, to doing business in California . . . it's the laid-back attitude to non-achievement in California'.[113] He pictured the call from Cricklewood 'that says "you've missed your monthly budget by 50 per cent" and the response is, "Well, don't worry about that sort of thing. By the way, what are you doing for the weekend? We're going to the beach." And all this sort of thing. It drove everybody absolutely bonkers here. We couldn't live with the laid-back response to failure.' IAS was sold to the Donaldson Company in Minneapolis in January 1987 after six years of fruitless perseverance.[114]

In 1983, Bill Mallinson, described by John Thompson as 'a very high-technology guy', championed the purchase of a small start-up company, Xionics, founded by Mike Bevan in 1978.[115] It was developing an 'open' architecture in office information systems, enabling previously incompatible systems to communicate, providing the user with access to word-processing, electronic mail, and database management. Alan Smith, company secretary and head of legal, remembered it as 'an early form of internet, if you like. But a dedicated one. We had it doing the word processing . . . some people thought it very good.'[116] There were some impressive installations—for example, the Cabinet

Office used Xionics, as did the GLC at County Hall, with the largest office automation system in the country.[117] Smiths was correct to anticipate there would be an explosion in information technology and Mallinson's zeal was another good example of the vital role of a champion for a transaction, but 'it didn't take us long to realize that we weren't Bill Gates, and they weren't either, and that they were therefore better off with someone else'.[118] It was sold back to management in December 1986.

Beginning to reshape industrial: mid-1970s to 1984

> *Following the recent disposals of certain businesses, I believe it is now important for internal and external reasons to show that SI has entered a period of stability and clarity of purpose.*
>
> (Roger Hurn, 1984[119])

Despite the closure of the motor accessories and clocks businesses, Smiths retained a diverse variety of companies outside its main medical and aerospace divisions. Some would be jettisoned, but a core group would remain long-term.[120] From the mid-1970s the original industrial division had been run by Bill Sykes, and included the tubing companies (Uni-Tubes and Flexible Ducting); the specialist roofers Uniroof; MacLellan Rubber, acquired in 1976 along with Flexible Ducting; Hypertac, the speciality multi-pin connector business, and Fliteline, which produced electrical harnesses and specialized hoses.[121] From 1978, Sykes also had responsibility for the marine division, comprising the Kelvin Hughes maritime charts operation (still supplying the merchant marine fleet with all its charts) and SI-Tex Marine Electronics, the radar, sonar, and echo-sounder business (which simply sourced Far Eastern products and sold them on—it was sold on itself in 1988).

With motors and clocks gone, a drive towards a simplified tripartite structure emerged—the 'three-legged stool' that Hurn was later to use frequently as an analogy for Smiths, offering stability. This was reflected in Sykes's election to the main board in August 1984, and the continued consolidation of the business, with small and complementary acquisitions in its connector and conduit businesses (e.g. the Superflexit group, comprising Aero-Electrical Connector and Icore International in 1984, both in the US, and Cam Profiles in St Albans).[122]

In September 1984, with the sale of Godfrey Holmes and Affiliated Factors to GKN, Hurn's memo to senior management outlined that there was 'an opportunity for a revision to the operating structure of SI'.[123] With Kelvin Hughes moved to aerospace, the industrial division now took on board the time controls operation that formed the last link to the clocks business, the precision fans and hydraulics businesses, and Xionics and Mecro—both of which were sold in MBOs in late 1986, after which margins in the group improved significantly.

Industrial ceramics and exports: 1970s–1987

We used to teach the world how to make spark plugs.

(Alan Smith, 1998)

Another important business moved to Sykes's division in 1984 was that of industrial ceramics, which John Thompson had been keen to develop from the mid-1970s. Although delayed by cautiousness at the time of the three-day week and darkening skies for the motor industry, the business had nevertheless continued to grow and develop. The original business of spark plug manufacture for cars faded out in the late 1970s, though industrial ignition continued to be successful, alongside igniters used in a wide range of aircraft engines, both civil and military.

While work continued at Putney, the major ceramics operation was located at Rugby. In mid-1978 a major advance was the acquisition of the isostatic press business of Olin Energy Systems from Sunderland. Olin's had patented the premier international design for a press to compact powdered ceramic material into components such as insulators, and this transaction gave Smiths leading-edge technology. The business joined the Rugby site in 1979, where two main lines were regulated. The industrial ignition business was eventually renamed Lodge Ceramics in 1984, recognizing the importance of the Lodge name in the town, and continued to enjoy success throughout the 1980s, alongside the spark plug machinery business, renamed as SIMAC in 1986.

John Thompson had first visited China in 1973 as part of a UK trade mission which sought to capitalize on the positive sentiment created after Nixon's visit the year before, and the apparent openness for improved trade with the West. It was a visit that would ignite a deep love for the country. During the trip, Thompson was taken to see the Nanjing Electro-Ceramic Factory, where he was shocked to see primitive production facilities, involving rough mixing of raw materials and the hand-pouring of ceramic mix into moulds. Discussions about possible licensing of Smiths' latest technology looked very promising, but the relative openness to foreign collaboration of the early 1970s became rapidly frustrated by the complicated political jockeying of the middle 1970s, and it was only in 1979 that Den Xiaoping's economic reforms reopened the possibility for international firms to become more deeply engaged within China. Meantime, following on from three transactions in the USSR, Stephen Gortvay had succeeded in negotiating the supply of another spark-plug-manufacturing facility to Kuwait in 1977–8, in a contract worth £1m.[124]

Following a trip to China by a Smiths delegation in 1978 to conduct a symposium on spark-plug manufacture, the Chinese embassy in London reopened contact with Thompson in 1979, resulting in an $8m contract signed the following year for the delivery of plant and machinery for a greenfield spark plug factory at Nanjing, with Chinese technicians brought to Rugby for weeks of training, thus fulfilling a long-held ambition of Thompson's to deliver a modern plant in China.[125] A ten-year technical support contract was also signed, and the transaction brought the total number of Smiths' international spark-plug licensing agreements to eighteen (including deals in Yugoslavia, Poland, Egypt, and Israel), many of which had been strongly supported by the UK's ECGD. Following the earlier Russian transactions, Trevor Leader remembers the Nanjing transaction as equally challenging, again mainly by reason of the distinctly alien environment in which there was virtually no precedent for a UK company to deliver high-technology plant.[126] A supplementary contract for further machinery followed in 1985.

Gortvay's pioneering of spark-plug licensing since his arrival at Smiths was honoured with the OBE in 1979 for his contribution to exports. Turning 75, he retired as chairman of the spark-plugs company in late 1980, leaving its direction and management largely to Leader, described by Thompson as knowing 'more than anyone else on the planet about spark-plug manufacture'.[127] In the 1956 Hungary uprising, Gortvay had lost the spark-plug factory he had built in the 1930s—but in his retirement year 'he experienced a curious mix of emotions when the managers of his old factory . . . contacted Smiths, to enquire tentatively about assistance with updating and expansion'.[128] In fact, the relevant plant was a replacement, next to Lake Balaton, and understandably Gortvay left it to his colleagues to complete, in late 1982.[129]

A final major contract for SIMAC was for General Motors' AC-Delco plant at Flint, Michigan, which Smiths contracted to re-equip from 1987. It was the last, largest, and most prestigious contract that Leader and Thompson were involved in. 'We designed and made with their very full cooperation some brand-new high-speed assembly machines to make a million spark plugs a day. It was controlled by solid-state cameras. This was the biggest thing I was involved in—apart from the disposal [to Lucas].'[130] Leader commented 'Here was a small British company showing the mighty AC Delco how to make spark plugs. It was quite something.'[131] The contract involved two parts: the equipment to mould the ceramic insulators, and then the equipment to manufacture the plugs, using the insulators. Five units were shipped, of which the first was installed and commissioned. Given the high degree of automation, requiring only 'minders, setters and controllers' by way of staffing, and probably reducing the number of staff needed from perhaps 450 to 50, AC Delco immediately ran into significant union opposition. Leader and Thompson's understanding is that the remaining four units were never unpacked, and the equipment remained unused.

In a nostalgic trip to Nanjing in 1997, Thompson recalls calling on the factory, which he opened in 1983 and which was now run by Bosch—'I asked the German manager if I could have a look round. The equipment we delivered was still there, still working.'[132]

Industrial progress: 1987–1990

> *Most of the hard work was internal, you know, getting the businesses set up really well, rather than disposals and acquisitions.*
>
> (Ron Williams, 1998)

The mid-1980s saw the industrial group still housing businesses that would be sold— Xionics, Mecro, subsidiaries in Australia and South Africa, for example—but a senior management team that had now been working together for many years gradually introduced stronger controls, better accounting, and more rigour for a range of sound companies that were retained. As the division became better rationalized, it homed in on simple targets, irrespective of the specific business involved—two of the most common denominators being high margins (which doubled to around 18 per cent by 1990) and (as a result) significant cash-generating ability, reflecting a mantra repeated by former Smiths executives—'cash is king'.

Sykes had been with Smiths since 1953 and was due to retire in April 1988. Planning ahead, Ron Williams became deputy chairman of the industrial group from April 1987, with a view to taking over, joining the main board in March 1988.[133] Tragically, Sykes's retirement was cruelly short, as he died soon after.

Ron Williams recalled his explanation to analysts, on his first appointment as chairman of the group. 'I told them I wanted to build on the businesses we had, and that one day I hoped Industrial would be a third of Smiths . . . I wanted the group to have a bit more clarity to it, rather than to be just a big mixture.'[134] Aerospace had recently doubled in size. The obvious place for another significant acquisition was the medical division that was growing strongly but nothing presented itself. Instead it was the industrial division that would see Smiths' next significant acquisition, where Williams identified and championed the purchase of Times Microwave in January 1989, bought from LPL Investment Group for $53.5m. This was a manufacturer of sophisticated custom transmission lines for military microwave systems and purpose-designed broadband co-axial cable. Its products were mainly of use to civil and military aviation clients, and its prospects were enhanced by new US legislation that required the fitting of collision avoidance radar, dependent on microwave technology. Williams, like Sykes before him, spent significant time, sometimes years, identifying businesses to bring into the stable, and which would benefit from the introduction of Smiths' rigorous management processes and a remarkable close attention to detail. It was his particular ability to analyse and improve the performance of such companies that was critical—as Hurn later remarked, 'it was one of my best decisions to persuade Ron to change from financial control to line responsibility for industrial—he excelled at running the companies in his division'.[135]

Medical: 1983–1990

> *A key focus was not to argue about the price of individual disposable items—if the argument ever came back that another product could be re-used, we would say 'If you do, here's the cost of antibiotics, here's the cost of staying in hospital.' The whole concept was not to talk about the price but instead to talk about reducing the risk of cross-infection.*
>
> (George Kennedy, 2013)

Kennedy's career changed gear in May 1983, and the medical division with it, following his appointment to the main board at the age of 42, just as he was completing the acquisition from Heathdyne Inc. of Laboratoire Lejeune, Seitz et Ameline (LSA), a French manufacturer that already distributed many Portex products.

For some time, Kennedy had been considering Downs Surgical plc. In January 1984, Kleinwort Benson and County Bank approached Smiths, offering parcels of shares amounting to nearly 14 per cent of the firm at an attractive price, which Smiths purchased immediately.[136] This led to a bid for the entire firm, closed out in March.[137] In retrospect, given the limited amount of time for due diligence in transactions involving public companies, Kennedy commented: 'Downs was a purchase · that didn't work out so well, even though we had some benefit from it.'[138] The firm produced hand-made surgical instruments—'It was archaic!'—and lost money doing so, but it also had a sideline in colostomy bags, which its management claimed was apparently 'only to tide us over', but nevertheless produced remarkable profit margins. It took time for Smiths to work through the purchase, and the UK surgical instruments business, which made inadequate returns, was later sold off to William Skidmore of Sheffield in 1988 (absorbed by Germany's Aesculap in 1989), but the ostomy business offered remarkable synergy with Smiths' next acquisition.[139] This was a small Glaxo subsidiary, Eschmann Bros & Walsh, another company that had been on Smiths' radar for years.[140] It made specialist surgical tables and sterilizing units, but also had an ostomy business. Eschmanns was bought at a keen price in October 1985. The existing sterilizer business of Surgical Equipment Supplies was merged into Eschmann, while the ostomy businesses of Downs and Eschmann were combined in a new company, SIMCARE, established in 1986 at Lancing in Sussex, using as part of its name the branding adopted from 1985 of SIMS—Smiths Industries Medical Systems.

While the UK was important as a marketplace, Smiths' export business continued to dominate—for example, more than 70 per cent of Portex's sales were overseas—and a fifth Queen's Award had come in 1984. North America remained a vital marketplace, but one in which competition increased markedly, emphasized from the early 1980s onwards by three factors in the US: (i) rapid growth in the emergence of group purchasing organizations (GPOs), allowing buyers 'to join together to leverage their purchasing strength', (ii) the rise in the number of for-profit hospitals, all keen to cut costs, and (iii) the introduction of Medicare's 'prospective payment system' in which hospitals are reimbursed a fixed price for a defined service, irrespective of their actual costs.[141]

In 1988, abandoning the original Wilmington location, US manufacturing was concentrated at the Concord site in Keene, New Hampshire, which became the HQ for SIMS North America. Strong competition in North America formed part of the backdrop for a period of consolidation after the Eschmann acquisition, but there was then a flurry of activity in early 1989, around the time Downs was being sold. First off, after tracking it through involvement in the same trade association, Smiths acquired Avon Medicals of Redditch in the UK from Smith & Nephew in January.[142] The firm manufactured dialysis and blood transfusion products, and operated in the single-use disposable field. The operation could be folded into Portex and in due course its premises were sold at a profit. Two months later, another long-running target was acquired, in Peter von Berg ExtraKorporale (PvB) from Munich—again a manufacturer of single-use equipment that fitted the Portex range, this time for treatment of cardiovascular conditions (pressure transducers, stopcocks, and cardiac catheters).[143] This was followed in April with the acquisition of Respiratory Support Products of California, maker of single-use temperature probes for determining whole-body temperature.[144]

1990 was spent consolidating these acquisitions and bringing new products under the Portex umbrella—for example bringing the PvB products from Germany into the UK market. The worldwide distribution of single-use products was now coordinated through one company—SIMS Medical Distribution (SMD)—which maintained offices in Australia, Singapore, and Japan.

Aerospace: 1986–1990

> *This was pretty exciting because it was far and away the biggest thing we'd ever done. It was right in the heartland of America, and it made us an onshore US defence contractor.*
>
> (Roger Hurn, 1998)

Throughout the early 1980s, Smiths aerospace exports to the US accounted for roughly 30–40 per cent of sales, and there was a desire to increase this. Hurn commented 'I was very keen to develop all our businesses in America, and less so in Europe. I knew we would have a fair crack of the whip in the US. So we favoured Boeing over Airbus, and American defence over French defence. [It was] free enterprise in America versus restrictive practices in Europe.'[145] It took a while to find the right opportunity to expand, but Pope pushed the development of more products and consideration of a major acquisition.[146] Tony Blackman, technical operations director in the aerospace division, recalls 'from the moment Hugh Pope arrived, he wanted the Aerospace Company to expand and we were constantly considering possible acquisitions. When Sperry at Phoenix, Arizona, came on the market the first time we became very excited, since they were our chief competitor', though with a US$1bn price tag, Sperry was beyond Smiths' pocket, and Honeywell secured it in late 1986.[147]

In December 1986, after several months of bidding wars, the leveraged-buy-out specialists Forstmann Little acquired Lear Siegler Inc., the US aerospace, automotive, and manufacturing conglomerate, for US$2.1bn. Within months, the private equity firm began the break-up process, putting the aerospace elements on the block. Alerted by Hedrick, who had worked for Lear Siegler before setting up Harowe Systems, a Smiths team travelled in spring 1987 to visit the main manufacturing sites in Michigan and New Jersey—'we went out for a week going round the plants . . . and we decided that parts of it were too flaky for us . . . high security areas that it was questionable if a British company would be allowed to own'.[148] This included the SkyEye pilotless drone, being used, for example, in surveillance in El Salvador.

At the time, both Marconi Avionics (GEC) and Plessey from the UK were also considering a purchase—indeed Blackman remembered meeting Ron Howard, the Marconi Avionics CEO, in June 1987 'at the Paris Air Show and listening to him recounting how well he was doing with the purchase of the whole company'.[149] Having kicked the tyres, Hurn recalls, 'we decided that we couldn't really pursue the whole, but what we would pursue . . . would be a cherry-picked two thirds of it'. Smiths bid US $350m (£219m) firm and expressed a willingness to close quickly. Smiths despatched Pope, Hornsby, and Mortimer, with a clear mandate to close a deal. Flying out two directors offered a competitive edge against Marconi's team of accountants. 'Forstmann Little got so fed up with the legal and other prevarications of Plessey and GEC that they said yes', and a deal with Smiths was announced on 23 July 1987, though not without a tense last-minute drama. Ron Howard of Marconi, who had 'had the cream taken from his saucer', muddied the waters by unnerving his Smiths contacts with doubts about potential tax and pension liabilities, but Cyril Miles, Hornsby's tax specialist, was adamant the deal was sound. Marconi concluded a deal one week later to purchase the remaining avionics businesses.[150]

Clearly an exciting and bold transaction, it also meant acquiring 3,600 more staff, in a business where 90 per cent of its revenues were from defence work. The transaction was financed with a rapid placement by Warburg's of £223m in shares, placed in a market which no one could predict would collapse so spectacularly, just two months later on 19 October 1987—Black Monday.

It may have been uncomfortable for Smiths, having just raised the money, but there were significant challenges to be met. For example there were onerous contracts relating to a 'self-contained navigation system' and a 'crash-survivable data recorder' (black box) which required renegotiation, and the financial reporting systems needed rapid upgrading. A potential dispute with the US Navy over sales to McDonnell Douglas at lower prices was brazened out through rapid direct contact with naval procurement officials—a course of action by the distinctly British Hornsby and Mortimer which ran directly contrary to their US counsel's advice.[151] Hurn felt the unusual approach of the British was crucial: 'The Americans loved the idea of being owned by us more than anyone else they could think of.'[152]

This was a substantial transaction for Smiths, doubling aerospace sales in a year from £189m in 1987 to £438m in 1988. Aerospace turnover increased from 44 per cent of the group figure to 66 per cent, while the profit contribution rose from 44 per cent to 58 per cent. Smiths had wanted to expand American sales and more than 75 per cent of Lear Siegler's turnover came from the US—combining all parts of the armed forces and civilian airlines among its clients. Smiths was also proud of the way it approached the issue of achieving a 'special security agreement' (SSA) with the US Department of Defense—in essence the method by which 'foreign-owned, controlled, or influenced' (FOCI) companies are permitted to own US companies with access to sensitive US military technology. Smiths contacted the US defence authorities directly to ask for advice—'They're used to clever lawyers approaching them with a clever deal they think is going to con them'.[153] The positive outcome was, at least for a time, 'the only SSA with a UK chairman of the committee'.

A short-term consequence of the acquisition was the marked increase in the military proportion of Smiths' aerospace turnover, which towards the end of the 1980s came from equipment for the Tornado, Harrier, Hawk, A4, F14, and F18 aircraft, the AH64 Apache helicopter as well as automatic systems for the EH101 helicopter, under development. There were benefits in other areas—for example, the airborne self-contained navigation system was adapted for the American Abrams M1A2 main battle tank, of which 4,000 were expected to be deployed by the mid-1990s.

The much longer term consequence came in relation to increased civil business. Hurn sees this as the crucial legacy of the transaction. 'It elevated us at a stroke to being a tier-1 supplier to Boeing. Lear-Siegler produced the flight management computer system for the 737, the most successful airliner series ever.' Over time, having this seat at the top table would prove hugely valuable. Indeed the value of equipment for the 737 series planes from Smiths and Lear Siegler was estimated at US$500,000 per aircraft in 1991, including the flight management system, autothrottle, engine instrumentation, and air data indicators.[154]

In 1989–90, to the external observer, the timing of the Lear Siegler acquisition did not look so good. Hurn's 'three-legged stool' was now heavily weighted towards the aerospace end of the business, and many issues combined to make this uncomfortable. On the labour relations front, the end of 1989 saw a large dispute between the Engineering Employer's Federation and the AUEW and CSEU in particular, centred on demands for a shorter working week. The aerospace industry was a particular focus for strike action, with Rolls Royce, BAe, and Smiths among particular targets. Out of 3,200 at Cheltenham, 1,000 workers came out on strike in November for three weeks, at an estimated cost of £3.5m before a settlement was achieved.[155] The costs of strike action continued however, since several clients' continuing disputes (e.g. BAe) prevented deliveries. Separately, a far more serious six-week strike at Boeing in late 1989 lost Smiths substantial revenues.[156]

Smiths looked briefly at various parts of Ferranti in late 1989, when its business started to unfold following the disastrous purchase of International Signal & Control, but took no action, leaving GEC to purchase Ferranti's radar business.[157] On the wider political scene, the importance of military contracts had exposed Smiths to significant risk as the Berlin Wall fell and the ending of the Cold War commenced, bringing with it the 'peace dividend' of reduced defence spending. It was clear the division was top-heavy and in July 1990, Pope presented a paper to the board on 'the restructuring of the Aerospace and Defence Group. The objective was to recognize the downsizing of the business consequent upon announced defence cuts as well as changes in defence practice. Management layers would be reduced, products discontinued and manufacturing facilities consolidated.'[158] In September, concrete plans were announced, including job cuts of around 1,000 (11 per cent of the division), fairly evenly split between the UK and overseas, though 450 were concentrated at Cheltenham, prompting claims from the unions of retaliatory job cuts. In context, BAe announced job cuts of nearly

5,000 (19 per cent) of its workforce at the end of 1990 and the closure of two plants, while Rolls Royce followed suit soon after with a plan to reduce staff by 6,000 (18 per cent).[159] Overall the aerospace industry suffered significantly, though arguably Smiths, as a leading provider of retro-fit equipment, was well-placed to meet the demands of clients with limited budgets, which might opt for upgrades versus new orders.

What was probably less obvious at the time to some analysts was how vital the Lear Siegler transaction may have been to Smiths' survival through a downturn in the industry. The Cheltenham and Basingstoke operations were very heavily military-oriented, and towards UK defence work, which was badly hit in the cutbacks that commenced from 1989 onwards. Lear Siegler itself had a strong military emphasis, but its relationship with Boeing was intensely close and the strength of its civil aerospace business offered a significant cushion through the tough environment that was emerging.

Financial summary: 1975–1990

> *Hardly anyone needs to be told that Great Britain is the sick country of Europe. Everywhere you look, the evidence abounds.*
>
> (Vermont Royster[160])

With the bulk of Smiths' turnover dependent on a waning sector, its margins in automotive fell and profitability with it. Negligible motor profits in 1975 recovered slightly by 1977, in line with the broader economy, but from then on declined, turning to losses from 1981 till disposal in 1983. A broadly similar pattern applied in the various distribution activities, including the diminishing clock business. Revenues remained relatively static from 1977 to 1981, but profits dwindled to very little. While the market was initially shocked to find Smiths exiting two of its most fundamental markets, the relevant financial performance made the disposals vital.

The industrial group would itself be reshaped over many years to come, but its existing diverse range of activities already offered a more stable performance in the late 1970s, with margins around the 10–13 per cent level, and sales of close to £50m. The medical division, though smaller, showed stronger growth, with turnover rising from £8.5m in 1976 to £20m in 1980, and profits rising from £1.5m to £5m (margins rising from 18 to 21 per cent, reflecting pricing for premium products). Aerospace showed the most spectacular rise, with turnover rising from £3m in 1976 to £53m in 1980, and margins moving from around 6 per cent to 11 per cent in the period, producing profits of £5.8m in 1980—20 per cent of annual total.

The end of the 1970s had seen the Labour government mired in the labour difficulties of the 1978/9 winter—the 'winter of discontent'—and inflation, though it had declined from the extremes of 1975 to below 10 per cent, had started rising rapidly again. When the figures are reconsidered using the inflation-adjusted current cost figures now presented as standard in the accounts, the decline in the real value of retained profits over the last half of the 1970s is marked, with the lion's share required simply to maintain the cost of inflated assets.

The Conservatives came to power in autumn 1979, committed to tackling inflation, but in the wake of the Iranian revolution earlier that year and the large rise in oil prices that followed, bolstered by the outbreak of the Iran/Iraq War from 1980, the UK's economy was subject to a broader international economic slump. In fact inflation doubled, and it took until 1983 to fall below 5 per cent. The relatively static profits for the whole group, at around £30m since 1980, reflect a series of problems—the drag of the motors and clocks businesses over the time taken to dispose of them; rapidly rising costs, pressuring margins (which halved in industrial, for example, to 7 per cent, between 1979 and 1983); and the deferral of both civil and military contracts in the aerospace division, where profits were static at around £12m from 1981 to 1984.

The medical division, starting from a low base, performed strongly throughout the 1980s, with margins reaching 15 per cent by 1985 and over 20 per cent by 1987, where they remained. Sales growth through to 1986 remained above 20 per cent per annum as well, though tailed off significantly in the latter half of the decade, in part reflecting the power of the US group-purchasing organizations. Likewise sales growth for the industrial growth was strong in the first half of the 1980s, occasionally boosted by acquisitions, while a decline in sales in the latter 1980s was attributable largely to divestiture of various businesses. From margins closer to 10 per cent, or lower, in the early 1980s, the latter part of the decade saw figures closer to 17–18 per cent, as the group became rationalized.

Overall, the figures for both turnover and profit increased more than three-fold between 1976 and 1990. Early increases were strongly influenced by inflation but a large proportion came from 1987 onwards, following the acquisition of the Lear Siegler businesses, which doubled the size of the aerospace contribution. Overall, from the mid-1980s to 1990, the relationship between Smiths' performance and the economies of the UK and US, forming the majority of its market, is distorted—partly by Lear Siegler, which increased sales and profits so significantly, and partly by the disposals and rationalizations still occurring in the industrial division, where though sales declined, margins and profits increased. The growth of the UK and US economies in the late 1980s offered a positive backdrop, but as the 1990s opened, nervousness emerged, both in terms of recessionary fears and concern over post-Cold War defence policy cutbacks.

In human terms, the effects of reshaping the business throughout the period are easily seen in Table 8.2. The 1980–2 recession saw cutbacks in staffing across the business, and the disposal of the motors and clocks businesses produced further

Table 8.2 Numbers of employees (1976–1990)

Year	Total Employees (000s)
1976	20.3
1981	17.5
1985	11.0
1990	13.1

Source: annual reports.

substantial reductions. The rationalization of businesses continued through until 1988, but acquisitions such as Lear Siegler reversed the trend to some degree.

Conclusions

> *The City were aghast initially. They won't tell you that now, they'll all say*
> *how brilliant they thought it was at the time . . . they jolly well didn't.*
>
> (Gerry Mortimer, 1998)

The firm celebrated its seventy-fifth year as a public company in 1989, and much was made in 1990 of the fiftieth anniversary of the Cheltenham site—there were two days of celebrations in May, with dramatic flypasts. While tradition was honoured with the Battle of Britain Memorial Flight, the clear emphasis was on the present, as the Tornado roared overhead. For Smiths, by 1990, the hi-tech clean rooms of aerospace and medical had replaced the lo-tech production lines of clocks and motors accessories.

That Smiths was now a hi-tech concern was emphasized each year by its R&D spend. When *The Accountant* surveyed twenty-six leading firms in 1987, it revealed Smiths' commitment, at 11 per cent of turnover for 1986, was the highest in the sample, which included GEC, Glaxo, BAe, Plessey, ICI, and other major names (and second highest in 1985).[161] Alan Hornsby, finance director, believes 'all the more impressive was our record of writing off R&D expenditure in the year it was incurred, rather than capitalising it over a longer period'.[162] He retired in late 1989, after thirty-five years with the firm—and reflects his most important contribution 'was to help promote the corporate finance function required in a decentralized structure'—essentially the discipline that saw people such as Ron Williams, Martyn Wenzerul, and Cyril Miles insist on a high level of accounting expertise, and together with Gerry Mortimer apply a greater degree of professional analysis to acquisitions. Overall, the 1980s saw Smiths refine its portfolio approach to owning businesses, developing greater professionalism in evaluation and management. Another firm believer in decentralization and a veteran of thirty-nine years was John Thompson, deputy MD, who was critical to the disposal of the motor accessories—'it was without question his finest hour'. He retired in 1988.[163]

By the late 1980s, Hurn had assembled his 'three-legged stool', with Pope, Kennedy, and Williams as his key generals. More rebalancing was envisaged, ideally with another medical acquisition, as the group felt top-heavy in aerospace, or at least the market thought so, with the share price suffering 'largely because of the prospect of defence cuts following political changes in Eastern Europe', but options for the 1990s were kept open. 'Mr Hurn felt that in the current climate, with the unscrambling of highly leveraged acquisitions, the number of opportunities would increase.'[164]

The previous fifteen years had witnessed remarkable events. From the mid-1970s the process of reorganization had seen staff numbers nearly halved over ten years before fresh acquisitions reversed the decline. Returns, however, increased—as Hurn puts it, 'we sold lots of sales, but we didn't sell much profit'.[165] Looking back on the Lucas transaction, Thompson summed up: 'it was an incredibly brave thing for the board to do, still loaded up with motor men—and Roger with all his roots in Cricklewood'.[166] Significantly, thirty years after Smiths' exit from the industry, ex-employees of the motor accessory division (from management down to 'the line') still meet regularly—in a club (the '2000 Club') that Roger Hurn continues to support—all testament to strong bonds formed over decades and the ethos built up by Frank Hurn and Dick Cave.

Despite the degree of inevitability in Smiths' decision to abandon its roots, Hurn is clear it was nevertheless a tough decision—'I had a lot of personal baggage. It was all my personal baggage.' It can be argued it would have been better to exit motors, clocks, and watches earlier, but it was also clear the motor accessory division would require significant and hugely risky investment, and 'we didn't want to put the money into it because it was not going to produce a viable return', added to which 'I could see what was happening in the other parts of the business much more clearly and I knew we could live through it.'[167] With the strong margins Smiths generated in medical and aerospace, and an ability to construct an exit from motor accessories that left the firm actually ahead on cash, the choice to focus the business in the mid-1980s where both growth and higher returns were possible made obvious strategic sense. Ahead, the 1990s now appeared to offer significant challenges, both in terms of the world economy and the uncertainties created by the dismantling of the Eastern Bloc, but Smiths was in considerably better shape to face those challenges.

Notes

1. TNA: PREM 19/71 (7 Dec. 1979).
2. For more detail, see table 3.1 and 'motor vehicles', Roderick Floud and Paul Johnson, *The Cambridge Economic History of Modern Britain* (Cambridge: CUP, 2003), iii. p59, 66–70.
3. 26 Mar. 1976, 20.
4. *The Times* (26 Mar. 1976), 17.
5. Hurn, interview (1998); *Financial Times* (6 Dec. 1986), 5.
6. *The Times* (6 Dec. 1986), 18.
7. Hurn, interview (1998).
8. Hurn, interview (1998).
9. Martyn Wenzerul, interview (21 Aug. 2013).
10. *Minutes* (9 June 1981).
11. Joan Berry, interview (17 Apr. 2013).
12. *The Times* (20 Feb. 1975), 5.
13. *Financial Times* (24 Feb. 1976), 6.
14. Geoff Hedrick, telephone interview (6 Aug. 2013).
15. CE Memorandum CE 14 (27 July 1982); *Minutes* (14 July 1981).
16. CE Memorandum CE 6 (12 Oct. 1981); Ray J. Abraczinskas, *Fifty-Five Trips around the Sun: The History of Smiths Industries Information Management Systems in Grand Rapids, Michigan* (Grand Rapids, MI: Smiths, 1999), 254.
17. Hurn, interview (2013).

18. *SI News* (Feb. 1975), 1; Kennedy, interview (9 July 2013).

19. *SI News* (May 1974), 1.

20. Kennedy, interview (2013).

21. *SI Digest* (Sept. 1977), 1.

22. *SI Digest* (July 1979), 1.

23. Kennedy, interview (2013).

24. Kennedy, interview (2013).

25. Mortimer, interview (1998).

26. Hurn, interview (1998).

27. Hurn, interview (1998).

28. SMMT figures.

29. Marcus Beresford, personal communication (July 2013); *Minutes* (10 Dec. 1980).

30. Beresford, pers. comm. (2013).

31. Beresford, pers. comm. (2013).

32. Nick Morgan, pers. comm. (July 2013); John Thompson, interview (1998).

33. Cochlin, telephone interview (3 Aug. 2013).

34. Miriam Glucksmann, *Women on the Line* (London: Routledge, 2009).

35. *The Times* (8 Nov. 1977), 27.

36. John Thompson, interview (3 July 2013); *Minutes* (13 Nov. 1979).

37. *Guardian* (6 Mar. 1980), 18.

38. *Minutes* (14 Apr. 1981).

39. Mortimer, interview (1998).

40. Beresford, pers. comm. (2013).

41. Dick Snewin, pers. comm. (July 2013).

42. TNA: FV22/70, 'visit report no. 665'.

43. Hornsby, interview (24 July 2013).

44. *SI Digest* (Jan. 1982), 1; *Minutes* (12 Jan. 1982).

45. Spencer, meeting notes (25 Aug. 1982), TNA: FV22/70; *Minutes* (8 June 1982).

46. Hurn, interview (1998).

47. *Minutes* (8 June 1982).

48. Hurn, interview (1998).

49. John Allen, 'Lucas Industries', notes for an Industrial Development Advisory Board presentation (16 Dec. 1982), TNA: FV22/72.

50. *HC Deb* (6 Apr. 1982), vol. 21, cc. 822–3.

51. *Financial Times* (23 Jan. 1982), 3.

52. Monopolies and Mergers Commission, *Car Parts: A Report on the Matter of the Existence or Possible Existence of a Complex Monopoly Situation in Relation to the Wholesale Supply of Motor Car Parts in the United Kingdom*, HC 318 (1981–2), 5; Tommaso Pardi, 'Do State and Politics Matter? The Case of Nissan's Direct Investment in Great Britain and its Implications for Great Britain', *Business and History*, 8, (2010), 8.

53. *The Economist* (10 July 1982), 10.

54. Cochlin, interview (2013).

55. Cochlin to Barker (3 Nov. 1982), TNA: FV22/70.

56. Manuscript additions, Fraser to Mountfield (16 Aug. 1982), TNA: FV22/70.

57. Cochlin, interview (2013).

58. 'Proposed joint company' (5 Nov. 1982), TNA: FV22/70.

59. 'Note of conversation', Cochlin and Wilkinson (15 Dec. 1982), TNA: FV22/71.

60. Paul Pennell-Buck, meeting notes (Nov. 1982), TNA: V22/71.
61. Cochlin to Mountfield (3 Dec. 1982), TNA: FV22/71.
62. Cochlin to Manzie (1 Dec. 1982), TNA: FV22/71.
63. 'Note of conversation', Cochlin and Wilkinson.
64. Evans to Barker (10 Dec. 1982), enclosures, TNA: FV22/72.
65. *Minutes* (11 Jan. 1983).
66. Barker, file note (19 Jan. 1983), TNA: FV22/72.
67. Andersen to Howse (25 Jan. 1983), TNA: FV22/72.
68. Spencer, meeting notes (25 Aug. 1982), TNA: FV22/70.
69. Thompson to Howse (18 Jan. 1983), TNA: FV22/72.
70. Riley to Cochlin (8 Feb. 1983), TNA: FV22/72.
71. Market capitalization was approx. £125m versus assets of £550m.
72. Cochlin to Baker (17 Mar. 1983), TNA: FV22/72.
73. *SI Annual Report* (1983); *The Times* (29 Mar. 1983), 19. Lucas contributed £30m in assets, and £75m in turnover.
74. Thompson, interview (1998).
75. Thompson, interviews (1998, 2013).
76. Beresford, pers. comm. (July 2013).
77. *Financial Times* (14 Jan. 1984), 3.
78. Sir Anthony Gill, pers. comm. (Aug. 2013).
79. Keith Wills, pers. comm. (Aug. 2013).
80. *Financial Times* (11 Apr. 1984), 1.
81. *Minutes* (16 Dec. 1986).
82. Cochlin, interview (2013).
83. Hornsby, interview (2013).
84. Hornsby, interview (2013).
85. Hurn and Thompson, interviews (1998).
86. Hurn, interview (1998).
87. Jones, interview (2013).
88. *SI News* (Mar. 1984), 11.
89. Pers. comm. (May 2013).
90. Barrett to Smith (29 Feb. 1980), courtesy Graham Smith.
91. Thompson, interview (1998).
92. *Minutes* (13 May 1980).
93. *Minutes* (10 June 1980).
94. CE Memorandum CE 28 (4 Oct. 1983).
95. Hurn, interview (1998).
96. Thompson (1998); *Minutes* (10 May, 14 June 1983).
97. Auction by Henry Butcher (12 Apr. 1984).
98. Hurn, interview (1998).
99. *Financial Times* (23 Apr. 1982), 34 and (30 June 1984), 3.
100. Andrew Lorenz, *GKN: The Making of a Business, 1759–2009* (Chichester: Wiley, 2009), 197.
101. *Financial Times* (20 Dec. 1984), 23.
102. Hurn, interview (1998).
103. Williams, interview (1998).
104. *Financial Times* (1 Aug. 1985), 26.

105. *Minutes* (9 Sept. 1986), closed 31 Dec.
106. Hurn, interview (1998).
107. *Minutes* (10 Nov. 1987).
108. Mortimer, interview (1998).
109. Hurn, interview (1998).
110. Hurn, interview (1998).
111. Williams, interview (1998).
112. Alan Smith, interview (1998).
113. Hurn, interview (1998).
114. CE Memorandum CE 58 (19 Jan. 1987).
115. Thompson, interview (1998).
116. Alan Smith, interview (1998).
117. *SI News* (Sept. 1984), 6.
118. Hurn, interview (1998).
119. CE Memorandum CE 38 (4 Sept. 1984).
120. Hurn, interview (1998).
121. *SI Digest* (Jan. 1976).
122. CE Memorandum CE 38 (4 Sept. 1984).
123. CE Memorandum CE 39 (4 Sept. 1984).
124. *SI Digest* (Nov. 1977), 1.
125. *SI Digest* (22 Aug. 1978), 1.
126. Trevor Leader, pers. comm. (July 2013).
127. Thompson, interview (2013).
128. *Financial Times* (29 Jan. 1980), 16.
129. *SI News* (Autumn 1982), 1.
130. Thompson, interview (1998).
131. Leader, pers. comm. (2013).
132. Thompson, interview (1998).
133. CE Memorandum CE 60 (11 Mar. 1987).
134. Williams, interview (1998).
135. Hurn, interview (2013).
136. *Minutes* (13 Jan. 1984).
137. *Minutes* (9 Mar. 1984).
138. Kennedy, interview (2013).
139. CE Memorandum CE 77 (20 Dec. 1988); *Minutes* (10 Jan. 1989).
140. *Minutes* (12 Mar., 9 Apr. 1985).
141. Robert Bloch et al, *An Analysis of Group Purchasing Organizations' Contracting Practices under the Antitrust Laws: Myth and Reality* (Washington, DC: Mayer, Brown, Rowe & Maw, n.d.), 5.
142. *The Times* (5 Jan. 1989), 20; *Minutes* (10 Jan. 1989).
143. *Minutes* (14 Mar. 1989); *Financial Times* (25 Mar. 1989), 8.
144. *Minutes* (11 Oct., 14 Dec. 1988); *Financial Times* (3 May 1989), 24.
145. Hurn, interview (2013).
146. *Minutes* (9 Oct. 1984).
147. Tony Blackman, *Flight Testing to Win* (Hamble: Blackman Associates, 2005), 304.
148. Hurn, interview (1998).
149. Blackman, *Flight Testing*, 304.

150. *Financial Times* (1 Aug. 1987), 1; Blackman, *Flight Testing*, 305; Hornsby, interview (2013); Wenzerul, interview (2013).
151. Mortimer and Williams, interviews (1998).
152. Hurn, interview (1998).
153. Mortimer, interview (1998).
154. Flemings Research, 'Smiths Industries' (12 Aug. 1991).
155. *Minutes* (12 Dec. 1989).
156. *Financial Times* (22 Nov. 1989), 4.
157. *Minutes* (12 Dec. 1989, 13 Feb. 1990); *HC Deb* (15 Nov. 1989), vol. 160, cc. 353–5.
158. *Minutes* (10 July 1990).
159. *Financial Times* (30 Nov. 1990). 1 and (9 May 1991), 1.
160. *Wall Street Journal* (20 Aug. 1975).
161. *The Accountant* (18 Feb. 1987), 4.
162. Hornsby, interview (2013).
163. Hurn, interview (1998).
164. *Minutes* (13 Feb. 1990).
165. Hurn, interview (1998).
166. Thompson, interview (1998).
167. Hurn, interview (1998).

CHAPTER 9

....

1991–2000

The End of an Era

....

Smiths Industries has been one of Britain's nimblest industrial players of the last decade. Under chairman Sir Roger Hurn it has made 30 acquisitions in nine years. Seven years ago its shares traded below 200p. Now they are 942½p. A fantastic record. But City followers are starting to wonder how Smiths can keep it up.

(*Daily Mail*[1])

THE 1990s opened with a global recession that hit hard in Smiths' main geographic markets. Once growth returned, the latter part of the decade witnessed the largest wave of merger and acquisition activity to date, culminating in the extraordinary market froth of the dot.com boom. The period 1998–2000 is particularly characterized by large-scale transactions in the internet and telecommunications sectors, involving remarkably optimistic price/earnings ratios—transactions that in many cases ended up destroying significant value.

Despite having little involvement in that late 1990s boom, or subsequent bust, the name Smiths Industries was nevertheless consigned to the past on 30 November 2000, marking the end of an era in the company's history, but also the end of a decade that offers a distillation of the classic Smiths Industries' model of operation. By 2000, a new model was needed, but during the 1990s, the company reaped a bountiful harvest, the result of both reshaping the group in the 1980s (eliminating low-margin activities) and successfully acquiring further profitable high-margin businesses. The results speak for themselves, in earnings and dividends that doubled over the decade, in real terms—the companies acquired in the 1990s notably accounted for half the profits figure for 2000. A senior management team, including members who had spent twenty or more years working together, moved towards retirement, and would leave by the end of the decade. They represented between them a remarkable reservoir of Smiths culture, and knowledge of the myriad subtle levers that could be used to manage a diversified portfolio of companies, and the people running them. The handover to a new team of managers would offer challenges, with changing styles and philosophies emerging.

Back to the beginning of the decade, though growth in the UK lasted slightly longer than elsewhere, overall 1990 saw the emergence of a global recession, influenced by restrictive monetary policies designed to dampen inflation accompanying the credit-fuelled boom of the late 1980s. Confidence declined, with the Gulf War, another oil-price spike, and credit limitations all contributing. For the UK, an important change came in October 1992, with the introduction of inflation targeting in place of exchange-rate stability. After a substantial fall, the slow rise of sterling that followed would later impact Smiths' exports from the UK.

In the first half of the 1990s, reduced defence spending, combined with intense civil aerospace competition among airlines, led to serious cutbacks in expenditure across the aerospace industry. Smiths' reinvestment of cash was broadly diverted away from the aerospace group and diverted into the other two groups, notably to medical. Its growth was marked, from 1991 to 1996, with sales more than doubling and margins reaching a record 24 per cent, influenced in part by the 1994 purchase of Deltec, heralding a move into a new area of health care products—used in the home—against a backdrop of significant health care budget problems in the US, and the resulting push towards solutions that reduced the burden of expensive care in hospitals.

Having taken over in 1988, Ron Williams, chair of the industrial group, hit his stride fully in the first half of the 1990s, consolidating the group and providing some focus on a more limited range of products, and adding complementary acquisitions that leveraged detailed knowledge of various chosen markets—interconnectors, specialist ducting, fans, and other specialist high-margin light-engineering—although it would be unwise to stress the notion of 'complementarity' too far. The real focus was on buying high-quality, cash-generating businesses, and then being able to manage them to produce their best. By the time he retired in February 1996, turnover and profits had already more than doubled from 1990 levels, with margins approaching 16 per cent.

Smiths entered the 1990s seen as an aerospace company, given the weighting of its three main businesses. By mid-decade, the benefits of the tripartite approach were clear, as the economic backdrop changed, and the contribution from the mix changed. The high-volume (though highly specialized) medical manufacturing business proved counter-cyclical and strengthened as aerospace weakened over the same period, before the fortunes of the two began reversing, towards the end of the decade. For the industrial group, the 1990s were described overall by one observer as 'a decade in the sun'.

The conglomerate nature of Smiths made it hard for the market to compare it with any peers. TI Group was one option, but comparisons were often made with more specialized companies—Meggitt, Goodrich, or Whittaker in aerospace, for example, or Mallinckrodt in medical. As the 1990s came to an end, ABN Amro concluded there were good prospects for growth at Smiths—'If the "old" economy stocks are to return to favour, then Smiths is arguably the "pick of the bunch".'[2]

Aerospace—some turbulence: 1991–1995

Our proximity to Boeing meant that we saw the writing on the wall.

(Roger Hurn, *Financial Times*, 1995)

Despite cyclical downturns, Smiths' view of itself in the 1990s included a strong weighting towards aerospace. With long-term annualized growth rates for air-passenger traffic in the region of 9 per cent, and a prediction that defence spending, despite varying with the economic backdrop, would continue, there was a long-term confidence that this was an absolute core business.[3] Notwithstanding downturns, it would be maintained and strengthened where possible.

Hugh Pope, chairman of the aerospace group, came to the end of a ten-year Smiths career in mid-1991, and on his retirement was replaced by Norman Barber, former head of the military aircraft division at BAe—an experienced aviation man. As one commentator noted, 'his many years at British Aerospace make him no stranger to trouble', and the first few years at Smiths offered little respite, as volumes, profits, and margins declined through to 1995 (though margins remained double-digit).[4] The group's performance was severely influenced in the first half of the 1990s on the civil side by the combination of the effects of global recession. For example, the scheduled US airlines lost an aggregate $13bn between 1989 and 1994, before finally posting profits in 1995.[5] Though the 737 held up well, Boeing's overall 1996 production was half that of 1991. In defence, there were severe cutbacks following upon the break-up of the USSR. The US government's spending on defence procurement peaked at $82bn in 1991, but by 1996 was 40 per cent lower.[6] This was all reflected in a decline in the S&P Aerospace/Defence index, from 1990 to the end of 1993, but then the rationalization of the industry notably fed through to a change in sentiment for the market and the index turned sharply positive.

The downturn of the early 1990s highlighted the value of the 'three-legged stool' approach, since firms that were purely (or mainly) aerospace-oriented suffered significantly more. Examples were Dowty Group, and particularly British Aerospace and Rolls Royce, both of whom significantly delayed payments to their suppliers in the 1991–2 period—at Smiths, Hugh Pope issued instructions not to press either firm for settlement.

Dowty is relevant for several reasons. It was the company most frequently compared with Smiths by the City analysts and the firms had a small joint venture, Dowty & Smiths Industries Controls. Despite retrenchment at Smiths, there was nevertheless a keenness to take advantage of circumstance where possible to grow its business, and Dowty, a possible acquisition target for many years, resurfaced as a possibility. Based in Cheltenham, it was best known for its landing-gear systems and the Rotol propeller business it had acquired in 1960, but the 1980s had seen diversification into wider avionics and advanced materials engineering, particularly in polymer seals, as well as telecoms and computer equipment, and even mining system solutions. In aerospace it entered the 1990s with a 60:40 mix of military/civil business and tried hard to reverse the balance, but with the overall decline in the industry its figures collapsed, prompting job losses of 2,500 (17 per cent) in 1991 and a boardroom shake-out, with both chairman and CEO leaving.[7]

Discussions had been held in the late 1980s between Smiths and Dowty on a possible tie-up, but Bob Hunt, Dowty's chairman, found his CEO, Tony Thatcher (formerly of Smiths), was against any such transaction. Then in mid-1991 Smiths took a further close look, assisted by Warburg's. It was natural in Smiths for the originators of acquisition transactions to be supported by their subordinates, and the system relied on checks and balances higher up the management chain. Dowty offered an example of a rare breed of transaction—felt to be sponsored by the chief executive (and therefore lacking a higher level of supervision). This led to a degree of code from the executive team analysing the transaction, offering support, while at the same time expressing 'issues'. Analysis of the potential deal filled weeks of early-morning meetings, but an advantage of working together for so many years was that Hurn was well accustomed to interpreting the code—he concluded the pricing was significantly too expensive, and withdrew.[8] The decision was strongly bolstered by advice from Kleinwort Benson, whom Smiths had engaged when its own long-term advisers, Warburg's, had declared a conflict of interest.[9] This arose from Warburg's also being house bank to the TI Group (formerly Tube Investments), where Christopher Lewinton, CEO since 1986, was still keen to break into the FTSE 100 and needed an acquisition. Like Smiths, TI had held informal discussions with Dowty, but unlike Smiths, Lewinton was prepared to launch a hostile bid, which finally emerged in April 1992, opening at £482m.[10] Dowty mounted a spirited defence, not least in highlighting the controversial accounting practices that TI employed in its acquisitions, explored in a case study in Terry Smith's recent book *Accounting for Growth*.[11] But Lewinton prevailed in June 1992, creating the second largest UK engineering firm behind BAe and propelling TI into the FTSE 100.[12] Dowty was then broken up, with various parts sold off immediately. A 1994 joint venture with Snecma, Messier-Dowty, absorbed the undercarriage business, which TI later exited entirely in 1997.[13] When Hurn came to look back in 1998 at possible deals that should not have been done over the years (and having, of course, no idea how things might unfold over the next two or three), he commented on being outbid for Dowty by TI— 'they're suffering for it now . . . so in terms of narrow escapes that might be one'.[14]

Despite a difficult marketplace, Smiths nevertheless pushed hard both to win new business and to protect its position, while undergoing serious rationalization, particularly by reducing staff numbers. Barber outlined the backdrop at a board meeting in early 1992:

> Unprofitable airlines were ordering fewer spares and cancelling or deferring the purchase of new planes. British Aerospace had experienced delays . . . EFA [Euro-fighter] production would be delayed. Rolls-Royce continued to experience difficulties . . . The break up of the Soviet Union had depressed sales . . . Work was now out of balance with a number of development contracts being undertaken at zero or low margins.[15]

The Gulf War itself had little effect on Smiths, though the aftermath had led to orders as equipment was replaced and restocked. A noticeable broader effect had been the highlighting of the role of technology in weaponry and particularly in military aircraft—for example, in the use of the self-contained navigation system (acquired with Lear Siegler), extensively used in the M1A2 Abrams tank and by the RAF and USAF in Desert Storm. Such an emphasis clearly benefited avionics firms such as Smiths. The hi-tech Eurofighter (EFA) project was expected to provide Smiths with orders worth £250,000 per aircraft, but in the early 1990s the numbers of aircraft under the programme were hit by reductions in orders from Germany (which nearly withdrew altogether), Italy, and Spain. While demonstrating for peace is a familiar notion, in October 1992 Londoners witnessed the remarkable spectacle of 2,000 workers marching on Parliament in support of a fighter aircraft, lobbying for resolute government backing for the EFA—including workers from Dowty and Smiths at Cheltenham, reflecting estimates that 25 per cent of families in Gloucestershire depended on aerospace and defence work for their income.[16] With reduced numbers and much debate, the programme finally moved forwards and the EFA made its maiden flight on 27 March 1994. The Typhoon, as the plane became known, still features some of the most advanced avionics. While the Europeans were debating the EFA project, the US pressed ahead with its latest hi-tech aircraft project, the F22, for which Smiths successfully bid to provide the electrical power distribution system.

On the civil side, Smiths continually updated its flight management system, offering profitable retro-fit business on the Boeing 737. Similarly, with fuel efficiency paramount, its improvements in fuel quantity indicating systems also gained regular upgrade contracts. On the military side, collapsing defence budgets promoted the use of retro-fitting, since upgraded avionics could extend the life of military aircraft by a significant margin. Analysts had predicted in the early 1990s this could be a major source of revenue for Smiths, though low-price disposals of combat aircraft by the US offered another option to the market—in addition to which there was not only increased competition from firms such as Rockwell but also the original manufacturers (e.g. Northrop Grumman and Lockheed), which were effective in resisting third-party upgrades without their involvement.[17] Nevertheless, an example of successful retrofitting was the self-contained inertial navigation system that Lear Siegler had originally contracted to provide to the USAF for its C130 Hercules aircraft. This had been another onerous contract that took Smiths time to renegotiate, but City analysts nevertheless estimated Smiths ultimately turned revenues expected in the late 1980s to be $250m into a programme with over $600m in revenues during the first half of the 1990s, with spin-offs in similar deliveries to the RAF.

As the aerospace industry contracted, there was widespread hope that it could redeploy expertise and already developed technology for civil use—what was termed 'conversion'—turning swords into ploughshares. But as Norman Augustine of Lockheed Martin admitted in 1992: 'The record of massive defense conversion is one unblemished by success.'[18] However, one outcome of the situation was a blurring of distinctions between some elements of the technology used in the defence and civil spheres, with the advantage that technology developed in military programmes, and therefore largely funded by Smiths' customers, could then be rolled out for civil application. This was of relevance in notable 1991 contracts from Boeing for the 777. Smiths had developed an electrical load management system (ELMS) for the AH64B Apache Longbow helicopter, focusing on central control of the electrical load and removing the need for much cabling and instrumentation. Smiths took the idea to Boeing at a time the design for the 777 was being developed. The ELMS has the advantage of reducing weight—1.5 tonnes in the case of the 777—and Boeing was persuaded, awarding an initial contract for 150 sets at $427,000 each. The associated development costs were nevertheless estimated at £15.4m over six years.[19] Another innovation, Smiths' fuel quantity indicating system (FQIS), which used ultrasonic detectors to monitor fuel tank contents, also won Boeing over, with an £85m contract, involving £6m in development costs.[20] With a further $35m contract for throttle actuators, Smiths could expect to deliver $1m of equipment per 777 completed, leading ultimately to revenues estimated at $400–600m over ten to fifteen years. The City welcomed the good news, though overall reaction was somewhat muted as many focused on the heavy development spend, which would impact profits in the near term, given Smiths' long-term policy of writing off R&D in the year it was incurred—a worry that perhaps ignored the fact Smiths had traditionally maintained a high rate of R&D and was not necessarily adding to figures previously budgeted. As matters turned out, though ELMS and FQIS had high long-term visibility, there were significant technical challenges along the way—reducing the profitability of FQIS, but allowing more revenue for ELMS as Smiths was able to recover its additional costs.

Still on the theme of engine and fuel management systems, Smiths formed a joint venture with Rolls Royce in February 1994—Rolls Smiths Engine Controls (RoSEC), which provided control units for Rolls Royce's BR700 engine—but this was a short-lived attempt to break into a highly competitive market, and after swallowing heavy development costs in 1996 (and organizing a significant resulting shake-up of the Basingstoke operation), Smiths sold its business to Lucas-Varity in July 1997.

Since the late 1980s, Kelvin Hughes had been moved into the aerospace group, largely for reasons of presentational tidiness, although using the argument that there was some technological crossover, with the bridge control systems for ships becoming more integrated, resembling patterns of development in avionic controls. The traditional chart business was being transformed by the adoption of GPS navigation, but also by digitalization and electronic displays. To enhance this business further, Smiths acquired Sestrel Observator BV in the Netherlands and Brown & Perring in the UK, during 1994.

With turnover and profits very close to those of the previous year, the nadir of the aerospace market for Smiths finally arrived in 1995, and the beginnings of a turn in the market began to show, with the first profits for US airlines since 1989. The 777 entered service and Smiths commenced a long production run, with development costs behind it, while significant revenues from the product support operation provided a further key element to the turnaround. The firm was also selected to develop the flight management system for the 737-700, Boeing's next generation of the long-running 737 programme.

Smiths could now look forward to increasing revenues from both civil and military programmes. On the military side, the EH101 and Apache helicopters, and the Hawk, F18, F22, and Tornado mid-life update all involved Smiths avionics—prospects for 1996 and onwards looked promising, and there was now a reasonable balance between the two spheres. Over the long term, Smiths had, in common with Rolls Royce (though quite independently), navigated a path from a heavy dependence on state contracts and aid, to independence from this through winning sufficient civil work.[21]

Industrial—a golden age: 1991–1995

Williams seems to be able to throw magic dust in the eyes of the companies he buys.

(Sir Peter Thompson[22])

When the 'three-legged stool' approach emerged, 'what we called the Industrial Group was, I suppose, in reality the things that were left that were not aerospace and were not medical', as Williams put it.[23] It included a diverse collection of companies, and could be perceived by some as the waiting room for businesses Smiths intended to sell. From the late 1980s, Williams had been working to dispel that image, though there had been and would continue to be disposals. At a cosmetic level the annual reports presented various evolving clusters of businesses, and as companies were acquired, the balance between those clusters changed, reflected in a gradual shift in the names of the industrial group subdivisions, designed in part to counter negative sentiment towards the notion of a conglomerate. The decade opened with two necessarily loose clusters: (i) Interconnect—businesses making things which connected one thing to another, ranging from the hugely expensive low-loss co-axial cables made by Times Microwave for fighter planes, to (imaginatively) the extending vacuum cleaner hose made for Dyson by Flexible Ducting; and (ii) Engineering—which included the gamut from specialist fans (SIFAN) to industrial ceramic ignition products (Lodge).

Things changed rapidly. The flexible ducting business had started small, with companies in Scotland and Germany, but significantly expanded in August 1991 with the £33m purchase of Flexible Technologies Inc., based in South Carolina, with several North American plants, the leading US maker of non-metallic flexible ducting and hoses (for air-conditioning and vacuums)—a company Smiths had first tried to buy two years earlier. Soon after, Smiths acquired Matzen & Timm of Hamburg, producer of silicone ducting used in the aerospace and vehicle industries. The emergence of an obvious network of ducting businesses—there were seven by mid-decade—led to the eventual creation of the Flex-Tek cluster, which included Kopex, with its roots in Smiths dating back to the late 1950s.

Williams was measured in his approach to acquisitions. Hurn recalls a poker player's demeanour: 'he was never willing to show that he wanted something in case he was tempted to pay too much for it, and so he would become very Druid-like and Welsh'.[24]

Mortimer remembered a similar uncertainty—did Williams really want the target business?—but also recalled dealing with the issue of a potential MBO. This was in late 1992, when Smiths once again bought a company it had known for years—a transaction that would lead to the creation of another cluster:

> The best one was Vent-Axia, where the management wanted to buy the business themselves, and this bloke [Williams] goes down (and I was recovering from an illness) and he goes down there, with the team, including me, and he says [heavy Welsh accent], 'Now,' he says, 'I . . . want . . . to . . . ask . . . you some . . . questions. But I want you to answer them very simply and very clearly, because I've got Gerry here, who won't understand . . . ' [laughter] and they couldn't believe this, and within two hours they wanted to sell to us.[25]

APV, the engineering group, was struggling after a decade of acquisitions that had not been integrated, and its newly appointed CEO, Clive Strowger, sold Vent-Axia to Smiths for £58m in December 1992 to release cash. Vent-Axia, the leading commercial fan manufacturer, complemented Smiths' existing business—SIFAN—another specialist fan maker (for boilers). By mid-decade, Vent-Axia was adopted as a collective term for the whole cluster of fan businesses.

The early 1990s did not offer an easy backdrop. The Conservative government returned to office in April 1992 faced serious problems, with unemployment rising, the economy in recession, and high interest rates leading to record numbers of mortgage defaults. It was a difficult backdrop against which to be trading—board minutes reveal Williams's concern that 'management morale needed constant stimulation throughout the Group'.[26] But it was also an environment that offered opportunities. A well-tried formula was maintained, of targeting high-margin, strongly cash-generating concerns that would benefit from what analysts detected was 'a rigorous management style'. Through 1993, the group felt the continuing effects of the global recession with some pressure on margins, though figures from Flexible Technologies and Vent-Axia fed through to strong increases in turnover and profits that year—indeed these two recent acquisitions accounted for half the group's sales and profits.

Owing to the new scale of the group, there were now more than just cosmetic notions behind the next change in its presentation, as from 1994 it was divided into three main clusters, with a modest management structure in each: Flex-Tek (combining all ducting and conduit businesses in the UK, US, and Germany), Vent-Axia (comprising all the fan businesses—Anda, Airstream, Benzing, and SIFAN), and Engineering, which grouped together the Interconnect businesses that had a good degree of relatedness, and a handful of other businesses (that would go on to be sold). Williams recalled: 'it was proving to be very difficult to handle the acquisitions and to run all the businesses—and so we split the business into three and had three mini group-MDs to allow us to grow, and that's how we coped'.[27]

In the period 1993–5, the overall size of the group doubled, with £134m spent on acquisitions. In the Flex-Tek division, purchases included Dura-Vent from Indiana and Compoflex in the UK in 1994, and then five further small ducting businesses across

Europe in 1995. By mid-decade, Flex-Tek comprised a large international portfolio of companies all involved in specialist ducting and hoses, with strong market shares in various niches, whether in fume extraction, low-smoke hazard, or flexibility—combining to produce margins of 15 per cent or more.

The engineering division was boosted in 1994 by the $32m purchase of Tutco, a large US manufacturer of heating elements, followed up with the purchase of Elkay in the UK, a manufacturer of plastic cable glands—both companies viewed by City analysts as 'classic Smiths industrial businesses': 'relatively small, highly cash-generative and with extremely strong market positions'.[28] Smiths also had a good track record with Hypertac connectors (remarkably reliable electric connectors suitable for demanding environments), which it had manufactured under licence since 1961. In June 1995 it finally acquired the licensor, FRB Connectron in France, plus three associated specialist connector companies in the US, Italy, and Germany. 'We paid a very reasonable price', recalls Robin Taunt, 'it was a great transaction'.[29] Two other businesses now moved under the engineering umbrella were Times Microwave and Icore, which suffered substantially from the defence cutbacks of the early 1990s. This resulted in some significant rationalization and a refocus towards civil communications.

Half way through the decade, the industrial group, which some analysts may have believed would be wound down, had increased sales from £100m to £250m, and with margins up to near 16 per cent, profits advanced from £15m to £38m. But another chapter was coming to an end. The autumn of 1995 saw Williams clock up thirty-six years with Smiths, the last twenty spent working closely with Roger Hurn, and the team that had been forged together over decades was beginning to fragment. Gerry Mortimer had retired in January 1995, after thirty-two years, and Williams retired a year later, in February 1996.

Medical—expansion in the home: 1991–1995

> Happily for Smiths, the medical business was sufficiently well developed by the late 1980s to fill the breach . . . it was generating cash and strong earnings just at the time civil aerospace went into free fall.
>
> (Financial Times[30])

The decade opened with business strong, and a Queen's Award in 1991 (and yet another in 1994). The Gulf War removed Middle Eastern business, and shortage of currency reduced Eastern European orders, but despite this sales were excellent. Health care spending in the highly developed markets continued to increase, despite the recessionary backdrop. In the UK, a new internal market was established with the NHS and Community Care Act 1990, leading to the establishment of the first NHS Trusts in 1991, but despite their implied independence, a trend towards more centralized purchasing also emerged. This offered a challenge comparable to that in the US, where, though the Clinton proposals for health care reform in 1993 failed, the pressure on the industry to 'heal thyself' led to further growth of 'managed healthcare', more consolidation, and stronger collective negotiation of pricing, as well as a focus on (cheaper) care outside the hospital.

Smiths' strategy remained largely unchanged in the early 1990s, with a focus away from hi-tech, major capital equipment and instead on single-use and specialized equipment, or complete kits for surgical procedures. The specialist or consultant remained the target customer, as Smiths found the detailed buying requirements of individual medical professionals continued to be met by large central purchasing bodies. The strategy of growth through acquisition continued as well. Japan remained a vitally important market, and in 1991 Smiths succeeded in gaining a 24.5 per cent stake in Japan Medico, its long-term Portex distributor—with Nomura taking 24.5 per cent as well. Unusually, rather than acquiring a company, Smiths purchased outright the technology for thermo-dilution catheters from 3M, allowing external monitoring of blood pressure and heart function.

In mid-1992, Smiths acquired H. G. Wallace for £16m in the UK—'one of the smaller ones, but now one of the gems', as Kennedy describes it—again a firm involved in disposable plastic products, used in infusion and dialysis. It is best known, however, for the Wallace echogenic catheter used by Robert Edwards, the Nobel laureate, in pioneering in vitro fertilization—resulting in the birth of Louise Brown. A larger transaction in the US, also in 1992, saw Smiths acquire Intertech for $110m, a leading provider of emergency resuscitation systems—a transaction that doubled the size of the firm's US medical systems business. The two acquisitions contributed approximately 20 per cent to overall turnover and profit, but a year of consolidation in 1993 yielded a remarkable overall rise of 40 per cent in income, making medical the largest contributor to Smiths' profits at £41.3m, slightly ahead of aerospace, but on a significantly higher margin and much smaller headcount. This was the beginning of a run through until 1998 that would see medical yield significantly higher margins and profits than the other two groups.

It was almost universally the case that Smiths' various medical units identified potential acquisitions and brought them to the attention of management. A significant exception occurred in 1994, with the introduction via Hambros of Pharmacia Deltec, based in St Paul, Minnesota. Deltec, a relatively small and outlying operation of the Swedish Pharmacia AB group, had developed a specialist niche in drug infusion devices— paperback-book sized pumps that are portable or wearable, known as 'ambulatory' pumps. These allowed medicines to be delivered in measured doses, in the home, thus relieving hospitals of a costly and labour-intensive operation—all part of a move in the health care sector (led by the US) to cut costs through developing 'care in the community'. Deltec's management had ambitions for the growth of the business through both increased exports and acquisitions, which Pharmacia was unprepared to fund as Deltec was definitely not a core business, and a sale therefore emerged as a possibility. Smiths purchased Deltec for $150m in mid-1994. The transaction was also the first time that Kennedy worked on an acquisition with Dr Robin Taunt, who took on the M&A role previously filled by Gerry Mortimer. The acquisition of Deltec was Smiths' largest medical acquisition to date, and opened up a new and significant business line in ambulatory pumps. While these were high-value items in their own right, they also brought with them the lucrative 'after-market' of cassettes, which typically contained each day's dose. A pump with a value of $3,000 might require $4,000 in cassettes each year—which were themselves subject to patent protection. Deltec represented a significant enhancement for Smiths, taking it into a new segment of the health care industry, offering both high margins and strong potential for growth.

A very small addition was made the same year with the purchase of the Kylie Kanga continence products business from Roche Products, and in early 1995, Smiths consolidated further its distribution channels with the acquisition of Boehringer Ingelheim Medizintechnik (BIMT), a European distributor of SIMS products in Germany. By contrast with these modest deals, in October, a very significant transaction was the acquisition of Level-1 for $60m, an innovative US company, based in Massachusetts, that manufactured equipment for maintaining the correct temperature of blood and fluids delivered to a patient during surgery, reducing the risk of hypothermia and shortening recovery times.

The first half of the 1990s, as for the industrial group, was characterized by substantial growth through acquisitions. With margins on the increase, the medical group's fortunes advanced, just as the economic cycle produced the opposite effect for the aerospace group, altering the balance and propelling medical into pole position. Reflecting its results, and to enhance further the profile of Portex, the medical group was in a position in 1993 to endow the Portex Chair in Paediatric Anaesthesiology at UCL, with Professor David Hatch the first incumbent.

Spotlight on management: mid-1990s

> 'It would be nice to be in the FT100. But whenever it looks likely, there's another privatisation,' he adds wistfully, 'and we get knocked down the list'.
>
> (Roger Hurn, interview, 1992)

For all sorts of reasons, the management of Smiths started to receive more press coverage in the 1990s. One journalist even attempted a semiotics of neckwear, focusing on the ties sported by the executives—Kennedy's 'swirling multi-coloured tie' suggested a flamboyance at odds with the deeply conservative Hurn, while Williams's 'tasteful floral number places [him] midway between Kennedy and the more conventional Barber, who sports a discreetly patterned red silk'.[31] More seriously, from the late 1980s onwards, attention focused on executive pay, as bonuses and stock options became more widespread, and levels of disclosure increased. With the reductions in staff numbers that occurred across industry as the recession took its toll in the early 1990s, focused in Cheltenham in the case of Smiths, the *Gloucestershire Echo* became a forum in which disgruntled former employees voiced their complaints, for example, with the 1994 headline 'Profiting from Wrecked Lives' above a letter from a recently redundant Cheltenham worker, complaining at 'immoral' pay increases at board level.[32] The *Echo* had something of an axe to grind with Roger Hurn and the location of GCHQ in Cheltenham did not help, given his appointment to chair a committee in early 1995 to investigate the agency's role, organization, and cost structure. The paper ignored the wider elements of the brief, focusing only on the issue of costs, leading to the claim that 'the man responsible for axing 1,556 jobs from Smiths Industries since 1990 has been put in charge of reviewing the future of GCHQ'.[33]

In London, Smith's public relations director succeeded in getting more positive coverage of the CEO—even down to the *Evening Standard* commenting on his retention of the 'old office furniture, with its patina of antique coffee stains' which he inherited from Dick Cave and which had originally been his father's—but the more substantive interest from the press began to centre around issues of succession.[34] Hurn had assumed the role of both chairman and chief executive, succeeding Sir Alex Jarratt as chair, in November 1991—a move presented as long-term preparation for the election of a new chief executive in due course. In the New Year's Honours list for 1996, Hurn was knighted for services to industry, and within months was engaged in the hunt for a new CEO.

The rating of Smiths' management by its peers in industry was revealed by a 1995 survey in *Management Today*, in conjunction with Loughborough University, in which 250 companies across twenty-five industrial sectors participated.[35] Smiths polled remarkably well—of the 'most admired' companies, it came third, behind Cadbury Schweppes and Unilever. It ranked highly in other categories—third in 'financial soundness', third in 'long-term value', first in 'use of corporate assets', and second in 'management quality'. However, there was a challenge ahead, since the careers of much of the management team were coming to an end over the next few years.

The two most senior executives still running business lines were George Kennedy and Norman Barber, but they were no more than two years younger than Hurn, in a firm that was now working on the basis of compulsory retirement at 60. So despite their obvious credentials, and given the lack of anyone else with sufficient seniority and credibility within the firm, Smiths had to look elsewhere for a new CEO. Its timing coincided with that of Keith Butler-Wheelhouse. Born in the UK, but moving to South Africa at 15, KB-W, as he is almost universally known, had spent twenty years with Ford, then moved to General Motors in South Africa, where he led a management buy-out of Delta Motor Corporation before moving to Sweden in 1992 for four years, running Saab Automobile. Looking to return to the UK, he was the obvious choice among candidates short-listed by Smiths, and his appointment was announced in June 1996. The news was greeted with caution by the City, surprised at 'the prospect of an industrialist without a UK record taking charge at one of the UK's most successful engineering companies', and KB-W admits 'it was quite daunting. Roger had recently received his knighthood for services to industry, and I wasn't known to his team.'[36] Joining in August, he took up the post of CEO after the AGM in November.

At the same time, Sir Alex Jarratt retired, relinquishing the role of senior non-executive director. His team of non-executives had seen fairly frequent changes in recent years. Departures in the early 1990s included Neil Shaw and 'Tin' Pearce. New arrivals were David Lyon, CEO of Bowater (who left again in 1994); Keith Orrell-Jones, CEO of Blue Circle; Alan Pink, a director of Zeneca; and Roger Leverton, CEO of Pilkington. In the later 1990s, Peter Hollins, CEO of British Energy came on board, to be followed by Robert O'Leary, the first American board member, bringing additional insight into the US health care systems through his position as president and CEO of PacifiCare Health Systems.

When Williams and Mortimer left mid-decade, another long-standing team member to retire was Martyn Wenzerul, the group financial controller, after thirty-six years. He was heir to the Hornsby tradition of insistence on the highest standards of accountancy and reporting, and had a vital role in revealing the true state of affairs behind any given set of numbers—valuable to Hurn, who commented: 'He had an encyclopaedic knowledge of the company's business and was a very shrewd judge of people. He was probably the most influential behind-the-scenes person of his generation.'[37] Another departing executive, who left a bit earlier, was not one of the old team. It was apparent that Christopher Taylor, the finance director since 1989, had not fitted the Smiths mould. Hurn was to comment of several people who joined over the years, and who turned out not to be a perfect fit, that 'the normal corporate rejection process sets in', likening it to a problematic organ transplant. Taylor was one such, leaving in 1995, to be replaced by Alan Thomson, recruited from the Rugby Group and previously of Courtaulds. Mortimer had enjoyed excellent relations with the City and its analysts, acting as court jester yet in command of his brief. Thomson, another showman, but also gifted with a prodigious memory, was able to rekindle the same confidence and respect from the City audience, although as one long-term observer noted, 'perhaps he just told us what we wanted to hear!'[38]

KB-W naturally spent 1997 becoming acclimatized to the Smiths' culture—and dealing with 'corporate rejection' for the newcomer. Given Smiths' conglomerate nature, and geographic spread, there were many locations to visit and people to meet, but he also underwent a baptism of fire through being immersed in the aerospace business from the beginning, taking responsibility for the group for three months during Barber's convalescence following heart bypass surgery. An interview in *The Times* in late 1996 reported on the results of a three-month review of activities. From early on, KB-W emphasized two themes for his vision of the path forward: greater internationalization and an emphasis on growing sales. Hurn had successfully focused on the familiar business mantra—'sales are vanity, profits sanity, cash is king'—but KB-W also recalls finding a culture dominated by engineers, certainly strongly focused on profits, but without the drive towards growing sales. Smiths were good at maximizing margins, but KB-W wanted greater focus on increasing the total volume of business through more aggressive marketing. Analysts and observers would from now on hear a lot about the drive 'to grow the top-line, without damaging the bottom-line'. It was a message that gradually took hold, *The Times* commenting a year later, under a headline

'Smiths changes focus as group sales top £1bn', the company had 'signalled that it needs to pay more attention to lifting sales if it is to sustain its strong record'.[39] On the international point, KB-W was quoted as saying 'Smiths is seen as an Anglo-American company in terms of sales, but I believe there are large opportunities in other markets.'[40] This was not without attendant tensions. For example, Kennedy recalls arguments over international expansion—his clear preference being to focus on the US, Japan, and the 'Commonwealth' markets (present and former), where brand recognition of medical products would be strongest.[41] Another aspect of KB-W's message to his managers was an emphasis on new product development, on taking more risks—encouraging people to move outside their 'comfort zone', and not to be so frightened of failure that new approaches or ideas remained untried.

There was another facet to the issue of new managers arriving, where the incumbents had decades of collective history. The retiring managers had spent years developing experience not only of the operations of several dozen companies, but also the personal foibles of the people running them. There were subtleties to the internal lines of communication, the budget process, and the analysis of outcomes that had been honed over many years. With external recruitment, rather than the promotion of time-served Smiths recruits, management knowledge was changing. Another factor that had bolstered close working relationships, especially since the move from 317 Edgware Road to Child's Hill in 1981, was the concentration of management in one place, with a strong open-door culture. A metaphor often used by Hurn was that of one castle, with all the barons inside. John Thompson recalls Hurn wanting a building 'that couldn't hold more than 110 people, and the way to make sure was to ensure it didn't have more car parking spaces than that!'[42] The teams running the three groups were tightly closeted with the central corporate staff. Flowerday remembers 'this led naturally to close working between group and corporate teams, and avoided baronial battles'.[43] It was an arrangement that clearly worked well when the natural location for the group management teams was still the UK. This would change over time as the centre of gravity of Smiths' overall business shifted strongly to the US and other international locations.

Hurn would reach forty years with Smiths in 1998, as well as the age of 60. In late 1995 there had already been City speculation he might succeed Lord Weinstock at GEC, but this role went to George Simpson of Lucas, also a co-director of Hurn's at ICI. In turn it was Simpson who later approached Hurn to take over as chairman at GEC, to replace Lord Prior, due to retire in the spring of 1998. Although he was expected to announce his plans in November 1997, at the Smiths AGM, Hurn surprised the City by confirming he would retire at the end of 1998, though confirmation of the GEC role, commencing December 1998, emerged soon after.[44] In turn, this led to the Smiths board appointing Keith Orrell-Jones as chairman elect.[45] Thus the succession issue was brought to a close.

It was at this point that a useful episode for the writing of this history occurred, in that Hurn instructed his PR director to engage two experienced engineering journalists to interview five executives with a collective perspective on Smiths' development since the early 1970s. The interviews could be used to illuminate a readable narrative. He told the writers: 'one day, when a future head of Smiths Industries says, "Let's have a history of the company", at least I will have left a record of this time—the last 25 years'.[46] It has proved to be a valuable decision.

There was one link to the past that was lost during the decade. Although the clocks and motors had disappeared in the 1980s, Ralph Gordon-Smith, now in his mid-eighties, lingered on, still president of the company. For some time after, as Sir Alex Jarratt recalled, he would still attend meetings—'but he would sit there, listening, though he never said a thing'.[47] His last board meeting was on 9 March 1993, and he died three weeks later, aged 87. As *The Times* recorded, he had been associated with the company for sixty-six years, twenty-two as chairman.[48]

Industrial—the rise of the interconnector: 1996–2000

Smiths stated that the aerospace, defence and telecoms markets account for around 75% of [industrial] sales. Inevitably it is the telecoms business that is the most exciting.

(ABN Amro, March 2000)

The new chairman of the industrial group from 1996 was Einar Lindh, who could already boast quite a long Smiths career. Joining in 1973, he had spent some time out from 1979, at Great Universal Stores, but rejoined in 1983 to end up as MD of SIMS Portex from 1990. His was a different style from Ron Williams. 'Ron would order another set of figures, not because he needed them—he knew the answer—but he wanted to nudge you to see if you could get there as well', recalls Donald Broad.[49] Lindh was far more direct and demanding in his management style. His arrival saw no let-up in the pace of growth for the group. There was also further tinkering with the cosmetic presentation of the group to the outside world. Although the notion of an 'interconnect' division had been used and abandoned in the early 1990s, it started to make a comeback, first as a Hypertac division, and then from 1998 onwards Interconnect was fully revived. It was under this grouping that Polyphaser of the US was acquired for £18m, in 1997. The mobile telephony market, while established, offered significant growth potential, both because 3G was on the horizon and there were still countries that had limited cellphone penetration. Polyphaser had a strong presence in the market for the lightning protection equipment used to protect mobile telephony base stations. Smiths' strategy was to avoid any obvious front-end involvement in the industry, but to build a strong position in components necessary for the anticipated infrastructural requirements that would necessarily follow. The purchase reflected a common theme in Smiths' history—the supply of parts in a growing industry avoided some of the risks absorbed by the main constructors and assemblers, and allowed for business with several different (potentially competing) customers in the same sector.

Back in 1996, additions were made to Flex-Tek with the £22m purchase of Adapta-flex, at Coleshill in Warwickshire, another specialist duct maker, and Vent-Axia was enlarged with the addition of Air Movement Group, at Dudley in the West Midlands, for £41m. These purchases were complementary to existing business groupings, but there was a continued willingness to hold other smaller and niche businesses—and by now it appears an explicit part of the strategy that the group could act as a form of incubator—as Lindh described such companies, 'some are the seed-bed for core competencies which may form a base for enlarging', while 'businesses which do not fit the future strategy will be given the opportunity to achieve success independently'.[50] This was the outcome for SIMAC, the spark-plug machinery manufacturer that Thompson and Leader had built up in the 1980s, now sold to a management team led by David Sced in 1996. Timeguard, maker of time switches and security products, was also sold in 1996—a disposal that meant, 145 years after the opening of the first shop on Newington Causeway, any surviving DNA of the Smiths clock and watch business finally died out.

The following year, 1997, the Vent-Axia division, already the major UK supplier of domestic, commercial, and industrial fans, was enlarged further with the £16m purchase of Swindon-based Torin, manufacturer of small-scale DC fans, for applications such as computers, and with an established European reputation. A period of profitable consolidation ensued in 1998 and 1999. The choice was taken eventually to present an even simpler structure to the group, coupling ducting and fans to form a new Air Movement division, alongside Interconnect. Small additions (Quartz Limited and Dan Chambers) were made in Air Movement in 1998, but the more significant acquisitions were in Interconnect towards the end of the year, with Transtector (£23m) and Engineered Transitions Company—Entraco (£3m) which complemented Icore and provided interconnectors on various major aircraft programmes. Transtector manu-factured surge suppressors, and in combination with Polyphaser formed part of the drive into the mobile telephony infrastructure field.

The business benefited from a strong US economy in 1999, with the majority of its interconnector businesses located there. A planned transaction, to acquire Trompeter, a specialist co-axial connector on the West Coast of the US, for as much as $150m, went nowhere, with its owner entrusting it to Citicorp Venture Capital to sell (where it remained for a long time). But Lindh then brought a series of four US-based Inter-connect deals to the board in the winter of 1999, totalling $135m, which all closed in the first months of 2000 (Sabritec in precision interconnectors, LEA in surge suppressors, EMC Technology in passive microwave systems, and Florida RF Labs in specialist military co-axial interconnects). Two small acquisitions were also made in the Air Movement division (Venair in silicone hoses, and Aerosonics in HVAC components), but the broader emphasis was clearly now on the interconnector businesses. Lindh's presentation to the board in early 2000 voiced an expectation they would be 'the main engine for growth over the next 5 to 10 years'.[51]

The financial year-end figures in mid-2000 showed yet again a 10 per cent increase in sales, but higher growth in profits, with margins nearing 18 per cent. Although the new

Interconnect businesses only contributed for a few months, their margins were report-edly above the average for industrial.

By the start of the new decade, Lindh had shifted the focus of the group he inherited from Williams more towards the Interconnect division. It was particularly in this division that he believed two broad avenues for growth presented themselves—the renewed growth in the aerospace industry with a demand for highly specialized components, and anticipated continued strong worldwide growth in communications infrastructure, which at the beginning of 2000 involved forecasts across the industry naturally still reflecting the exuberance of the current boom and a high point of international M&A activity.

Medical—a more competitive environment: 1996–2000

They never let me have as our business slogan, 'We stick our business into other people's noses'. I felt it was a winner.

(Gerry Mortimer, 1998)

The years 1996–7 saw Smiths' medical group treading water somewhat, albeit still producing profits in excess of the other two groups, at around £75m. Margins were still comfortably the highest in the group by far, at 24 per cent or more, but underneath the headline figures, business was becoming harder. Health care spending continued to grow in the main markets, but both competition and budgetary pressures were increasing, and the rise of sterling did not help the UK operation, given its 70 per cent export focus. Smiths needed to combat this with greater efficiency, new products (to cope with copycat ranges from the competition), a potential drive into new markets, and perhaps further acquisitions.

In spring 1997, Robert Fleming floated a potential transaction, to acquire Graseby plc, arguing the medical pump part of its wide-ranging business would complement the drive towards out-patient care seen with Deltec. The key banker on project 'Gravity' was Kennedy's former employee from Portex, Bernard Taylor, who left Smiths in 1985 for Baring Brothers, joining Flemings in 1994.[52] Not particularly wanting to deal with a diversified conglomerate, Smiths naturally just wanted the medical business, but this proved impossible, and in August 1987 it launched a public bid of £136m for the whole firm, closing the deal in October. There were some micro-circuit engineering busi-nesses that could be fitted in to the aerospace group, but a range of other industrial businesses were rapidly put up for sale (except for Graseby Dynamics, dealt with later). Rationalization was quickly implemented for the medical business itself, with a move of Graseby's US production into the Deltec plant at St Paul, but there were significant costs in both 1997 and 1998—indeed the main pump business, which was pole-mounted, was somewhat outdated and lacked features offered by competitors, and a small line in ambulatory pumps (much simpler than the Deltec product) was a disappointment, selling into less sophisticated markets. Quickly on the heels of Graseby came a much smaller deal to acquire pneuPAC Ltd, based in Luton, for £8m—a manufacturer of pneumatically powered, portable resuscitation devices—a transaction not without its eventual headaches, which resulted in proceedings being issued by Smiths, alleging pneuPAC's accounts had not presented a true and fair view.

Despite these reversals, Smiths retained an appetite for significant further acquisitions and late on in 1997 was homing in on a large transaction to acquire Valleylab from Pfizer—an important manufacturer of diathermy (electrosurgical) equipment based in Boulder, Colorado—as a complement to the surgical table business of Eschmann. Kennedy was authorized to bid $405m, and shook hands on a deal in early December, but US Surgical Corporation had $20m more in last-minute firepower, and Smiths came home empty-handed, though within months US Surgical was itself bought by Tyco for $3.3bn.[53] This was symptomatic of the market and may have been on the mind of Alan Smith, company secretary, when he said, soon after, 'It's certainly the case that medical companies in the US are sold for a multiple of earnings that we haven't so far persuaded ourselves is something we can approach as an acquisition price.'[54]

While these transactions were happening, a new and more efficient Portex factory at Keene was completed for $15m, including 33,000 ft² of 'clean room' manufacturing space. With Japan still an important market, the firm had already increased its stake in Japan Medical from 24.5 to 50 per cent, and then boosted this further to 62 per cent, but this was against a backdrop of an unfolding crisis across most Asian markets, starting in Thailand in early 1997 and finally reaching Japan with three major financial institutions failing in November. The resulting problems virtually halted sales to, and within, Japan.[55] Another factor was the strength of sterling, which continued to impact the UK business in its exports to Europe and Japan. Sales growth and profits were therefore held fairly static in 1998, and symptomatic of a need to reduce costs, some of the production capacity of Respiratory Support Products (purchased in 1989) was moved south from California to a nearby maquiladora facility in Mexico. At the turn of 1999, Smiths added to its respiratory products portfolio with the acquisition of Biochem International in Wisconsin, for £42m—a leading manufacturer of hand-held devices for measuring blood oxygen levels.

Despite sales increases, partly through acquisitions, profits for 1996–9 remained in the £73–76m range, with margins declining, reflecting a difficult market backdrop of increased price pressure, particularly in the US, overvalued sterling impacting UK exports, and the effects of the Asian crisis. To achieve efficiency gains, more US volume manufacturing was moved to the maquiladora in Tijuana, from Deltec and Portex Inc. Having taken majority control of Japan Medico from 1997, excess stock levels, a long-standing problem, were progressively dealt with, and the problem finally cleared by 2000, but de-stocking naturally took its toll on profits.

For the balance of 1999 and early 2000, the last months of Kennedy's Smiths career, the environment continued to be challenging, with Portex UK suffering from the strength of sterling. Cheaper priced competition hit Deltec's pump business, and redundancies followed as it scaled back its operations—there was a group-wide focus on cutting costs, and building on the maquiladora success the idea of low-cost manufacturing in Eastern Europe was first mooted.[56] Eschmann, the surgical table manufacturer, was struggling and Smiths eventually put it up for sale in April 2000.[57] As he prepared for retirement, Kennedy's presentations to the board focused on the restructuring of the group, measures to cut back the cost-base and the drive for efficiency. The mid-1990s had been the zenith of the group's operations to date, with record margins, and the later 1990s had been challenging, with organic growth proving difficult to achieve and margins coming off their peaks. Nevertheless, the analyst community viewed the medical group as having some significant strengths.

Aerospace—the question of scale: 1996–2000

> *The defence industry could prove very profitable for its long-term survivors.*
>
> (*Financial Times*[58])

While the trend of falling sales from 1990 was finally reversed with an increase in 1996, the relative position of the group within Smiths still declined, with its contribution to the bottom line falling to third place, reflecting in part the acquisitions in the other two groups that bolstered their figures. The split of business was still weighted more to defence than civil work (60:40), but the plan was to move this to nearer a balance over time.

A significant improvement in margins came in 1997, up from 12 per cent to over 14 per cent, with profits similar to the industrial group at close to £60m. The commercial business was the strongest driver, with Boeing increasing its production of the 737 at a fast rate. By mid-1997, the firm had delivered 120 of the electrical load and fuel quantity management sets for the 777. In the first purchase of any size for several years, Leland Electrosystems of Ohio was acquired for £16m. Leland made electric power generators, which Smiths integrated into a package with its existing power management systems.

In 1998, the aerospace group achieved a remarkable set of results, pulling back to being the major contributor to profits, having been the junior partner in the two previous years. Margins increased again, to 16.6 per cent, a record for the group. This was on the back of a strong recovery in the wider industry, driven by airline profitability and new aircraft demand, though only half the firm's business came from original equipment for new aircraft—the balance coming from the upgrading and retro-fitting of avionics in existing aircraft.

Two trends were becoming clear across the industry and these had far-reaching long-term consequences for Smiths and its plans for growth. With a blurring between civil and defence technologies, there would be less room in future for defence customer-led (and funded) R&D to spill over into later commercial applications—the traditional path. Defence buyers were keener to purchase ready-developed systems, rather than fund long-term development projects, while the sophistication of commercial airliner avionics advanced rapidly. This led to a reorganization of the group around its product types, rather than the long-standing arrangement which divided commercial and defence products, leading inevitably to further redundancies at Cheltenham.[59]

An area of the business growing in importance and visibility was Health & Usage Monitoring (HUMS), a proprietary technology designed to assess the performance of a large number of parameters in an aircraft's operation—initially for helicopters. The system for the Chinook monitored more than 200 such inputs, allowing for regular analysis—leading to a better understanding of wear and service requirements and improved predictive capacity for failure, leading to higher safety and more efficient maintenance. Adopted by the RAF for the Chinook from 1997, the system was expanded to the RAF's other helicopters. The business was enhanced in 1998 with the purchase of Signal Processing Systems in San Diego.

Customers increasingly wanted more integrated systems of avionics, removing the need to assemble the cockpit with parts from separate specialists, challenging Smiths' historic focus on discrete components. Its competitors were assembling ever larger complete cockpit systems, not individual instruments, thus pressuring Smiths to consider what it could do strategically to acquire other businesses, forge joint ventures, or somehow build the capacity to offer more comprehensive avionics. The aerospace business had last doubled in size in 1987 with the purchase of the Lear Siegler businesses. What prospect was there of another game-changing move of this sort? Relationships were close with Sextant Avionique and with Rockwell Collins. Analysts wondered what possibilities there might be for closer ties.

As 1999 unfolded, with the aerospace group experiencing sales at a level not seen for ten years, developments elsewhere in the market offered possibilities.[60] Under George Simpson, GEC was fast implementing its decision to focus on telecommunications, leading to the sale of its non-core businesses, including Marconi Electronic Systems, its defence arm. It was bought by BAe and merged to form BAe Systems. Barber was hopeful of securing elements of the former Marconi operation, including its display business, but Smiths was only one potential buyer and BAe resisted moving quickly. It was only in March 2000 that Smiths finally acquired Marconi Actuation Systems for $99m, a business involved in the electronic control of aircraft systems. This followed on the January 2000 purchase of the aerospace division of Invensys for £111m, comprising five US-based companies focused on electrical power management and utilities. Here the logic was clear—bringing these businesses together, Smiths aimed to simplify the entire power system of an aircraft in a unified package, involving its power supplies, with computer control, reduced cabling, and using specialized actuators which interfaced between the computer and the relevant device requiring control.

Before Simpson had taken over at GEC, he had run Lucas Industries, and had engineered its merger with Varity Corporation in 1996, forming Lucas-Varity, which in turn was sold to TRW of the US in 1999, in a £4bn transaction in which TRW was widely thought to have overpaid. Barber was hopeful that TRW would focus on the automotive business of Lucas-Varity and might dispose of the former Lucas Aerospace (which specialized in flight controls, engine controls, power generation, and cargo handling systems), so an approach was made even while the TRW purchase was being negotiated.[61] But no transaction occurred. TRW was later to sell its aerospace business, in 2002, to try to deal with a mountain of debt it had accumulated, but it would be Smiths' competitor, Goodrich, that would win out. On another front, a line of communication was opened up in early 1999 with Thomson CSF, to explore a potential acquisition of a controlling stake in Sextant Avionique, Smith's partner in the development of a new flight management system for the Airbus range. This had some potential to be the 'mega-deal' that analysts and observers felt Smiths needed, but the relationship remained one of simple collaboration, since the Elysée Palace made very clear it would not countenance Smiths getting involved. A similar outcome emerged when Smiths came close to acquiring Intertechnique, another French aerospace business, where the government intervened to encourage its purchase by Zodiac, better known for its rubber boats. Other transactions were aborted at the last minute for different reasons, and an interesting feature that KB-W found remarkable in Smiths' culture was the lack of any shame in an executive deciding to abandon a transaction after all final board approvals had been issued. One such was the planned acquisition of Whittaker Controls in the US, where due diligence pointed out potential litigation claims relating to environmental issues, and Smiths decided it could not proceed.[62] In May 1999, ABN Amro's analysts pointed out Smiths had indicated back in 1997 the need to double the size of its aerospace business 'to be taken seriously by the likes of Boeing', yet two years later 'Smiths has done little to address the issue of size'.[63] It was operating against a much changed backdrop, by comparison with a decade earlier. The US industry in particular had responded to the early 1990s recession through significant rationalization and a series of mega-mergers (e.g. Northrop/Grumman; Lockheed/Martin Marietta; Boeing/McDonnell Douglas), meaning Smiths' customers were now significantly larger and more powerful, while its competitors (e.g. Honeywell, Rockwell Collins, Sextant) also enjoyed a strong second half to the decade. With the market dominated by these firms, Smiths appeared to have limited options for a transaction that would achieve the desired effect.

Threat Detection—a serendipitous gain: 1997–2000

You'd be mad to think of selling it.

(Paul Lester)

When Flemings brought Graseby to Smiths as a potential acquisition target, and it became clear Smiths could not cherry-pick the medical pump business but would have to mount a bid for the whole firm, it was obvious subsidiaries would be resold, neatly providing Flemings with more transactions and fee income. These fell in two broad parts: the technical division (Graseby Dynamics) which manufactured chemical agent monitors for the defence industry; and the environmental and product monitoring divisions, which achieved margins significantly lower than Smiths' threshold of acceptability. It was understood Flemings would immediately resell both. However, a conversation between David Flowerday of Smiths and Paul Lester, who had recently quit as Graseby's CEO, revealed Lester's clear assessment the threat detection business was by far the best part of the whole concern, with significant and immediate potential. It had spent years developing technology 'that was about to break, with the chance for greatly increased scale. And he was completely right.'[64] At a regular Monday morning meeting of the board, soon after the Graseby purchase, the directors made clear their position that the medical business was the only piece to keep, but Flowerday pressed the case that threat detection had significant potential. The memory of Saddam Hussein's chemical attacks on his own people remained, and UN inspection teams were still operating in Iraq. The threat of chemical warfare remained potent and governments worldwide would have a growing interest in workable technologies to help address it. They were persuaded to keep Graseby Dynamics by this argument. Nevertheless, by early 1998 a separate deal was in place to sell the unwanted environmental controls businesses to Thermo-Electron of Massachusetts, for £44m. For the time being, Graseby Dynamics was slotted, perhaps somewhat uncomfortably, under the control of the aerospace group. The firm had immediate and lucrative business in the pipeline, and even by year-end 1997 Smiths received a substantial pre-payment from the Swiss government for equipment. Through to the end of the decade, the business neverthe-less remained off the radar, little mentioned by the firm or analysts, till early 1999, when Barber brought a potential acquisition to the board—Environmental Technologies Group of Baltimore—a manufacturer of sensors and systems for detecting chemical hazards. The purchase concluded late that year and this in turn led to the decision in early 2000 to form a new division within aerospace—Protection and Detection Systems—headed by John Shepherd.[65]

Financial summary: 1991–2000

> *Roger Hurn called it a 'purple patch'—the data for the decade supports this—earnings and dividends doubled in real terms.*
>
> (David Flowerday, 2013)

The inflationary booms in Smiths' main markets during the late 1980s (UK inflation peaked at 10.9 per cent in late 1990), and the corrective action taken by central banks, raising interest rates, coupled with various external shocks, gave rise to a recessionary period that dominated the early years of the decade. The downturn in the worldwide aerospace industry lasted significantly longer, and Smiths was exposed, having greatly expanded its aerospace operation. With wages running at roughly 50 per cent of cost of sales, headcount was an obvious target for cutbacks, and by 1992, job cuts of 1,100 had reduced headcount in the aerospace group to 7,330. Smiths' overall headcount peaked at 14,000 in 1989, and reached a trough of 11,200 for 1992–3, before acquisitions increased numbers again. Despite the downturn being anticipated, the combination of cutbacks in both civil and military programmes inevitably meant falling sales, which declined from a peak of £455m in 1990 to £374m in 1995, and margins from around 13–14 per cent to 10 per cent in the same period. This trend reversed in the second half of the decade, with various programmes moving into construction and the whole industry pressing ahead strongly, resulting in a 56 per cent increase in sales between 1995 and 2000, and margins climbing to above 18 per cent. By the end of the period, aerospace had clearly re-established itself as Smiths' lead activity.

The medical group's decade showed the opposite curve, since though sales increased year-on-year, the spectacular growth occurred up to 1995, with margins peaking over 24 per cent for two years. Increasing provision of health care and ageing populations were just two broad factors on the demand side. With a growing emphasis on out-patient care, Smiths' move into ambulatory pumps with Deltec contributed solid results, but increasing competition and price pressure exerted by central purchasing organizations put pressure on margins, which declined to closer to 20 per cent by 2000. Previous strong support from Japanese distribution tailed off as problems with overstocking emerged, and overall medical group sales remained fairly flat at around £75m for four years, finishing on £86m in 2000. With organic growth hampered by competition, Smiths had achieved a scale where growth through acquisition was now seriously hampered by the lack of potential targets of an achievable size.

In the industrial group, a 'decade in the sun' saw a diverse group of companies rationalized and focused progressively on its own tripartite structure of different subdivisions by mid-decade. Acquisitions continued, with the result that industrial, which had accounted for 15 per cent of Smiths' turnover and profits in 1990, doubled in numbers of companies, sales, and profits by the end of the decade, contributing £82m in profits, up from £16m in 1991. Margins varied to a degree over the 1990s, dropping below 14 per cent during the recession, and peaking near 19 per cent in 1998, easing to about 18 per cent by 2000.

For Smiths as a whole, sales over the decade increased 118 per cent to £1.46bn, while profits were more spectacular, growing 180 per cent to £276m, reflecting success in driving margins from around 15 per cent early in the decade to close to 18 per cent by 2000. Along the way, the 1996 figures benefited from a one-off dividend of £14m, the result of finally disposing of Smiths' interests in all the housing association assets that had been built up post-war to support the creation of factories in Witney, Basingstoke, and Cheltenham—signalling yet further the passing of an age.

Management challenges: 1997–2000

> There's a certain amount of pressure on them to go out and spend some
> significant amounts of money—that's a risk.
>
> (Salomon Brothers[66])

Towards the end of the decade, external speculation began to focus on Smiths' overall strategy—was it time for Butler-Wheelhouse finally to drop Hurn's three-legged stool and focus on one activity, most likely aerospace? Commenting on the 1998 results, a long-term observer said 'the reservation that we harbour is that the market is probably looking for clear evidence that Smiths has carved out a strategy for long-term growth'.[67] For some, this put both medical and industrial groups in the spotlight as potential sales targets—the *Financial Times* commenting in March 1999: 'Smiths Industries has been long expected to move towards a disposal of its medical and industrial divisions, and to use the money to buy into aerospace.'[68]

With the arrival of KB-W, strategy meetings became more intense. In May 1997, the focus was on the reliance Smiths appeared to have on acquisitions, and the relative lack of organic growth in existing businesses. KB-W returned to this theme in April 1998, stressing the market valuation of Smiths was closely related to expectations for long-term growth. Smiths was losing much of its senior management, who were retiring. There was a challenge to recruit the best possible replacements. There was also the issue that the firm had joined the FTSE 100 in 1996, but was now bouncing along the bottom, and there was concern at what might happen should it fall out. Alan Thomson in particular had worked hard to promote the company with new institutional investors, and he and KB-W had travelled to the US to do the same, since the company's shareholders were almost entirely based in the UK, yet more than half its markets lay in the US. It would take years to alter this mix. When Smiths exited the FTSE 100 in September 1999, KB-W recalls, 'We were all amazed at how the price drifted and how interest in the company just faded away. It's something not to be taken lightly.'[69]

When the board gathered for a strategic review in May 1999 (the first prepared by David Flowerday), KB-W commented on the historic stability that had been brought by the three groups, and that recent acquisitions made the industrial group strong and profitable, but the market seemed to like the medical and aerospace businesses more—come what may, though, the firm needed to take action to ensure growth, probably with a major acquisition. However, 'the transforming "big deal" would necessarily be opportunistic and therefore difficult to plan'.[70] Reflecting the view of Smiths as predominantly an aerospace company, a name regularly identified by analysts as a logical acquisition target was Rockwell Collins, but recent discussions confirmed there were many possibilities for technical cooperation, but nothing more.[71] The approach to Thomson CSF did not progress either.[72] Various ideas for growth through a major acquisition were therefore not working out. In particular there was a feeling the evolution of the aerospace market might reach a pace Smiths presently could not match. Despite a note of concern from the analyst community that Smiths might be tempted to make a bold move it would regret, nevertheless the internal view had crystallized that doing nothing was not an option.

Conclusions

> The aerospace and medical operations of the group are curious bedfellows but have proved a winning combination. Throw in the company's light industry division, which now embraces vacuum cleaner parts and household extractor fans, and it is clear that most of human life is here.
>
> (*The Times*[73])

Smiths handled the downturn of the early 1990s remarkably well, rebalancing activities to produce excellent overall results. In the second half of the decade, it again produced very good results, but then its competitors and peers had done likewise, so the outcome was less remarkable. Aerospace continued to be the strong focus, and by 2000 the firm appeared to be back in a familiar position, feeling the need to address the issue of 'scale'.

With earnings and dividends doubling in real terms over the decade, the headline figures were clearly strong. Within them, Smiths' organic growth was acceptable, taken across the three groups, but unspectacular. What was spectacular were the returns from the acquisitions made in the decade—reflecting a remarkably effective acquisition machine, which often pursued the purchase of smaller companies, from specialists and entrepreneurs, for which there was limited bid competition. Smiths avoided paying premium prices, but believed, often correctly, that with its management a business could perform better. The standard presentation of acquisitions, or mergers, involves attempting to persuade the market the whole is greater than the sum of the parts— there are savings to be made in stripping out duplicated management or administrative costs; benefits will accrue from greater scale and so forth, summed up in the catch-all 'synergy'. Perhaps recalling his time at Harvard Business School, where Cave had sent him years before, Hurn had a view on synergy: 'It's the name given to the set of things which—if they were real—would cause a business to be worth what you paid for it, as opposed to what it is worth.' This in part reflected a jaundiced view of advisers, whose fees related to concluded transactions and who might press synergistic arguments. In the case of a business worth x, but available only for (higher) price y, there is a temptation to hypothesize a set of things (potential cost-savings, higher efficiencies, etc.) that will over time cause the value of the business to increase from x to y. In Smiths' case, there were rarely synergies to be pursued—its experience of transactions pursued on grounds of potential synergy was not wholly positive. Indeed the strength of its acquisition policy lay in maintaining discrete companies with their own systems, their own culture, their own vision, and their own highly driven management. This successful strategy therefore lay at odds with the approach analysts and commentators generally believed Smiths should pursue, which was to target larger, highly recognizable companies, where premium prices would be involved, and synergies were argued to be part of the game.

However, one of the realizations that dawned, perhaps best exemplified by the industrial group where a second tier of management was introduced in 1995 to help administer a much enlarged portfolio, was that the current model was not infinitely scalable. By the end of the 1990s, Smiths had taken the model of growth through non-synergistic acquisition to its natural conclusion. Something else would need to come next.

Notes

1. 16 Oct. 1997, 67.
2. ABN Amro, 'Smiths Industries' (20 Mar. 2000).
3. Based on RPM data for US airlines (1960–90), Bureau of Transportation Statistics.

4. Helen Kay, 'Smiths Forge Ahead', *Management Today* (Jan. 1992), 33.
5. *Flight* (10 Jan. 1996), 12.
6. *Financial Times* (9 Jan. 1996), 15.
7. *Financial Times* (1 June 1991), 8.
8. David Flowerday, interview (5 Sept. 2013).
9. *Minutes* (9 Apr. 1991).
10. *Financial Times* (24 Apr. 1992), 18.
11. Terry Smith, *Accounting for Growth* (London: Century, 1992), p. 29–34.
12. *Financial Times* (11 June 1992), 23.
13. *Financial Times* (11 Dec. 1997), 22.
14. Hurn, interview (1998).
15. *Minutes* (11 Feb. 1992).
16. *Financial Times* (30 Oct. 1992), 13.
17. UBS, 'Smiths Industries' (1 June 1995), 19.
18. *Foreign Affairs* (1 Mar. 1992), 25.
19. *Minutes* (12 Apr. 1991).
20. *Minutes* (9 Apr. 1991).
21. David Smith, 'Defence Contractors and Diversification in to the Civil Sector: Rolls Royce 1945–2005', *Business History*, 49/5 (2007), 637–62.
22. Interview (22 July 2013).
23. Williams, interview (1998).
24. Hurn, interview (1998).
25. Mortimer, interview (1998).
26. *Minutes* (14 July 1992).
27. Williams, interview (1998).
28. UBS, 'Smiths Industries' (1 June 1995), 28.
29. Robin Taunt, telephone interview (22 Nov. 2013).
30. 25 Oct. 1995, 30.
31. Kay, 'Smiths Forge Ahead', 33.
32. *Gloucestershire Echo* (11 Nov. 1994), 8.
33. *Gloucestershire Echo* (27 Mar. 1995), 1.
34. *Evening Standard* (20 Oct. 1995), 35.
35. *Management Today* (Dec. 1995), p. 41–4.
36. *Financial Times* (11 June 1996), 21; KB-W, interview (20 M. 2013).
37. Hurn, interview (1998).
38. Sandy Morris, interview (21 May 2012).
39. *The Times* (16 Oct. 1997), 27.
40. *Financial Times* (19 Nov. 1996), 24.
41. Kennedy, interview (2013).
42. Thompson, interview (1998).
43. Flowerday, interview (2013).
44. *Financial Times* (28 Jan. 1998), 15.
45. *Minutes* (17 Mar. 1998).
46. Hurn, interview (1998).
47. Sir Alex Jarratt, interview (27 Aug. 2013).
48. *The Times* (17 Apr. 1993).
49. Donald Broad, interview (24 Sept. 2013).

50. Annual report (1996).
51. *Minutes* (8 Feb. 2000).
52. Taylor had been Graseby's adviser at Barings.
53. *Minutes* (25 Nov. 1997, 10 Feb. 1998).
54. Alan Smith, interview (1998).
55. *Minutes* (14 July 1998).
56. *Minutes* (27 Apr. 1999).
57. *Minutes* (11 Apr. 2000).
58. 9 Jan. 1996, 15.
59. *Minutes* (8 Sept. 1998).
60. *Minutes* (9 Feb. 1999).
61. *Minutes* (16 Mar. 1999).
62. Meggitt plc, *Annual Report* (2000).
63. ABN Amro 'Smiths Industries' (27 May 1999).
64. Flowerday, interview (2013).
65. *Minutes* (14 Mar. 2000).
66. Quoted in *The Times* (24 Nov. 1997), 47.
67. ABN Amro, 'Smiths Industries' (19 Oct. 1998).
68. *Financial Times* (13 Mar. 1999), 2.
69. KB-W, interview (20 Mar. 2013).
70. *Minutes* (18 May 1999).
71. *Minutes* (9 Feb. 1999).
72. *Minutes* (27 Apr. 1999).
73. 26 Oct. 1995, 28.

CHAPTER 10

....

2000–2007

Shocking the Markets Again

....

Managements looking for new growth have two routes: strategic planning (thinking through the options and choosing one or more with reasonable chances of success), or opportunistic investments (reacting to events or external proposals when they appear sufficiently promising).

(*Financial Times*[1])

UNLIKE other chapters, which describe somewhat larger blocks of years, this covers just seven, bounded by Smiths' two largest ever transactions, each of which came as an immense surprise to the market, and each of which wholly transformed the company. It also brings to an end the coverage of Keith Butler-Wheelhouse's eleven years as CEO, and therefore arrives at a natural break in the Smiths story. Although a change in strategy had been needed, the market was nevertheless shocked to discover in September 2000 that this involved a £4.3bn merger with TI Group, a company whose shares had recently fallen out of favour. Over the next seven years, significant effort went into reshaping the resulting new company—reducing the substantial debt that arrived with the merger, making new acquisitions and disposing of non-core activities. The proceeds from the sale of businesses totalled over £4.5bn, with £1.4bn reinvested in new acquisitions. Events followed a different path from that expected by observers—the part of the business that was centre-stage at the beginning of the decade was not the one chosen for further investment. Instead businesses initially considered peripheral came to occupy this position via a mix of internal growth and acquisition. In the process, Smiths had to rebuild a reputation in the City for sound management and stewardship of a diverse group of businesses.

This was achieved against an unpromising backdrop. With the FTSE peaking at 6,930 on 30 December 1999, the next decade opened with wobbles in hi-tech stocks, followed by internet companies beginning to fail. Only a few months before the Smiths/TI deal was being conceived, Lastminute.com had floated, losing 80 per cent of its value over the coming months. Many others, particularly in Silicon Valley, entered their death throes—from dot.com to dot.bomb. In 2001, as the rot spread to computer hardware companies, so negative sentiment spilled over into a crash in telecom stocks.

The terrorist attacks in September 2001 had a profound further influence on markets, as did the failure of Enron in December, leading to criminal proceedings against Arthur Andersen, its accountants—but Enron was just one of many accounting scandals. The markets were rocked time and time again by announcements—Cable & Wireless, for example, saw its value halve over a few months in 2002, announcing record losses of £4.7bn, and suffering the indignity of shareholders shouting abuse at the board during the July AGM. From above 5,000 in early 2002, the FTSE tested 4,000 in the autumn, but held up for a while before collapsing to 3,500 in early 2003, reaching a low with the onset of the invasion of Iraq. From then on, markets began a long and slow recovery to the highs of 2007 (with a notable correction in mid-2006). The 1980s and 1990s had seen the supremacy of 'shareholder value' as the key desideratum, but had ended with an M&A boom that had destroyed rather than created significant value. In the wake of the collapse of the dot.com boom, there was a challenge—to find the correct path forward to achieve sustainable growth. By late 2006, having outperformed the FTSE100 by about 20 per cent since the merger, Smiths realized that its shareholders were best served by another ground-breaking transaction, in which once again its best known business would be sold. But unlike in 1983, this was not a loss-making concern—quite the reverse, and a significant gain was crystallized and passed back to its shareholders.

The path to TI

> Smiths had no US listing, so they couldn't issue paper in the US to pay for things in the way Tyco could. If they were to do a big deal, it had to be closer to home. Looking around carefully, TI was the obvious candidate.
>
> (Bernard Taylor[2])

Thinking had gradually moved on from the May 1999 strategy meeting, and a transition in management was well under way as Norman Barber and George Kennedy sat with their replacements, John Ferrie and Lawrence Kinet, at the April and May 2000 board meetings. An important meeting was the May strategy day at the RAC Club at Woodcote Park where the team reviewed a valuation of the component parts of the group, prepared by UBS Warburg.

Smiths had exited the FTSE 100 in June 1999, having been a premium stock for much of the 1990s, but now beginning to fall behind in price/earnings comparisons. The outlook for the aerospace industry was not good, in both the civil and defence spheres. Various paths forward, adopted by other firms, were reviewed. For example there was the transformation approach adopted by GEC, dismantling the Weinstock-era conglomerate to focus on telecoms; or the aggressive route of acquisition followed by major surgery, epitomized by Tyco. Flowerday, the strategist, outlined another path as 'bulking out', which he dubbed 'the TI Group approach', which might achieve corporate size, but risked failure in achieving operational gains. Another factor was the continued market dislike of conglomerates.

The conclusion was that the firm had to steer a path among these strategies. Of the three main businesses, aerospace had easily the most to gain from increasing scale. The medical division needed to continue reducing its manufacturing costs and adopt a more global approach, targeting e-commerce. The industrial division was doing well, with its highest margin businesses growing at the fastest rate. Overall, with organic growth proving difficult to achieve, acquisitions would need to continue.

Behind the scenes, a transaction had slowly been bubbling up. Various aerospace-led transactions had been considered, but nothing ever proved possible. Bernard Taylor at Robert Fleming (owned by Chase Manhattan, soon to acquire JP Morgan) had continued to discuss potential transactions with KB-W since the Graseby acquisition, and understood the need to achieve greater scale. His suggestion of a deal with TI Group just before Roger Hurn left Smiths had not been taken up—after all, Hurn had overseen an exit from motor accessories, and was not about to return—but now it was time to look again.[3]

Who was TI?

I remember it was at Rocky Lane, the Tubes Ltd office, and Arthur Chamberlain was chairman. It was a long meeting but before the meeting ended agreement was reached on what was considered a fair settlement of the claims of the merging companies. And that was the start of TI.

('The Story of TI')

The roots of TI Group lay in mid-nineteenth-century Birmingham, in various tube-making businesses which later merged to form Tubes Limited during the bicycle boom of the 1890s. At the turn of the twentieth century, their products were mainly used in shipbuilding, bicycles, and electrical conduit, and other market players included Accles & Pollock, Simplex, and Credenda. All these firms were heavily engaged in the Great War (e.g. in gun mounts and airframes), but before the end of hostilities were already discussing amalgamation, fearful of a deeply competitive post-war environment. In July 1919 they merged to form Tube Investments, creating an integrated manufacturing business with Simplex and Credenda offering distribution. Arthur Chamberlain (uncle of Austen and Neville) was the first chairman.

In the difficult post-war period, Tube Investments struggled, like Smiths, but it successfully amalgamated and rationalized businesses, absorbing smaller manufacturers. Just before the Second World War, it purchased a controlling interest in Crane Packing, the UK operation of Chicago's John Crane. The latter part of the 1930s saw the firm inextricably drawn into military production, followed by a good war, in which its products ranged from Sten gun barrels, to torpedo hulls, through boiler tubes to hypodermic needles. Post-war, under the leadership of Ivan Stedeford, an acquisitions programme added bicycle manufacturers, machine tool makers, and rolling mills—much of the resulting mix falling into the broad 'metal-bashing' category. The strategy was part defensive—buying Raleigh to counter over-capacity in the cycle market, and moving into aluminium as it posed a threat to steel. A stand-out moment came with the 'aluminium war' of 1958, when Siegmund Warburg advised a consortium of Tube Investments and Reynolds from the US in the purchase of British Aluminium, regarded as the first high-profile hostile takeover in the London market and a driver in the formulation of the City Takeover Code.[4]

Lord Plowden, a distinguished civil servant and former MAP colleague of Allan Gordon-Smith, succeeded Stedeford as chairman in 1963, inheriting one of the largest general engineering companies in Britain, alongside GKN and Vickers, at a time of falling earnings and returns, prompted by intensifying foreign competition and excess steel manufacturing capacity. Into the 1970s, further expansion through acquisition produced strong results against a positive economic backdrop, before the bubble was pricked in 1973 and the FTSE turned south, taking Tube Investments with it. From a price near £5 in mid-1973, the shares fell to £1.80 over the next year, still heading south. In 1978, with Brian Kellett in charge and fortunes briefly revived, TI acquired Reynolds' stake in British Aluminium, headed by Ronnie Utiger, in a year that saw profits peak at £80m.

With the early 1980s recession, sterling strength, a steel strike, and falling aluminium demand, the figures collapsed to an overall loss in 1981 when the shares fell below par. In 1982, the *Financial Times'* LEX column commented 'buying TI on the anticipation of an upturn has been a most efficient way of losing money', while an internal corporate history from the 1990s comments wryly that, actually, it had been that way since the 1950s, allowing for inflation.

Utiger became MD of Tube Investments in 1982. With a symbolic change of name to TI Group, he took corrective action, selling traditional businesses and the stake in British Aluminium, held since 1958—possibly at an overall loss on inflation-adjusted terms—but despite disposals, problems multiplied, with losses in machine tools, cycles, and gas cylinders. Utiger replaced Kellett as chairman in 1984, but his determination to stop the rot was immediately checked by a substantial loss at Raleigh, blamed on computer failure, undoing much positive public relations work. However, the shares roared ahead in mid-1985 on the strength of a 20 per cent stake taken by Evered, a small and audacious Birmingham-based engineering company. Over the next ten months, TI's shares moved from £2.30 to over £5, at which point Evered cashed out.

Utiger meantime closed more businesses. Recognizing the group needed further revitalizing, his solution was the recruitment of Christopher Lewinton from Allegheny in July 1986. He joined as CEO and deputy chairman, immediately commencing a complete reorganization. The bloated Birmingham head office (echoed in other businesses, such as Dunlop or Lucas) was closed by late 1986, ultimately replaced by a small office in Mayfair's Curzon Street in London. The new strategy was 'to become an international group concentrating on specialized engineering businesses, operating in selected niches on a global basis', which could equally have described Smiths. By the end of 1988, a major UK disposal programme was largely complete, with most of the well-known names in TI's pantheon of traditional businesses sold—including Raleigh,

Creda, Russell Hobbs, Tower Housewares, New World, Parkray and Glow-worm, TI Machine Tools, Cold Drawn Tubes, and Seamless Tubes.

The proceeds were recycled in a major acquisition programme, including Armco (automotive brakes and fuel lines), Houdaille (which owned the 49 per cent of John Crane in the UK that TI did not already own), and Bundy (automotive and refrigeration tubing). Houdaille was acquired from KKR, establishing a personal link between Lewinton and Henry Kravis (whom he admired greatly, following an introduction by Eric Gleacher of Morgan Stanley), and after the John Crane element was extracted, the husk was resold to KKR, not without comment. In these acquisitions, Lewinton cemented relationships with the Warburg and Morgan Stanley bankers that would support him through to the end of his TI career.

In less than a year, Lewinton had disposed of long-term TI core holdings, promoted John Crane to become one of the principal lines, and added Bundy. These two strands to the business would contribute 80 per cent of TI sales by 1996. Echoing Smiths' tripartite structure, Lewinton tried adding a third leg with Thermal Scientific in 1988, but this was short-lived and resold later. A third business was established in specialist aerospace engine components, but this was then substantially expanded with the acquisition of Dowty in a 1992 hostile takeover, propelling TI into the FTSE 100. Its undercarriage business was then transferred to a joint venture with Snecma, forming Messier Dowty.

In 1996, expanding the polymer engineering business in the John Crane division with the purchase of Forsheda, Lewinton also sold Accles & Pollock, completing the disposal of businesses owned at the time he took over. The following year saw TI sell its underperforming stake in Messier Dowty, unable to buy out its French partner. When Brian Walsh—a forceful and demanding finance director—finally retired in 1997, Lewinton surprised commentators by recruiting a City high-flier—Martin Angle, formerly of Warburg and Kleinwort Benson. The polymer engineering business had now become a fourth unique business line—renamed Forsheda, while succession planning saw Bill Laule move from running Bundy to group CEO from 1998 onwards, cementing his arrival with the purchase of the aircraft engineering firm EIS, which boosted Dowty (through the Hamble aerostructure business) and John Crane with a wider range of seal products.

Several major transactions occurred in 1999—the purchase from GE of Tri-Manufacturing (jet engine components); the acquisition of Walbro (and later the balance of Marwal not already purchased) which expanded the automotive business significantly; and the purchase of Busak + Shamban, which substantially increased Forsheda's capacity in polymer products. Leveraging the link established through the earlier Houdaille transaction, Lewinton secured a cash injection of £94m in March 1999 from KKR for a 4.9 per cent stake in TI—but significantly more important in terms of validation, Henry Kravis joined the board.

Lewinton would be 68 in January 2000, relatively old to be running a plc, and he needed to make a significant move. But TI Group's momentum had been lost. ABN Amro had commented in 1998: 'It would seem there has been a loss of faith in TI

Group'.[5] The results for 1999 showed a small margin improvement at the specialty polymer business, but John Crane, Dowty, and the automotive businesses (representing near 90 per cent of profits) all showed declining margins.

The options for a major transaction—whether major acquisition, merger, or ordered break-up (an MBO was even briefly considered)—were limited.[6] Over the course of the 1990s, TI's credibility had slowly slipped, and its US-dominated share register revealed UK institutions had abandoned it. It was therefore not a premium stock that could pay up, with its own paper, to make major acquisitions work. In 1998–9, several attempts were made to tie up with BF Goodrich in the US, but despite significant efforts, no workable structure could be found. Another idea, in late 1999, was a merger with BBA Group, run by Roberto Quarta, and Lewinton advanced talks quite far, but these were two diversified conglomerates, with no overlap, and the board finally chose to abandon the initiative—a decision welcomed by the firm's advisers at Warburg's.

Considering possible sale options, the obvious candidate was the remaining Dowty business. Even without Messier Dowty, TI's aerospace business was still regarded as a strength. Robin Budenberg, then one of its bankers, explained, 'there were a number of business lines, each with its own problems, but aerospace was the best. We could sell it, but then what on earth would we do with the rump?'[7] A strategy not to sell Dowty, but the automotive business instead, would make TI altogether a more attractive proposition in any proposed further corporate activity.

Probably around the time the BBA/TI merger talks failed, and a couple of years since the idea had last been floated, Bernard Taylor urged KB-W to consider whether buying TI might meet Smiths' goals. Smiths wanted scale in aerospace and knew Dowty well, both from previous failed acquisitions and the fact that they were simple neighbours in Cheltenham. TI's value had dropped substantially in recent years—perhaps Smiths might now acquire Dowty, but at a discount, by virtue of the TI wrapper in which it was held. Budenberg's analysis tallies: 'TI was coming to the end of its natural life. It was generally unlikely that someone would bid for a conglomerate with three or more business lines. With two, it could make sense if one of those could be sold, but three was a challenge.' If Smiths could buy TI, Taylor reasoned, but dispose of unwanted parts, this might prove a neat move. A first discussion between Lewinton and KB-W led nowhere, but in the summer of 2000 a catalyst for further talks was the decision by TI to auction its automotive division, through UBS Warburg. Initial soundings suggested TI could secure £1.2bn, probably from a financial buyer, the most likely being Blackstone, Doughty Hanson, Bain Capital, CVC, or Cinven, while Visteon was the single target trade buyer. News of this reached both Flemings and Smiths, and Taylor arranged a private dinner for KB-W and Lewinton at the Connaught, followed up with a further dinner at Mark's Club, including a small circle of advisers. The notion of a Smiths/TI merger began to form, but there were obstacles. The automotive businesses would have to be sold, but even the broad terms of a deal would not be easy to agree. Lewinton had a reputation as a tough negotiator—some analysts referred to him as 'the great white shark'—and KB-W recalls 'unsurprisingly, he had an unrealistic idea of the value of what he owned'.[8] Nevertheless, project 'Toronto' was born. In late August,

KB-W revealed the plan to his executive team, where it did not meet with instant approval.

Curzon Street joins Finchley Road

Cap'n Butler-Wheelhouse unsettles the crew.

(*Daily Telegraph*[9])

As France and the UK entered a fuel crisis in early September 2000, with widespread protests, particularly by lorry drivers, at the rising cost of diesel and petrol, negotiations between Smiths and TI continued behind closed doors, and reached the point it was time to introduce the senior management teams to each other (without the non-executive directors). They met at the Intercontinental Hotel at Hyde Park Corner on Wednesday 13 September. Secrecy was still being maintained—Lewinton in particular was desperate not to be spotted in company with KB-W. On a rainy day, as '200 truckers park up along Park Lane, bringing parts of central London to a standstill' according to the BBC, the parties entered the hotel by a discreet side entrance in Hamilton Place. David Flowerday recalls arriving to find two groups of chauffeurs loitering—one group were recognizably from Smiths, the others all sported TI golf umbrellas. 'So much for confidentiality', he thought. It was a tense meeting—UBS Warburg had just dropped the bombshell it would be advising its other client, TI, so KB-W and his team found themselves facing their usual corporate brokers across the table.

The Smiths executive directors met the next day to consider formally the proposed merger. The principal rationale was not the opportunity for growth—TI's businesses 'were acknowledged to be mature'—but instead the deal 'would significantly increase its financial firepower and enable it to make further acquisitions of a size which it could not now contemplate'.[10] In effect, this deal would be a stepping stone to even larger business. So far, Bill Laule (TI's CEO) and David Lillycrop (TI's chief counsel), who led the negotiations from the TI side, had tried for a deal structure that valued the two companies near to 50:50, but it was clear this significantly undervalued Smiths, and its board would only support a transaction at nearer a 60:40 ratio, in Smiths' favour. Lewinton's benefits package also attracted significant comment, the view emerging that various arrangements which would vest on a change of control of TI might be problematic. There was also the issue of asbestos-related litigation at John Crane, and the need for Smiths to sign off that it had conducted any necessary preliminary due diligence. At this stage, David Flowerday was worried that the deal pricing was wrong and urged KB-W to tread warily. Recognizing that there were significant risks as TI's businesses were rated significantly lower by the market than Smiths, and that more should be done to ensure the sale of TI's automotive business, it was nevertheless agreed discussions should continue and that the board would meet again, if necessary, on the coming Sunday.

Smiths' immediate reaction to losing its corporate broker was to contact Cazenove's to secure its services, and a conference was hastily arranged for the Friday afternoon with David Mayhew, chairman at Cazenove's—indeed such was the haste, KB-W recalls Mayhew's chief concern was to ensure Smiths genuinely understood the scale of fees to which it was committing. Mayhew's reputation lay partly in a legendary ability to forecast market sentiment for transactions, and his opinion was sought, but such appeals rarely resolve a dilemma. Having heard arguments for and against, he opined the market would not find the merits of the proposed merger compelling at first—the negatives would probably be given more weight than the positives, and the share price would come off—which in turn meant, should Smiths choose to proceed, it would need to work very hard to build a convincing case and to communicate it well. This advice, perhaps opaque viewed with the benefit of more than a decade's distance, was taken to mean the transaction could indeed be sold to the market, and a determined effort was the key.

The whole board duly met on Sunday, with Cazenove's, PwC, and JP Morgan/Chase present. Smiths had by now negotiated the ratio to be used in issuing new Smiths shares to TI shareholders on the basis of a relative Smiths/TI valuation of 57.6:42.4. It was understood that expressions of interest were lodged for the automotive business, and that Smiths would retain £900m of the proceeds, with the next £300m returned to TI shareholders under a complicated contingent structure. Cazenove's reported it had approached three of Smiths' main shareholders, which had apparently reacted positively to the transaction, though with reservations about the proposed board structure, and one shareholder had been concerned over the potential emergence of a competing bid—should TI, for example, be acquired by another firm, this would leave Smiths significantly damaged.

PwC reported on its limited due diligence, concluding 'there were no "black holes" in the Toronto accounts although their results were less conservative' (than Smiths'). The subject of asbestos-related claims against John Crane, Inc. was explicitly covered. Both Alan Thomson and Einar Lindh voiced strong reservations about the transaction, prompting a wry comment from Peter Hollins that he had never before encountered an acquisition where the non-executives needed to persuade the executives to move ahead. Nevertheless, when the meeting broke up, the board had resolved to press ahead the following morning.

People were an issue—there was bound to be some potential duplication and both KB-W and Lewinton had clear ideas on which executives should survive. A last-minute change engineered by Alan Thomson and KB-W that Sunday night was the retention of John Langston from TI, whom they realized would be best qualified to manage both the John Crane and polymer engineering businesses. With Thomson remaining as finance director, Martin Angle was slated for a role as strategic director, while Lillycrop would also join the board, nominally taking the additional role of company secretary vacated by Alan Smith who was retiring. John Ferrie would run the amalgamated aerospace business. Bill Laule would continue to run the TI automotive business, now being sold, taking Allan Welsh of the TI board with him.

At the heart of the City, 12 Tokenhouse Yard had since 1937 been a principal shrine of haute-banque finance—Cazenove's office—from which thousands of transactions had been masterminded. It was there at 6.30 a.m. on the Monday morning that KB-W, Alan Thomson, and Alan Smith met to review the documentation and a press release, issued shortly afterwards. It was exactly a year since Smiths had dropped out of the FTSE 100—now they would roar back in.

The stock exchange announcement of 18 September fired the starting gun towards closure several months later, but it was not to be an easy ride. Visits to institutional investors in both firms by their respective advisers apparently produced little negative sentiment towards the transaction, but several analysts were very negative and Smiths' share price came off markedly—12 per cent within the day, and briefly down 24 per cent a month later. There was a momentary up-tick in TI's price, but it too fell within a couple of days, eventually losing 11 per cent by late October. From these lows, both shares then gradually regained ground, against a backdrop of the FTSE oscillating in a roughly 3 per cent range between 6,200 and 6,400 towards December. It should be borne in mind that the shares of both firms were very largely locked up with institutions and that the free float would have been relatively small. It did not take much selling pressure to cause the falls to occur. It is also possible that both firm's previous share prices included some speculative element.

When the board gathered a week later, Cazenove's reported on the deal reception: 'the markdown in the Company's share price had been more severe than anticipated, though it should be seen against the general fall in prices between 18 and 21 September'.[11] Fortunately, there were so far no indications of a competing bidder—'feedback from institutions had, with one or two exceptions, been reasonably positive'. With regards the response from TI shareholders, it 'had been one of disappointment rather than hostility'. As one analyst put it, 'the proposed merger offers TI shareholders an inelegant and somewhat complex exit route from their investment'.[12]

In mid-October, Mayhew of Cazenove's turned up in person to discuss the unfavourable reaction to the deal, which was definitely harsher than expected, with concerns over the sale of automotive business the major factor. Another early factor was strongly negative sentiment towards the multi-million pay-out Lewinton was entitled to receive, resulting from the crystallization of various benefits. Having spoken at length with both KB-W and Mayhew, and unhappy at the prospect of serving as non-executive chairman of the merged firm but at the same time attracting significant adverse comment, Lewinton decided in mid-October both to negotiate a reduced compensation amount and also to retire altogether from the board, ahead of the closure of the deal, leaving Keith Orrell-Jones as chairman, with KB-W as CEO.

It became apparent that, on the announcement of the deal, the various bidders in UBS Warburg's auction of TI's automotive business had backtracked. The press reported TI had narrowed the range of possible buyers to Blackstone, Doughty Hanson, and Bain Capital.[13] For any potential purchaser, their reading of the situation will have been that both Smiths and TI had an urgent need to dispose of the business, and this played into their hands, suggesting a cheaper price could be achieved. A potential transaction for £1.2bn rapidly disappeared, with the receipt of three definitive bids of £750m, which were rejected. Having exited the automotive business in the early 1980s, it was uncomfortable for Smiths to be back in part of it, and the market did not like it. The interim solution was that the division would be held for sale, and that TI shareholders would receive any excess above £900m received for it in due course (after various defined adjustments).

Integration of the businesses was clearly a priority. The market had been promised £25m in immediate cost-savings and these were targeted with the move of several corporate offices into Smiths' north London offices. At Cheltenham, where Smiths and Dowty had been neighbours for decades, there were obvious savings to be made. An integration committee was appointed, with three representatives from each side, and October and November were spent working out how to eliminate duplication. Candidates from both companies were interviewed for retained positions on a meritocratic basis. It was an expensive process, with the rationalization of corporate offices alone costing £40m owing to higher than expected long-term incentive and redundancy pay-outs.[14]

By mid-November, the proxies already received were overwhelmingly in favour of merger, but the large shareholders had not yet voted. As regards the analysts, Sandy Morris at ABN Amro had voiced his disapproval early—heading his report 'TIorpedoed'—but more positive views existed, for example, at Credit Suisse which rated Smiths a buy, with a target price of £10. However, one concern that had emerged in analytical coverage was over the use to which additional 'firepower' arising from the merger might be put.[15]

A decision was taken to change the name of the firm—both to mark the emergence of the new entity but also to emphasize the move towards hi-tech and away from metal-bashing, so that 'Industries' was dropped, and 'Smiths Group' adopted. When the deal closed on 4 December, just two of the TI executive directors elected to join: John Langston (placed in charge of all sealing solutions businesses) and David Lillycrop. Martin Angle, the finance director, decided against taking up a seat in charge of strategy. On Smiths' board, Alan Pink had died in September, while Peter Hollins and Roger Leverton, who had been crucial to the decision to agree the merger, needed to resign to make way for three TI non-executives—Sir Nigel Broomfield, Sir Colin Chandler, and John Hignett.

The first evaluation: May 2001

> *Those first few months were awful. We had the automotive business we hadn't wanted to take, and we had debt we wanted to pay down. It was a very uncomfortable time.*
>
> (Keith Butler-Wheelhouse, 2013)

By February 2001, it was clear no new offers would emerge for automotive, and Bernard Taylor was already working on an idea. He presented his plan in March—to demerge TI Automotive, backed by new debt financing (syndicated by JP Morgan), allowing the payment of £615m in cash to Smiths, added to which it would receive preference shares with a nominal value of £325m, and 19.9 per cent of the ordinary equity of the demerged firm (and thus not consolidate it).[16] This notionally provided for 15 per cent dividends on the preference shares (subject to various deferrals and performance hurdles), and the possibility for further proceeds should the company be acquired in the future. Laule would continue to manage the demerged firm, and Taylor would have a seat on the board, representing Smiths.

Morgan's managed to complete the debt-raising exercise by mid-year, allowing the demerger to occur prior to the financial year-end. The net result however fell a long way short of the notional value originally placed on the business, pre-merger. With a significant write off in goodwill, the demerger created a £300m pre-tax loss on disposal—just one of several large exceptional items in the year-end figures. At this stage, however, Smiths still held at par £325m of TI Automotive's preference shares, representing 37 per cent of capital employed, so the story was far from over.

When the board met for a strategic review in May 2001, the Smiths world had changed radically from a year earlier. The firm was essentially twice as big, having to a degree achieved the greater scale in aerospace it had sought, but at some cost—the assumption of several businesses that did not form part of the core strategy, higher debt levels, and an increased scepticism on the part of the market. Synergies were being achieved but slowly, and external market forces had hit several TI businesses hard, as well as Smiths' original telecoms-related industrial companies.

A range of strategic options presented themselves. The City view, articulated by Cazenove's, included the observation that the declining contribution of medical over five years contributed negatively towards sentiment, which in turn bolstered interest to achieve a major acquisition for the medical division. Further large acquisitions for the aerospace division might well also be needed, because the issue of scale, whilst partly met, had not disappeared. But KB-W's initial goals were to consolidate and improve the present position: management resources should in fact be focused on the necessary disposals to clean up the group. John Langston's proposed strategy to prioritize the sale of John Crane–Lips Marine was endorsed, but the balance of the sealing solutions businesses would require serious study to determine what the right strategy should be. For the industrial division, given the changed market circumstances for several of its component parts, it needed rebalancing, and some disposals were needed.

Aerospace: 2001–2006

One thing that was always true about Smiths was that we punched significantly above our weight.

(John Ferrie, 2013[17])

The Smiths/TI merger can very largely be seen as an aerospace-led transaction, designed to give more scale in the market. Traditionally, Smiths had provided hi-tech cockpit equipment, while TI had a fair-sized engine components business, and produced various bits of specialized engineering (propellers, actuators, etc.). While the transaction therefore delivered more overall sales, technically it did nothing to provide a more integrated package of equipment. It did however diversify the client base, since it immediately brought more work from Airbus, which was in turn determined to reduce its reliance on Honeywell.

The £75m acquisition of Fairchild Defense from Orbital Sciences Corp that closed as the merger was under way brought more data recording and analysis capacity for military applications. After this, the division was understandably slightly quiet on the acquisition front, as Ferrie worked hard to bring together the Smiths and Dowty businesses, eliminating overheads and duplication, while winning some important contracts in 2001–2, such as the hydraulic actuation package for the Airbus A380 landing gear.

What turned out to be a problematic transaction arrived in 2002 with the winning of a contract to supply the refuelling system for the Boeing B767 Global Tanker Transport Aircraft. Muscling in on territory (in-flight refuelling) that was traditionally the province of Cobham, Smiths acquired Able Corp in the US for $25m, the engineering firm that would provide the necessary hose system. As Ferrie later commented, 'you don't know what you don't know', and the transaction unravelled over time, partly because the development costs escalated as the technological challenge became apparent.[18] Able had developed a digitally controlled refuelling system, arguably more sophisticated than Cobham's traditional electro-mechanical system, but the systems integration challenge proved overwhelming and cripplingly expensive. Even at the eventual development cost of $132m, there would have been some chance of at least recovering the investment, given original estimates of lifetime sales of $1bn, but owing to irregularities being uncovered in the award of the GTTA contract by the US government to Boeing, the entire programme was suspended from late 2003, leading to a substantial write-off, with a minimal recovery of costs from Boeing. It was symptomatic of the increasing risk profile to which aerospace suppliers were becoming subject.

There was also the aftermath of the attack on the World Trade Center in September 2001—essentially a significant reduction in civil aerospace demand. In 2002–3, weak airlines delayed orders, and orders for spares and retro-fits declined, though there was some offset from increased (though lower-margin) military sales. In the technical arena, Smiths had developed sophisticated electronic systems for the Boeing 777 in the 1990s, but the evolution of the next generation, the 7E7 (Dreamliner), was revealing a marked change in the field.

Until now, the constructors had retained responsibility for aeroplane design, and subcontracted the design and supply of individual components or systems packages. Increasingly the burden was moving to the suppliers for the development, manufacture, and supply of entire systems designed to meet a specified function—partly as a function of cost-cutting at the airframe manufacturers, who wanted to cut (expensive) design staff. This meant Smiths and others 'now had to learn a range of aircraft integration issues they had never previously had to worry about'.[19]

Smiths competed head-to-head with Honeywell, Rockwell, and Thales in bidding for a common core system (CCS) for the Dreamliner. Now a supplier would provide an open-architecture 'mainframe' computer and associated design tools for the manufacturers of various key devices around the aircraft (e.g. systems for flight management, electric load management, fuel measurement, etc.), the controlling software for which would be hosted on the CCS. Honeywell had provided an earlier version of the CCS on the 777 airliner, but integrated with their cockpit, providing something of a stranglehold on upgrades, and Boeing wanted to widen their field of suppliers. This was one among six different elements of the Dreamliner for which Smiths bid, winning contracts for the CCS, landing-gear, and high-level lift systems, as well as winning further business on the A380 landing-gear system. The anticipated shipset value per Dreamliner rose to $1.5m in electronics, and $1m via the engine manufacturers.

It was a period of limited M&A activity for Smiths, one exception in late 2004 being the acquisition of Integrated Aerospace of California, for £75m, which expanded the landing-gear business. But if there were limited opportunities to grow by acquisition, there was nevertheless a focus in increasing margins though cost-cutting. Smiths announced a company-wide restructuring plan in 2004, in which the greatest focus was on the aerospace division, particularly in reducing US costs. Looking to move to lower cost environments, Smiths acquired a large site at Suzhou, Jiang Su province, in China, for a factory to specialize in engine components which opened in 2005, by which time the downward trend in commercial jet construction, in evidence since 2001, was finally reversed. But the industry as a whole had suffered several years of reduced activity, putting severe pressure on sales and margins. The late 1990s had seen Smiths recover to around 19 per cent as a margin in aerospace, but within three years this had declined to 11 per cent.

The work on the Boeing tanker was one obvious user of R&D funding, which for Smiths as a whole had been rising throughout the decade, the bulk occurring in aerospace. The rise in self-funded R&D as a proportion reflected a long-term trend of risk transfer from the constructors to the suppliers, and the analysts understood and accepted this. What attracted less positive sentiment was the necessary corollary of the adoption of IFRS accounting standards for the 2006 accounts, which forced a change in the accounting treatment of R&D. For years it had been Smiths' boast that it wrote off expenditure in the year it was incurred. Donald Broad recalls 'one of the most difficult analysts' meetings I ever attended was when we explained the enforced change of policy'.[20] As one analyst commented, there was a 'general suspicion of R&D capital-ization as an accounting policy (even though all peers have similar policies)'.[21] This was one of several glitches in analyst contact that led to a decline in confidence in management in the analyst community, providing a challenge for the incoming finance director, John Langston, who replaced Alan Thomson on his retirement in September 2006.

Overall, the board's strategy for aerospace, implemented by Ferrie over the first six years of the decade, was to develop a balance of business on Airbus programmes as well as Boeing. This meant coping with the obvious process of de-risking that both manufacturers were undertaking, with a rising requirement for self-funded R&D and an increased risk profile for Smiths. Technological challenges also remained ahead with the A380 and Dreamliner programmes, arising from the changed methodology of the constructors subcontracting not only component and system design and manufacture but the entire issue of system integration. What had not been foreseen were the problems and delays a lack of in-house integration capacity might create—in the case of the Dreamliner, it entered service in 2011, some four years later than originally planned.

Detection: 2001–2007

Combined with Smiths' other acquired detection-businesses . . . Heimann will give Smiths an unsurpassed detection capability.

(Credit Suisse, 2002)

John Ferrie inherited from Norman Barber a responsibility for the protection and detection business, run by John Shepherd. The business remained relatively low-profile but its importance was markedly influenced by the events of 11 September 2001. Just a few months before, there had already been a significant acquisition, of Barringer Technologies of Toronto for £39m, a specialist in explosive and narcotic detection. The detection business was effectively doubled in late 2002 with Smiths' largest acquisition to date, beating GE to the purchase of Heimann Systems from Rheinmetall of Germany, for £256m, the world's leading manufacturer of X-ray equipment for mail, baggage, and cargo. This led to the creation in August 2003 of a separate Smiths division—Detection—which reported sales for 2003 of £273m, up from £119m a year earlier. John Langston, who had been running Sealing Solutions (essentially John Crane and the old Dowty polymer business) was moved to run the new division, partly to use his German-language skills in a business with a new German emphasis. By now, analysts could talk of 'an unsurpassed detection capacity', and noted Smiths had 'the only integrated metal and explosive detection system on the market'.[22]

Mid-2004 saw the division expand further with two US acquisitions totalling $90m, of SensIR and Cyrano Sciences, manufacturers (respectively) of technology to identify chemicals (e.g. using spectroscopy) and to sense chemicals (in effect, with an electronic nose). By now, the most significant customer was the US Transport Security Administration, but others included the US mail service and various other foreign administrations, including the Greek government, which required screening technology for the Athens Olympics. The downside of the product and relevant client mix was the tendency for sales to be made up of smaller numbers of bulk orders, and for these to be timed in relation to governmental agency timetables—a feature that produced 'lumpy' figures, thus distorting short-term like-for-like comparisons.

Still the smallest division in 2005, sales growth was nevertheless impressive, even taking account of acquisitions—the latter comprising Farran Technology from Ireland (millimetre wave technology to detect hidden threats, complementing trace and X-ray screening); Echo Technologies Inc.—ETI of Boston, MA (optical sensors for biological and chemical agents), and LiveWave of Newport, Rhode Island (networking of sensors and CCTV). In the autumn of 2005, Smiths decided to merge the biometric business of Heimann with Cross Match Technologies of Florida, taking a 43 per cent stake in the resulting enlarged group. With Stephen Phipson (formerly of Interconnect) in charge from mid-2004, with his whole career spent in hi-tech electronics (and also a good networker), the group's profile was enhanced in the market.

The division participated in the group-wide restructuring programme of 2004–5, leading to some consolidation of manufacturing facilities, but these were then enlarged in 2006 with the addition of a new factory in St Petersburg, reflecting the expectation of significant investment by the Russian authorities in detection equipment.

From 10 per cent of Smiths' sales in 2003, the contribution had risen to 12 per cent by 2006, and nearly 15 per cent of headline operating profit. The business entered 2007 as the clear global leader in threat detection equipment manufacture, enjoying supply relationships with a large number of governments, in a business dominated by transportation security. With the United States as a vital target market, one cloud on the horizon was that Smiths' equipment did not use the technology specified by some US authorities in certain circumstances—it was to become topical in the consideration of a major transaction, dealt with elsewhere.

Industrial/Specialty Engineering: 2001–2002

> *Glorious hopes on a trillion-dollar scrapheap.*
>
> (*Financial Times*[23])

The simplified presentation of the industrial division had resolved itself into Interconnect and Air Movement by the end of the 1990s. Within these, Lindh had significantly boosted Interconnect with purchases that were telecoms-related, and in the wake of the collapse of the dot.com era and the global telecoms industry, Smiths could not escape some consequences, especially given the near-recessionary backdrop of the US economy in 2000–1. However, elements of Interconnect held up well, especially in the field of 'mission-critical connectors', reflecting new growth in defence budgets. In addition, there were still areas of telecoms that Smiths believed had prospects, leading to the late 2000 purchase of Radio Waves in the US for $25m, a maker of high-frequency microwave antennae, but the telecoms market collapse meant its prospects declined dramatically and its value was written down heavily. A long-term legacy business in hydraulics in the UK was sold to SPX for £12m in early 2001. Later that year, two of the flexible hose businesses, Induplas and Flexiplas, were also sold, to Petzetakis SA of Greece.

The following year—2002—was more uncomfortable with both parts of the business suffering from market downturns, leading to an overall 13 per cent drop in sales, which the company met with a 12 per cent reduction in employee numbers. Lindh remained convinced the move into sophisticated electronics had been correct, but now felt it to be the right time to explore disposals, resulting in a significant sale in December 2002, in which the Air Movement businesses, bundled together with the cable management operations, were sold to HSBC, for £125m. This included names such as Kopex, which dated back to the late 1950s, as well as acquisitions from the 1990s, such as Vent-Axia. With these disposals, the size of the original industrial group was now much reduced, and it was timely to gather together the remaining companies with parts of the old TI, to form a new Specialty Engineering division.

When the Smiths/TI merger had been put together, as well as selling the automotive business, there was an anticipation the whole sealings solutions division would be sold as well. In March 2001, when John Langston presented on the four constituent businesses, it was clear the EIS vacuum and filtration business line would go. In a series of transactions later in the year, they were sold to SPX Lightnin and Harris Watson Holdings, for a combined £15.2m. Margins were declining in John Crane-Lips Marine, and it was therefore also under a cloud. Leveraging off the existing alliance between John Crane-Lips and Wärtsilä of Finland, the business was sold outright to Wärtsilä for £235m in April 2002.

The main mechanical seals business and the polymer division were still performing satisfactorily, if unable to grow, and by early 2002 Langston believed Smiths might be best served by the disposal of the remainder of the division.[24] At mid-year the figures showed divisional sales had declined by 8 per cent to £822m, although profits were largely unchanged, at £100m, or a margin of over 12 per cent. To evaluate prospects, Bain & Co. were brought in as consultants, and their involvement is discussed later. By September 2002, it was decided John Crane should be retained, while the old Dowty polymers business should be sold, with a target price of £450m, though it was recognized this would be dilutive. A market-testing process for Project Walrus was commenced by JP Morgan in the spring of 2003, leading to a deal in July with Trelleborg AB, closed near year-end, for £495m. From the four original businesses, just John Crane remained, and the proceeds of the various sales had helped to pay down debt significantly.

In August 2003, John Langston ceded responsibility for John Crane (although temporarily), to look after the new detection division. A new division—Specialty Engineering—now brought together John Crane, the Interconnect businesses (which enjoyed a strong year in 2004), the Flex-Tek ducting and hose operations, and Marine Systems (i.e. Kelvin Hughes charts and marine electronics). Einar Lindh ran the division till mid-2004, before handing back over to Langston, ahead of his retirement.

In the 2004–5 period, the division enjoyed the benefits for Interconnect of renewed demand in the telecoms sector (with the roll-out of infrastructure for 3G) and increased military budgets, while strong global oil and gas investment increased sales for John Crane. The microwave cluster of businesses was expanded significantly in mid-2004 with the $112m purchase of TRAK Communications of Florida, specialists in microwave subsystems and antennae. In early 2006, the purchase of Lorch Microwave of Maryland further expanded capacity in microwave filters—as part of a strategy to build a cluster of companies around microwave communications, including Florida RF Labs and EMC, purchased in the 1990s. Boosting Smiths' abilities in millimetre wave technology with a components manufacture, Millitech Inc. of Massachusetts was acquired in 2005. At the same time, the Flex-Tek range of businesses added Farnham Custom Products of North Carolina, a specialized heater producer. With the focus moving to the hi-tech Interconnect companies, Icore, which made specialist conduit, was now less of a fit, and was sold for £20m in 2004.

Looking to locate itself closer physically to the Asian component of its customer base, and to reduce costs, John Crane invested in new manufacturing and service facilities in Bangalore in 2006. By the end of the year, John Crane accounted for half the sales in the division, while Flex-Tek and Interconnect accounted for about 21–3 per cent each, with a small balance of around 6 per cent from the marine business, which by mid-2007 was held for sale on the balance sheet. Analysts could point to John Crane's strong global market share—at around 35 per cent, it was more than double that of its nearest competitor.[25]

John Crane, Inc. (JCI), a subsidiary of the John Crane division of Smiths Group, continues to be one of many co-defendants in US asbestos litigation. The litigation began more than thirty years ago and typically involves claims for a number of diseases, including asbestosis, lung cancer, and mesothelioma. The JCI products generally referred to in these cases consist of industrial sealing products, primarily packing and gaskets. The asbestos was encapsulated within these products in such a manner that, according to tests conducted on behalf of JCI, the products were safe. JCI ceased manufacturing products containing asbestos in 1985.

Medical: 2000–2007

If Smiths is to sustain the growth over the last five years, it is essential that we see a return to sustained growth in the Medical division.

(ABN Amro, March 2000)

Lawrence Kinet inherited a medical division built up over twenty-five years by George Kennedy, which reflected a broader Smiths' policy of retaining niche businesses within the division, in separate silos. This was alien to Kinet's philosophy, which tended towards a more centralized approach. He was unhappy with the large number of different facilities and units, both in manufacturing and sales, and set out from 2001 onwards to rationalize. In 2001 this involved the move of more manufacturing to the maquiladora facility in Tijuana, while Eschmann, which had been through a lean phase, arguably no longer fitted in the Smiths product mix with its surgical tables, and was sold in mid-2001 to a consortium, advised by George Kennedy.

In terms of presentation, Kinet chose to focus the division on therapy types, creating nine different groupings (e.g. ambulatory infusion, needle protection, airway management, etc). More radically, in 2003, the old name of SIMS was dropped, and a new one,

Smiths Medical, created, to present a unified presence to the market, and arranged around two broad product categories: (i) medication delivery and patient monitoring, and (ii) anaesthesia and safety devices. In this latter category, the US authorities had passed the Needlestick Safety and Prevention Act in April 2001, which provided a substantial boost to Smiths' needle protection business. In the same year, Kinet managed to find further acquisitions with the purchase of Bivona (silicone tracheostomy tubes) and the anaesthesia kit and tray business of Abbott Labs.[26]

Capitalizing on Deltec's success in developing medical devices for home use, in December 2001, Jim Stitt of Deltec and Kinet presented plans for a significant addition to the product range. This was a new ambulatory pump, tailor-made for diabetic medication, the market for which was already large, but growing. The field was dominated by Disetronic and MiniMed (i.e. Medtronic), but the proposed Cozmo device (named after the marketing manager's dog) would offer greater personalization and programmability. The pump was developed throughout 2002, launching the following year. With the product selling well, and Disetronic in difficulties, Cozmo might be expected to have a bright future, but instead by the autumn of 2003 Smiths found itself resisting a patent infringement suit from Medtronic.[27] This rumbled on for more than a year and was finally settled in mid-2005. While Kinet would have fought on, David Lillycrop, Smiths' general counsel, believed the potential costs of losing substantially outweighed any upside. Technically Smiths could continue to manufacture the pump, but under a licence agreement that effectively meant Medtronic had all the benefit. The pump was withdrawn a number of years later.

Trying to fend off competition from Mallinckrodt, Abbott Labs, Baxter Labs, and Sulzer Medica, as well as devoting resources to product development, Kinet pursued several potential acquisition transactions. He and Robin Taunt presented a strategy in late 2003, suggesting the economics of purchasing mature mid-sized medical companies were the most attractive—of which a range of possible options ranged in size from £100m to £1bn.[28] One of these was Arizant, operating in the medical heating device market, like Level-1. Smiths valued the business at $205m, but lost out to Court Square Capital, a Citigroup venture capital arm which bid $255m. Almost immediately, consideration was given to Hudson RCI, a respiratory care products manufacturer, for which Smiths agreed to bid up to $425m, but was again beaten to the post, by Teleflex with a $460m bid in May 2004.[29] Even as this deal failed, another was being pushed forward, and DHD Healthcare, another respiratory care device maker, was successfully acquired for $55m from Riverside Capital in July 2004.

The next transaction was, however, very significant. There was a history of contact between Medex and Smiths. The firm had been through several transformations over many years, first having offered to sell itself to Smiths back in 1982.[30] A long-standing and important product line was its Medfusion syringe pump, complementary to Smiths' infusion business. Kennedy had taken another look in 2000 but nothing transpired. In 2001, a management buy-out saw the senior staff and employees acquire the firm from Saint Gobain Performance Plastics Corporation. The new owners expanded the business in 2003 with the purchase from Johnson & Johnson of its Jelco and ProtectIV lines, both leading market products with loyal customer followings. To enable the purchase, Medex sold an 83 per cent stake in itself to One Equity Partners in 2003, the private equity arm of JP Morgan.

In September 2004, Kinet outlined to the board a potential bid for Medex. One Equity was now preparing it for a potential flotation, but would consider a straight sale. Morgan Stanley, Smiths' adviser, believed it might float for an amount in the $850–950m range. After an initial bid was rejected, Smiths sharpened its pencil and a deal was eventually agreed and announced in early December, at $925m, though subject to regulatory approval, which delayed the closing until March 2005. Cheuvreux summed up, 'Smiths has finally made a meaningful acquisition.'[31]

The integration plan for Medex was complicated, and crucial in Kinet's plan was the role for Dominick Arena, the Medex CEO, whom he rated highly. Kinet wanted to move away from the traditional Smiths' strategy of retaining individual businesses in a division, with their own identity, frequently known by their long-standing brand names. He believed the division should be organized not around products, but around its customers—so that, for example, in dealing with group-purchasing organizations in the US, there would be a single Smiths' contact point, someone who would be able to contract and sell all Smiths' products to a customer. Arena was Kinet's suggested head of an integrated US organization for Smiths (where the bulk of the firm's medical sales were made). The risks, and costs, of such an integration were very significant, as well as being alien to Smiths' culture, and it was here that Kinet met entrenched opposition from KB-W, who firmly believed in the strategic strengths of retaining different brand identities—his argument being this protected better against pressure to reduce prices, to which Smiths might be subject if organized with a single market presence. A lack of common ground on the correct path forward led to Kinet's decision to leave Smiths and return to the US in July 2005, and within months the departure of Arena from Medex as well.

Einar Lindh, who had retired a few months before, but who had worked in the medical division for years, was drafted back in on a temporary basis while the firm recruited a replacement, which took until January 2006, when Smiths announced it had hired Srini Seshadri, former chief marketing officer of GE Healthcare, to run the medical business. A chemical engineer, with a strong background in the medical screening and X-ray fields, he had worked for GE for over twenty years. On arrival at Smiths, there were challenges to be met. The headline operating profit for the division in 2006 was 57 per cent ahead on 2005, but the increase was dominated by contributions from Medex and DHD, with limited organic growth from existing businesses, requiring attention. The market view of the division was that it had under-invested so far in the decade, both in terms of R&D and in acquisitions. As regards the latter, it was clear that Smiths tried, but it was nowhere near as aggressive as some competitors, notably in the US. On R&D, the numbers increased, from around 2 per cent in 2000 to over 3.5 per cent in 2007 and on an upward trend, levels regarded as important to deliver organic growth.

To reduce costs, manufacturing was restructured in 2006, with further expansion in Ohio and Mexico allowing the closure of facilities in Duluth and Wampsville, New York, as well as at Hythe in the UK, the site of the original Portland Plastics operation from the 1950s. The original Peter von Berg operation, now pvb Critical Care, was also sold to meet competition requirements in Germany. The disruption of the factory closures and general restructuring had the effect of reducing sales in 2007 versus 2006, but the medical division entered the year with close to a 20 per cent global market share for its medical devices, with over half its sales occurring in the US. The fall-off in margins in the late 1990s was halted in the early part of the decade, but the heavy cost of launching the Cozmo pump combined with currency losses took their toll in 2003, taking margins below 20 per cent for the first time in fifteen years. From then on, they remained in the 18–19 per cent range, and therefore the highest in the group.[32]

TI Automotive: 2001–2007

The decision to write down the value of the TI stake to zero, amid a weakening US auto market, cuts the sole canker from an otherwise healthy group.

(*Independent*[33])

There was considerable success in the wake of the TI merger in disposing of businesses, or achieving improvements, but one disastrous outcome was the hangover from the failed initial sale of the automotive business. It was demerged from July 2001, and Smiths retained two forms of investment—some ordinary equity, and £325m in preference shares, nominally offering a 15 per cent dividend, 5 per cent payable annually in cash and the rest deferred until redemption, which was anticipated when TI Automotive repaid its initial bank debt. Smiths held the ordinary shares at zero in its balance sheet, but recorded the preference shares at par, making no accruals for dividends.

The economic slowdown of the early 2000s knocked the business, and in 2002 it had to restructure the debt arranged only a year earlier, having unsuccessfully tried to launch a bond issue in the US.[34] Relations between Smiths and the firm were not always easy. With Bill Laule running it quite independently, Smiths' only leverage was an ability to appoint the chairman, the first being Richard Lapthorne, on the suggestion of Bernard Taylor who had known him for many years through their joint banking careers. In 2003, Lapthorne attempted to introduce a significantly enhanced executive incentive programme, much to Smiths' consternation, leading to his removal as chairman, to be replaced by Colin Chandler from the Smiths board.

Having tried to solicit some interest for the equity through CSFB in late 2005, without success, and deciding by mid-2006 there was no reasonable prospect of any dividends being paid, particularly with the 'recent material deterioration in the automotive components market (particularly in the US)', the preference shares were written off, at a loss of £325m.[35] In 2007, a syndicate of investment funds, headed by Oaktree Capital Management and Duquesne Capital Management acquired the firm, partly through a conversion of debt to equity. Smiths agreed to sell its shares for just £15m, which it recorded as a gain, together with £9m resulting from a release of various provisions.[36]

Gorillas in the midst

> *Gorilla: A company that dominates an industry without having a complete monopoly.*
>
> (Investopedia)

Players that enjoy significant market power, or some dominance in a market segment, are sometimes colourfully described as gorillas. A gorilla makes competition harder for smaller players—for example, through aggressive pricing policies, or entrenched relationships with key customers. Smiths has found itself sometimes enjoying the benefits of a large market share, at others having to face the difficulty of building businesses where gorillas already dominate. In the inter-war years, it dominated the British horological industry. For much of the twentieth century, it occupied a similar position with certain motor accessories, alongside Lucas which dominated its own sector of the automotive market. Smiths has also habitually dominated niche markets—a strategy similarly pursued by Lewinton at TI Group—exemplified by the industrial group, where the individual businesses have often been a powerful force within their own niches.

A process of coming to a better understanding of Smiths' position in its various markets, and where it wanted to end up, was assisted by a number of projects involving external consultants. One of these occurred in 2000, when the consultancy firm, Health Advances, undertook a strategic review of the medical division. A notable finding, focusing on the respiratory-related businesses, was presented in a matrix. It charted relative market share for product types against potential market capacity, revealing a number of weaker positions in markets where the outlook was for little growth or even contraction. However, Level-1 was a marked exception—enjoying both a strong market share in blood warming products, and significant growth potential. The exact opposite applied for the ostomy and urology businesses—hence their later sale to Mentor Corporation in the US.

In April 2002, when a disposal of parts of the sealings solutions business was mooted, Keith Orrell-Jones suggested Robin Buchanan of Bain & Co. might help Smiths evaluate its options.[37] From this first contact, and having impressed KB-W, the idea for a deeper involvement was presented by Julian Critchlow of Bain at the strategic conference in May 2002, as usual held at Woodcote Park. A further project, led by Bain's Jimmy Allen, would explore the potential for the medical division and help devise a growth strategy, building on the earlier work of Health Advances. If successful, this would lead to a company-wide evaluation and the development of an overall strategy. This matched KB-W's goal to see Smiths move on from what he described as a culture of 'grafting and grinding'. He was keen to foster instead a culture that could make imaginative leaps forward, aided by a dose of fresh and external thinking. David Flowerday remembers KB-W asking, whenever the conversation turned to strategy, 'What do we want to be when we grow up?'

At the heart of Bain's methodology was a process it termed 'Full Potential Review', which started with two broad questions; (i) what was the potential market available (i.e. was there market headroom available for capture?), and (ii) what realistic capacity was there to improve market share and margins? After exhaustive information gathering, analysis would highlight strengths, weaknesses, threats, and opportunities. From this an action plan could be devised to achieve 'full potential', with quantifiable outcomes, expressed in terms of capital value—a business should be worth more, by a quantifiable factor, at the end of the process.

In September 2002, Bain completed evaluations of both the sealings solutions and medical businesses. The sealing solutions exercises showed contrasting prospects for Crane and Polymers. Crane was the clear global leader—here Smiths owned a gorilla. Furthermore, a path could be plotted to exploit this leadership position, growing both organically and by acquisition, with potential for the value of the business to grow significantly. The Polymer business by contrast had a reasonable rather than leading market share, and there was no obvious path to materially increasing the value of the business. Bain's review suggested Crane's value could be increased by as much as £200m, and it was therefore clearly to be retained.[38] In the case of the medical business, valued at around £1.1bn, Bain saw more value, mainly through better exploitation of certain market niches, achieving synergies within the portfolio, and increased R&D.

The favourable experience of these projects led to a company-wide 'full potential review', presented at the May 2003 Woodcote Park strategy meeting. Various important insights emerged. A first issue was the difference between (i) the current valuations of the separate divisions, and (ii) projected 'full potential' values for the same business, the latter assuming it would be developed by a series of demanding actions. Where the comparison showed significantly higher full potential value, the necessary actions should be pursued vigorously.

Given their scale, the aerospace and medical businesses received most focus. A valuable outcome was the way the process effectively held up a mirror to the company, forcing a realization of the market position it enjoyed in various specialist and niche segments. For ease of presentation, Bain utilized a highly visual approach. This involved coloured Marimekko charts depicting the players and their market shares in each of Smiths' many product niches. Two in particular for the aerospace division were highly striking. One showed the global market for electronic systems, giving a market size of £6.8bn per annum.[39] Smiths' offering included systems for flight management, electronic load management, power distribution, fuel gauging, etc. It was visually immediately apparent (even for non-specialists) that in certain niches, Smiths, as expected, was a major player. But cumulatively these niches formed only a very small part of the global market. For big ticket items (communications, navigation, primary generation, and engine control systems), the market was entirely dominated by

Rockwell Collins, Goodrich, Honeywell, and Hamilton Sundstrand—the gorillas. With pressure from the airframe constructors on their suppliers to consolidate their product offerings into integrated systems, the territories of flight deck avionics, power, and utilities were rapidly becoming the playing field of a very small number of larger companies, of which Smiths was not one.

Intriguingly, a completely different picture applied for engine components—the aerospace businesses Smiths acquired with TI. In the £2.3bn market for engine fabrications, complex machining, rings, and rigid aero tubing, and absent the engine manufacturers themselves, Smiths was the gorilla. Bain further pointed out that the return on capital for the major constructors (Boeing and Lockheed) was both cyclical and on a decline. If they were having a lean time, it was natural for them to put increasing price pressure on their fat suppliers (whose returns had been more stable), to preserve their own returns. Bain believed winning future civil aerospace business was increasingly dependent on making a decreasing number of risky big bets (i.e. the Airbus A380 and Dreamliner), as a result of the convergence of technology. They described the concept of the 'winner's curse', in which firms (including gorillas) bid for large contracts where development is a major component, with both costs and timetable hard to quantify. With the likelihood of these huge contracts being bid on the basis of winner-takes-all, prices would likely be bid down to a level where the winner faced little upside and significant downside, increasing the probability that winning would become a curse. KB-W adopted the phrase and the aerospace team would come to understand it forcibly in relation to the Boeing tanker contract, where the planned investment increased three-fold. Bain predicted some contracts for the A380 and Dreamliner might carry such a curse.

The analysis of the medical division revealed the traditional Smiths approach to running its divisions—significant separation between the businesses and brands, with companies run on a standalone basis to incentivize management strongly and to create an entrepreneurial spirit—while R&D expenditure had typically been modest. Bain suggested a stronger focus on promoting cross-selling opportunities, partly through a restructuring of the salesforce, as well as a reduction of manufacturing costs through consolidation. It was also suggested that product development should be customer-led to a greater degree. Analysis confirmed the earlier Health Advances' study: the highest margins occurred where Smiths enjoyed both a strong market share, and where the product was routinely distinctly specified by medical professionals—Level-1 being the stand-out example. While acquisitions to bolster Smiths' position in various markets were desirable, it was also clear that the P/E ratios for medical device companies had radically moved up, from around 20 in 1996–7 to the mid-30s. Acquisition economics looked less and less favourable, and the market was dominated by several gorillas that would be difficult to displace.

In the case of the detection business, the global market was assessed at a much smaller size—£745m per annum. Yet within this, Smiths was the undisputed gorilla, with strong representation in almost every part of the market, from baggage scanning through to biochemical attack diagnosis. Nevertheless, Bain still argued it would be 'a white knuckle ride', where market demand might fluctuate wildly, and investment in advancing the science of the business would be expensive. John Crane, another gorilla, likewise dominated the global market for industrial seals—valued at £1.4bn per annum. Of this total, two segments (North America, and Europe, Middle East, and Africa) accounted for 70 per cent, and Crane's market share in each was 30–5 per cent. Polymer Seal Systems also had a reasonable market share, but it was already slated for sale.

KB-W's decision to employ Bain and the presentation to the 2003 conference was a significant one, and helped shape much thinking going forward. In a modified form, the Bain terminology framed the core of Smiths' annual budgeting process, so that performance would in future be measured against financial 'full potential' targets. From 2004, Flowerday's annual strategy reviews were influenced by Bain's approach, in examining both performance and charting potential paths forward. The rhetoric also appeared in external presentations of the firm, commencing with KB-W's 2003 annual review. By 2005, the annual report set out clearly the elements to deriving value from Smiths' 'Full Potential Programme'. Importantly, it clearly stated that, where others had the opportunity of creating more future value, Smiths would sell. Conversely Smiths would acquire, where there was an opportunity to increase the value of an acquired business.

Another legacy was a phrase favoured by Bain, the private equity acid test—generally attributed to James Coulter of Texas Pacific Group: 'Every day you don't sell a portfolio company, you've made an implicit buy decision.' This translated to the question going forward, for all of the divisions, 'If we did not already own it, would we buy it?'

Changes at the top

An accomplished gun, Sir Roger was given a double-barrelled shotgun as a leaving gift—which gave him the chance to joke about the double-barrelled Keiths which he was handing Smiths over to, and the 'firepower' they brought to the job.[40]

After Roger Hurn's retirement, KB-W enjoyed the support of Keith Orrell-Jones over the following years, especially through the TI transaction, and the two enjoyed working together. Orrell-Jones had been on the board longer than anyone else and had gathered around him a diverse group of non-executives, with Robert O'Leary (who joined in 1997) bringing directly relevant experience from the US health industry. Several new non-executives arrived within months of each other in 2000, first with Julian Horn-Smith (director of Vodafone), and then a team that came with the TI merger: Sir Nigel Broomfield (former UK Ambassador to Germany), Sir Colin Chandler (formerly of Racal, Vickers, DESO, BAe, and a noted figure in UK defence sales) who became Orrell-Jones's deputy, and John Hignett (former TI deputy chairman and investment banker, ex-Lazards, and former Glaxo finance director), whose place was taken by Peter Jackson (CEO of Associated British Foods) in late 2003. It was during 2003 that the board took various steps to implement the combined code on corporate governance, part of which involved moving to majority non-executive representation, in turn leading to the appointment of Lord Robertson (former UK Defence Minister and recent Secretary General of NATO). Colin Chandler, chairman of TI Automotive from July 2003, retired from the Smiths board in late 2004.

It had earlier become clear that Orrell-Jones's health was suffering, leading to a search for a replacement following the November 2003 AGM. In the spring of 2004, Smiths announced the recruitment of Donald Brydon, 'one of the City's best connected executives', according to *The Times*, though described as 'more "Edinburgh Mafia" than City grandee'.[41] He had spent a long career in investment management, with over twenty years at Barclays, running the asset management company, ending up as deputy CEO of BZW. For most of the 1990s he served as a director of the London Stock Exchange. Moving from BZW to AXA, he ran the investment management arm, becoming chairman of the division in 1997, the same year he joined the board of Amersham. Becoming chairman in 2003, he oversaw its acquisition by GE Healthcare in 2004. At the time of joining Smiths, other City posts included directorships of Allied Domecq and Scottish Power, and chairmanships of the London Metal Exchange, the Financial Services Practitioner Panel, and the Code Committee of the Takeover Panel. As the press pointed out on his appointment, a key task would be overseeing succession planning on the Smiths board, where four key executives (Thomson, Kinet, Ferrie, and Lindh) would all retire within three years, a situation partially addressed in 2003 with the decision to defer KB-W's retirement by two years to 2008.

Brydon took up post in September 2004. A long-time adviser and friend of Keith Orrell-Jones, David Challen, joined the board at the same time—well-known to Brydon from shared directorships at Amersham and positions on the Takeover Panel. Challen brought further City experience as a former chairman of Schroders and senior positions at Citibank.

The need for a majority of non-executives, and the gradual retirement of various executives, gave rise to a new desire to reshape the board, to prevent it becoming unmanageable. In future, the heads of each of the main businesses would not necessarily join the main board. As result, Stephen Phipson (who ran detection after John Langston), Paul Cox (who was recruited from Andrew Corporation in Chicago, replacing Einar Lindh in Specialty Engineering), and Srini Seshadri (who had arrived to run Medical) did not join the board.

In 2006, the board saw several changes, losing three non-executives, with the retirement of Lord Robertson and Julian Horn-Smith, and the death of Robert O'Leary following a long illness. On the executive side, Alan Thomson retired. New arrivals were Sir Kevin Tebbit (recently retired as permanent under-secretary from the Ministry of Defence) and Stuart Chambers (CEO of Pilkington). Peter Löscher (President and CEO of Siemens, and former chief operating officer at Amersham) joined in June 2007.

Thinking the unthinkable

We were ranked as an aerospace firm, alongside Rolls Royce and British Aerospace. Here I was, a Johnny-come-lately, from an entirely different industrial background, suggesting we cut off our own head. It was heresy.

(Keith Butler-Wheelhouse, 2013)

From 2002 onwards, there had been a change in strategic thinking, Smiths now being seen as the wrapper for a series of businesses, which it would not necessarily hold for all time, or until they ran out of steam (e.g. the motor business in 1983)—a natural tendency to be on the buy-side would be balanced by a willingness to sell in the right circumstances. This thinking was reinforced by Bain's input, and consideration was now given to the potential benefits of major disposals, even of an entire division, and the resulting outcome for the remainder of the company. KB-W challenged the board to 'think the unthinkable' and recalls heated exchanges on the topic of disposals. Nonetheless, despite the mind-stretching exercises, the clear decision was to prioritize driving for the 'full potential' available to the existing mix of divisions.

In 2005, the strategic review highlighted the different market positions enjoyed by the divisions. John Crane, detection, and clusters such as Interconnect and Flex-Tek were already dominant in their given markets or niches. In the case of aerospace and medical, there were different ideas for how to move forward. In medical, there were no concerns over the future of the market—health care budgets were forecast to expand well into the future—and growth seemed possible, both organically and through synergistic acquisitions. Had the Cozmo diabetic pump not been challenged by Medtronic, it would have offered a good example of the way forward—a new product offering both high initial sales revenues and a large after-market in supplies. If the challenge of growing sales could be met, the market offered containable risk.

A different assessment began to emerge for aerospace, where in both systems and components there were growing worries about the impact of converging technology and future price pressure. Nevertheless there were still significant gains to be made by achieving the full potential goals, much of which depended on achieving cost savings and efficiencies. Thus the priority remained as before to maximize the performance of the division, but with a realization it was conceivably advantageous to consider the sale of the division, if concerns over the risks posed by the market increased.

A year later, in April 2006, once again at Woodcote Park, the board considered whether it wanted to explore further the desirability and feasibility of the sale of the aerospace division. By now the experience of the Boeing tanker project was an influence, highlighting the significant risks to which the company could be exposed. Flowerday presented an analysis of the values he believed might be achievable in a sale, and it was agreed that external validation of these values would be the next stage in a feasibility study.

KB-W then embarked on a process to select an external adviser, and since he wanted a known and trusted financial adviser looking at a potentially highly sensitive transaction, he chose Braveheart, a new corporate advisory business that Bernard Taylor and Julian Oakley had established after leaving JP Morgan—though within a short space of time Braveheart was in turn acquired by Evercore.[42] Taylor recalls the first stages of the project, essentially challenging KB-W and his team to consider if they really wanted to dispose of a key business.

By September, Flowerday had compared his analysis with Evercore's. It confirmed there was a possibility to dispose of the business at a premium, though there were numerous qualifications and the next logical step would be to sound out some prospective buyers, as a reality-check. Such a process had to be conducted in the utmost secrecy, and KB-W and Taylor travelled to meet the CEOs of a small group of selected companies—Finmeccanica, Snecma, United Technologies, Rockwell Collins, and Thales. Taylor recalls, 'We were a sort of double-act. We explained that Smiths was undertaking a strategic review, said that they had expressed an interest in the past, and asked if they still might be interested.'[43] But KB-W made clear there was no auction process envisaged. Should anyone be interested, the price was $5bn. In November, some interest had emerged, with requests for more information and several firms working on due diligence, but the next development came as a surprise.

Bill Castell was well-known to Taylor through the earlier sale of Amersham (where Castell had been CEO) to GE, of which Castell was now a vice-chairman. Over lunch, Castell commented, 'There's a rumour Smiths is contemplating the future of its aerospace division', and went on to ask, 'Do you think they could be persuaded to sell?' This led to a call from Jeff Immelt, GE's CEO, who then travelled to London to meet KB-W at Taylor's offices on 15 December.

Immelt was keen to proceed and, sensing he was possibly in competition, looked for ways to secure a transaction. This led to a wider discussion, in which the acquisition of Smiths' detection business was mooted. GE had assembled Homeland Protection from two US businesses—Ion Track acquired in 2002, and then InVision Technologies, purchased for $900m in 2004—and Smiths' business would be a natural complement. Tactically, KB-W focused on securing an aerospace deal first, and deferred discussions involving the detection business for the time being.

GE then commenced extensive due diligence, over the end of 2006 and into January 2007, tabling a firm bid for the aerospace business (subject to completion of due diligence) and, in addition, seeking to enter into a joint venture in detection, where Smiths would have management control, and ownership would be split 64:36 in Smiths' favour. In a board meeting held at Allen & Overy's office on 10 January 2007, the board heard the latest on the proposed transactions and negotiations, and listened to presentations from Evercore, Cazenove's, and Credit Suisse on expected market reaction. A critical consequence of the aerospace sale, now agreed at $4.8bn, was that £2.1bn would be returned to shareholders.

The board met again on Sunday, 14 January, where it decided in favour of completing the sale of the aerospace business, and entering into a letter of intent to create the joint venture with GE in detection—acknowledging that the latter would take many months to progress. The deal was announced early on the Monday morning, with a plan for a conditional agreement on the detection joint venture to be signed on 21 March.

The end game

Disposing of a business no one knew was for sale, for a much higher price than seemed possible, is something of a coup for the little-loved management of Smiths Group.

(*Financial Times*, LEX)

There were seven appearances of the deal in the Tuesday edition of the *Financial Times* alone. One was headlined 'Sigh of relief', reflecting unenthusiastic coverage of the group in previous months, following the TI Automotive write-off of £325m in September. The natural reaction to the latest news was positive, but another predictable headline ran 'Speculation of break up starts'. It was also taken as read that, with the aerospace sale sealed, the proposed joint venture in detection would naturally occur.

After the launch of the formal process of the sale in January, there were nevertheless significant practical hurdles to overcome, such as submissions to, and approval from, the US anti-trust authorities, but early May soon emerged as a target date for closure, with the proceeds, subject to adjustments, now expected to be $5.1bn. Finally, on 4 May 2007, the transaction duly closed, and John Ferrie resigned from the Smiths board, to join GE—leaving KB-W with just two fellow executive directors, both out of the TI stable.

It was now that a more subtle element of the entire story began to play out. The desire to create the detection joint venture had mainly come from GE. Evercore had been happy its client was negotiating two deals at once with GE, since this would deter other market gorillas from launching a hostile bid for Smiths. GE's tanks were effectively on Smiths' lawn, facing out. However, once the aerospace deal had closed, there was room to deploy Smiths' forensic capacity in more detailed due diligence of the GE Homeland Security assets, which would be GE's contribution to the joint venture in return for a 36 per cent stake.

Having visited GE in the US for a joint review of future prospects, David Flowerday submitted a paper to KB-W in July, which highlighted significant reservations, confirming earlier suspicions from the deal team in London. At the time, Smiths' scanning technology used 'multiview' X-ray scans, whereas GE employed the competing computer tomography (CT) approach. CT scanning was mandated by the US Transportation Security Administration (TSA), whereas in most other geographies multiview was preferred. However, it became apparent the TSA was considering a move towards using a mix of technologies. This diminished the strategic value of GE's business and enhanced Smiths'. In addition, the joint venture was expected to rely in future for technical development upon the resources of GE's medical division (source of the CT technology), and there was some scepticism as to whether this was a viable structure. Flowerday's analysis was that (absent any change in TSA policy) and based on valuing Homeland Security, GE's shareholding in the joint venture should not exceed 23 per cent, and if the TSA's policy did change, it should reduce to 17 per cent. Persuaded of the logic, KB-W arranged a conference with Brydon to brief him. It was abundantly clear GE could never agree to such a pricing structure, and it was therefore agreed Smiths should call off the planned joint venture, which KB-W succeeded in doing diplomatically. Understandably, since GE would want to be able to construct an alternative transaction for Homeland Security in due course, Smiths could not elaborate for the market its reasons for withdrawing, and it was simply announced on 19 September that the two sides had failed to reach agreement. The perceived failure of Smiths to close the transaction gave rise to negative coverage in the press and from analysts. Tellingly, GE subsequently disposed of its investment in 2009 at a significant loss, reflecting having entered the market at a peak, shortly after the September 2001 terrorist attacks in the US.

The aerospace deal had been safely put to bed, and what would have been a very poor transaction in detection had been neatly sidestepped. But there was still housekeeping to be done. An in-house analysis (with one page mischievously headed 'Hari Kari') highlighted the transformation Smiths had undergone over the decade, rising to a middle ranking in the FTSE 100 and building the in-house infrastructure to suit. But now it was radically smaller, with corporate overheads—largely the cost of a small group of high-ranking head office executives—that were no longer appropriate. The workload needed to be reapportioned and Smiths would need to cut its coat according to the new cloth of the post-aerospace world. As a result, a significant number of the head office team retired on 31 July 2007.

KB-W had extended his retirement from March 2006 to July 2008 to ensure continuity on the board when other directors had been slated to retire, and when strategic planning had assumed a new significance, but by the autumn of 2007, Brydon, as chair of the nominations committee, had already been running a search process for a new CEO, and analysts and the press were aware of this. With the abandonment of the detection joint venture, Brydon took the view it was important to move forward and to send a strong signal to the market that someone new was at the helm. As a result, the appointment of Philip Bowman, who had recently left Scottish Power, was announced just a week after the abandonment of the joint venture, to coincide with the release of Smiths' figures. KB-W retired on 10 December, bringing to an end a remarkable and transformational eleven years at the helm.

Financial summary

Smiths has delivered operating margins in the mid-teens and gross margins of around 35–40%. These margins were slightly diluted by the merger with TI, but progress has since resumed at the gross-margin level and in our view operating margins should return towards historical levels.

(Credit Suisse, 2006)

The TI transaction was expected to yield cost savings, with an initial £25m target, which the team managed to exceed over time. The immediate closure of TI corporate offices provided close to the overall target, but it was also true that a large part of the TI head office cost had been associated with TI Automotive, so would have disappeared anyway. There were additional business reorganization savings which steadily accumulated. In presenting the 2002 results, the company confirmed merger savings of £50m had been achieved, and that further savings of £44m were planned over the coming two years. These savings were clearly substantial in relation to the operating profits of around £190m generated by the acquired TI businesses. True, these savings were not reflected in increased profits, but major action had been taken which in turn outweighed any premium in the price paid for the incoming TI businesses.

By 2002, it was clear that, whatever the merits of the TI deal, the timing had been unfortunate as TI's more civil-orientated aerospace activity was more impacted that Smiths defence-biased business. Similarly, an industry downturn had hit the seals business badly, so that, together, the TI elements of the new company produced some 40 per cent less profit in 2002 versus 2001. Which is not to say the original Smiths businesses escaped lightly—the telecoms crash was largely responsible for reducing profits from the industrial division by the same amount.

For 2004, dollar weakness hit the figures, and despite continued cost-cutting, aerospace reported a fall in earnings. For detection, the unpredictable nature and timing of large government orders, driven by reactive policy changes, showed in the 2003–4 figures, where the earlier year included a significant government order and the resulting 20 per cent reduction in profits in the following year. For medical, the decision to back the Cozmo pump product meant significant expense and 2003's figures suffered as a result.

From a low in 2004, most of Smiths' figures began to improve, from overall profitability to earnings per share. Increased R&D reflected contract wins and increased market shares. For 2005–6, the margins in aerospace and detection both improved, and profits advanced well, reflecting increased production rates at Boeing and Airbus, and detection's increased business with both US civil airports and the US military. For medical, the 2005 acquisition of Medex fed through to stronger headline profits, but £10m of integration costs and the Medtronic settlement took their toll. A further £19m of integration costs hit in 2006, with a further £20m still anticipated. The most significant element in the 2006 accounts by far was however the exceptional

Table 10.1 Earnings per share (pence), 2000–2008

2000	2001	2002	2003	2004	2005	2006	2007	2008
59.0	57.4	52.3	45.6	45.9	52.8	64.8	47.0*	74.5

Source: Accounts: 2000–2004 (GAAP), 2005–2008 (IFRS). * the 2007 figures are distorted by the aerospace sale. Stripping out the effects, a more realistic pro-forma EPS would be 67.8.

loss of £325m taken in writing off the preference shares in TI Automotive. The figures for 2007 look remarkably different, given the absence of the aerospace division. The figures for detection and medical were both skewed by exceptional costs, but these were most significant for John Crane, where a large litigation provision largely wiped out profits for the year, even after taking account of income from the commutation of insurance policies.

Earnings per share (EPS) for the period (shown in Table 10.1), at a headline level (i.e. stripping out exceptional items) show the effect of acquiring the lower-margin TI businesses, and the time it took to bring earnings back to pre-merger levels—some six years.

Total reported earnings were significantly more volatile, particularly influenced by exceptional items such as gains and losses on businesses sold. The results of normal trading were dwarfed by the sale of TI Automotive, with a resulting goodwill write-off, producing a loss of 31 pence per share in 2001. Likewise, the high point of the exceptional £1.5bn profit on the sale of aerospace boosted earnings to 314 pence per share in 2007.

Conclusions

> *The 11 per cent surge in the share price yesterday reflected the previous undervaluation of the aerospace business, as well as a bit of rethink on the quality of the management.*
>
> (*Financial Times*, LEX[44])

Despite the fact that KB-W presided over the last few years of the 1990s, which continued to exhibit the 'purple patch' commenced under the previous management, posterity associates his term almost solely with two distinct transactions, in 2000 and 2007. If the abandonment of motor accessories in 1983 was a surprise, the veil of the temple was rent in twain, twice, by the later events. It is clear the reception for the aerospace sale was highly positive, but the TI merger was deeply unpopular with many, immediately on its announcement, and human nature dictates such a first impression is a deep and lasting one. First impressions may be deceptive, despite the fact that, at the time, both Smiths and the broader market were going through a highly volatile period. With such dramatic events—broadly doubling the size of the company in 2000, and then broadly halving it again in 2007—it is natural to ask what benefits accrued to the shareholders. Was value created or destroyed?

The TI merger involved Smiths shareholders being diluted in favour of TI shareholders, with this dilution made good by subsequent cost synergies. The scale of the immediate dilution, based on the assumption of realizing the expected £925m for TI Automotive and the most recently published 2000 profits, can be calculated at about 4 per cent. Observers who believed the former Smiths Industries businesses were of higher quality, or who doubted that the automotive business would realize £925m, would have considered the value dilution to be higher.

The progress of the share price indicates the market's judgement (see Figure 10.1, comparing Smiths' performance with a range of indices). Smiths' shares fell immediately on the announcement, and continued to drift down, to a low of £6.32 after a month—a fall of 24 per cent. A fall of such magnitude is very likely to remain in the memory, and after more than a decade it was still talked about. What is forgotten is that share price weakness persisted for a while, but by May 2001 the price climbed above pre-merger levels, even though the FTSE 100 had declined.

But this was a time of high volatility in markets and wild swings in sentiment for different sectors, with the majority of shares dropping significantly following a period noted for its 'irrational exuberance'. The benchmark revealing the market reaction most clearly is the FTSE Aerospace index—since aerospace avoided the extreme swings in telecoms and various other volatile stocks. This comparison shows an initial 20 per cent relative decline for Smiths, half of which was recovered over the next three months. The resulting 10 per cent relative decline was maintained for about a year, until progress on synergies and disposals led to the shares regaining their initial relative position during the second year.

By the second anniversary of the merger, using the share price from the day before the merger announcement as a benchmark, Smiths had outperformed the aerospace sector by a whisker, and outperformed both the FTSE 100 and the broadly based FTSE Industrial sector by 30 per cent. Overall, the share price suggests broad market approval of the steps and measures that had been taken.

Beyond the two-year point, the outlook for other industrials and for pure aerospace players improved more quickly than at Smiths, so the relative gains versus those indices in the early period were eroded. Rolling forward to the consummation of the aerospace sale and the resulting return of capital to shareholders, the comparative picture changes again. Making a simple comparison, for the period from the day before the merger announcement to the end of September 2007, following the results announcement (seven years and a few days), Smiths' shares advanced from 835p to 1069p—a gain of 28 per cent, and this after allowing for a gross provision of £142m in the 2007 accounts in relation to John Crane, Inc. litigation. Over the same period, the FTSE 100 moved from 6,417 to 6,467—a rise of just 1 per cent. But the broadly based FTSE Industrial sector had done better still, rising from 2,201 to 2,978—some 35 per cent. Measured against the broader FTSE 100, it is clear that, over the seven years, Smiths' shareholders did well.

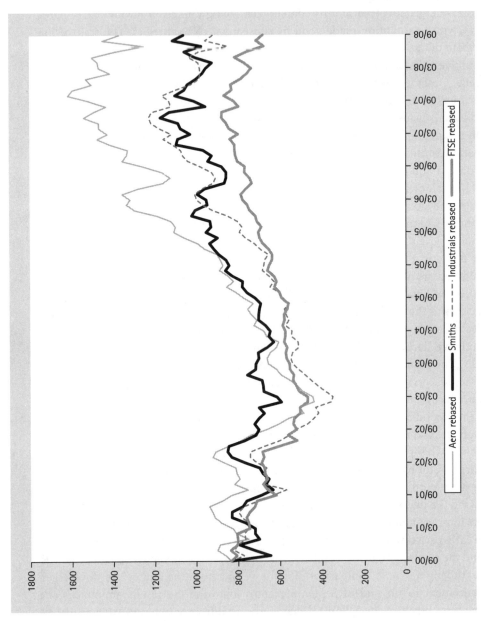

FIGURE 10.1 Smiths' share price vs. FTSE 100, FTSE Aerospace and FTSE Industrial indices, all rebased to September 2000.

Source: Smiths Group

Strictly speaking, it is true that TI shareholders benefited more over the period from their investment transforming into a holding in Smiths, but the shareholders of both original companies came out well ahead. Observers in 2007 may have equated KB-W's departure with the announced abandonment of the proposed GE detection joint venture—not realizing this represented the avoidance of a poisoned chalice. While it is exceedingly speculative to contemplate the counterfactual of a Smiths which had failed to acquire TI, the threat from the convergence of aerospace technology (and the gorillas) was most keenly felt in Smiths' original electronic systems business, and the prospects for a theoretical sale of the division in late 2006 (without the TI businesses) would have been markedly poorer.

Looking at external perspectives, Smiths had been known as a mid-sized engineering company, with a well-respected management, regarded as being conservative. It was noted—even criticized—for making cautious steps forward, and generally not spending more than £100m each year on acquisitions. It was also notably frugal in its use of debt, which stood at £285m in 2000. Growth and acquisitions had built a group with some 16,000 employees.

In one bound, this changed dramatically. The merger with TI Group took headcount immediately to 60,800, and debt mushroomed more than six-fold to £1.9bn. From then on, reorganization was intense, and new activity continued. A further thirty-three businesses were acquired, at a total cost of £1.4bn—the most significant being Heimann, which radically transformed and enhanced the detection business. Some twenty-five significant disposals were made (plus numerous other small units), with total proceeds of £4.5bn. This largely contributed to reducing employee numbers, to 21,400 in 2007, only about a third larger than in 2000. The exceptional items associated with some of the disposals severely distorted the historic track record of steadily accretive numbers in each year's accounts. Several successive restructurings were put in place, to cut costs and increase efficiencies, which themselves cost more than £200m to implement. Debt was radically reduced, closing at under £600m in 2007, while shareholders saw roughly £2.2bn flow back to them.

If this markedly altered the external aspect of the company, inside Smiths the culture changed significantly during the period of KB-W's tenure. As well as urging his management team to 'think the unthinkable' and perhaps sell core assets, he also encouraged them to accept the challenge of more risk. He recalls a message along the lines of 'I'm not going to come down on you if we try really hard for something new and it doesn't work out, but I'm sure as hell going to come down on you if we do nothing.'[45] The willingness to back the detection business proved far-sighted—developing a new diabetic pump in a market dominated by a gorilla did not work.

What of value? For the shareholders, what can be said is that the 28 per cent gain in the share price over the period was much better than many other companies achieved. Acquisitions and disposals played their part, but so did organic growth, which (stripped of the effects of currency) averaged 5 per cent over the period—a healthy achievement against a backdrop of low inflation and troubled economics at the start of the decade.

Notes

1. 9 Aug. 2004, 11.
2. Interview (16 Sept. 2013).
3. Alan Thomson, interview (8 Oct. 2013).
4. Niall Ferguson, *High Financier: The Lives and Times of Siegmund Warburg* (London: Allen Lane, 2010), 183–99.
5. ABN Amro, 'TI Group' (11 Mar. 1998).
6. *Financial Times* (15 Sept. 2000), 23.
7. Robin Budenberg, interview (20 June 2012).
8. *Financial Times* (13 Mar. 1997), 24.
9. 19 Sept. 2000, City editorial.
10. *Minutes* (14 Sept. 2000).
11. *Minutes* (26 Sept. 2000).
12. Schroders, 'TI' (18 Sept. 2000).
13. *Financial Times* (27 Nov. 2000), 20.
14. *Minutes* (13 Feb. 2001).
15. *Minutes* (14 Nov. 2000)
16. *Minutes* (13 Mar. 2001).
17. Interview (24 Sept. 2013).
18. Ferrie, interview (2013).
19. Ferrie, interview (2013).
20. Broad, interview (2013).
21. Credit Suisse, 'Smiths Group' (17 Mar. 2006).
22. Credit Suisse (7 Oct. 2002).
23. 5 Sept. 2001, 12.
24. *Minutes* (12 Mar. 2002).
25. Credit Suisse (29 Nov. 2006).
26. *Minutes* (11 Dec. 2001).
27. *Minutes* (23 Sept. 2003).
28. *Minutes* (11 Nov. 2003).
29. *Financial Times* (3 June 2004), 22.
30. *Minutes* (13 Oct. 1982).
31. Cheuvreux, 'Smiths Group' (7 Dec. 2004).
32. Credit Suisse (24 Sept. 2007).
33. 28 Sept. 2006, 46.
34. *Financial Times* (13 Nov. 2002), 26.
35. *Minutes* (26 Sept. 2006).
36. *Minutes* (16 May 2007).
37. *Minutes* (13 May 2002).
38. *Minutes* (24 Sept. 2002).
39. OEM sales, not after-market.
40. 'Smiths Industries (1973–1998)', unpublished.
41. *The Times* (1 Apr. 2004), 25 and (20 Sept.), 23.
42. *Minutes* (11 Sept. 2006).
43. Bernard Taylor, interview (16 Sept. 2013).
44. 16 Jan. 2007, 16.
45. KB-W, interview (2013).

CHAPTER 11

....

A Fortune in Change

....

Survival is an unquestionable, perhaps the ultimate, mark of success. Business history has often been accused of being a 'success story' discipline, of being primarily interested in companies which have survived to the present day and celebrate the event with an appropriate jubilee volume.

(Cassis, *Big Business*[1])

WHILE Cassis goes on to point out business history has long since moved on, this is clearly just such a jubilee volume—and it is likely that long surviving companies will continue to mark major milestones in this way. But having surveyed sixteen decades of history and more, and having charted some of the main features in the Smiths landscape, it is natural to pose a few broader questions. In considering the history of entrepreneurs and the social sciences, Leslie Hannah pointed out that the occupational hazard of the business historian is to descend into anecdote, and the foregoing text is no exception. But there is a role for the single company monograph in providing evidence to support broader conclusions that are otherwise dependent on large assemblages of data. Perhaps most useful are those specific company stories that do not fit broader patterns and which give us cause for more thought.[2]

So at a simple level, we can ask if the particular story of Smiths supports or runs counter to any themes of broader business history scholarship, and vice versa whether any wider observations on relevant business types help to illuminate the Smiths story further? In this more reflective chapter, I begin by sketching the stages through which the enterprise passed. Building on this, I discuss the topic of the 'family' business and the transition to a managerial enterprise, highlighting the strengths and weaknesses of the family element in the business. This leads to a discussion of the main features of Smiths' culture, and the way this influenced and shaped the management of the company, using a 'social intelligence' that was an aspect of the family culture. A discussion of conglomeracy follows, and the evidence the Smiths example offers for its legitimacy as a model. It will be seen that Smiths often fits within general patterns observable across British industry, but it also offers occasional and interesting differences from the norm. Overall, the inevitability of yet further change is emphasized, as Smiths continues to pursue shareholder value.

The first century and a half

I think it is especially pleasing that a company which started life in the Victorian era as a small family-run business should have evolved and adapted to changing circumstances so successfully.

(Roger Hurn, 75th anniversary address)

The history of the company falls into four broad phases: (i) the second half of the nineteenth century; (ii) and (iii) the two halves of the twentieth; and (iv) the period since the TI merger. Appendix II offers a simple visual guide to the growth of various business lines over the company's life. The first period was the most distinct and different from the others, and belongs very much in the world of the family business—focused in the world of retail jewellery, with a small staff, and two generations of single entrepreneurial owner/managers who were successful in growing a business, in both status and income. It appears clear that Samuel Smith (junior) succeeded in accumulating substantial material wealth for himself and his immediate family, signified most obviously by the grand properties and domestic staff he and his children enjoyed. He had the typically dynastic ambitions of the head of a successful family enterprise, in which his sons would carry on and grow the retail jewellery empire he had established. His own path had taken him from the Elephant and Castle to the West End of London, and his vision stretched much further, for example to the Far East, where operations were commenced in Siam. With four sons, succession must have seemed assured, but plans did not unfold as expected. The two eldest sons, born into luxury, were soon to disappoint in a business sense, but by marked contrast, the third proved to have all the qualities needed to perpetuate the family business, though the direction in which he chose to take it was probably another source of family conflict.

Allan Gordon-Smith (as he became), like his elder brothers, certainly acquired a taste for the high life from a wealthy upbringing, but a more important and vital trait, keenly observable in a school record of intense overachievement, was his intensely competitive spirit. Whether or not the short period of watchmaking training in Switzerland was his father's idea, or perhaps his own, it exerted a long-term influence over his life, providing a source of important network relationships, crucial in later life—a strong networking ability was what would now be called a core competence of this intensely clubbable man.

Allan Gordon-Smith's ascendancy as the principal controlling mind of the company from the early years of the century marks the second phase of the company's history—which he was to dominate. It is unclear what his motives were for the radical move from retailing to the formation of an entire, vertically integrated manufacturing business, doing everything from making to selling motor instruments, and we are therefore regrettably left with speculation, but there are some possible clues to the influences involved. It is unlikely that he was influenced directly by developments in motor-car manufacture, since the impact of the moving assembly line method of production (e.g. Ford at Trafford Park) only became apparent after Smiths'

Speedometer House was already in operation. More likely he was aware that the historic craft methods of watch production, previously standard in Switzerland and the UK, had been supplanted by the volume production methods of Waltham in the United States. The Swiss had paid attention, and Gordon-Smith will have seen at first hand in his short sojourn in Biel the resultant transformation, with the wholesale adoption of standardized and mechanized methods by the Swiss. Back in London, and now selling speedometers, it may thus have been Gordon-Smith that influenced Robert Benson North, his supplier, to build a new factory in Watford. Whichever way, it was clear from early on that demand for speedometers would vastly outstrip the capacity of the Clerkenwell craft-based system. Gordon-Smith must then have realized by 1912 that he had an opportunity to grow a business substantially beyond the scale of anything Robert Benson North could help him with, and hence arrived at the decision to become a manufacturer in his own right.

Whatever the original motivations and inspirations for this strategy, the Great War altered everything. When the firm was floated, ceding half the ownership to the public, there would very likely have been a plan to retain family control of both equity and management. Any such plan had failed within months, with successive capital raisings causing ownership to pass nearly entirely out of the family—though crucially not control. Over the course of a short space of time, the company increased in scale by an order of magnitude to meet the demands of munitions production.

Emerging from the war, ambitious plans forged in the heat of the post-war boom rapidly placed the company in serious difficulties through over-indebtedness, and it would be several years before the company would once again control its own destiny and devise a new strategy. That post-war need to pay down debt significantly, in order to return to equilibrium, anticipates the early 2000s, when post-TI merger net debt hit a peak (see Figure 11.5).

It was in the late 1920s that one can see the next transformation of Smiths. The Edwardian shift had been from retail to vertically integrated manufacturer. The transformation during the Jazz Age would involve the stripping out of non-core businesses (notably factoring, magneto, and vehicle lighting manufacture) and a tighter focus on mainstream products, as well as a new business in clocks—effectively the creation of an entirely new UK industry. It was achieved with the close cooperation and support of Allan Gordon-Smith's Swiss friends—though within a few years this effort took on a public policy slant in the context of national interest, as part of the 1930s rearmament effort.

Whereas the Great War was a shock that transformed the company unexpectedly, the long build-up to the Second World War meant much planning was involved. Indeed Smiths' management was likely aware of the militaristic backdrop to the efforts of Black Forest industry from relatively early on—perhaps as early as 1933, although this deserves more research in its own right. With an early involvement in promoting the Territorial Army, building shadow factories, and supplying equipment and mater-iel, the company's development was shaped to match government requirements, before, during, and then after the Second World War, when close relationships had been forged between senior management and important officials in the new Labour government. The post-war creation of new factories in the development areas of Wales and Scotland supported public policy goals of promoting employment in troubled locations, in addition to which the incremental business was geared chiefly to the export of goods and the earning of valuable foreign currency.

Rubinstein talks of this post-war period demonstrating a lack of British entrepreneurship, when it failed 'to capitalize on the strong position she enjoyed as a manufacturing nation ... following 1945 when most of Europe and Japan were first in total ruin and then rebuilding'.[3] Smiths' particular example offers a further perspective, since account needs to be taken of changing foreign policy goals towards Germany. Smiths was at the heart of immediate post-war planning for the dismantling of German industry—its key staff toured Germany as part of crucial working parties—but though French interests were advanced significantly with the systematic looting of Black Forest machine tools, such locations fell outside the British Zone.[4] From an instinctive aim to advance British industry at the expense of Germany, policy shifted, encouraged by eloquent liberal opinion, and by 1947 the importance of the reconstruction of Germany worked against measures that would have allowed British firms such as Smiths to achieve any sustainable advantage. In the long run, all Western mechanical clockmaking industries would be dead, but the Black Forest clockmakers enjoyed a post-war recovery which contrasted strongly with the experience of their British counterparts.

Hope for a new Jerusalem continued to fade further—after enduring the pre-war dumping of German clocks, the post-war period led not only to renewed German competition but then large-scale dumping from countries such as Hungary. Smiths' main goal was to export, but despite being the gorilla of the UK clock industry, it was hamstrung by wider market distortions.

The third phase of Smith's history, after Allan Gordon-Smith's death and from the 1950s onward, saw the end of export dominance by the UK motor industry—an industry in which Smiths' fortunes, as a supplier, were determined by those of the assemblers. After a brief period as the world's largest vehicle exporter, the thirty-year decline in the British motor industry is a story that has been well-documented, and there is therefore a degree of inevitability to the end of Smiths' involvement. An involvement in aerospace, by contrast, grew to become the mainstay of the company's business in the latter part of the twentieth century, indeed through to 2007.

In one of the most important examples of the role of serendipity in Smiths' fortunes, a first step towards its wider diversification was made in 1958 with Uni-Tubes' apparently unauthorized purchase of Portland Plastics, thus bringing a medical business into the group. Taking steps to deal with the decline of its primary business lines, and against an unfavourable economic backdrop, Dick Cave then presided over further diversification from 1970, with the move into wholesale motor accessory trading and factoring—even the establishment of a high-street retail presence (thereby reversing the trend of the 1920s when Smiths had exited those markets). From the 1970s the systems and organization were put in place to support a diversified conglomerate, not only operating in the UK but beginning to expand significantly on an international basis.

Cave can therefore be said to have sowed the seeds of the conglomerate business that survives to this day. What has grown most strikingly is the proportion of staff employed outside the UK, which after many years of running at between 5 and 10 per cent started to increase and most recently reached a level of 92 per cent (see Figure 11.1). In dropping its increasingly unprofitable involvement in sectors such as the motor industry, and the clock and watch industry, the firm was better able to focus on activities with better growth prospects—in aerospace, health, and specialist engineering. In the case of aerospace, the firm concentrated particularly from the 1980s on expanding into the US. This was at a time when the perceived wisdom suggested UK companies did not prosper in the US, but as we saw in Chapter 8, Hurn believed its free enterprise environment offered substantial advantages versus a European backdrop of restrictive practices.

Having enjoyed significant growth in the 1990s, and adding new businesses which made a large contribution to earnings, the company was nevertheless subscale in a number of its markets—in other words it did not have, in all its divisions, the size of operation and/or market share to ensure sustained growth. The solution, taken by a new team of managers, was the bold step of merging with TI in 2000—a watershed that defines the commencement of the fourth and most recent phase of the overall history. This has obviously seen a large change in the range of businesses, but more fundamentally a new approach to the selection and ownership of business lines—a subtle change has meant that rather than running a strategy of essentially 'buy-and-hold', Smiths now assesses whether or not it is the best owner of any given business. Thus, while the 1980s disposal of the motor business was largely inevitable, the disposal of the aerospace business in 2007 was not forced by immediate circumstance, but was nevertheless judged to be the best strategic move for shareholders. This stemmed from an analysis that aerospace technologies were converging, favouring the largest players in the market, capable of supplying fully integrated systems. Smiths currently enjoyed a privileged supplier status with the airframe companies, but it had only a small part of the jigsaw. Nevertheless, given the value this would have for others still assembling their integrated offerings, the logical step was to realize the potential premium value—spectacularly achieved through a sale of some 37 per cent of the company's activity at a price equal to just over 50 per cent of its market capitalization, bringing to a close the events covered in this volume.

Having thus surveyed the history at speed, it is instructive to consider a few long-term statistics and metrics which illuminate elements of the story. The increasing size of the company's business appears most simply in nearly a century's growth in turnover, adjusted for inflation (see Figure 11.2).

While the Great War had a profound effect on the management of the company, it is clear that the scale of the business was really transformed from the outbreak of the Second World War. From then on, dips in the figure show the influences of wider political and economic events. The downward trend from the mid-1970s to the latter part of the 1980s reflects the downturn in the motor industry and then the cutting back of activity in the firm through disposals. The acquisition of the Lear Siegler businesses

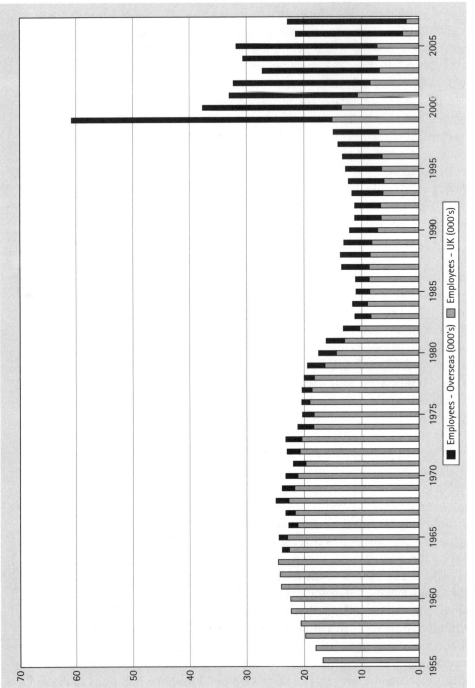

FIGURE 11.1 Smiths' staff numbers (UK and overseas) 1955–2008.

Source: annual reports

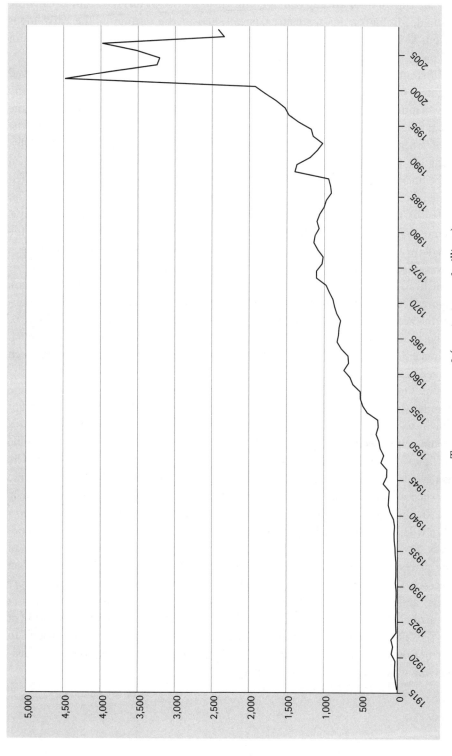

FIGURE 11.2 Turnover 1915–2008 (constant 2010 £millions).
Source: annual reports (NB 1920–55 estimated, based on debtors)

in 1987 are shown dramatically with a commensurate rise in turnover, but equally the unfortunate timing of the acquisition is reflected in the decline of the early 1990s recession. This was followed by the 'purple patch' of the 1990s, and then the drama of the TI merger, and subsequent disposals that followed.

A different picture emerges in considering the margin the company achieved throughout the period. In Figure 11.3 we can see the dramatic slump of the early 1920s when the firm had to restructure its capital, having lost so much money in the bust that followed on the brief post-war boom. Recovery was rapid however, and on the back of strong contracts with Morris and others, margins widened substantially, allowing the financing of the growth of the business into new areas, without a need for debt financing. Again, wider political and economic events make themselves felt (e.g. the 1920s depression and the Second World War), but there is a distinct period indicated by the graph that could well qualify to be called a 'golden age' for Smiths. There are distortions in the late 1940s figures, but after a peak in the mid-1950s the figures show the declining margins being earned in the motors and clock businesses. This was offset with the addition and growth of higher margin activities in the 1970s (e.g. medical) and then with the disposal of low-margin and loss-making businesses, the figures for the latter half of the 1980s were boosted. The graph similarly demonstrates the acquisition of higher margin businesses in the 1990s. The marked drop for 2000 illustrates the acquisition of what were initially low-margin TI businesses, which were then either disposed of, or improved, leading to an upward trend, which has been continued since.

Finally, Figure 11.4 examines the performance of Smiths' share price against the FTSE index (or near equivalent) from 1951 to 2007. This amply illustrates the significant growth in value throughout the 1950s (with a wobble, stemming from car industry misfortune), followed by a relatively flat, though inconsistent, performance in the 1960s, following the market closely, largely responding to 'stop-go' economics. The market events of the 1970s which most directly affected the motor trade, with external events such as the oil-price shock, and then the crisis of British Leyland, are clearly shown. In the entire sixty-year period of the graph, this era demonstrates the most significant loss of value, leading to the company's abandonment of much of its core business. The long positive run to the turn of the century is punctuated by the effects of issuing shares in 1987 to pay for the Lear Siegler units, the stock market crash, and then the recession of the early 1990s, in which the aerospace sector (now Smiths' core business) suffered in particular—though it was results from the aerospace division that contributed strongly to two clear periods of out-performance. With the addition of strong selection in acquisitions made throughout the 1990s, performance through to the turn of the century saw the zenith of the long-standing model of bolt-on acquisition, giving way to a new era, post-TI merger.

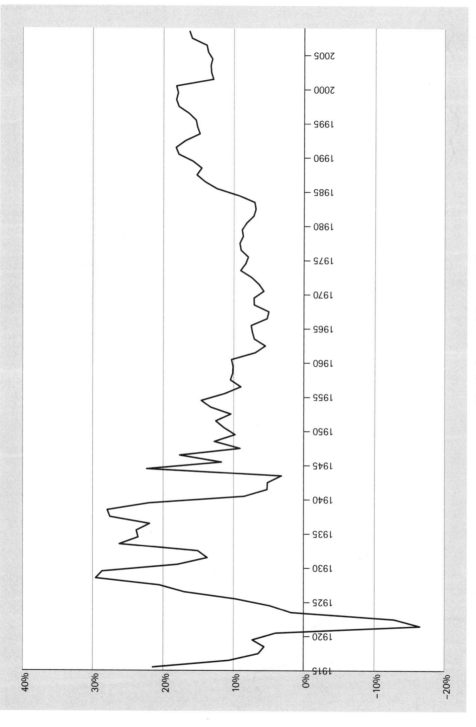

FIGURE 11.3 Margin (per cent) (1915–2008).
Source: annual reports

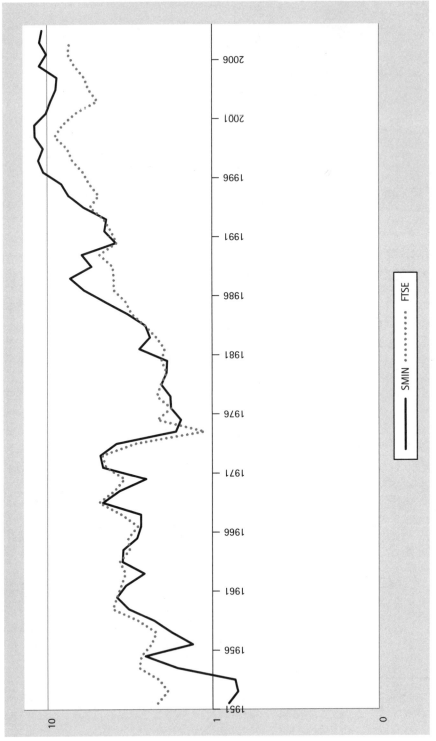

FIGURE 11.4 Smiths' share price (rebased to 1960) vs. FTSE all share index (constant 2010 £, log-scale) (1951–2007).

Source: SMAA, Global Financial Data

Smiths—the 'family business'

Mr Ralph Gordon Smith joined the company on 29 August [1927]. Previously he had spent two years with Whitehill, Marsh in London and Birmingham; a year with Kodak; a course of motoring mechanics; some six months in the Talbot factory in Suresnes (France) and a shorter period with the Paris Agency ... mainly spent in selling KLG plugs in North Africa.

(Cann[5])

How much of an issue was it that Smiths started as a family business? And how did the transition to what Chandler characterized as a 'managerial enterprise' take place? Once the company had done so, was there nevertheless any broader notion of 'family' that survived the transition and which was of significance in the continued development of the company? Did the pace of transition to a managerial enterprise hold back the development of a functional management hierarchy or a viable multi-divisional structure for the company, as might be expected under a typically Chandlerian characterization of British industry? These are all interesting questions, the answers to which illuminate further characteristics of the company.

Though the family lost any meaningful ownership through dilution very soon after the 1914 flotation, it did not lose managerial control for at least another forty years, if not longer, although there was pressure from the banks to add non-executive directors from the 1920s. The transition to a combination of both public ownership and professional management was not standard, because although the family (very largely through Allan Gordon-Smith) derived a large income from the company, it was not in the traditional form (i.e. dividends) but through a remarkably privileged set of financial arrangements, which allowed for substantial discretionary bonuses and a preferred ability to make valuable sales of intellectual property to the company. In a common path from family business to managerial enterprise, there is a divorce between ownership and control, with the family retaining an appreciable equity participation (or shares with some preferential treatment), while the increasing complexity of corporate operation necessitates layers of salaried middle managers who effectively secure significant control. Allan Gordon-Smith, by contrast, engineered the opposite—since without equity he both retained supreme executive authority and an income stream sufficient to fund a lavish lifestyle, complete with country estates, a string of racehorses, and all the trappings of wealth. At the same time, he was not a distant manager, but remained involved at the heart of business travel, client negotiation, and the winning of new business.

Explanations of this state of affairs are likely to focus on the force of his dominant personality, and the correctness of a vision for the future of the motor industry, but must also recognize the value of the network which he did so much to foster—combining elements such as the master salesman, Charles Nichols, who delivered the critically important Morris contracts; P. O. Dorer and other technicians who delivered new inventions and designs; Hubert Marsh the accountant, who steered the finances of the firm; and Frederick Szarvasy, the *éminence grise* who influenced the company's banking relationships, among many others.

When the company faced near-death in the early 1920s through mistimed expansion and consequent crippling indebtedness, the extensive efforts of this combined network allowed a recovery to the point where the business was generating substantial cash, sufficient to fund a new wave of more profitably directed expansion. This experience of the 1920s allows for discussion of the first of two weaknesses that are commonly ascribed to family businesses—an inherent and hobbling resistance to innovation and change, potentially leading to an erosion of market position as more dynamic competitors evolve and develop.

At one level, the difficult recovery from 1921 to 1927 appears to have led to a significant conservatism in financial management thereafter—the high margins of the late 1920s (see Figure 11.3) led to surpluses in the late 1920s that were converted into sizeable reserves. It meant the firm recovered from being heavily indebted to being net cash positive by 1927—a position that was then maintained through to the Second World War, despite the development of new business lines, the construction of new factories, and the substantial expansion of the business (see Figure 11.5).

A charge of financial conservatism is well supported on the evidence. But in terms of entrepreneurial dynamism, the Smiths' story offers a contrast. Allan Gordon-Smith remained a pioneering spirit throughout his life, gathering around him inventors and engineers that would propel the company's business forward—adding innovative aircraft instruments (e.g. the automatic pilot) and devising and growing a new clock and watch industry, as well as constantly developing new motor accessory products. That the team was close-knit is evidenced further by the share those engineers took in the income from selling their joint patents to the company—in a curious hybrid arrangement that bridged between the Schumpeterian inventor/entrepreneur and the in-house R&D laboratory. While a family-controlled business, Smiths did not stand still in terms of research and development, or product development.

A second common flaw of family businesses relates to managerial succession, owing to the limited pool from which leaders may be drawn and a potential lack of natural talent or ability. Here Smiths offers a more conventional example of the problems of family enterprise. Samuel junior had already proved himself to be dynamic in taking his father's jewellery business up-market and growing it substantially by the 1870s and he was the natural successor. His continued success led in turn to dynastic consider-ations, and I suggested the influences on his thinking in Chapter 2. Incorporation formed part of the strategy, but it was obvious that Samuel junior expected his sons to follow him into the business. The elder two were to disappoint him. Evocative of the 'third generation' or Buddenbrook's syndrome, these wealthy and probably spoiled young men chose different paths. It is striking that both, having married and had children, tried building new lives in distant parts (Canada and New Zealand), breaking up their families through adulterous affairs in the process—just the sort of dissolute behaviour the syndrome anticipates.

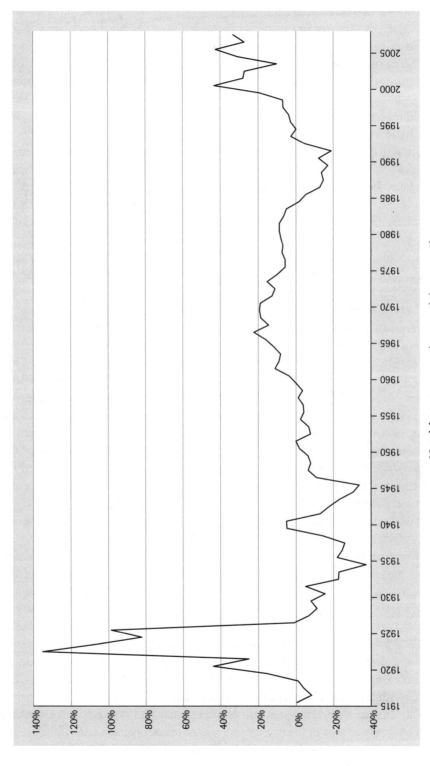

FIGURE 11.5 Net debt to turnover (per cent) (1915–2008).

Source: annual reports

Samuel junior had taken steps to provide some early training in the business, with his eldest son Herbert placed in a responsible role in the West End shops alongside one of the most experienced of Samuel's senior staff, but the main feature of this episode was a notorious jewel theft, reported around the world. The experience with the third son, the future Allan Gordon-Smith, was quite different. Forcing the early abandonment of watchmaking training in Switzerland, Samuel brought his third son home and installed him at the heart of the business, delegating substantial responsibility, and being rewarded with notable success for the firm at the next two international expositions. Here was a son whose vision and energy stretched far beyond that of the father, with the result the business soon began a large transformation, of both scope and scale, from retail jeweller to motor accessory manufacturer. If he is correctly identified as representing the third generation running the family firm then, by contrast with his older brothers, Allan Gordon-Smith turns on its head the classically articulated Buddenbrook's syndrome, since, even stripping away the natural hagiography of corporate memory, his tenure at the helm saw Smiths' successful emergence as a major force in UK light engineering—but the 'third generation' syndrome of failure has in any event been extensively challenged as a concept.[6]

When in turn Allan Gordon-Smith came to consider the succession issue, he faced a problem. As with his own experience, as was standard across UK commerce, university training was not the norm. Instead he arranged for Ralph, his only son, to receive a wide training within parts of the group, in various external companies, and also, interestingly at Marsh Whitehill, the accountants—mindful no doubt of the critical role Hubert Marsh had played in rescuing the company in the 1920s and guiding its financial management thereafter. Yet father and son apparently did not get on well, with Allan Gordon-Smith favouring Rex, his nephew—apparently most like him in character—leading to family frictions. Thus, despite a nominal handing over of the reins of power to Ralph during the war, as the minutes make clear, Allan Gordon-Smith attended every board meeting and continued to run the company, despite any public presentation otherwise.

Predictably, when he died in 1951, there was no effective succession plan. Though Ralph was officially managing director, and had enjoyed an early and diverse exposure to a range of other businesses, he was ineffectual and had none of the drive and vision which had propelled the company forward under his father—it was a failure of the fourth generation in this particular case, not the third—though not through dissolute behaviour, simply a lack of entrepreneurial flair and authority. Instead, through a lack of leadership, Ralph allowed two powerful managerial factions to develop, divided not only over issues of power but over fundamental issues of business philosophy—whether to centralize or decentralize, at its heart a conflict between outdated and modern modes of management. This led to a wasteful and divisive leadership struggle in the mid-1960s, the resolution of which robbed Smiths of important talent. The battles fought for power beneath Ralph finally decided the new path of succession, with the rise of Dick Cave, and the company finally moved in the late 1960s from technically being a family business to being a managerial enterprise—but very likely not having met its full potential over much of the interval since Allan Gordon-Smith's death.

However, the extended transition from a family business had not hindered the creation of a functional managerial hierarchy, nor the division of the firm into a multi-divisional structure. Back in 1944, and in a clear manifesto for post-war operation, the existing structure, which already contained a series of separately arranged and managed units, was formally restructured into four distinct divisions, each with its own management hierarchy, responsible via tiers of managers to a divisional director, represented on the board. The formality of the structure was probably influenced by Allan Gordon-Smith's wartime experience in the Ministry of Aircraft Production—which he nominally left to rejoin Smiths coincidentally in 1944—and by his close friend, the minister responsible, Stafford Cripps, who was at the forefront of urging factory modernization, and a scientific drive for efficiency and better management.[7] Thus while Smiths was still in the phase where it would have been firmly regarded both internally and externally as a family company, it nevertheless adopted the machinery of the modern enterprise—another small example supporting Hannah's observation on Chandler's 'curiously implausible notion that Britons proved serially incapable of developing or managing professional management hierarchies'.[8]

The rise of the extended family

After Marlborough and a two-year apprenticeship at Rolls-Royce—'the move from public school to night school at Crewe Technical College was quite a culture shock'—he joined his father in 1958 at Smiths Industries.

(*Evening Standard*[9])

Despite the waning of Smith family influence, nevertheless the network that had grown up under first Allan and then Ralph Gordon-Smith's tenures continued to flourish and to be the source of a continuing management framework and pathway for succession. Frank Hurn, who joined the company in 1919, had long been the driving force and dominant controlling mind of the motor accessories division—the largest part of the company's business—and therefore the source of power and influence. Dick Cave had joined at the end of the Second World War through a Hurn family introduction, and though Ralph may have been wavering at the very top, succession planning in the powerful motor accessories division in the early 1960s was well under way, and it was explicit by 1962 that Cave was to succeed Hurn in charge.

The pathway for Frank Hurn's son Roger originally commenced as an apprenticeship at Rolls Royce—widely regarded as a solid career foundation—though the young Hurn discovered after a couple of years that he was not cut out to be an engineer. But making the transfer into Smiths allowed him to play to his strengths in languages, and also satisfied a liking for international postings and travel, offering useful early sales experience. Another important early experience was being sent by Dick Cave to Harvard Business School on an intensive training course, in exports, an experience Hurn found useful in benchmarking himself against others with educational qualifications he lacked, having come up by a different route.

Being sent on any kind of management training to Harvard had not been the norm for Smiths management, where leadership development followed a fairly traditional pattern, and this prompts a momentary diversion into the issue of education and training, and the question of how the business leaders of Smiths were educated over time, and whether there were changes. Cassis commented in 1997 'there is little doubt left about the narrow social recruitment of business élites' and described the debunking of 'myths of spectacular social mobility offered by business life'.[10] The early pattern of leadership succession at Smiths falls squarely in Cassis's description of family capitalism, but its later managers offer some counterpoint to the conclusion the overwhelming majority of 'business leaders have been recruited among the privileged classes'.

In the case of Samuel junior, who had very little formal education, he nevertheless achieved significant wealth, and followed a well-trodden path in sending his sons to public school—Christ's College Finchley. He expected them all to follow him into the family business, but as we have seen, the elder two took other paths. Allan Gordon-Smith's competitive nature and personal interests give rise to another comment. On the wider business history front, Berghoff and Rubinstein have rebutted the arguments advanced by Wiener, Coleman, et al. that public school, humanities-oriented education played a role in hindering the economic growth of the UK, but a feature of that education little mentioned in the literature is that of sport. Allan Gordon-Smith was intensely competitive—his school career was defined by his sporting prowess, and then his business life was woven around a continued involvement in, or promotion of, sport, whether football matches between shop and factory (with him playing—as a successful centre forward, naturally) or myriad sporting tournaments, clubs, and fixtures arranged by the firm from the 1920s onwards. The social character of Smiths, which I move on to discuss, was no doubt significantly shaped by Allan Gordon-Smith, who was in turn influenced by an education with a strong sports emphasis—if Wiener were correct that 'few future businessmen emerged from these [public] schools', Gordon-Smith offers one example, at least.[11]

In general, the educational pattern for Smiths' management was standard for British industry. A few—some who were marked out early for possible advancement—shared with the Smith family the training of a highly regarded public school (e.g. Roger Hurn at Marlborough and Marcus Beresford at Harrow), but it appears Philip Bowman, CEO from 2007, was the first to run Smiths having completed a university degree before entering industry. Before him, a long succession of leaders all started their careers straight from school, albeit frequently in apprenticeship schemes that provided excellent technical educations (e.g. Roy Sisson at Hawker's, Roger Hurn at Rolls Royce, and KB-W at Ford), and in the case of Dick Cave on a foreshortened wartime degree course at Cambridge which he did not complete.

From the death of Allan Gordon-Smith in 1951, through to the 1990s, the issue of succession of executives at Smiths was very largely handled through in-house promotion of long-standing employees. This did eventually change, and ties in to wider issues of the company's culture.

Smiths: the culture of the family

You know that I am a man who is tremendously keen on fostering the
family spirit. Given this, it does not matter what product you are making
. . . whatever comes along you have the ability to succeed.

(Ben Haviland, Smiths dinner and dance, 1938)[12]

Continuing with the notion of family and the rhetoric associated with it, it is relatively easy to find examples of companies either where management was internally highly regarded, or alternatively held in low esteem. One does not need to look further than the British motor industry of the 1970s to find examples of the latter. In the most unionized and militant environments, the notion of family did not extend vertically, but merely horizontally—everyone was a 'brother', and it was less appropriate to talk in terms of paternalism or of a familial relationship between the company and the employee. By the 1970s, a wholesale shift in attitudes had seen the workers' earlier position as stakeholders in a company erode significantly, as the interests of shareholders advanced.

While Smiths did not escape this entirely—and Miriam Glucksmann's *Women on the Line* makes this clear for Cricklewood in the late 1970s—nevertheless the company had succeeded over several decades in creating and sustaining a deeply paternal environment—yes, there was still unionization, and some of the same disputes, but as Gil Jones, former industrial relations director, pointed out, Smiths escaped remarkably lightly in his time (1970s/1980s), and the evidence right back to the General Strike is one of only relatively moderate industrial unrest. That Eddy Downey should recall colleagues bursting into tears across the factories when Gordon-Smith's horse fell in the 1950 Grand National speaks volumes of the relationship between the shop-floor and management and the stakeholder culture the company had fostered in the middle part of the century.

How else did this broader sense of family express itself? What was the language of aggregation that meant Smiths employees thought in terms of 'we' not 'me' and how was a valuable sense of belonging instilled? This came in part from the huge emphasis on sports (both in-house but also in local leagues), social clubs, group outings, summer holiday camps, the wartime Hard Luck Fund, the Isle of Wight rest home, suggestion boxes in the factories that offered significant prizes for winning contributions (a Mini car on one occasion), beauty competitions, annual dinners, long-service awards, features in the in-house publications covering business units around the world or writing up the stories of 'old-timers' with decades of service behind them (serving to cement as well the company's long heritage). All these features of everyday Smiths life built a strong sense of belonging, something that continued in retirement—another regular feature of in-house publications was the letter from a retiree, looking back on marvellous times, missing the camaraderie. Even in the twenty-first century, long after the closure of Smiths' motor accessories operations (some thirty years past), the 2000 Club still exists to bring retirees back together again regularly. Similarly, former employees in Cheltenham, Wishaw, and around the old geography of the former Smiths Industries, continue to meet—a noticeable characteristic of the retirees being a fierce loyalty to the company and a deep pride in the company's products. It was of course possible for some newcomers to join the company at later stages of their careers and to be adopted into the family, but it is also noticeable that on occasions this clearly did not work—witness Joan Berry's comment on Bill Mallinson in Chapter 8 that 'he never really fitted in, not having come up through Smiths', or Roger Hurn's comment that 'the normal corporate rejection process sets in' when people did not quite fit, such as the specialists brought in by Dick Cave in the 1970s to help run the motor factor businesses.[13]

The 2000 Club's continued existence is testament to a spirit built throughout the twentieth century, through to the third quarter at least, but the ethos of the company will have started to change from then on—from the Dick Cave era. 'Cutting out the fat', as Gil Jones called it, involved dismantling the physical structures that embodied the 'sports and social' element of Smiths—selling the sports grounds, cricket pavilions, and letting go the green-keepers. The social lives of employees earlier in the century included significant time for the company and activities with fellow workers—something that was gradually eroded in tandem with rising standards of living and changing patterns of leisure time. The character of the workplace changed, though this varied widely among the different locations. In Cricklewood, the vision of hell articulated by Miriam Glucksmann's study offers a stark portrait of 1970s mass production assembly lines, and an organizational structure characterized not by familial language but simply by 'us and them'. By contrast, the sense of family and a strong camaraderie survived to the end in locations such as Wishaw. In Chapter 8 we heard about the frequent evenings out, the running of an in-house hairdresser's, and the pride taken by the women in being the best turned out of any of the regional factory workers—as the secretary of the local history society commented, 'you had a better class of girl at Smiths Wishaw'.

Another contrast became clear as a result of an appeal for information to ex-Wishaw employees. Letters made a point of describing not only the strong collegiate spirit of the workforce, but also the fact Smiths paid the best wages locally—a comment echoed in contact from retirees associated with other UK locations around the group. This view from the shop-floor contrasts in part with Glucksmann's assessment from Cricklewood (she rated the wages as relatively low), but also runs counter to a message that came across clearly from more than two dozen former senior managers that were interviewed. Almost to a man (and they were all men), the phrase emerged identically—'Smiths were never a good payer'. The impression left is that, as careers advanced in Smiths, managers did not necessarily attract the rewards they believed were attainable elsewhere in comparable UK industrial firms. It could be argued, of course, that one reason for the relatively collegiate atmosphere in many parts of Smiths was influenced by this combination of, on the one hand, higher wages for shop-floor workers and extensive non-monetary benefits, and on the other, relatively low wages for senior managers, which led to a less polarized community in terms of economic reward and perception of collective interest. But again, this is a topic which deserves its own and further research.

Information flows

I don't think anybody ever really knows why a particular team comes together and works—but you know whether it does or doesn't. And we were very fortunate in that our team did gel, and one of the big advantages of working so closely with people . . . was that you developed an instinctive feel for one another's reaction.

(Roger Hurn, 1998)

A crucial element of any managerial enterprise is that set of various mechanisms by which information and signals travel through the organization and influence decision-taking and management practice. Some of these are entirely standard and formulaic, but others are informal and depend significantly on the particular culture of the organization.

At a formal level of monitoring performance, the two Samuels who ran the early retail business of Smiths probably had a good understanding of their business at any time—knowing the state of the cash book and their inventory. They will have known all their staff personally and met them regularly. By contrast, after the Great War, with thousands of newly arrived workers, the situation was entirely different. With a large factory in Cricklewood, it becomes clear from the minutes that the management relied heavily on its external accountant to understand the company's finances—in his absence, finance was not discussed, and it is obvious the financial reporting system largely revolved around Hubert Marsh himself. It was he who largely saved the day in the early 1920s—both through offering advice on management of the balance sheet but also mediating with the banks. Significant internal accounting mechanisms were clearly developed over time, but at the same time there is a suspicion that these reporting systems were not properly effective until Colin Proctor arrived as chief accountant after the Second World War.

With Proctor's arrival on the board in the early 1960s, an emphasis on improving the quality of financial data emerged, yet despite Alan Hornsby describing Proctor as 'one of my heroes at Smiths' it is clear it was ultimately Hornsby himself who significantly improved standards. With the move by Dick Cave to diversify the business by acquisitions in new sectors, yet to retain businesses as separate entities, the requirement for high-quality management reporting increased significantly. If Smiths' success thereafter reflected in part the successful running of a range of diverse, unique, and segregated businesses, this depended in great measure on the quality of the systems for (i) ensuring adequate analysis of the business prior to acquisition and (ii) adequate oversight and financial reporting thereafter. As described in Chapter 8, the enhancement and promotion of what Hornsby refers to as the 'corporate finance function' was his chief contribution. Which is not to say that financial analysis supplanted all other evaluative tools—the personal element of business remained critical, and it is notable that several interviewees discussed potential acquisitions being abandoned not because the numbers did not stack up, but because there was a sense the owners of the target business might not fit the Smiths' ethos.

This touches on the theme of 'social intelligence', one particular aspect of the notion of 'family' but of use in a managerial sense. Smiths was not uncommon in having members of staff who spent their entire careers in the company. The tight management team that particularly characterizes the 1980s/1990s offers a particularly good example of what John Thompson argued was the advantage of a properly managed and diversified business—the ability for the best candidates from the far reaches of the corporate empire to make it up the ladder, to reach the centre, and indeed the top of the organization. With Thompson called to London from Technical Sales in Coventry, Ron Williams brought to London from Anglo-Celtic in Wales, and George Kennedy brought to London from Portex, led by Roger Hurn, who had travelled extensively and worked as export manager for various elements in the business, a team was forged over many years of growing up together. It knew its own strengths and weaknesses, and through close attention to detail it had far-reaching and deep knowledge of both the people and the nature of the separate companies of the conglomerate, controlled from the centre. The long-developed social intelligence meant the team knew what levers were available to exercise management. There was an ability to interpret what the financial statements from subsidiaries really meant—what the rhetoric of middle management revealed or attempted to hide—aided by the inheritors of Hornsby's mantle (e.g. Wenzerul and Flowerday) who had their own ways of unravelling what was happening in the business.

One of the metaphors mentioned in Chapter 9 was that of the castle—the Finchley Road office—with all the barons inside. The company has moved on from this model, partly through design, and partly through its unsustainability. The maintenance over the long term of the same culture depended on replacement managers of the right age, available to progress through the system, and in the case of the board there was a clustering of retirement ages falling in the second half of the 1990s. Unable to repeat the process of bringing leaders in from the periphery to the centre, the fundamental management culture of Smiths was transformed as the 1990s came to an end, first with a new CEO, Keith Butler-Wheelhouse, drafted in from the wider public company market, and then the heads of the various divisions, similarly recruited from industry, all over the space of a short number of years.

With the rapid pace of acquisitions that characterized the 1990s, it was also the case that a large percentage of the company's staff would in any event be new to the Smiths' 'culture'. There was the factor of a growing internationalization as well, with the staff spread over a more diverse geography. There was therefore a transformation, from a period in which the board could tap into a deep social intelligence and long-standing tacit knowledge to understand both people and businesses around the group, to a new era in which the board comprised a team of professional managers whose careers had been developed elsewhere, running a diversified conglomerate in which many of the companies had themselves only joined the group in the relatively recent past.

While there were some prima-facie disadvantages to losing a long-standing store of management knowledge, there were nonetheless gains to be had. Some of these relate to a changing attitude to the overall stewardship of a diversified group, and introduce another important theme—the value and legitimacy of the conglomerate model of business.

Why not break it up?

While investors have welcomed the moves by Smiths as providing much needed streamlining of the industrial conglomerate, many are still hoping that a private equity buyer could be interested in buying the rest of the company at a healthy premium.

(*Financial Times*[14])

Allan Gordon-Smith radically altered Smiths by transforming it into a light engineering company, and the vehicle he shaped evolved gradually, but retained natural links and synergies between its component parts. Three industries provided a focus—motor accessories, aircraft instruments, and clocks—one common thread being the presentation of measurements on precisely calibrated instruments. This focus was based on a (correct) prediction that motor cars and aircraft would become ubiquitous and populist, and that the markets for both would provide long-term demand for Smiths' products. The rationale for a belief in a future for clocks and watches is more complex. We can predict there was a degree of sentimental attachment to an industry in which Gordon-Smith first enrolled as a teenage student, and which formed a link to the early heritage of the firm. In the 1920s–30s, there was perhaps a convenient blend of commercial interest and patriotism in working to ensure Britain had a capacity to compete with foreign production; and then in the wake of the Second World War the patriotic rhetoric came to the fore with the company's involvement in the reconstruction and development efforts promoted by Gordon-Smith's close associates in government.

The diversification that followed, particularly in the 1960s and 1970s, was agglomerative. It did not seek to replace business activities with alternatives—it sought to add diversification and more sources of profit when existing business lines were suffering. At this time the philosophy was strengthened under which subsidiaries were left to be highly independent, remotely managed, and expected to remain entrepreneurial—left alone, as long as targets were met, but if they were not, then there was a lot of 'help' available from the centre, from long-standing London-based managers who worked hard to instil a systematized approach to managing stock ratios, cash collection, and the like. Thus the modus operandi for acquisitions was to buy and hold, and nurse where necessary.

The major transformation that occurred with the transition from the Hurn era to the KB-W era was the move to a concept more fully akin to private equity—a notion of being the owners of businesses 'for the time being' and returns to financial capital alone determining acquisitions and disposals. Rather than being buy-and-hold biased, the framework moved to being one of 'if we didn't own this business, would we buy it'? This view of stewardship will be crucial to the future of Smiths and will likely continue to determine the composition of its portfolio of businesses.

At the end of the 1990s, Smiths concluded it could not continue with a model that involved consistently bolting on additional small- and medium-sized companies. But with the prevailing mergers and acquisitions boom, and P/E ratios becoming stratospheric, it was also faced with a difficult task to identify and successfully conclude transactions that would deliver true scale in any of its divisions—in other words, acquisitions that would ensure improved market share and the capacity to ensure sustainable growth. To move forwards, a bold move was needed and Chapter 10 described two remarkable and major transactions which shocked markets in 2000 and 2007, reshaping Smiths significantly once again. The transformation is all the more striking for the fact that the business regarded as dominant—aerospace—was the one sold, and a business which arrived in the Smiths stable at a time when it was not doing well, and which therefore was considered for sale—John Crane—is now the world leader in its field.

While conglomeracy or the 'diversified industrial' path has remained more of an accepted business model in the US markets than London (in particular), its validity remains open to debate. The arguments for conglomeracy are relatively few and simple: diversification is the most obvious advantage proffered, in that a mix of activities offers the possibility that different business lines will respond to different phases of the economic cycle, and produce a blended and less volatile overall result. This was the 'three-legged stool' analogy favoured by Roger Hurn, in which a leg could be longer or shorter at any given time, but the stool would offer stable support—and Smiths would argue its experience over the long term has proved this to be the case, through the recession of the early 1990s and particularly through the 2007–8 financial crisis and its continuing after-effects.

By contrast, a common criticism of conglomerates is that diversification of risk can be achieved by investors themselves through adequate stock selection, and indeed that diversification can be achieved with much lower cost. Smiths' counter to this rests on a track record of producing solid results (even against an adverse backdrop, as recently). A struggle it certainly faces is the common problem for conglomerates that derives simply from a lack of market understanding of their activities—sell-side analysts are typically focused on a single sector, probably demonstrated in the high historic covariance between Smiths' share price and the FTSE aerospace index, when it was treated solely as an aerospace stock. There is a further tendency to evaluate conglomerates purely on a short-term or 'snapshot' basis—focused on the notional sum-of-the-parts valuation if the component parts could be broken up and sold or listed separately, a scenario which is arguably often unrealistic.

Philip Bowman, the present chief executive, argues conglomeracy has another important advantage, which is the ability it confers to act as an incubator—the detection division offering an interesting example of a world-class business, fashioned from virtually nothing in a decade.

That business would have been very difficult to develop outside a larger enterprise with very strong cash flow, because it consumed a lot of capital, required a lot of resources, and the lead time to bring new products to market and have them certified is significant. Smiths the conglomerate could make that possible, because the company could choose to allocate capital when needed.[15]

There are other advantages. Beyond coping with the ebb and flow of the economic cycle and the ability to fund capital intensive growth through reliance on other divisions, a successful conglomerate business will likely develop proven common systems of management, which can then be deployed in new businesses as they are acquired, to monitor and improve performance. There should also be real efficiencies derived from the provision of a range of services from a single corporate centre, especially as communications and other support and operations technologies become more advanced. The corporate centre can also be small—the London head office of Smiths employs just fifty staff.

Conclusions

> What we are interested in is can we provide shareholder value ... will we continue to review where we can best do that? Absolutely. Have we got a plan today to sell something else? No, we don't. Will that change? Yes. It's a process that one goes through.
>
> (Keith Butler-Wheelhouse, *Financial Times*.[16])

Despite launching its flotation at one of the worst possible times—the outset of the Great War—Smiths survived, and has clocked up a century being listed on the London stock exchange, having emerged yet a further sixty years earlier than that. It is now one of the hundred most valuable listed UK companies. If the obvious question is 'why has it survived?', the foregoing account should reveal there is no great mystery. It is entirely plausible to argue that its independence lies largely in its diversity and conglomerate nature. Anyone interested to acquire a single business could not conceive of buying the whole firm, in view of the scale of the premium likely required. In addition, there are few natural buyers of diverse conglomerates in their aggregate form. However, this is not the reason commonly advanced. Ask anyone associated with the company in the last half century why it has survived and they almost invariably offer the same explanation—that Smiths has constantly reinvented itself, developing or acquiring new business lines, and abandoning others when necessary, to rebalance its activities in order to remain relevant to a changing business environment. The evolutionary nature of its history strongly suggests adaptability is a key strength, and one that can be predicted to be a necessary enduring characteristic. If the experience of the 2000s showed the value of an ability to 'think the unthinkable', it is a lesson that must not be unlearned.

Another observation is that the issue of scale emerges with a cyclical predictability. It dates back a long way in the company's life: even the retail business went through its own significant expansion to capture new markets, but in the twentieth century it is noticeable Allan Gordon Smith's demands first led to North's factory being created in Watford, and when this was not sufficient, Smiths establishing its own. Two significant expansions of scale were the necessary by-products of war, and had the effect of transforming the business on each occasion. Having established new businesses and built new factories after the Second World War, a long period of more gradual expansion stretched over thirty years, until the 1987 acquisition of various Lear Siegler units, which once again transformed the company—notably elevating it to tier-1 status as a supplier to Boeing. But this transformation lasted only a decade before the need emerged again to take significant action, and the TI merger resulted in 2000. The course of Smiths' development has naturally changed substantially over the decades, reflecting changing opportunities and threats. This will surely be ongoing—the focus of investment might presently favour John Crane, but another business might in time move to the forefront of opportunity. Things will continue to change, and perhaps radically—though equally perhaps not as dramatically as in 2007, with the sale of the aerospace business.

During the time its operations were largely based in the UK, Smiths succeeded in building a remarkably strong collective ethos that remains reflected in a fierce loyalty and pride among its former employees, and which over the years will have contributed to its remarkable survival story. In terms of employer brand, the post-war Smiths, through at least to the 1970s, was one of the most highly regarded UK light-engineering employers, attracting high-quality applicants. Since then, with diversification of business lines, and the accelerating internationalization, Smiths' visibility, whether as an employer or as a recognizable UK brand, has steadily diminished, to the point that it remains virtually unknown in its country of listing—and is perhaps best known in the US.

So the rich history of Smiths is bound up in a wide variety of twentieth-century consumer products—and some less visible products and instrumentation familiar to a range of specialist professionals—coupled with a remarkably strong sense of belonging and familial spirit among its large pensioner community. This was the outcome of the implementation of a particular management approach across a range of mainly UK-based companies and across many decades—the consistency of the approach doing much to establish a historic brand. But the twenty-first-century Smiths is a remarkably different animal. Managed from a lean corporate office in the UK, but overwhelmingly international in its business—the barons now inhabit their own distant castles—its modern legacy will rest on a changed set of tools. With management devolved overseas to the local level, a common thread linking the portfolio of companies, imposed from the corporate centre, will nevertheless be the continued pursuit of the full potential of each business, achieved in a wide variety of ways—whether through an emphasis on lean production, or the use of benchmarking methods to enhance performance, or the deployment of secure and effective mechanisms for knowledge management and transfer. Much will depend on the ability of the company to remain nimble and adaptable to changing market circumstances, and its skill in seizing opportunities to acquire new companies advantageously, or to extract a premium in realizing existing value in its portfolio.

Notes

1. Youssef Cassis, *Big Business: The European Experience in the Twentieth Century* (Oxford: OUP, 1997), 102.
2. Leslie Hannah, 'Entrepreneurs and the Social Sciences', *Economica*, 51/203 (Aug. 1984): 229.
3. W. D. Rubinstein, 'Cultural Explanations for Britain's Decline: How True?' in Bruce Collins and Keith Robbins, *British Culture and Economic Decline* (London: Weidenfeld, 1990), 76.
4. See e.g. TNA: BT 211/37, EIPS, 'Establishment of a Working Party on the German Watch and Clock-Making Industry' (19 Dec. 1945).
5. Cann, 'Chronological Record', i. 117.
6. Andrea Colli, *The History of Family Business, 1850–2000* (Cambridge: CUP, 2003), 13, 73.
7. Noel Whiteside and Robert Salais, *Governance, Industry and Labour Markets in Britain and France: The Modernising State in the Mid-Twentieth Century* (London: Routledge, 1998), 54.
8. Leslie Hannah, 'Strategic Games, Scale, and Efficiency, or Chandler Goes to Hollywood', in R. Coopey and Peter J. Lyth, *Business in Britain in the Twentieth Century* (Oxford: OUP, 2009), 18.
9. 20 Oct. 1995, 35.
10. Cassis, *Big Business*, 123.
11. Quoted in Rubinstein, 'Cultural Explanations', 81.
12. *Smiths Home Journal* (Apr. 1938), 9.
13. Berry, interview (2013).
14. 3 May 2007, 20.
15. Philip Bowman, interview (6 Dec. 2013).
16. 16 Jan. 2007, 19.

Appendix I

Simplified Smith Family Tree

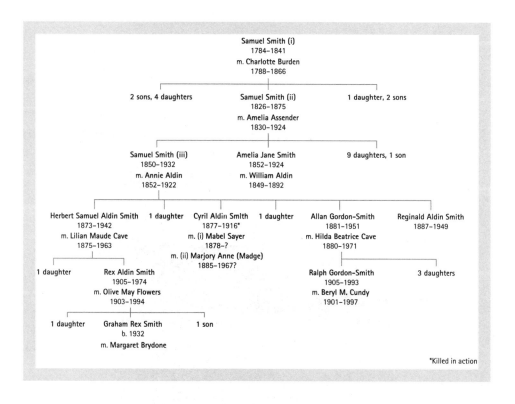

Samuel Smith (i)
1784–1841
m. Charlotte Burden
1788–1866

2 sons, 4 daughters — Samuel Smith (ii) 1826–1875 m. Amelia Assender 1830–1924 — 1 daughter, 2 sons

Samuel Smith (iii) 1850–1932 m. Annie Aldin 1852–1922 — Amelia Jane Smith 1852–1924 m. William Aldin 1849–1892 — 9 daughters, 1 son

Herbert Samuel Aldin Smith 1873–1942 m. Lilian Maude Cave 1875–1963 — 1 daughter — Cyril Aldin Smith 1877–1916* m. (i) Mabel Sayer 1878–? m. (ii) Marjory Anne (Madge) 1885–1967? — 1 daughter — Allan Gordon-Smith 1881–1951 m. Hilda Beatrice Cave 1880–1971 — Reginald Aldin Smith 1887–1949

1 daughter — Rex Aldin Smith 1905–1974 m. Olive May Flowers 1903–1994 — Ralph Gordon-Smith 1905–1993 m. Beryl M. Cundy 1901–1997 — 3 daughters

1 daughter — Graham Rex Smith b. 1932 m. Margaret Brydone — 1 son

*Killed in action

Appendix II

Overview of development of activities (1851–2014)

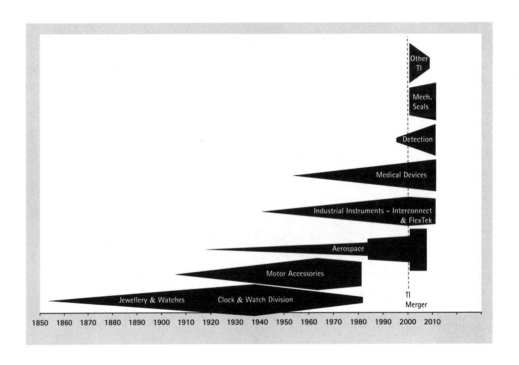

Appendix III

Main financial data (1915–2008)

All figures are drawn from Smiths annual report and accounts. Figures for a given year are from the accounts for that year, and do not take account of later restatements of prior years (relating to acquisitions or disposals). Turnover figures were not reported for 1920–55. However, figures for debtors were reported, and turnover typically equated approximately to five times debtors. Turnover figures for the missing years are calculated on this basis.

	Turnover (000s)	Profit (000s)	Shareholders' Funds (000s)
1915	118	25	118
1916	396	42	239
1917	747	48	348
1918	868	49	355
1919	813	59	669
1920	2,465	98	1,369
1921	1,773	(293)	1,036
1922	2,027	(258)	772
1923	397	7	779
1924	490	23	215
1925	570	56	271
1926	432	73	344
1927	493	101	832
1928	374	111	979
1929	398	114	1,127
1930	538	97	1,129
1931	388	53	1,109
1932	408	62	1,124
1933	383	100	1,158
1934	533	125	1,284
1935	578	137	1,586
1936	802	176	1,676
1937	909	250	1,960
1938	790	220	1,979
1939	1,059	233	2,011
1940	2,353	200	2,007
1941	3,289	171	1,961
1942	3,338	172	1,965

(continued)

	Turnover (000s)	Profit (000s)	Shareholders' Funds (000s)
1943	3,244	103	1,931
1944	5,739	1,281	1,974
1945	4,513	529	2,005
1946	4,577	809	2,777
1947	7,568	687	3,228
1948	6,738	858	3,575
1949	8,778	860	3,882
1950	9,718	1,102	4,382
1951	12,127	1,520	5,790
1952	12,011	1,248	6,250
1953	12,651	1,678	6,931
1954	19,539	2,854	8,632
1955	23,322	2,635	9,756
1956	26,035	2,333	10,773
1957	27,223	2,847	11,737
1958	33,380	3,382	13,008
1959	35,720	3,604	14,471
1960	40,588	4,191	15,941
1961	38,365	2,660	16,713
1962	40,515	2,226	17,245
1963	46,850	3,311	18,021
1964	52,000	3,821	19,210
1965	53,300	4,012	20,769
1966	54,950	2,876	25,205
1967	54,800	2,738	24,184
1968	61,250	4,350	26,261
1969	66,900	4,760	27,215
1970	72,950	4,162	28,077
1971	84,550	5,431	28,803
1972	94,550	7,056	32,725
1973	117,000	10,548	35,782
1974	135,750	11,300	42,800
1975	157,500	12,500	56,400
1976	180,800	16,200	64,500
1977	224,100	20,500	76,700
1978	254,800	22,100	102,700
1979	284,600	25,100	111,300
1980	319,800	26,100	125,200
1981	367,600	26,300	139,500
1982	385,900	26,500	142,800
1983	380,700	26,800	151,200
1984	388,700	36,200	153,600
1985	383,000	47,600	160,200
1986	401,200	56,500	173,400
1987	429,900	65,700	197,400
1988	666,400	97,200	254,300
1989	704,900	111,700	273,200
1990	673,000	120,000	300,400
1991	655,500	119,500	309,300
1992	635,300	107,300	330,000

1993	725,800	107,800	266,700
1994	759,300	115,400	212,000
1995	899,300	138,500	225,500
1996	1,008,400	165,400	211,800
1997	1,076,200	192,100	240,400
1998	1,198,500	218,100	221,700
1999	1,323,900	237,500	352,300
2000	1,463,700	266,300	787,400
2001	3,466,200	448,100	831,300
2002	3,070,100	406,000	832,600
2003	2,629,200	349,400	857,200
2004	2,678,400	350,300	1,122,500
2005	3,016,800	412,600	1,483,800
2006	3,522,900	488,800	1,362,900
2007	2,160,900	345,000	903,300
2008	2,321,200	378,600	915,900

Appendix IV

Companies acquired/formed and sold (1917–2007)

Some smaller acquisitions and disposals may be omitted, while a limited number of company formations or reorganizations are included (marked *). In the interests of simplicity, no distinction is drawn between minority and majority shareholdings. Companies are located in the UK unless otherwise stated.

Purchases and formations

		Location
Pre-1930		
1917	Trier & Martin	
1917	Frederic Hollocoombe Clift's airspeed indicator business	
1917	S. Smith & Sons (Siam) *	
1918	Smith & Teagle (joint venture)	
1919	M-L Magneto Syndicate	
1920	H.W. Smith	
1925	Johnson Motor Company	
1927	Ed. Jaeger (London)	
1927	Robinhood Engineering (becomes KLG in 1929)	
1928	All British Escapement Company (ABEC) *	
1928	A.T. Speedometer Co.	
1930s		
1931	Richard & Co.	
1932	Smiths English Clocks *	
1932	Synchronous Electric Clocks *	
1932	English Clock and Watch Manufacturers	
1932	Williamson Clock Co.	
1933	Enfield Clock Co.	
1934	S Smith & Sons (England) *	
1935	Tucker, Nunn & Williamson	
1935	Henry Hughes & Son	
1937	Sessions Holdings	
1937	Stevenson Jacks	
1937	Synchro-Time Systems (becomes English Clock Systems in 1939)	
1937	Pullars Electric	
1938	Smiths Jacking Systems	

1938	Richard & Tucker Nunn
1938	French Clock House
1939	S. Smith & Sons (Cheltenham) *
1939	J.E.V. Winterbourne

1940s

1941	Marine Instruments
1941	United Kingdom Clock Co.
1942	British Precision Springs *
1942	Clock Components
1942	Furzehill Laboratories
1944	David Harcourt
1944	Petro-Flex Tubing Co.
1944	Smiths Motor Accessories *
1944	Smiths Aircraft Instruments *
1944	Smiths Industrial Instruments *
1945	Kelvin, Bottomley & Baird
1945	Radiomobile (joint venture with EMI)
1945	Anglo-Celtic Watch Co. (joint venture with Ingersoll and Vickers-Armstrong)
1946	Autop
1947	Synthetic Jewels *
1947	Grimshaw Baxter & J.J. Elliott
1947	Kelvin & Hughes

1950s

1950	Ming Ware
1950	Dennis & Robinson
1952	Tyme
1953	Uni-Tubes
1957	World Radio
1957	R.M. Papelian
1958	Portland Plastics
1959	Camron Engineering

1960s

1960	Cribb Associates	
1961	Waymouth Gauges & Instruments	
1962	Lodge Plugs	
1965	Payne & Griffiths	
1965	Canadian Formwork (later Concrete Formwork)	
1965	Air-Shields	
1965	Gap Instrument Corporation	USA
1966	Specto Avionics	
1966	Kelvin Electronics (KECO)	
1966	Smiths Industries (Pty)	South Africa

1970s

1970	Yorkshire Factors
1970	Longlife Accessories
1972	Godfrey Holmes
1972	Affiliated Factors
1972	Defence Equipment Company (joint venture with Thorn EMI Automation and Laurence, Scott & Electromotors)

(continued)

Purchases and formations (continued)

		Location
1972	Auto Finish	
1972	Fred Medcalf & Co.	
1972	Battery Electrics (Herefordshire)	
1973	Claude Rye	
1973	Masons Motor Factors	
1972	Micro Circuit Technology *	
1973	Lancasters (St Helens)	
1973	Car Radio Services (Otley, Leeds and York)	
1973	G. Caldwell & Co. (Wrexham)	
1973	Tudor Accessories	
1974	Flight Navigation (joint venture with Decca)	
1974	Furnco Holdings	Australia
1975	Romulus *	Guernsey
1975	Marine Audio Visual Instructional Systems	
1976	Kuraray-Portex Co. (joint venture) controlling Japan Medical	Japan
1976	Anglo French Offshore Surveys (joint venture)	
1976	MacLellan Rubber	UK and USA
1976	Flexible Ducting	
1976	Hypertac	
1976	Fliteline	
1976	Simonsen & Nielsen	Denmark
1977	Dowty & Smiths Industries Controls (joint venture with Dowty)	
1977	Miller & Edwards	
1977	John R Stephenson Group	Australia
1977	Injex (Pty)	South Africa
1977	Surgical Equipment Supplies	
1978	Medcraft Brothers	
1978	Harowe Systems	US
1978	Technisch Bureau M Weijerman BV	Netherlands
1978	Wood Enterprises	Australia
1978	Denwenjen Pty	Australia
1978	S.I.D.K. Pty (joint venture with Diesel Kiki)	Australia
1979	Smiths Industries Aerospace and Defence Systems	
1979	Concord Laboratories	USA
1979	Currency Handling Systems Pty	
1980s		
1980	Efco Manufacturing Co.	Australia
1980	Grosvenor Surgical Supplies	
1980	K.G. Flexschlauch Produktions GmbH & Co.	Germany
1981	Mecro (merger of Miller & Edwards and Claude Rye bearings businesses)	
1981	Integrated Air Systems	USA
1981	Unifurn Pty	Australia
1983	Lucas Electrical Electronics & Systems (LEES) (minority interest from the contribution of the Automotive Instrument Systems division)	

1983	Xionics	
1983	Laboratoire Lejeune, Seitz et Ameline	France
1983	Cape Industries (17 branches only)	
1984	Aero-Electrical Connector Co.	USA
1984	Superflexit Group	
1984	Icore International	UK, France, Germany, and USA
1984	Cam Profiles	
1984	Lodge Ceramics	
1984	Downs Surgical	UK and USA
1985	Eschmann Bros & Walsh	UK, France, Germany, and Singapore
1985	Unitex	
1985	Newman-Tonks Pty	
1986	Camper & Nicholsons Marine Equipment	
1986	J.D. Potter	
1987	Lear Siegler (avionics systems companies only)	USA
1987	Pyzotec (joint venture with EDO Corp)	
1988	Avon Medical	
1989	Times Microwave Systems, Inc.	USA
1989	Louis Newmark plc (aviation division)	
1989	Peter von Berg extrakorporale Systeme GmbH and Telos Medizintechnik GmbH	Germany
1989	Respiratory Support Products, Inc.	USA
1990s		
1990	Lokata Limited	
1991	Japan Medico Company Limited (24.50%)	Japan
1991	Mednova Company Limited (30%)	
1991	AI (Holdings), Inc. (Flexible Technologies)	USA and Canada
1991	Gorizont-Kelvin Hughes (joint venture with Gorizont)	Russia
1992	Matzen & Timm KG	Germany
1992	Ashling Engineering Limited	
1992	A & D Fluid Power Limited	
1992/93	H.G. Wallace Limited	
1992	Medical-Assist Limited	
1992	Intertech Resources, Inc.	USA
1992	Vent-Axia	
1992	Anda	
1992	Vent-Axia Ventilation Limited (Eire)	Ireland
1992	Benzing Ventilatoren GmbH	Germany
1994	Qubit Limited	
1994	Compoflex	
1994	Brown & Perring	
1994	Sestrel Observator N.V.	Netherlands
1994	Kylie-Kanga	
1994	Tutco, Inc.	USA
1994	Elkay Electrical Manufacturing Company Limited	Wales
1994	Dura-Vent, Inc.	USA
1994	Pharmacia Deltec, Inc.	USA
1994	Applied Medical Concepts	

(continued)

Purchases and formations (continued)

		Location
1994	Belhen S.A. (Sodiama S.A.; Sodiama-Expansion S.A.; Sodiamex-International S.A.;)	France
1994	Interplas S.A. (Induplas SpA.; Flexiplas S.A.; and Euro-Hose Limited)	Switzerland, Italy, France, and UK
1995	Boehringer Ingleheim MedizIntechnik division	Germany
1995	Brevetron S.A. and FRB Connectron S.A. (Asari Holding S.A.; Connei SpA; Interconnectron GmbH; Hypertronics Corp.)	France, Germany, Italy, and USA
1995	Level 1 Technologies, Inc.	USA
1995	M.J.A. Dynamics Limited	
1996	Air Movement (Holdings) Limited	
1996	Adaptaflex Limited (Harnessflex Limited; Adaptaflex Pty Ltd; and Adaptaflex GmbH)	UK, Australia, and Germany
1997	Leland Electrosystems, Inc.	USA
1997	Prostab International Limited	
1997	Torin Holdings Limited	
1997	PolyPhaser Corp.	USA
1997	Graseby plc	
1997	pneuPAC Limited	
1998	Dan Chambers Limited	Ireland
1998	Quartz Limited	
1998	Signal Processing Systems	
1998	ChartCo Limited (joint venture with Fugro)	
1998	Stewart Hughes Limited	
1999	Transtector Systems, Inc.	USA
1998	Engineering Transitions Company, Inc.	USA
1999	Biochem International, Inc.	USA
1999	Hemex Medical AB	Sweden
1999	Strategic Technology Systems, Inc.	USA
1999	Metchem Technologies, Inc. (Environmental Technologies Group, Inc.)	USA

2000 to 2007

		Location
2000	Sabritec	USA
2000	LEA International, Inc.	USA
2000	Barber-Colman Aerospace (Tech Development Inc.; Aerospace Avionics, Inc.; Lambda Advanced Analog, Inc.; and Lambda Novatronics, Inc.)	USA
2000	EMC Technology, LLC	USA and Costa Rica
2000	Marconi Actuation Systems, Inc.	USA
2000	Venair Technik AG	Switzerland
2000	Aerosonics, Inc.	USA
2000	Florida RF Labs, Inc.	USA
2000	Fairchild Defense division of Orbital Sciences Corp.	USA
2000	Merger with TI Group plc	
2000	Radio Waves, Inc.	USA
2001	Chapman Avionics	Australia
2001	Barringer Technologies, Inc. and subsidiaries	USA and Canada

2001	Bivona, Inc.	USA
2001	Summitek Instruments, Inc.	USA
2001	Triveni Flexibox Limited (residual minority interest acquired)	
2001	Abbott Laboratories (anaesthesia tray kit business)	
2002	Able Corp.	USA
2002	Heimann Systems GmbH	Germany, Canada, France, Singapore, and USA
2002	MPS Acacia	
2003	General Seals S.A.	Chile
2003	Joint venture company between John Crane (40%) and Iskra and Gaztekhsnab	Russia
2003	Kelvin Hughes Services AS	
2004	Cyrano Sciences, Inc.	USA
2004	Smiths Medical Japan Limited (residual minority interest acquired)	Japan
2004	Dynamic Gunver Technologies, LLC and shares of DGT Europe, LLC	USA and Poland
2004	Trak Holdings Corp	USA and UK
2004	SensIR Technologies, Inc.	USA
2004	DHD Holding Company	USA
2004	Integrated Aerospace, Inc.	USA
2004	Tianjin Timing Seals Co. Ltd	China
2005	ChartCo (residual minority interest acquired)	UK
2005	Farran Technology Limited	Ireland
2005	US Seals	USA
2005	MedVest Holdings Corp. (Medex)	USA, UK, Brazil, France, Germany, Italy, and Mexico
2005	Gryphon Management Group Pty Limited	Australia
2005	Hi-Tech Holdings, Inc.	USA
2005	Sevit SpA	Italy
2005	ETI Technology, Inc.	USA
2005	Cross Match Technologies, Inc (joint venture from the contribution of Heimann Biometrics)	USA
2005	Farnham Custom Products	USA
2005	Millitech, Inc.	USA
2005	Live Wave Inc.	USA
2005	John Crane Tianjin Limited (residual minority interest acquired)	China
2005	Lorch Microwave	USA
2006	Smiths Detection Montreal Inc. (residual minority interest acquired)	Canada
2006	Comet Costruzioni Metalliche S.r.l.	Italy
2006	Tecnicas Medicas MAB SA	Spain
2006	Morphosys UK	
2007	CDI Energy Services, Inc.(Global Energy Products LLC; Global Energy Products LP)	USA and Romania
2007	Sartorius Bearing Technology GmbH	Germany

Disposals

Pre-1980s

1930	M-L Magneto	
1966	Air-Shields	
1979	Tudor Garden Products	

1980s

1980	English Clock Systems	
1980	Thomas Richfield	
1982	Longlife Accessories	
1983	S. I. Automotive Instrument Systems division (contributed to LEES)	
1982	Radiomobile	
1982	World Radio	
1982	S. I. Pressure Gauge (industrial pressure devices unit – formerly David Harcourt)	
1982	Dennis & Robinson	
1983	S. I. Vehicle Heater Co.	
1984	Affiliated Factors	
1984	Godfrey Holmes	
1984	EMWE	Netherlands
1984	Enterprise	Netherlands
1984	Simonsen & Nielsen	Denmark
1985	Overseas Cars	
1985	S.I.D.K. Pty (joint venture)	Australia
1985	Autosound	
1985	Smiths Industries (Pty)	South Africa
1986	Mecro	
1986	Xionics	
1986	Integrated Air Systems	USA
1986	Cam Profiles	
1987	Contents Measuring Systems	
1987	Avonicom Systems	
1987	Integrated Air Systems	USA
1987	Uniroof	
1988	SLI International Corp. (Aviquipo assets)	USA
1988	various Australian businesses	Australia
1988	Smiths Industries Belgique SA	Belgium
1988	SI-Tex Marine Electronics, Inc.	USA
1988	Downs Surgical instrument business	
1989	The Aero-Electric Connector Company, Inc.	USA
1989	MacLellan Rubber	Scotland
1989	Automated Engineering Products	
1989	Medcraft Brothers	

1990s

1992	Lodge Ceramics Limited	
1993	SIMS S.A.	Spain
1993/94	OIS Optical Imaging Systems, Inc. (formerly Ovonic Imaging Systems, Inc.)	USA
1996	SIMAC Limited	
1996	Aero Quality Sales businesses	USA, UK, and Singapore

1996	Timeguard Limited	
1997	Smiths Aerospace Engine Controls business	
1997	Lucas & Smiths Industries Controls Limited (minority)	
1997	Rolls Smiths Engine Controls Limited (joint venture)	
1998	Graseby Product Monitoring; Environmental; and Allen businesses	
1999	Benzing Ventilatoren GmbH	Germany

2000 to 2007

2000	Lambda Advanced Analog Inc.	USA
2001	Smiths Industries Hydraulics Co. Limited	
2001	Kylie Kanga	
2001	Eschmann Bros & Walsh Limited and SIMS Pte Ltd	UK and Singapore
2001	TI Automotive (minority interest in demerged company)	Global
2001	Plenty Group (GSF Europe BV; Plenty Products, Inc.; Plenty Treveni Limited; Plenty Uniquip Pty Limited; and Plenty Limited)	UK, France, India, Australia, and USA
2001	Induplas SpA and Flexiplas S.A. and EuroHose business	Italy, Switzerland, and UK
2001	Cambridge Vacuum Engineering Limited; Wentgate Dynaweld Limited; and Wentgate Dynaweld, Inc.	UK and USA
2001	Woodville Airbags business (part of TI SPP Limited)	
2001	Hortsmann Defence Systems Ltd, Aeronautical & General Instruments Ltd, and AB Precision (Poole) Ltd	
2001	Hick Hargreaves & Co. Limited (Hibon International SA; Wilhelm Klein GmbH; 3H Czech; and Stokes Vacuum)	UK, Czech Republic, France, Germany, and USA
2002	John Crane Lips businesses	UK, France, Germany, India, Italy, Japan, Netherlands, Norway, Portugal, Singapore, and USA
2002	Dan Chambers Limited	Ireland
2002	Urology and ostomy businesses of Portex Limited	
2002	Fans and Spares group companies	
2002	Mixing Solutions	
2002	Precision Handling Systems	
2002	Lodge Ignition	
2002	Air Movement businesses (Vent-Axia, Roof Units, Sifan-Torin, Airstream and Quartz)	UK and Ireland
2002	Cable Management businesses (Adaptaflex, Kopex, Elkay and Harnessflex)	UK, Australia, and Wales
2003	C. & F. Millier	UK
2003	Matzen und Timm	Germany
2003	Polymer Sealings Solutions	USA, UK, Malta, Poland, Scandinavia, and Italy
2003	Lapmaster International	UK and USA
2004	Icore International	UK; Germany and USA
2004	Sodiamex	France
2005	EBTEC Corporation	USA
2005	pvb critical care GmbH	Germany
2005	Smiths Heimann Biometrics GmbH (contributed to Cross Match Technologies)	Germany

2006	John Crane Safematic bearing lubrication business	Finland
2006	Beagle Aircraft	
2007	Smiths Aerospace Group (sale of the Aerospace division to GE Aviation)	UK, USA, Canada, and China
2007	TI Automotive (sale of minority interest)	
2007	Kelvin Hughes and ChartCo	UK, Denmark, Norway, Netherlands, Singapore
2007	John Crane Automotive and Cyclam	France, Germany, and Mexico

Summary of acquisitions/formations and disposals

	Business acquired/formed	Businesses sold
Pre-1930	11	3
1930s	18	
1940s	17	
1950s	8	
1960s	10	
1970s	40	
1980s	28	35
1990s	50	11
2000–2007	51	35

Appendix V

List of officers

Chairman

Samuel Smith	1914–1923
Charles Percy Newman	1923–1924
Walter Henderson-Cleland	1924–1945
Sir Allan Gordon-Smith	1945–1951
Ralph Gordon-Smith	1951–1973
Sir Richard Guy Cave	1973–1976
Sir Roy Sisson	1976–1985
Sir Alex Jarratt	1985–1991
Sir (Francis) Roger Hurn	1991–1998
Keith Orrell-Jones	1998–2004
Donald Hood Brydon	2004–2013
Sir George William Buckley	2013–

Managing Director/CEO

Sir Allan Gordon-Smith	1914–1947
Ralph Gordon-Smith	1947–1967
Sir Richard Guy Cave	1967–1973
Sir Roy Sisson	1973–1976
William Arthur Mallinson	1976–1978
Sir (Francis) Roger Hurn	1978–1996
Keith Oliver Butler-Wheelhouse	1996–2007
Philip Bowman	2007–

Directors

Samuel Smith	1914–1932
Sir Allan Gordon-Smith	1914–1951
Reginald Aldin Smith	1914–1922
George W. Arnold	1914–1922
Charles William Nichols	1914–1962
Charles Percy Newman	1914–1951

(continued)

Directors (continued)

Walter Henderson-Cleland	1922–1945
Sydney Dawson Begbie	1924–1945
Ralph Gordon-Smith	1933–1978
Charles Molyneux Carington	1945–1961
Sir Frederick Stewart	1947–1950
James Reid Young	1950–1967
(Francis) Frank James Hurn	1951–1972
Dennis William Barrett	1954–1968
George Brian Gibbon Potter	1954–1960
Sir Joseph Flawith Lockwood	1959–1978
Colin St. Clair Proctor	1961–1972
James Anthony Blair	1963–1967
Sir Richard Guy Cave	1963–1976
Alastair Michael Adair Majendie	1963–1967
Stanley Ernest Burlington	1967–1973
George Patrick John Rushworth, Earl Jellicoe	1967–70; 1973–1986
David Lucas Breeden	1967–1987
Sir Roy Sisson	1969–1985
Donald Edward Robson	1970–1978
Sir Barrie Heath	1970–1986
William Arthur Mallinson	1972–1985
John William Thompson	1973–1988
Sir (Francis) Roger Hurn	1976–1998
John Derek Birkin	1977–1984
Sir John Lidbury	1978–1985
Alan Kenneth Hornsby	1978–1989
George MacDonald Kennedy	1983–2000
Austin Hugh Pope	1983–1991
Sir Alex Jarratt	1984–1996
William Fillans Sykes	1984–1988
Sir James Hamilton	1985–1993
Neil McGowan Shaw	1986–1990
Sir Peter Thompson	1986–1998
Sir Austin William Pearce	1987–1992
Ronald Williams	1988–1996
Christopher Skidmore Taylor	1989–1995
John David Richard Lyon	1991–1994
Norman Victor Barber	1991–2000
Keith Orrell-Jones	1992–2004
Alan Ind Harvey Pink	1993–2000
Roger Frank Leverton	1994–2000
Alan Matthew Thomson	1995–2006
Einar Lindh	1996–2005
Keith Oliver Butler-Wheelhouse	1996–2007
Robert White O'Leary	1997–2006
Peter Thomas Hollins	1999–2000
Lawrence Henry Neil Kinet	2000–2005
Julian Michael Horn-Smith	2000–2006
John Ferrie	2000–2007
Sir Nigel Hugh Robert Allen Broomfield	2000–2007
Sir Colin Michael Chandler	2000–2004
John Mulock Hignett	2000–2002

John Langston	2000–2010
David Peter Lillycrop	2000–2008
Peter John Jackson	2003–2009
Rt. Hon. Lord George Islay MacNeill Roberston of Port Ellen	2004–2006
Donald Hood Brydon	2004–2013
David John Challen	2004–
Sir Kevin Tebbit	2006–
Stuart John Chambers	2006–2012
Peter Löscher	2007–2008
Philip Bowman	2007–
Anne Cecille Quinn	2009–
Peter Andrew Turner	2010–
Bruno François Jules Angelici	2010–
Tanya Dianne Fratto	2012–
Sir George William Buckley	2013–

President

Ralph Gordon-Smith	1973–1993

Vice–Chairman

William Arthur Mallinson	1978–1985
Sir Colin Chandler	2000–2004
Sir George William Buckley	2013–2013

Deputy Managing Director

Sir Roy Sisson	1971–1973
John William Thompson	1978–1988

Company Secretary

Frank (Francis) Cotterell	1914–1922
Murray A Carson	1922–1923
Henry Warwick	1923–1945
Bruce Arthur Charles Hills	1945–1951
George Stuart Sturrock	1951–1959
James Anthony Blair	1959–1967
John Grenville Dean	1968–1970
Raymond Tulip	1970–1986
Alan Smith	1986–2000
David Peter Lillycrop	2000–2008
Sarah Louise Cameron	2008–2014

APPENDIX VI

LIST OF INTERVIEWS

2012–13

Barber, Norman
Berry, Joan
Bowman, Philip
Broad, Donald
Brodie, Chris
Brydon, Donald
Budenberg, Robin
Butler-Wheelhouse, Keith
Clegg, Aidan
Cochlin, Michael*
Downey, Eddy
Ferrie, John
Flowerday, David
Hedrick, Geoff*
Hornsby, Alan
Hurn, Sir Roger
Jarratt, Sir Alex
Jones, Gil
Kennedy, George
Kinet, Lawrence
Lillycrop, David
Manzie, Sir Gordon*
Morris, Sandy
Nicholls, Paul
Smith, Graham
Tapner, Rory
Taunt, Robin
Taylor, Bernard
Thompson, John
Thompson, Sir Peter
Thomson, Alan
Wenzerul, Martyn
Williams, Ron
* by telephone

1998

Hurn, Sir Roger
Mortimer, Gerry
Smith, Alan
Thompson, John
Williams, Ron

BIBLIOGRAPHY

I PRIMARY SOURCES

Archives

1. Smiths (unpublished)

Anon, 'The Story of TI' (c.1992).

Board minutes (1914–2007).

Cann, Wilfrid M., 'Robert Lenoir 1898–1979' (1980).

Cann, Wilfrid M., 'Smiths Industries Limited: A Chronological Record', 2 vols (1962 revised 1967/8).

Lenoir, Robert, and Wilfrid M. Cann, 'The Introduction of Jaeger Speedometers and Clocks into Britain, 1920' (1976).

Chief executive's memoranda (CExx/MDxx).

Original speedometer orders records (1904).

'Smiths Industries: Aerospace, Medical Systems, Industrial (1973–1998)' (1999).

Walton, Sydney, 'A Brief History' (1945).

2. Smiths (published)

Abraczinskas, Ray J., *Fifty-Five Trips around the Sun: The History of Smiths Industries Information Management Systems in Grand Rapids, Michigan* (Grand Rapids, MI: Smiths, 1999).

Annual reports (1914–2007).

FATHOM (1949–55).

'Programme' (16 June 1906) and (29 June 1907) [sports day programmes].

PIVOT (1943–57).

Portex Communiqué (1977).

Roadcraft [1920s].

S. Smith & Sons, *Guide to the Purchase of a Watch* (London: Smiths, c.1900).

S. Smith & Sons, *Motor Accessories Catalogue* (London: Smiths, 1910).

School Digest (Cheltenham school newsletter).

Share prospectuses (various).

SI News (1966–89).

Smith's Home Journal (1930–9).

Smiths News (1957–65).

Souvenir of your association with S. Smith & Sons (M.A.) Ltd (London: Smiths, 1934).

The Year 1950–51 (London: Smiths, 1951).

3. Ecclesiastical Commissioners archive

Papers relating to Samuel Smith's lease of 151–153 Newington Causeway, ECE/7/1/95012.

4. Guildhall Library

'S, Smith & Son (Motor Accessories) Limited', *Loan and Company Prospectuses–Stock Exchange* (1914).

5. House of Commons Library

'Air Transport Statistics', *Commons Library Standard Note*, SN03760 (July 2011), 1–19.

6. National Archives

BT 31 series for company records.

7. Schroder Archive

Papers relating to S. Smith & Sons and Smiths Industries, SH851 and SH270.

8. Southwark Archives

Minutes of St Mary Newington Vestry Governors and Guardians (1865–75).

9. Westminster Archives

St Marylebone Borough Council Minutes (1912).
St Marylebone Borough Council Rates (April–September 1913), Ward 7.

Parliamentary Papers

Monopolies and Mergers Commission, *Car Parts: A Report on the Matter of the Existence or Possible Existence of a Complex Monopoly Situation in Relation to the Wholesale Supply of Motor Car Parts in the United Kingdom*, HC 318 (1981–2).

Monopolies Commission, *Report on the Supply of Electrical Equipment for Mechanically Propelled Land Vehicles*, HC 21 (1963–4).

Report of His Majesty's Commissioners for the Paris International Exhibition 1900, P.P. 1901, Cmd. 629, 630, vol. II.

Private papers

Papers of Lawrie and Alys Nickolay, held by Stella Nickolay.

Miscellaneous

Peter Graham, 'Reflections on a life influenced by Smiths', kindly communicated to the author (Mar. 2013).

II SECONDARY SOURCES

1. Analysts' research

ABN Amro, 'Smiths Industries' (19 Oct. 1998, 27 May 1999, and 20 Mar. 2000).
ABN Amro, 'TI Group' (11 Mar. 1998).
Cheuvreux, 'Smiths Group' (7 Dec. 2004).
Credit Suisse, 'Smiths Group' (7 Oct. 2002, 17 Mar. 2006, 29 Nov. 2006, and 24 Sept. 2013).
Flemings Research, 'Smiths Industries' (12 Aug. 1991).
Schroders, 'TI' (18 Sept. 2000).
UBS, 'Smiths Industries' (1 June 1995).

2. Books

Ackrill, Margaret, *Manufacturing Industry since 1870* (Oxford: Philip Alan, 1987).

Andrews, P. W. S., and Elizabeth Brunner, *The Life of Lord Nuffield: A Study in Enterprise and Benevolence* (Oxford: Basil Blackwell, 1955).

Anon, *Programm* (Biel: Schüler, 1898).

Anon., *Glasgow International Exhibition 1901: The Official Guide* (Glasgow: Charles P. Watson, 1901).

Barty-King, Hugh, *AA: A History of the First 75 Years of the Automobile Association 1905–1980* (London: Automobile Association, 1980).

Blackman, Tony, *Flight Testing to Win* (Hamble: Blackman Associates, 2005).

Block, Robert, et al., *An Analysis of Group Purchasing Organizations' Contracting Practices under the Antitrust Laws: Myth and Reality* (Washington, DC: Mayer, Brown, Rowe & Maw, n.d.).

Buxton, Tony, Paul G. Chapman, and Paul Temple, *Britain's Economic Performance* (London: Routledge, 1994).

Cassis, Youssef, *Big Business: The European Experience in the Twentieth Century* (Oxford: OUP, 1997).

Church, R. A., *The Rise and Decline of the British Motor Industry* (Cambridge: CUP, 1995).

Colli, Andrea, *The History of Family Business, 1850–2000* (Cambridge: CUP, 2003).

Collier, Richard, *The City that Wouldn't Die* (London: Dutton, 1959).

Coopey, R., and Donald Clarke, *3i: Fifty Years Investing in Industry* (Oxford: OUP, 1995).

Creagh, O'Moore, and E. M. Humphris, *The Distinguished Service Order, 1886–1923* (London: J. B. Hayward, 1978).

Dictionary of Business Biography, ed. David J. Jeremy, 5 vols (London: Butterworths, 1984).

Edge, S. F., *My Motoring Reminiscences* (London: Foulis, 1934).

Edgerton, David, *Warfare State: Britain, 1920–1970* (Cambridge: CUP, 2006).

Edwards, Ronald S., and Harry Townsend, *Business Enterprise: Its Growth and Organisation* (London: Macmillan, 1958).

Ellis, Chris, *Smiths Industries at Cheltenham: The Story of Fifty Years at Bishop's Cleeve 1940–1990* (Surbiton: Kristall, 1990).

Evans, Geoffrey, *Time, Time and Time Again* (Barry: Quinto, 2008).

Ferguson Niall, *High Financier: The Lives and Times of Siegmund Warburg* (London: Allen Lane, 2010).

Floud, Roderick, and Paul Johnson, *The Cambridge Economic History of Modern Britain* (Cambridge: CUP, 2003), iii.

Frow, Edmund, and Ruth Frow, *Engineering Struggles: Episodes in the Story of the Shop Stewards' Movement* (Manchester: Working Class Movement Library, 1982).

Gere, Charlotte, *Jewellery in the Age of Queen Victoria* (London: British Museum, 2010).

Gere, Charlotte, and John Culme, *Garrard* (London: Quartet, 1993).

Glucksmann, Miriam, *Women on the Line* (London: Routledge, 2009).

Goldsmith, Stephen Spencer, *The History of Christ's College: The Victorians* (forthcoming).

Hannah, Leslie, *Electricity Before Nationalisation* (London: Macmillan, 1979).

Holmes, Thomas Henry, *A Brief History of the National College of Horology and Instrument Technology* (London: NCH, 1960).

Hooley, Ernest Terah, *Hooley's Confessions* (London: Simpkin, Marshall & Co., 1925).

Lattek, Christine, *Revolutionary Refugees: German Socialism in Britain, 1840–1860* (London: Routledge, 2006).

Lewis, W. Arthur, *Economic Survey 1919–1939* (London: Allen & Unwin, 1949).

Lines, Mark, *Ferranti Synchronous Electric Clocks* (Milton Keynes: Zazzoo, 2012).

Lomax, John, *The Diplomatic Smuggler* (London: Arthur Barker, 1965).

Lorenz, Andrew, *GKN: The Making of a Business, 1759–2009* (Chichester: Wiley, 2009).

Marden, Thomas Owen, *A Short History of the 6th Division, Aug. 1914–March 1919* (London: Hugh Rees, 1920).

Mass Observation, *War Factory: A Report* (London: Gollancz, 1943).

Mayhew, Henry, *London Labour and the London Poor*, 4 vols (London: Griffin, Bohn, 1862), iv.

Mercer, Vaudrey, *The Frodshams: The Story of a Family of Chronometer Makers* (Ticehurst: AHS, 1981).

Miles, Robert H. A., *Synchronome: Masters of Electrical Timekeeping* (Ticehurst: Antiquarian Horological Society, 2011).

Morrison, Kathryn, *English Shops and Shopping: An Architectural History* (London: Yale University Press, 2003).

Mortimer, Gavin, *The Longest Night: Voices from the London Blitz* (London: Weidenfeld & Nicolson, 2005).

Nockolds, Harold, *Lucas: The First 100 Years*, ii. *The Successors* (Newton Abbott: David & Charles, 1978).

Nutland, Martyn, *Brick by Brick* (Google eBook, 2012).

Passmore, Michael, *The AA: History, Badges and Memorabilia* (Princes Risborough: Shire, 2003).

Pevsner, Nikolaus, and Bridget Cherry, *Hertfordshire*, 2nd edn, rev. Bridget Cherry (Harmondsworth: Penguin, 1977).

Ridout, Martin, *English Clock Systems Limited*, Antiquarian Horological Society, Electrical Horology Group, technical paper, 68 (2005).

Roberts, Andrew, *Eminent Churchillians* (London: Phoenix, 1994).

Roberts, Richard, *Schroders: Merchants and Bankers* (Basingstoke: Macmillan, 1992).

Roberts, Richard, *Saving the City: The Great Financial Crisis of 1914* (Oxford: OUP, 2013).

Roberts, Richard et al., *Sharpening the Axe* (London: Lombard Street Research, 2010).

Scott, J. D., and Richard Hughes, *The Administration of War Production* (London: HMSO, 1955).

Setright, L. J. K., *Drive on! A Social History of the Motor Car* (London: Granta, 2004).

Slinn, Judy, *Clifford Chance: Its Origins and Development* (Cambridge: Granta, 1993).

Smith, Terry, *Accounting for Growth* (London: Century, 1992).

Society of British Aircraft Constructors, *A British Technical Triumph* (London: SBAC, 14 Dec. 1944).

Stamper, C. W., *What I Know: Reminiscences of Five Years' Personal Attendance upon His Late Majesty King Edward the Seventh* (London: Mills & Boon, 1913).

Streeter, Patrick, *Streeter of Bond Street* (Harlow: Matching Press, 1993).

Survey of London, xli. *Brompton* (London: English Heritage, 1983).

Tansey, E. M., and D. A. Christie (eds), *Looking at the Unborn: Historical Aspects of Obstetric Ultrasound*, Wellcome Witnesses to Twentieth Century Medicine, 5. (London: Wellcome, Jan. 2000).

Thorold, Peter, *The Motoring Age: The Automobile and Britain 1896–1939* (London: Profile, 2003).

Turner, Graham, *Business in Britain* (London: Eyre & Spottiswoode, 1969).

Vielle, E. E., *Almost a Boffin* (Thatcham: Dolman Scott, 2013).

Whiteside, Noel, and Robert Salais, *Governance, Industry and Labour Markets in Britain and France: The Modernising State in the Mid-Twentieth Century* (London: Routledge, 1998).

Wigham, Eric, *The Power to Manage: A History of the Engineering Employers' Federation* (London: Macmillan, 1973).

Wotton, Pam and Peter, *Birth of the Synchronous Motor Clock*, 2 vols (self-published, n.d.).

3. Book sections

Clifford, Helen, 'The Myth of the Maker: Manufacturing Networks in the London Goldsmiths' Trade', in Kenneth Quickenden and Neal Quickenden (eds), *Silver and Jewellery* (Birmingham: UCE, 1995), 5–11.

Eichengreen, Barry, 'The British Economy between the Wars', in R. Floud and P. Johnson, *The Economic History of Britain since 1700* (Cambridge: CUP, 2004), 314–43.

Hannah, Leslie, 'Strategic Games, Scale, and Efficiency, or Chandler Goes to Hollywood', in R. Coopey and Peter J. Lyth (eds), *Business in Britain in the Twentieth Century* (Oxford: OUP, 2009), 15–47.

Rubinstein, W. D., 'Cultural Explanations for Britain's Decline: How True?', in Bruce Collins and Keith Robbins (eds), *British Culture and Economic Decline* (London: Weidenfeld, 1990), 59–90.

Wilson, Shelagh, 'Art and Industry: Birmingham Jewellery or "Brummagem"?', in Kenneth Quickenden and Neal Quickenden (eds), *Silver and Jewellery* (Birmingham: UCE, 1995), 41–8.

Wright, J. S., 'The Jewellery and Gilt Toy Trades', in Samuel Timmins (ed.), *The Resources, Products and Industrial History of Birmingham and the Midland Hardware District* (London: Robert Hardwicke, 1866), 452–62.

4. Journal articles

Astrop, Arthur, 'Avon House Works', *Retort! Bulletin of the WIAS* (Summer 1998), 3–10.

Booth, Alan, 'Corporatism, Capitalism and Depression in Twentieth-Century Britain', *British Journal of Sociology*, 33/2 (June 1982), 200–23.

Booth, J. B., 'Tracheotomy and Tracheal Intubation in Military History', *Journal of the Royal Society of Medicine*, 93 (July 2000), 383.

Buxton, Neil, 'The Role of the "New" Industries in Britain during the 1930s: A Reinterpretation', *Business History Review*, 49/2 (1975), 205–22.

Church, Roy, 'Advertising Consumer Goods in Nineteenth Century Britain: Reinterpretations', *Economic History Review*, 53 (Nov. 2000), 621–45.

Close, Roy, 'A Short History of Newman Hender', *Journal of the Gloucestershire Society for Industrial Archaeology* (1994), 11–23.

Dietrich, Ethel, 'British Export Credit Insurance', *American Economic Review* (June 1935), 236–49.

Edwards, Frank, 'Military Timepieces', *Horological Journal* (July 1994), 453–7.

Gordon, R. A., 'Experience with Vinyl-Plastic Endotracheal Tubes', *Anaesthesiology* (July 1945), 359–61.

Green, David R., Alastair Owens, Josephine Maltby, and Janette Rutterford, 'Lives in the Balance? Gender, Age and Assets in Late-Nineteenth-Century England and Wales', *Continuity and Change* (July 2009), 307–35.

Hannah, Leslie, 'Entrepreneurs and the Social Sciences', *Economica*, 51/203 (Aug. 1984), 219–34.

Lenoir, Robert, 'Progress of High-Grade Watch Production', *Society of Engineers' Journal*, 51 (1960), 59–77.

Little, Stephen E., and Margaret Grieco, 'Shadow Factories, Shallow Skills? An Analysis of Work Organisation in the Aircraft Industry in the Second World War', *Labor History*, 52/2 (May 2011), 193–216.

Pardi, Tommaso, 'Do State and Politics Matter? The Case of Nissan's Direct Investment in Great Britain and its Implications for Great Britain', *Business and History*, 8 (2010), 1–13.

Parker, P. W., and P. M. D Gibbs, 'Accounting for Inflation: Recent Proposals and their Effects', *Journal of the Institute of Actuaries* (Dec. 1974), 353–4.

Parker, R. A. C., review of *Churchill and Consensus*, *Historical Journal*, 39/2 (June 1996), 563–72.

Saltzman, Rachelle, 'Folklore as Politics in Great Britain: Working-Class Critiques of Upper-Class Strike Breakers in the 1926 General Strike', *Anthropological Quarterly*, 67/3 (1994), 105–21.

Shay, Robert, 'Chamberlain's Folly: The National Defence Contribution of 1937', *Albion*, 7/4 (1975), 317–27.

Smith, David, 'Defence Contractors and Diversification in to the Civil Sector: Rolls Royce 1945–2005', *Business History*, 49/5 (2007), 637–62.

Thornton, H. L., 'Vinyl "Portex" Tubing', *British Medical Journal* (1 July 1944), 14–18.

Trotman-Dickenson, D. I., 'The Scottish Industrial Estates', *Scottish Journal of Political Economy*, 8 (Feb. 1961), 45–61.

Watson, Isobel, 'A Very Large Speculator in Building: The Double Life of EJ Cave', *Camden History Review*, 24 (2000), 26–31.

Wylie, Neville, 'British Smuggling Operations from Switzerland, 1940–1944', *Historical Journal*, 48/4 (2005), 1077–102.

Zeitlin, Jonathan, 'Americanization and its Limits: Theory and Practice in the Reconstruction of Britain's Engineering Industries, 1945–55', *Business and Economic History*, 24/1 (1995), 277–86.

5. Newspapers

Achievement
Anglo American Times
Auckland Star
Autocar
Cheltenham Chronicle
Daily Mail
Daily Telegraph
Dover Express
Evening Standard
Fine Arts Journal
Foreign Affairs
Gloucestershire Echo
Guardian
Horological Journal
Illustrated London News
Independent
Journal Suisse d'Horlogerie
Lloyds Weekly News

London Gazette
Management Today
Manchester Guardian
Motoring Illustrated
New Scientist
New York Times
Pall Mall Gazette
Singapore Free Press and Mercantile Advertiser
South London Chronicle
South London Press
The Accountant
The Auto Motor Journal
The Bradford Era
The British Clock Manufacturer, supplement to *Watch and Clockmaker*
The Car
The Church Weekly
The Economist
The Engineer
The Flying Lady
The Lancet
The Motor Trader
The Straits Times
The Times
Watch and Clockmaker
Westminster Budget
Willesden Citizen

Index of Names

Note: **bold** page numbers refer to figures or tables.

Index of Subjects

Note: **bold** page numbers refer to figures or tables.